ILLUSTRATING WITH MACROMEDIA® FLASH™ PROFESSIONAL 8

ILLUSTRATING WITH MACROMEDIA® FLASH™ PROFESSIONAL 8

ROBERT FIREBAUGH

CHARLES RIVER MEDIA
Boston, Massachusetts

Cover Design: Tyler Creative
Cover Image: Robert Firebaugh

CHARLES RIVER MEDIA
25 Thomson Place
Boston, Massachusetts 02210
617-757-7900
617-757-7969 (FAX)
crminfo@thomson.com
www.charlesriver.com

This book is printed on acid-free paper.

Robert Firebaugh. *Illustrating with Macromedia Flash Professional 8*
ISBN: 1-58450-477-3

Library of Congress Cataloging-in-Publication Data
Firebaugh, Robert (Robert Russell).
Illustrating with Macromedia Flash Professional 8 / Robert Firebaugh.-- 2nd ed.
p. cm.
Includes index.
ISBN 1-58450-477-3 (pbk. with cd : alk. paper)
1. Computer animation. 2. Flash (Computer file) 3. Web sites--Design. I. Title.
TR897.7.F495 2006
006.7'8--dc22
2006002913

Printed in Canada
06 7 6 5 4 3 2 First Edition

TO THE FLASH ARTIST

Contents

ACKNOWLEDGMENTS

This book would not have been possible without the dedicated and talented people at Charles River Media. Most important, I would like to graciously thank David Pallai for his continued support and interest in my work. This book would still be sitting in my head collecting dust without his help.

I would like to thank all the fans of *vectorkid.com* who have showered me with kind words and given me support to continue creating photorealistic illustrations in Macromedia® Flash™. A special shout out goes to Catur Prayogo, CeeCee, co_kla_t, dravalanche, echopathy, jankratochvil, mixedtrigeno, morganwill, Neal Prentice, Ozbo, ritalin, and soopanova. Let us hope this second book continues to inspire many more people to come.

A special thanks to Jobe Makar for his continued support and being a positive influence in my life. I am grateful for the constant support and encouragement from my family—Mom, Dad, Renee, Pickles, and Patches. A warm hug to Angela—thank you for being there through the late nights and long weekends; your support and love keeps me going.

PREFACE

Welcome to the second edition of *Illustrating with Macromedia Flash*™, which proves you don't have to be an artist to create high-quality, photorealistic illustrations. In fact, not being artistically savvy can work to your advantage, since you will not have any pre-conceived ideas on how something should be drawn, nor will you skip a section because you feel you may already know it.

Although not necessary, some knowledge of Macromedia Flash, its basic functions, and certain programs terms will be a plus, as less beginner material is included here.

If you do have previous experience with the program, keep an open mind when learning new concepts and techniques presented here—they are unique to this book and not commonly taught. Every chapter is important, and contains cutting-edge processes and explanations that will help you become more efficient when working with Flash. Because there is a lot of content to cover, some details are not repeated, so read the chapters in order so you don't miss something important.

This book was created for the sole purpose of educating the Macromedia Flash industry and its developers about the illustrating possibilities you can achieve with Flash's drawing tools. The work and views in this book are the author's, and reflect seven years of experience with Flash. With the program constantly evolving, every new version of this book communicates innovative techniques and unique solutions developed from an artist's point of view.

Thanks to the overwhelming feedback received through *Vectorkid.com* about the first edition of this book, we are proud to be back with a second edition that focuses more on advanced illustrating projects. A new concept in this edition is the presentation of exercises at the end of each chapter to help you hone your Flash skills and expand your illustration capabilities.

So, sit back, relax, and be amazed by what you can do with Macromedia Flash.

About the Author

Robert Firebaugh, a.k.a. Vectorkid, is the founder of *vectorkid.com*, where he continues to be a pioneer in the Flash arts field. *Vectorkid.com* is a vector art community site that educates developers of Flash's illustration possibilities. With over 10 years of illustration and game design experience, Robert is creative director and cofounder of Electrotank, Inc. The games he has designed have won numerous international awards and have been acknowledged by many publications. He is an active member in the graphics community, publishing many other Flash works in magazines such as *Computer Arts, Computer Arts Projects, Web Designer, Practical Web Projects*, and many others, and contributed a chapter on graphics in games for *Macromedia® Flash™ MX Game Design Demystified*.

CHAPTER

1

GETTING STARTED

Macromedia® Flash™ is the only vector-based program that can achieve photorealistic quality graphics, fluid animations, and advanced programming with very little file size. The latest version—Macromedia Flash Professional 8—reaches whole new levels with its programming capabilities, and delivering of dynamic content. In the beginning, what made Macromedia Flash so popular were the entertaining animations and the fun visual toys it brought to the Web browser. But without its wide variety of drawing tools, extensive timeline, and tweening capabilities, Macromedia Flash would not be where it is today, and as a Macromedia Flash developer, you have to wonder why more people are not talking about Macromedia Flash and its possibilities as an illustration or animation tool. Yes, we have seen our share of Flash animation books, but illustrating in Flash? This book, *Illustrating with Macromedia Flash Professional 8*, breaks new grounds and continues to open your eyes to the truly jaw-dropping illustration possibilities you can achieve with Macromedia Flash.

INSPIRATIONAL START

We are still told to do our illustrations in other vector illustration programs and import them into Macromedia Flash. Why hassle with the exporting and importing when it can all be done in Macromedia Flash initially? Why work with noncreative pen tools in those other vector illustration programs when you can work with Flash's artistic drawing tools? Flash is such a creative illustration program that with the Brush tool, you can paint vectors. How cool is that? Well, there is something cooler: feast your eyes on Figure 1.1, which shows you the true illustration potential of Macromedia Flash and proves that it is the most powerful vector-based illustration program on the market. All the concepts, techniques, and tutorials needed to create these illustrations follow in this book.

ILLUSTRATION STYLES

There are all types of illustration styles, ranging from photorealistic to simple line art. Illustration styles for the most part are created by the tool or medium used and how the artist applies the stroke of color. For instance, drawing with a crayon will give you a different look than drawing with a pencil. If you are looking for a cartoon effect, applying black outlines to your graphics will do the trick. Some other traditional tools and mediums are airbrush, chalk pastel, oil pastels, color pencils, pen, watercolors, and a computer. With the computer and the digital medium, and programs like Macromedia Flash, more illustration styles are easier to achieve. In this chapter, we review several popular illustration styles, and

FIGURE 1.1 CD, Jar, Serving Board, Cardboard Box, Chrome, Manga Character, and Human Figure. Manga Character courtesy of Electrotank, Inc.

explain their attributes and what makes them special. We show some examples and where they are most often used.

Line Art

Line art is a graphic comprised of many lines, most often in a single color. Some examples are technical drawings you may see in product manuals, and black-and-white illustrations found in books or newspapers. Although Macromedia Flash is primarily a Web publishing tool, because of its extensive and easy-to-use vector drawing tools, it is a great illustrating tool for print as well. There will always be a need for line art, because not all print material can be produced in many colors; to keep the price down on product documentation, companies print them in one color—black. Since Flash is a vector-based illustration tool, exporting these illustrations at print resolution—300 dots per inch (dpi)—and in popular print file formats such as

AI or EPS is not a problem. Achieving this illustration style is quite easy with Flash's Line tool. Following are examples of line art created in Flash.

Assembly Diagram

The assembly diagram in this section was created primarily with the Line and Selection tools. The Line tool was used to create the vanishing points and any extra lines needed, as shown in Figure 1.2.

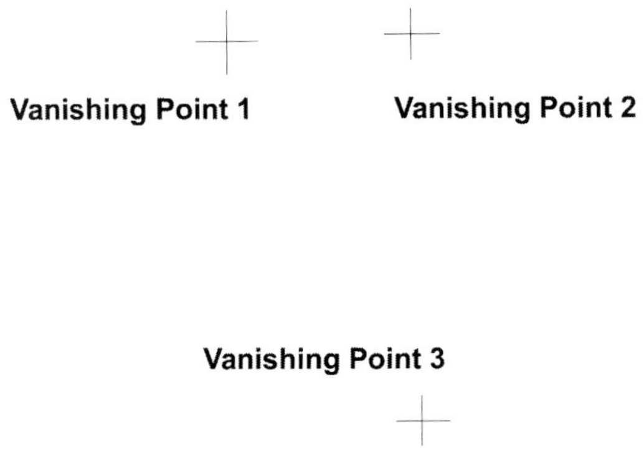

FIGURE 1.2 Vanishing points plotted.

To create the actual lines that define the shape of the object, the Selection tool was used to grab and place the lines from the vanishing points in the desired position, as shown in Figure 1.3.

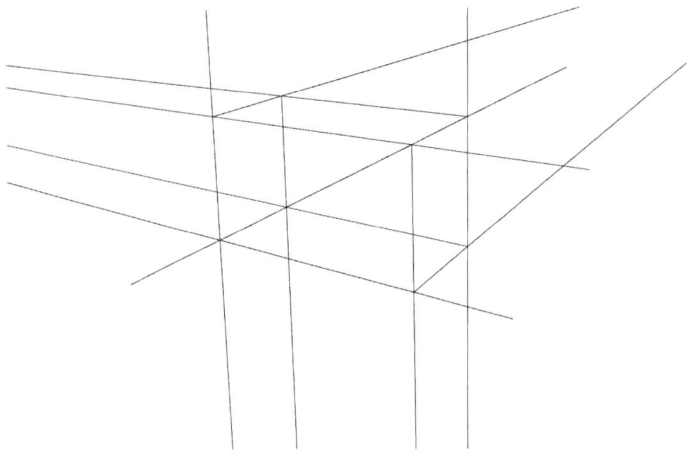

FIGURE 1.3 Place the lines to form the basic shape of the object.

Once enough lines have been placed, detail is added and unwanted lines are deleted, the result of which is similar to Figure 1.4. If you want to achieve a similar 3D perspective, review the three-point perspective technique found in Chapter 4, "Illustration Techniques."

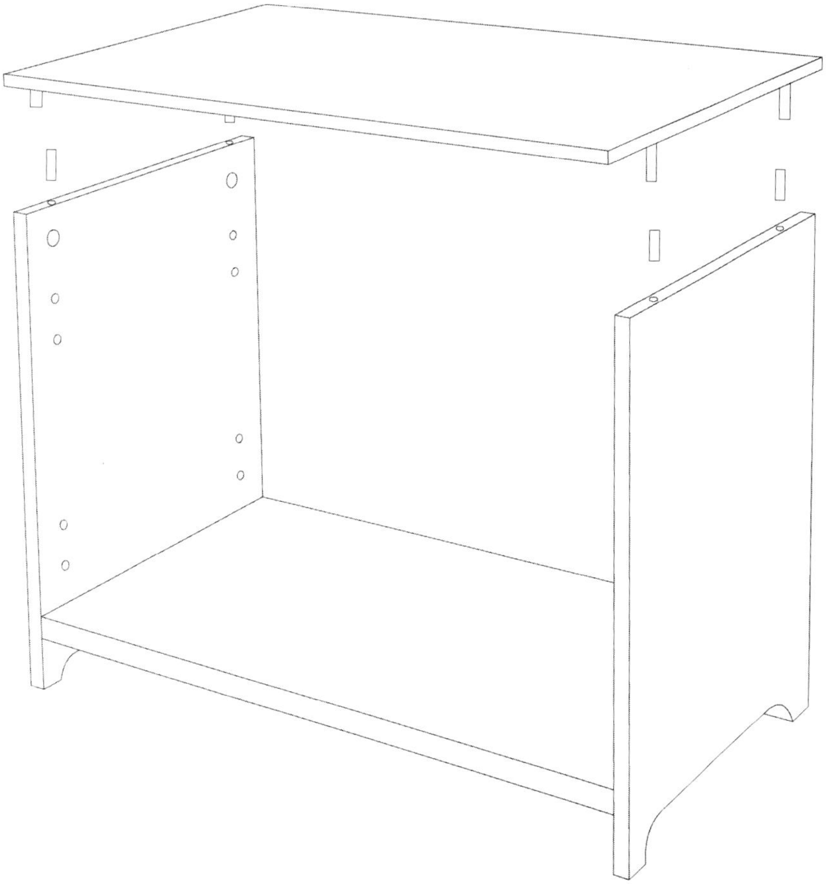

FIGURE 1.4 The finished diagram of how to install the top shelf.

Product Line Drawing

Similar to the assembly diagram, the product line drawing presented here was created primarily with the Line and Selection tools. The Line tool was used to create the lines you see in Figure 1.5. The Selection tool was used to modify any of the lines by moving, deleting, and applying a curve to an existing line.

FIGURE 1.5 A car illustrated using the Line and Selection tools.

Solid Fill Art

The solid fill art style appears in hip, cutting-edge ad campaigns that try to capture tech-savvy and next-generation audiences. Being comprised of solid colors, a graphic of this type works well for print and GIF banner ads. This style can be achieved in several ways, discussed here and in the following subsections. You can use Macromedia Flash and its Trace Bitmap feature, which lets you convert a raster image into vectors. There are several settings to play with, but for the most part, because the process is automated, you can tell if a bitmap graphic has been run through it. Although Trace Bitmap is easy to use, the result is unoptimized, and for the most part provides you with points and curves that are not placed correctly. Since a Trace Bitmap vector image will need much editing and optimization, in most instances it will be much faster to trace the graphic in Flash manually. Following are examples of solid fill art and the best way to create them.

Video Game Console

The video game console shown in Figure 1.6 was sketched on paper, scanned in, and imported into Macromedia Flash.

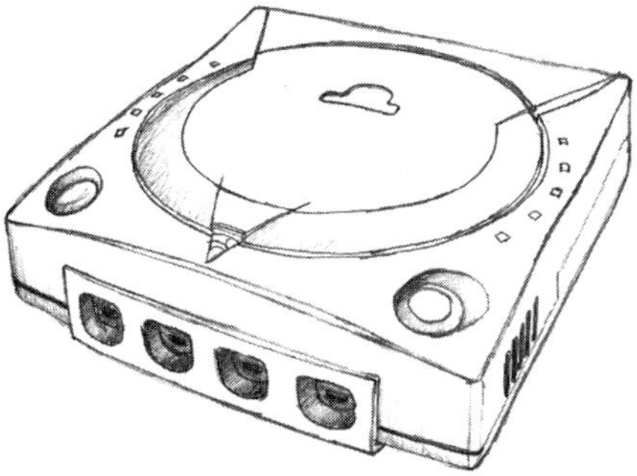

FIGURE 1.6 Sketch the object you want to illustrate.

To illustrate the solid fills, an outline has to be drawn with the Line and Selection tools. If we were to start with the Brush tool and draw the shape of the object, we would end up with a fill that is not the exact shape we are looking for and would contain more vector points than needed. Fixing it would require extra time editing with the Selection tool and optimizing it. Once the basic shape of the object has been outlined, more detail should be added with the Line tool, as shown in Figure 1.7.

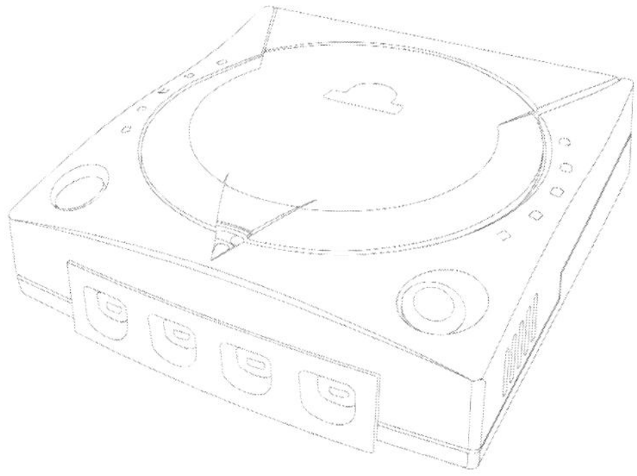

FIGURE 1.7 Adding more detail with the Line tool.

Now that we have all the outlines, it is time to fill them in with the Paint Bucket tool, as shown in Figure 1.8. We will be using the Color Mixer panel, which is where you will be choosing the colors you will be applying. If you want to learn how to use the Color Mixer panel more efficiently, review the *Coloring* section in Chapter 2, "Illustration Concepts."

FIGURE 1.8 Apply solid fills with the Paint Bucket tool and delete all outlines.

F-14 Fighter Jet

The F-14 fighter jet illustration was created with the same process as the video game console, beginning with the basic shape of the object and finishing the details. Use the Color Mixer panel to prepare the color swatches you will be using, and apply them between the outlines with the Paint Bucket tool. The result is shown in Figure 1.9.

FIGURE 1.9 F-14 fighter jet illustrated as solid fill art.

Cartoon

Everyone is familiar with cartoons, whether in your daily newspaper or Saturday mornings on television. Most traditional cartoons start as ink drawings, are then colored in with ink or paint, and contain distinct outlines. If you were to illustrate a cartoon-like bouncing ball in Macromedia Flash, it would contain an oval outline and a solid fill coloring in the center. Since cartoon-style graphics are comical in nature, they tend to over exaggerate a character's facial expressions and body movement. Flash provides you with great drawing tools that make creating cartoon-style graphics quite easy. We next review several steps to getting into cartoon drawing mode and get you used to being able to identify some cartoon graphics drawn in Flash.

Shark

Several sharks were sketched before the shark in Figure 1.10 was drawn. The one chosen was scanned in and imported in Macromedia Flash MX 2004 for reference.

Figure 1.10 is a typical illustration of a cartoon-style graphic. To illustrate the solid fills, an outline has to be drawn with the Line and Selection tools. If we were to start by using the Brush tool and draw the shape of

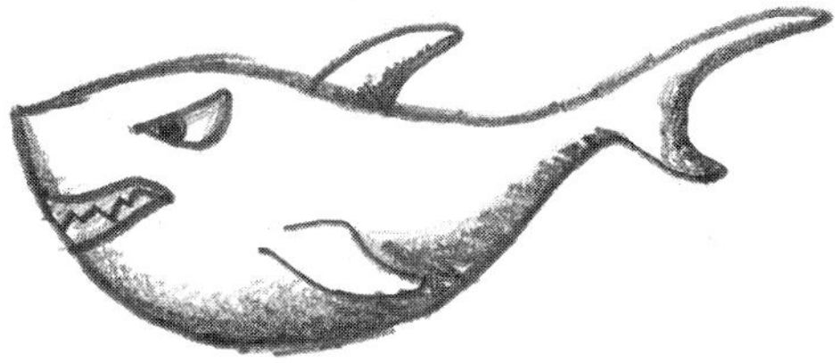

FIGURE 1.10 Sketch the object you want to illustrate. Courtesy of Electrotank, Inc.

the object, our result would be a fill that is not the exact shape we are looking for, and would contain more vector points than needed. Fixing it would require extra time editing it with the Selection tool and optimizing it. Once the basic shape of the object has been outlined, more detail should be added with the Line tool, as shown in Figure 1.11.

FIGURE 1.11 Adding detail with the Line tool. Courtesy of Electrotank, Inc.

Now that all the outlines have been illustrated, it is time to fill between the lines with the Paint Bucket tool, as shown in Figure 1.12. To do so, we will use the Color Mixer panel, which is where you will be choosing the colors you will be applying with the Paint Bucket tool. To learn how to use the Color Mixer more efficiently, review the *Coloring* section found in Chapter 2.

FIGURE 1.12 Apply solid fills with the Paint Bucket tool and delete all outlines. Courtesy of Electrotank, Inc.

Zombie

The difference between the zombie graphic and the shark is that the zombie graphic contains all fills. This illustration was used in a tile-based online game with a resolution of 25 pixels by 25 pixels, so it required little detail. The black outlines were illustrated with the Line tool and filled in with a black solid fill. Its colors were chosen in the Color Mixer panel and applied with the Paint Bucket tool, resulting in Figure 1.13.

FIGURE 1.13 Cartoon graphic with all fills.
Courtesy of Electrotank, Inc.

Manga

Manga is a style of illustration associated with the Japanese style of comics and the Asian culture. *Anime* refers to the Japanese style of animation. Since this is a book on illustration, we will be focusing more on the art of Manga. The Manga style of art has become very popular in the United States, and around the world, many artists are drawing in this style. Similar to the cartoon style with its simple outlines and solid fills, what really sets this style apart is the way the stroke of color is controlled and a character's facial features are drawn. The stroke of color is controlled by how the artist applies it on the paper, which means, depending on the artist, you could have a slightly different-looking Manga style. Since the cartoon style is fundamentally similar to anime style, it can be drawn in Macromedia Flash just as easily. The following examples show two Manga styles and explain how one can be replicated fairly quickly with the Brush tool.

Drawing the Face

The Manga illustration discussed here was drawn for an online game called *Electro Air Hockey* created by Electrotank, Inc. The game is an air hockey simulation-type game wrapped around a tournament-style fighting theme, which required 16 Manga-style characters to be drawn. The character face shown in Figure 1.14 is just one of them. To create this graphic, you first want to illustrate the face on paper with a pencil; that way, you can focus

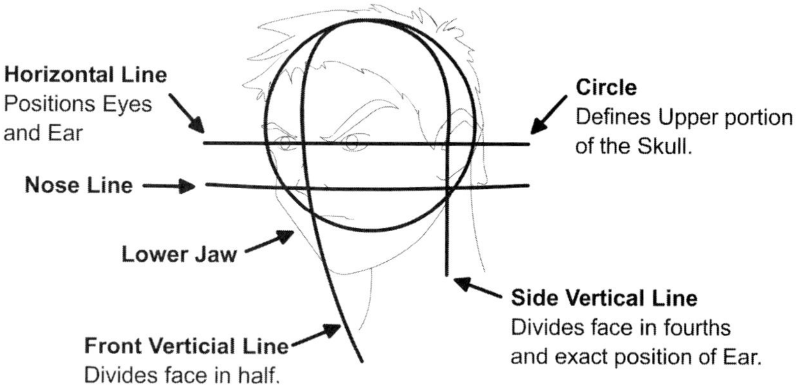

FIGURE 1.14 The guidelines of the face. Courtesy of Electrotank, Inc.

more on the strokes you will be drawing and how the face is constructed. Study the guidelines that make up the major parts of the face. The human face is comprised of two major parts: the upper portion of the skull and the lower jaw. The circle defines the upper portion of the skull, and the organic chin-shaped line defines the lower jaw. Notice the vertical, horizontal, and nose lines that divide the face and map out where the eyes, ears, and nose will be placed.

Now that the basic shapes of the face are plotted out, continue to define the face with more detail, including the hair, mouth, and any accessories (in our case, goggles), as shown in Figure 1.15. Feel free to erase the guidelines as you finalize your sketch.

FIGURE 1.15 The details of the face. Courtesy of Electrotank, Inc.

Once the sketch is finalized, it is scanned in and imported into Macromedia Flash to be traced with the Brush tool. You could use the Line tool, but here we used the Brush tool to get the brush outline look, which makes the drawing look as if it were sketched. To outline the shadows and highlights of the character, the Line tool was used, as shown in Figure 1.16.

FIGURE 1.16 Trace the sketch with the Brush tool, and outline the shadows and highlights with the Line tool. Courtesy of Electrotank, Inc.

Now that the character is outlined, use the Color Mixer to create colored fills and gradients you will be using to color between the outlines. Apply the fills with the Paint Bucket tool, and make any edits to those gradients with the Fill Transform tool. The result should resemble Figure 1.17. Delete the lines that were created with the Line tool.

FIGURE 1.17 Apply fills and delete the lines that were created with the Line tool. Courtesy of Electrotank, Inc.

Character Illustration

The Manga character discussed here was drawn for the online game *Digikid*, created by Electrotank, Inc. The illustration was used on menu screens where a detailed illustration of the character was needed. Although this character was illustrated with the sketching process used in the previous section, notice that the final illustration as shown in Figure 1.18 does not contain black outlines. If you want to make your illustrations seem more realistic, do not keep the black outlines in your finished illustration.

FIGURE 1.18 Manga cartoon graphic illustrated with all fills. Courtesy of Electrotank, Inc.

Photorealistic

Illustrating a realistic-looking object does not take much talent, and if you analyze what is involved, you will find it is much easier than you may have thought. Broken down to its basics, a photorealistic graphic is comprised of several layers of gradient fills and shapes of color orchestrated in such a way that the result appears real. For an object to look real, it must resemble something found in the real world, and reflect light and cast shadows. Otherwise, it would look less believable. If there were no light cast upon the object, your object would be black, and if there is no light, a shadow could not be cast. In the following subsections, we review two examples of photorealistic illustrations achieved in Flash and discuss how they are achieved. To explore more examples of photorealistic illustrations created in Macromedia Flash, see Chapter 8, "Novice Tutorials."

Penguin

Penguins are interesting creatures and fun to watch. The little guy in Figure 1.19 was sketched and photographed at the zoo. Several sketches were done before the one shown was chosen.

The sketch was traced in Macromedia Flash with the Line tool and the Selection tool to create the outlines, as shown in Figure 1.20. Notice the detail in the penguin's fur. The Pencil tool, set at Smooth, was used to illustrate those small curvy lines. Since the Pencil tool produces an unoptimized line, because it is manually drawn, you must optimize it as much as you can without losing the desired path. To optimize any vectors, select them and run them through the Optimize feature, located under Modify > Shape > Optimize. To learn the Optimize feature in more depth, review Chapter 2.

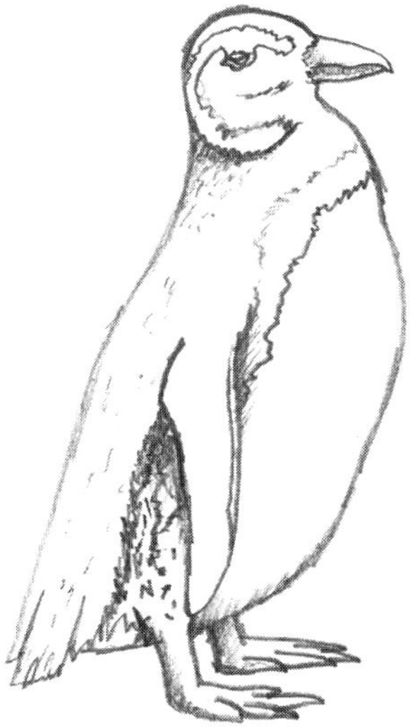

FIGURE 1.19 Sketch of a penguin at the zoo.

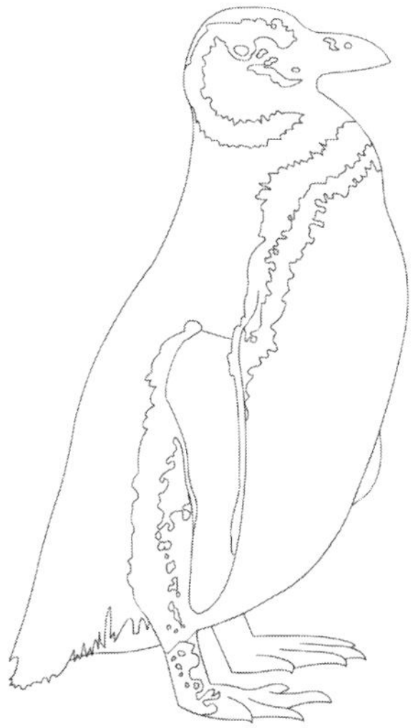

FIGURE 1.20 Outlines were drawn from the sketch with the Line tool.

It is time to color between the outlines. Use the Color Mixer to create your solid fills and gradients. Use the Paint Bucket tool to apply the fills, and the Fill Transform tool to edit the placement of the gradients. Delete the outlines when you are finished applying the fills, as shown in Figure 1.21.

FIGURE 1.21 Solid fills and gradients were applied to the outlines, a shadow was drawn, and the outlines were deleted.

Apple

The apple shown in Figure 1.22 was illustrated with the same process as the penguin. Since the apple has a detailed textured surface, more layers of gradient shapes were used to get that look. Refer to the Apple tutorial in Chapter 9, "Advanced Tutorials," for a more detailed analysis.

FIGURE 1.22 Photorealistic apple illustrated in Macromedia Flash MX 2004.

Experimental

You may have thought that drawing in Macromedia Flash could only be done with its drawing tools. In fact, with ActionScript you can program lines and fills to be drawn. Three-dimensional-looking vector shapes can be created with the help of 3D software such as Swift 3D™, 3D Studio Max™, or Maya™. Importing the 3D geometry into Flash as vectors is just another way to achieve 3D-looking interfaces or objects with accurate perspective. The following examples explain how you can achieve these experimental styles and what other software you might need to do so.

3D Interface

You can get 3D geometry such as vector graphics into Macromedia Flash in several ways. One method is to find a 3D program like Swift 3D that can export an SWF file of your geometry. Another is to find a plug-in for a 3D program that lets you export an SWF file. Swift 3D makes plug-ins for 3D Studio Max, Softimage™, and NewTek LightWave®. Following is a quick review of the plug-in process and how a final interface is illustrated in Macromedia Flash.

In 3D Studio Max, six stretched-out cubes are placed in a group and the camera is positioned at the desired angle, as in Figure 1.23, with the Swift 3D plug-in for 3D Studio Max installed, an SWF is rendered. The settings are adjusted to include only the edges, black lines are set to hairline width.

FIGURE 1.23 Boxes are placed in 3D Studio Max for an interface.

By importing the SWF into Flash, you will get a result like that in Figure 1.24. The vector graphic will be grouped rather strangely, so you will have to break it down if you want to edit it.

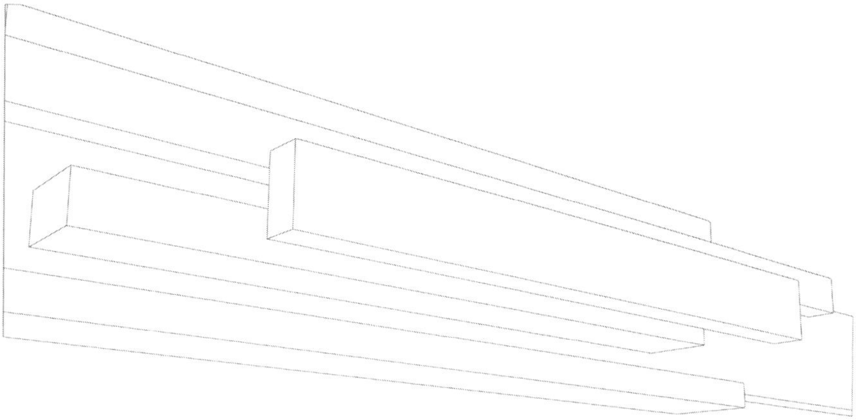

FIGURE 1.24 The SWF imported into Macromedia Flash MX 2004 with the grouped vector graphic broken down.

Once the vectors are broken down and the graphic can be edited, the Paint Bucket tool is used to add the colors between the lines. The lines are then deleted and distorted text is added, which completes the 3D interface, as shown in Figure 1.25.

FIGURE 1.25 Apply solid fills with the Paint Bucket tool, delete all outlines, and add distorted text.

Programming Vectors

Illustrating vectors with ActionScript is not as extensive as illustrating with the drawing tools. You are limited to coding lines and fills as shown in Figure 1.26.

FIGURE 1.26 Triangle, square, and circle created with ActionScript.

This feature could be used in an online application with which the user can make a line drawing to illustrate an idea or collaborate with another user. The following ActionScript is used to create a square and is added to the first frame of the movie. To make sure you understand the code, let's look at it in depth. `_root` states that the code will be executed on the main timeline. `lineStyle` states that we will be drawing a line. The first number `10` controls the stroke width, and `0x00FF00` sets what HEX color that stoke will be. `75` is setting the alpha % of the stroke. `moveTo` states where the cursor starts. The first number `100` is the x location of the cursor, and the second `100` is the y location of the cursor. `lineTo` creates a point. The first number `200` is the x location of the point, and the second number `100` is the y location of the point.

```
_root.lineStyle(10, 0x00FF00, 75);
_root.moveTo(100, 100);
_root.lineTo(200, 100);
_root.lineTo(200, 200);
_root.lineTo(100, 200);
_root.lineTo(100, 100);
```

Vector versus Raster

Which is better, vector graphics or raster graphics? Is there a definitive answer to this age-old question? To even come close to an answer, one must understand what these two types of graphic formats are and the environment in which they are used.

Vector

Vector graphics are defined by mathematical statements and properties such as fill, outline, and color. Being comprised of mathematical statements and properties makes this file format quite small in size, and it can be scaled and published at any resolution and not lose its quality. Since vector graphics require calculations to be shown, displaying a vector image can be processor-intensive depending on the image's complexity. The SWF file format of Macromedia Flash has introduced other properties such as alpha color (transparency), grouping of graphics, symbol color settings, and filter effects. Some common vector-based illustration programs are Macromedia Flash MX 2004, Macromedia® FreeHand® MX, Adobe® Illustrator® CS2, and CorelDRAW® 12. Common vector formats include AI (Adobe Illustrator), CDR (CorelDRAW), CGM (Computer Graphics Metafile), SWF (Shockwave Flash), and DXF (AutoCAD and other CAD software).

Raster

Raster graphics are defined by pixels in a grid. Each pixel in the image contains information about the color to be displayed. The larger the resolution of the raster image, the larger the file size may be. Since raster images have a fixed resolution, they cannot be resized without losing image quality. Raster graphics are not as processor-intensive to display, since no mathematical calculations are needed. Some common raster-based illustration programs are Macromedia® Fireworks® 8, Adobe® Photoshop® CS2, Corel® Painter™ IX, and Microsoft® Paint. Common bitmap-based formats are JPEG, GIF, TIFF, PNG, PICT, and BMP.

Now that we know a little more about vector and raster graphics, it is time to compare actual graphics files and their file size and see which is superior. As shown in Figure 1.27, we have three graphic files, all of which were created from a vector illustration drawn in Macromedia Flash. The two raster files, the GIF and the JPEG, were optimized in Adobe Photoshop, and still cannot match the file size and quality of the SWF file. Therefore, if you plan to use any graphics in your Macromedia Flash projects, consider using vector graphics. Company logos, user interfaces, product screen shots, and product imagery can all be vector images, and you will benefit from the small file size and high-quality images. Of course, there are exceptions, such as creating photorealistic vector graphics of humans and landscapes—too time-consuming to convert to vector. However, stylistic vector illustrations of humans and landscapes have been done that look amazing.

FIGURE 1.27 Comparison of GIF, JPEG, and SWF files of similar graphics.

BE AN EFFICIENT ILLUSTRATOR

There is a difference between *using* a certain software package and *mastering* it, and being an efficient Flash user is one step closer to mastering it. Efficiency is broken into two areas: use of your hardware, and how you use Flash, the software. Depending on what type of hardware you use and how you use it can determine how much production time you could be saving. How you use the drawing tools and panels could determine whether you will be successful in achieving a certain graphic quality.

Recommended Hardware

Anyone who has a computer most likely uses a mouse peripheral device to interact with his or her computer. When it comes to navigating through your files on your personal computer or using a word processing program, a mouse does the trick. However, if you have tried to use your mouse to create graphics in a drawing program, you know it can become awkward. This transition between media can be difficult, but with the help of certain devices, getting your illustrations into Macromedia Flash can be a cinch. Although it is possible to use a mouse to draw in Macromedia Flash, some features cannot be executed with a mouse alone. Several hardware devices are available that will save you time and give you more control over your illustrations.

Scanner

You should always sketch your ideas on paper first. Working with pencil and paper is a great place to start brainstorming your ideas and focus on what you want. If you plan to get your sketches into Macromedia Flash, you will need a scanner, as shown in Figure 1.28. Scanners are now relatively affordable and lightweight. Make sure it scans at least at 300 dpi and 32-bit color depth. In case you did not know, computer monitors display at 72 dpi, and depending on your monitor, the color setting can range from 16- to 32-bit color depth, so you do not need the hottest scanner on the market. Installation and compatibility when running Windows XP or Mac OS should be no problem when installing with a USB (Universal Serial BUS). The BUS is a pathway that allows for multiple devices to connect and communicate. USB connection allows the device to be used right out of the box, without having to reboot the computer. If you are running any other operating system, review the requirements on the side of the scanner box.

FIGURE 1.28 A flatbed scanner.

Getting a scanned image into Macromedia Flash may seem simple, but if you are not familiar with the scanning process, you can run into trouble. You can use the scanning software your scanner comes with, or Windows XP, which has a scanning utility. Another option is a plug-in that can be downloaded and installed, which will give you the ability to use a utility in Adobe Photoshop to scan your images. Before you import the scanned image into Flash, make sure you have cropped it to include only what you need. *Cropping* is a graphics term that means to reduce the resolution of an image to display only the content you want to show. For example, if your scanned image contains a lot of white space on top of the image, cropping that white space will reduce the dimensions of the image, making the file size quite small. Importing a huge image will only slow the performance of Macromedia Flash. Your scanned image should be edited and optimized in a raster drawing program such as Macromedia Fireworks or Photoshop. What you plan to do with this image in Macromedia Flash will dictate whether you need to compress the image. If you want to use the image in your Flash movie, it should be optimized. If you do not intend to use the scanned image in your Flash movie and just need it to trace or "eyedrop" certain colors, compression does not matter. Once you are done with the image, make sure you delete it from your library because it will increase the size of your FLA.

Graphics Tablet

A graphics tablet is a peripheral device that consists of a tablet surface and a stylus pen, as shown in Figure 1.29, and replicates a pencil and paper experience. The monitor screen is mirrored onto the tablet surface, so if you position the stylus pen in the lower right corner, you will see your cursor in the lower right corner of your monitor screen. Technically, you will not see your display on the tablet. If you want to illustrate in Macromedia Flash and use the pressure sensitivity feature, a tablet is highly recommended. Using a tablet will increase the precision of your lines and shapes and save you time, whether you are tracing an image or drawing from scratch. In addition, a tablet is ergonomically correct, since as you are using a stylus pen to navigate, the underside of your wrist does not make contact with the surface of your desk. Graphics tablets come in different sizes and are reasonably priced. If you are thinking about purchasing a tablet but are used to using a mouse, it will take several hours to get used to, but the rewards are worth the learning curve. If you use a two-monitor setup or a wide-screen display, get a graphics tablet with a similar desktop space ratio. The Wacom Intuos 2, 12x18 is an excellent option.

FIGURE 1.29 A typical graphics tablet.

Interactive Pen Display

An interactive pen display is an LCD monitor with pressure sensitivity on the display so you can use a stylus pen to interact right on your monitor, as shown in Figure 1.30. Working with one of these is similar to working with a paintbrush and canvas. You can adjust the incline so you can work with the display flat or standing up. Although these devices may not be affordable for everyone, they do bring a lot of value. They are great for tracing images, and since you work directly on the display you have complete control over your lines and the shapes you are drawing. They can also be used to sketch right into Macromedia Flash, versus sketching with pencil and paper and having to scan in the sketch. The pressure sensitivity is half as sensitive as on the graphics tablet, but it is not noticeable.

FIGURE 1.30 An interactive pen display in horizontal position.

Setting Up Your Workstation

If you have used Macromedia Flash before, you will understand the importance of memorizing the shortcut keys. Having to look them up will slow your work pace significantly. Use Flash at least 30 minutes a day to become more familiar with the shortcut keys, and you will become a more efficient worker. When it comes to drawing in Flash, knowing your shortcut keys and the position of your fingers on the keyboard are very important if you want to execute your key commands swiftly.

Shortcut Keys

Everyone has certain commands he or she uses the most; if you have not memorized them in Flash yet, a good way to start is to look them up under Edit > Keyboard Shortcuts > Tool Panel, as shown in Figure 1.31. Edit them as you wish, and once satisfied with the configuration, type them, and print them out. Place the printout next to your keyboard for reference. It sounds somewhat silly, but having the shortcut terms visible really helps increase your productivity. If you prefer previous versions of Macromedia Flash, you can edit shortcut keys to suit your taste under the Keyboard Shortcuts panel. Since shortcut key settings have a history of changing with new versions of Flash, it is a good idea to create your own keyboard shortcuts and use them in other graphics programs you use. That way, you can avoid confusion when working with multiple graphics programs.

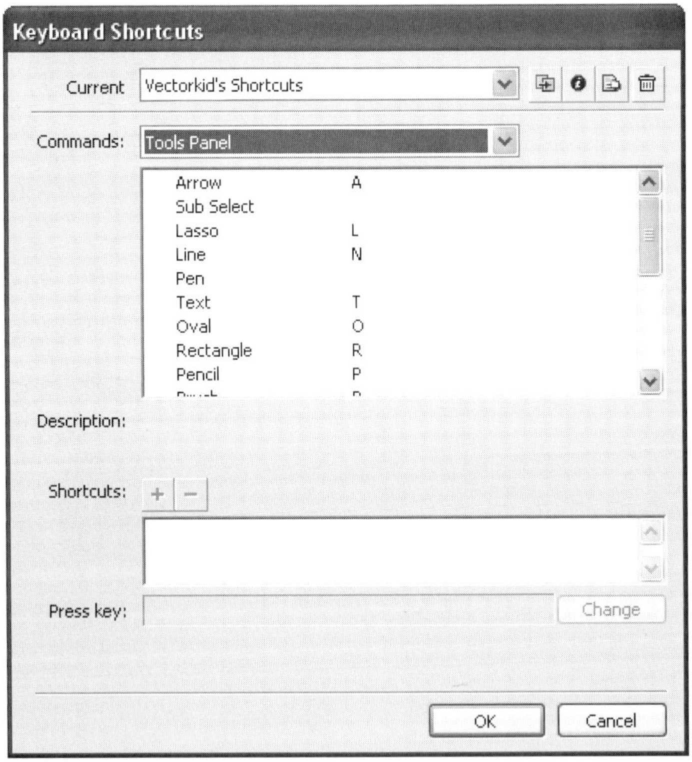

FIGURE 1.31 Editing keyboard shortcuts.

Recommended Hand and Finger Positions

Using a specific hand and finger position may sound a bit strange, but can be quite effective. Just as in driving a car (automatic) with two hands on the steering wheel and your right foot on the accelerator (or brake), you are able to respond rapidly to whatever the conditions may be. The same is true with Macromedia Flash, where you have to execute key commands quickly and precisely. Figures 1.32, 1.33, and 1.34 show different setups. Of course, if you change your shortcut key commands slightly, the finger positions may not be accurate. Figure out the hand and finger position that works best for you.

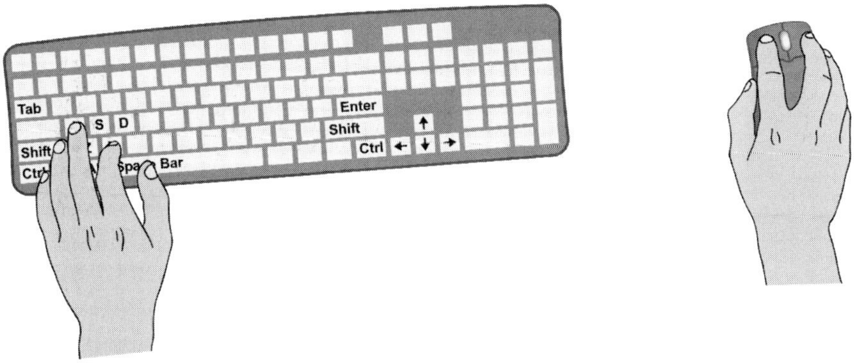

FIGURE 1.32 Recommended setup if you are using keyboard and mouse.

FIGURE 1.33 Recommended setup if you are using keyboard and graphics tablet.

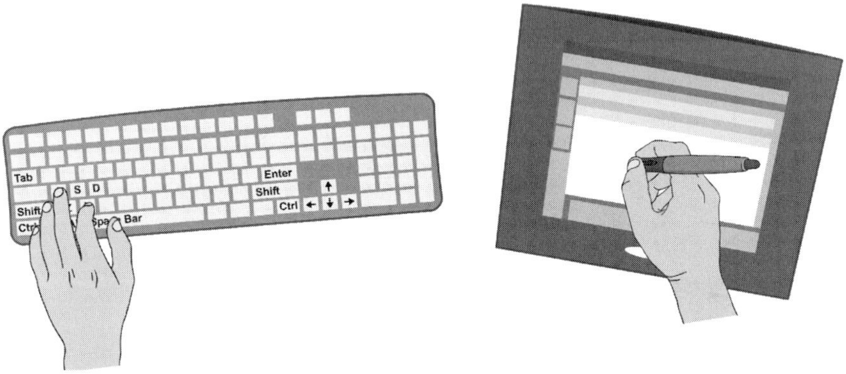

FIGURE 1.34 Recommended setup if you are using keyboard and interactive pen display.

Understanding the Drawing Tools and Panels

Upcoming chapters refer to certain Macromedia Flash drawing tools located in the Tools panel, and you will need to be up to speed on what they do, and this book teaches you how they should be used. Flash has tools similar to those in other programs you might be using—which does not mean you should use them the same way. To better understand the potential of Macromedia Flash as a vector drawing program, you have to understand the basic drawing tools. Sure, they are simple to understand—the Line tool makes a line, the Paint Bucket tool creates a shape fill—but do you know how to use Flash's drawing tools to control the vectors so your graphic will be optimized for the Web? If you need to edit the shape of a graphic, do you know the most efficient and fastest way to do so?

Selection Tool

The Selection tool has many uses. Normally, it can be used to select and edit objects, but if needed, you can also straighten and smooth your lines. By using this tool to select and modify your vectors, you will have more control and your vector graphics will look more precise.

Selecting Objects

With the Selection tool, you can select lines, shapes, grouped objects, symbols, raster graphics, and text fields. Once you have selected something, the Properties panel will tell you what you have selected, along with other settings related to the selected object, as shown in Figure 1.35. If you want to select more than one object, hold down the Shift key as you are selecting. Try it yourself—create a square with the Rectangle tool. Select the Rectangle tool located in the Tools panel, and click and drag on the stage to create a square. Switch to the Selection tool, and click and drag to create a bounding box around the square. Once you unclick, the graphic will be selected.

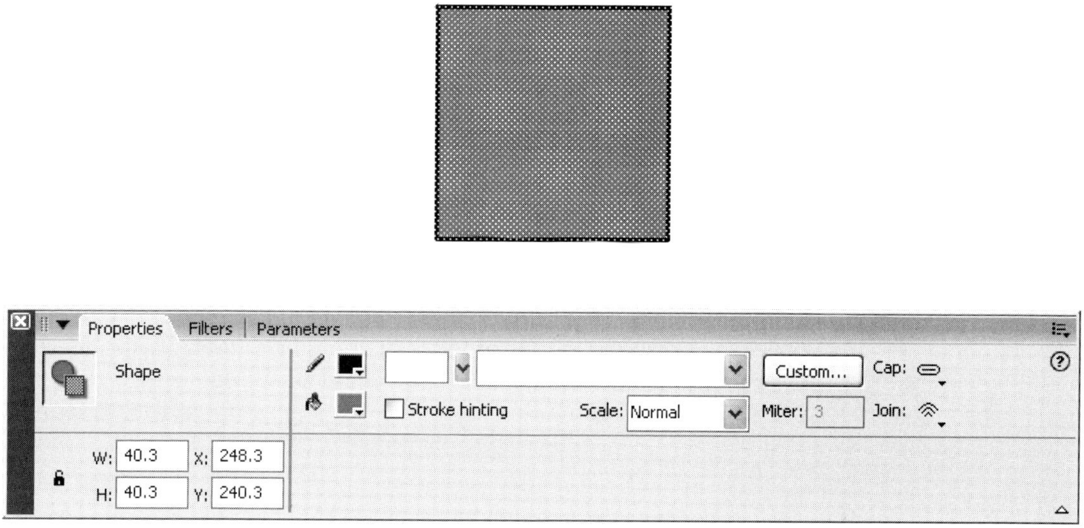

FIGURE 1.35 Square selected and properties displayed.

You can select lines that are connected and of the same color and line width by double-clicking any part of the lines. This tip will come in handy later in the book.

With the Selection tool still active, hold down the Shift key, and click on the objects you wish to keep on that key frame to have them deselected. Holding down the Shift key works in reverse by deselecting what you have already selected. Use the appropriate shortcut keys to move or delete based on what you want to do. To move selected objects, use the arrow keys. To delete a selected object, use the keyboard shortcut to delete. This tip can be applied to many tasks, and although it may seem simple, it can accomplish such complicated tasks as deleting hundreds of unwanted objects.

Manipulating Lines and Shape Outlines

The Selection tool allows you to make modifications to vector points and curves. If you edit a line or shape outline too much, Flash may add unnecessary vector points to the curve you are modifying. If you are looking for a more complex curving line, try to add more points in your line as you are creating it and edit the curves from there. Create the four different lines as shown in Figure 1.36. With the Line tool, create two lines connected at one end, like the "2 Curves" line shown in the figure. To make sure the two lines are connected, the Snap to Objects feature needs to be on. That option can be accessed by choosing View > Snapping > Snap to Objects. Once the "2 Curves" line is drawn, switch to the Selection tool, click and drag your mouse on the center part of one of the lines, and drag back to see the line curve. Unclick to apply the desired curve to the line. Apply a similar curve to the other line and you should have a line curve similar to "2 Curves Modified." To create the other two lines, start with the "5 Curves" line and apply curves to your lines to create the "5 Curves Modified" line.

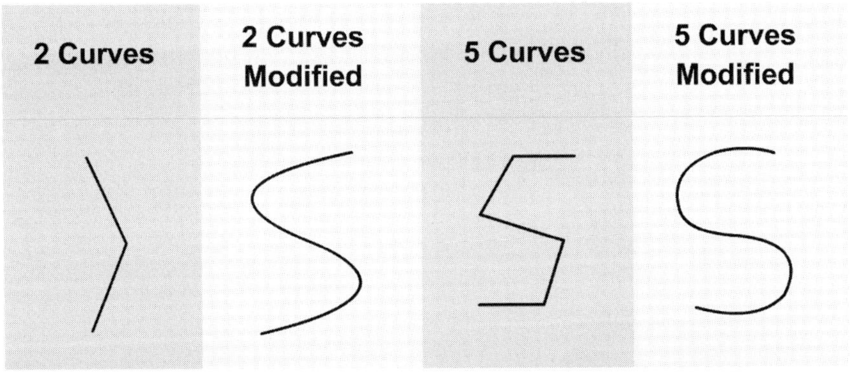

FIGURE 1.36 To draw a path that resembles an S, more points are needed.

When editing a line or shape, the Selection tool will change its appearance based on what part of the line or shape your cursor is hovering over. If your cursor is over a vector point, the Selection tool will display a right angle line, as shown in Figure 1.37. Create a line with the Line tool and hover your mouse over a vector point to see your mouse cursor change in appearance, similar to Figure 1.37.

If your cursor is over the curved part of the line, the Selection tool will display a curved line, as shown in Figure 1.38. Move your mouse cursor over the curved part of the line to see your cursor change appearance.

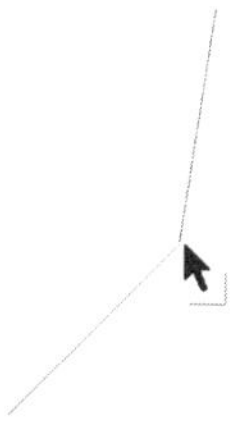

FIGURE 1.37 Working with the Selection tool as the cursor is over a vector point.

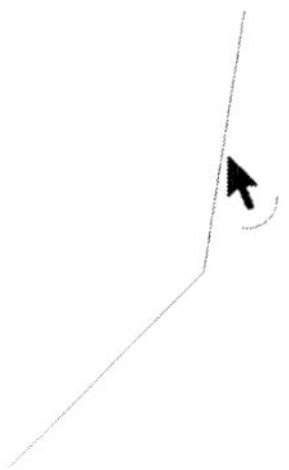

FIGURE 1.38 Working with the Selection tool.

Snap to Objects

When using the drawing tools, and especially when moving objects around, the Snap to Objects feature lets you constrain your object to other objects, which lets you be very precise. There are four other Snap features: Snap Align, Snap to Grid, Snap to Guides, and Snap to Pixels, but they are not as important when illustrating with the drawing tools. This feature can be disabled by holding down the G key on your keyboard while using the Arrow tool or Line tool. (If Snap to Objects is turned off and you hold down the G key, the feature will not turn on.) It can also be turned on or off by clicking the Snap to Objects button in the toolbar Options box. This allows you to better determine the precision of your vectors. Being able to turn this feature off at any time is efficient because you did not have to stop what you are doing and execute the shortcut key. This feature was last seen in Flash 4, but Macromedia has now reimplemented it.

See it in action in these next four steps. With the G key not pressed (up), you can see the Snap to Objects feature if currently on as shown in Figure 1.39.

With the G key still up, the line snaps the lower line in Figure 1.40.

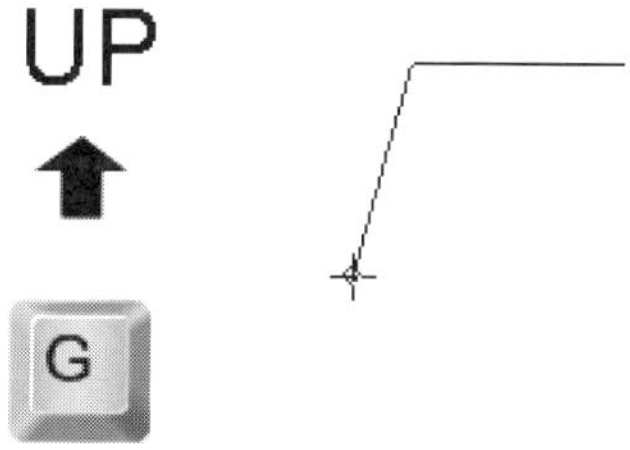

FIGURE 1.39 Adding a line connecting the top and bottom lines.

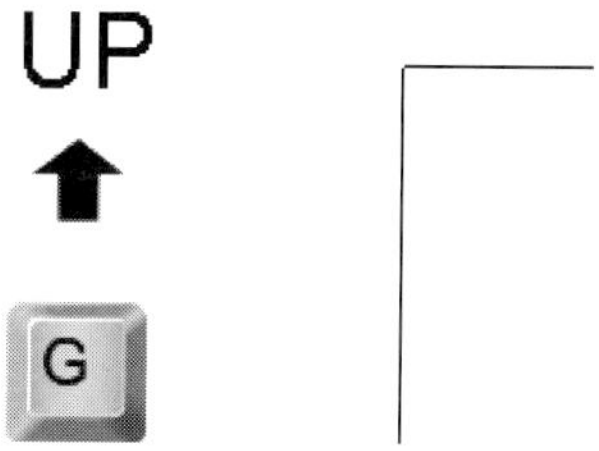

FIGURE 1.40 The top and bottom lines are now connected precisely.

When connecting the line on the right, hold down the G key, turning the Snap to Objects feature off. The line can be placed close to the other line without the Snap feature interfering with your placement, as in Figure 1.41.

Now, release the G key, enabling the Snap to Objects feature, and the line snaps to the other line, as in Figure 1.42. Snap to Objects and the G key are very effective when creating more complicated graphics where this feature needs to be switched on and off while using the Line, Arrow, and Fill Transform tools.

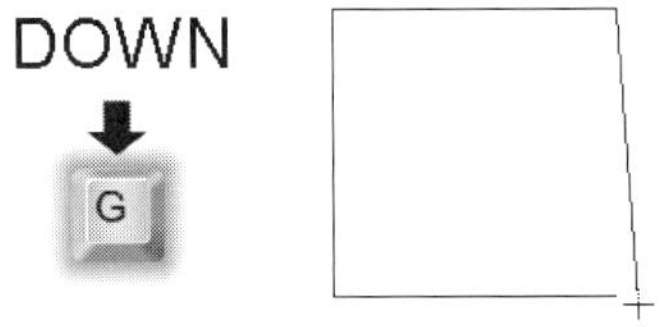

FIGURE 1.41 While holding the G key down, the Snap to Objects feature is turned off.

FIGURE 1.42 With the G key not pressed, the Snap to Objects feature is enabled.

Straightening and Smoothing Lines and Shapes

Once a line or shape is selected by using the Selection tool, two buttons will be active in the toolbar Options box: Smooth and Straighten. Smooth removes the points used in the selected line or shape. You can continue to execute the Smooth feature on the same line or shape to achieve the object you want. Straighten takes out the curves in your object, making an "s" shaped line into a "z" shaped line.

Lasso Tool

Using the Lasso tool and its Polygon Mode modifier, you can select objects by drawing a freehand or a straight-edged selection area. This tool really comes in handy when you need to select a graphic placed next to another graphic, or a graphic on top of another graphic, as shown in Figure 1.43.

Select the Lasso tool and press down as you circle around the line, as shown in Figure 1.44.

FIGURE 1.43 A line needs to be deleted.

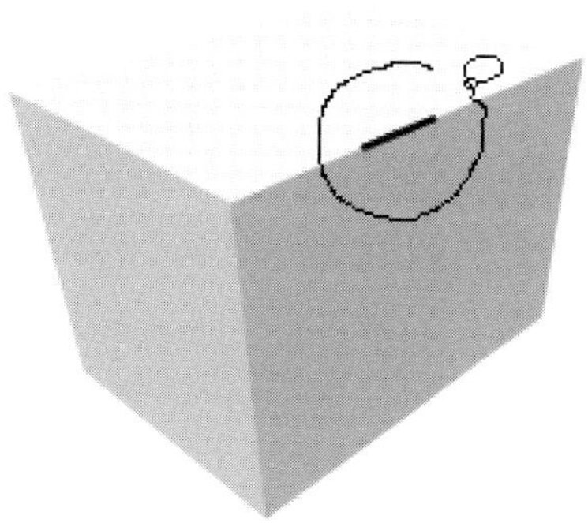

FIGURE 1.44 Use the Lasso tool to select the line to be deleted.

Unclick the mouse button and the area will be selected. You now have three pieces selected: the line, and two fill pieces as shown in Figure 1.45.

Switch to the Selection tool, and as you hold down the Shift key, deselect the two fills, as shown in Figure 1.46.

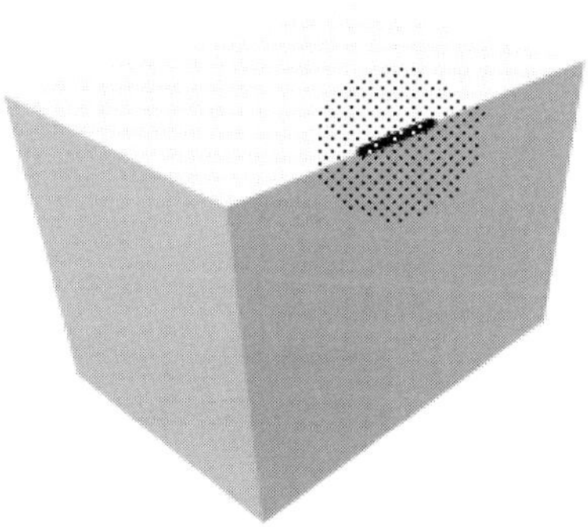

FIGURE 1.45 Using the Lasso tool allows you to select more than just the line.

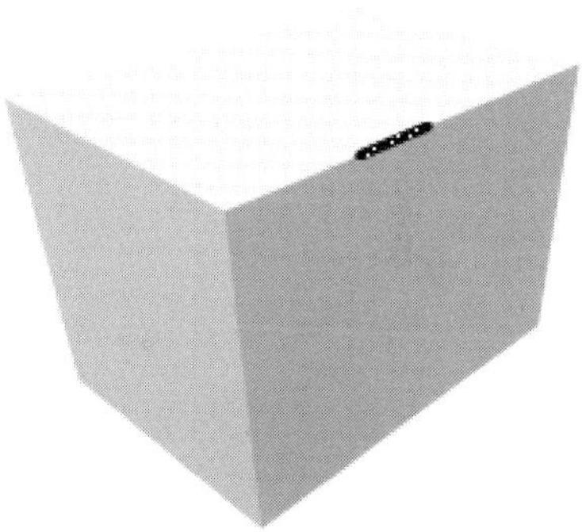

FIGURE 1.46 Use the Selection tool to deselect the two fill pieces.

After the graphics you do not want are selected, execute the shortcut key to delete, as shown in Figure 1.47.

FIGURE 1.47 The line is deleted.

This procedure may seem a bit complicated, since you could have selected the line instead with the Selection tool, but if you are working with more complex graphics, the Lasso tool will save you time when selecting what you want. The Lasso tool lets you be more intricate in your selection and can be used in areas in which the Selection tool cannot be used. Grouped objects and symbols will not be selected if they are not fully circled.

Polygon Mode

By drawing a straight-edged selection, you can select an area in a more angular way by clicking once to start the point, then positioning the pointer to where you want the first line to end, and clicking. Keep setting end points for additional line segments. If you want to close the selection area, just double-click. If you are using a mouse, this mode could be an advantage because it is click-oriented, which could give you more control.

Improvements

The Polygon Mode feature has great potential for precisely selecting graphics and objects, although while closing the selection it is hard to tell if you will be closing the Lasso shape. It would be helpful to see some type of small graphic appear when you move your mouse over the beginning of the Lasso, similar to how Fireworks' Lasso polygon tool works. Canceling a Polygon selection is awkward. You have to right-click, which brings up the right-click pop up, or press the Esc key and left-click to start selecting again—which gets quite confusing. Fireworks' Lasso tool polygon feature is much more intuitive and less stressful to use.

Magic Wand

The Magic Wand lets you change the fill of a selected area of a broken-apart bitmap. With the Magic Wand settings modifier, you can edit the threshold and smoothing of how the Magic Wand selects. Although this is an interesting feature to experiment with, we recommend that you do all your raster image editing in Fireworks or Photoshop. Since those programs' focus is on raster graphics, you will be able to achieve higher quality, optimized images, and precise editing with them.

Line Tool

The Line tool draws lines, but has more uses. It can allow you to create optimized shapes and become more precise at editing your graphics.

Create Complex Shapes

As you all know, a line is comprised of two vector points, and those points, when connected, make one curve. Technically, if you connect four lines, you can make a square, and if you edit the curves, you can make a circle. Follow the first four steps shown in Figure 1.48. With the Line tool, draw two lines to form a right angle, as shown under "2 Curves." Complete the square and connect two more lines to the bottom half, as shown under "4 Curves." Switch to the Selection tool, click and drag the curved part of the top two lines, and apply a curve to them, as shown under "2 Curves Modified." With the Selection tool, click and drag the bottom two lines and apply a curve to them, as shown under "4 Curves Modified." Since four curves are not enough for a circle, use the Oval tool to create a perfect circle that consists of eight curves, as shown at the far right in Figure 1.48.

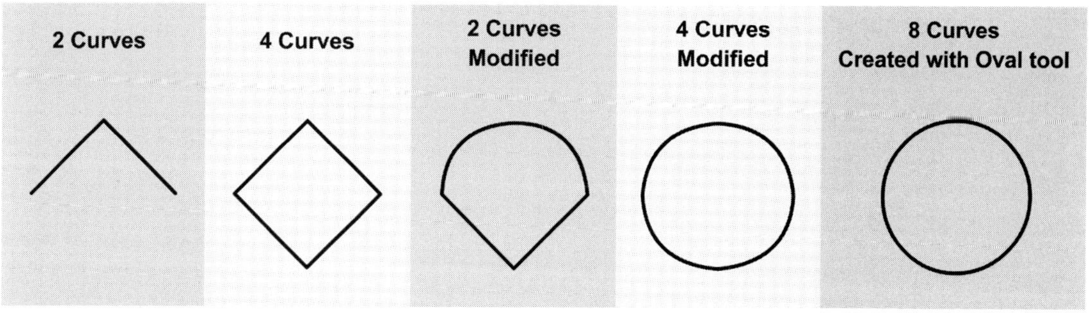

FIGURE 1.48 Comparing the number of curves it takes to create a circle.

The four-curve circle may not be a perfect circle, but that is not the point. The point is that the Line tool has the potential to make basic and complex shapes if used correctly, which enables you to illustrate optimized graphics in Macromedia Flash. If you take your Paint Bucket tool and fill in the circle of four lines, you will have a "4 Curves Modified" circle. Now that you know that plotting your own vectors with the Line tool is the most optimal approach, we will review many shapes that can be achieved in Chapter 2. Besides benefiting from the Line tool, you can also achieve precise positioning of graphics and objects.

Creating a circle with eight vector points is quite simple, and knowing how to do so will help you understand how to keep your vector shapes optimized and can give you a head start to creating more complicated shapes. With the Line tool, start creating an octagon, estimating where the lines should be. To connect the next line you plot with the previous one, make sure the Snap to Objects feature is on, as shown in Figure 1.49. With your octagon complete, adjust only the vector points with the Arrow tool.

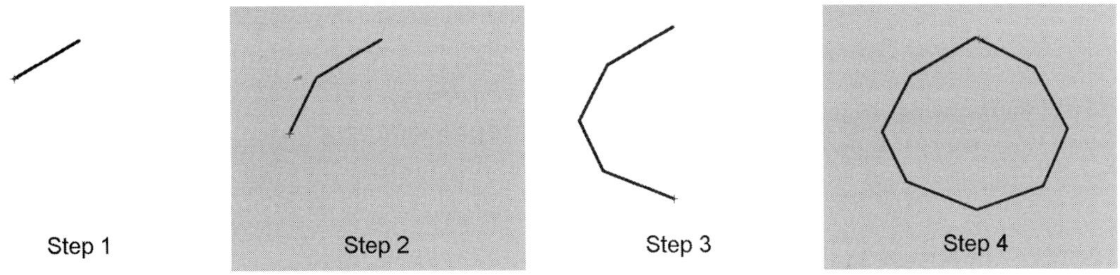

FIGURE 1.49 The first four steps in creating a circle from scratch.

Now that the lines are created, it is time to add the curves to them with the Arrow tool. Click and pull on the center part of the line; only a little bit of curve is needed. Work your way around adding a slight curve to all the lines. Once you are done, make the final adjustments to have the result in step 8 in Figure 1.50.

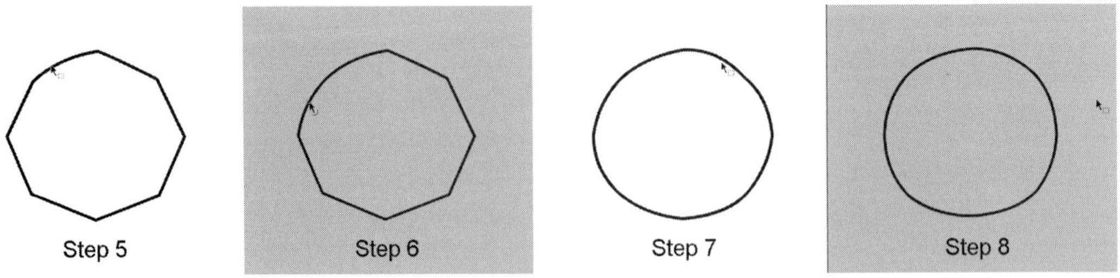

FIGURE 1.50 The last four steps adding the curve shape to the circle.

Oval Tool

The Oval tool lets you create ovals and perfect circles if you hold down the Shift key as you use it. If you use the Oval tool with a little help from the Line and the Selection tools, you can create a cylinder, as shown in Figure 1.51. The first step is shown on the far left, where you use the Oval tool to create a horizontal oval. In the second step, use the Line tool to connect a straight vertical line to the left side of the horizontal oval. In the third step, use the Selection tool to select and duplicate the first vertical line and move the copied line to the right side of the oval. In the last step, use the Selection tool to select the bottom half of the oval, duplicate it, and move it down to the bottom, closing the cylinder.

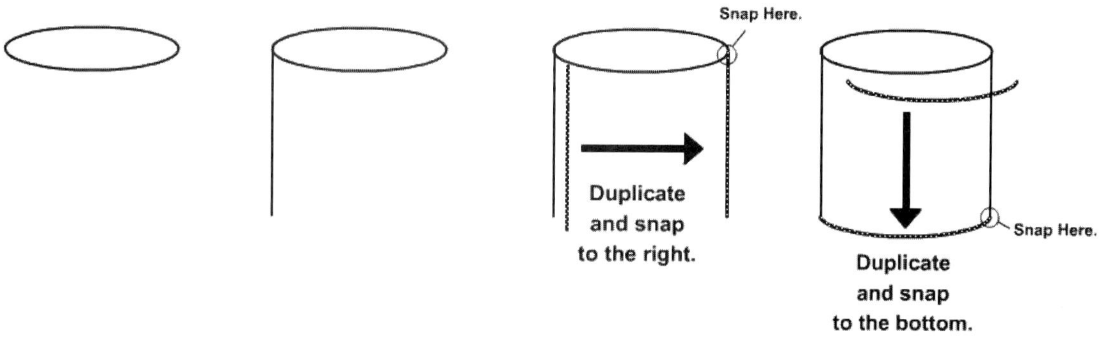

FIGURE 1.51 Create a cylinder in four easy steps.

Rectangle Tool

The Rectangle tool lets you create rectangles, and perfect squares if you hold down the Shift key. You can create a simple cube with the Rectangle tool and a little help from the Line and Selection tools, as shown in Figure 1.52. First, use the Rectangle tool to create a perfect square. Second, using the Selection tool, select the square, duplicate it, and position it as shown in Figure 1.52. Third, use the Line tool and connect the six corner points defining the sides of the cube. Finally, use the Selection tool to select and delete the unwanted lines.

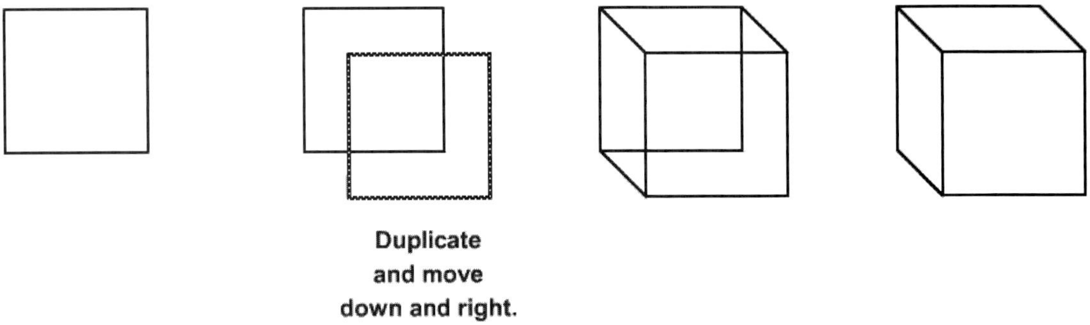

FIGURE 1.52 Create a cube in four easy steps.

PolyStar Tool

The PolyStar tool lets you create two basic shapes, all in one tool. Depending on what you set it at, it will let you create polygons or stars. This tool contains three key options: Style, Number of Sides, and Star Point Size. Style lets you choose between creating a polygon or star. Number of Sides lets you choose how many sides you want your polygon or star to have. Star Point Size sets how sharp or dull your star will be. To create a shape with the PolyStar tool, drag your mouse up to create a star or polygon standing up, and drag it down to draw the figure upside down. With the PolyStar Style option set at star, you can make a shooting star with the help of the Line and Selection tools, as shown in Figure 1.53. First, use the PolyStar tool to create a five-sided star. Second, use the Selection tool to select the star and duplicate it. To scale the star graphic down, use the Transform panel, which can be accessed in the menu under Windows > Transform. Check the Constrain box, enter a value of 30 in any of the percentage boxes, and press the Enter key on your keyboard to execute the scale. Position the scaled star as shown in the second step in Figure 1.53. Third, use the Line tool and connect the 12 corner points defining the sides of the stars. Last, use the Selection tool to select and delete the unwanted lines.

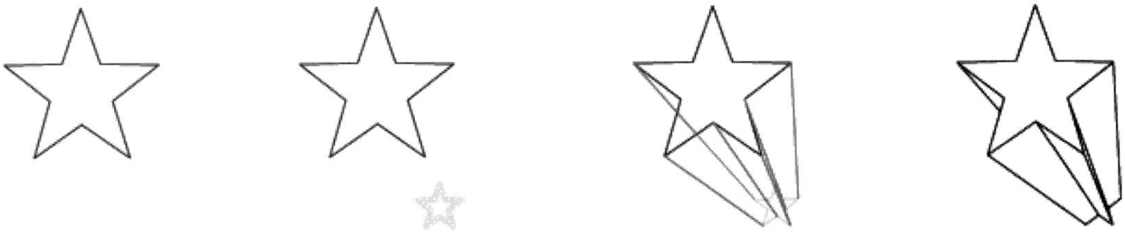

FIGURE 1.53 Create a shooting star in four easy steps.

With the PolyStar Style option set at Polygon, you can make a honeycomb graphic with the help of the Line and Selection tools, as shown in Figure 1.54. First, use the PolyStar tool to create a five-sided polygon. Second, using the Selection tool, select the polygon and duplicate it two times, connecting the three polygons. Third, using the Selection tool, select all three polygons, duplicate them, and reposition them down and to the right. Fourth, use the Line tool to connect the 26 corner points defining the sides of the polygons. Last, use the Selection tool to select and delete the unwanted lines.

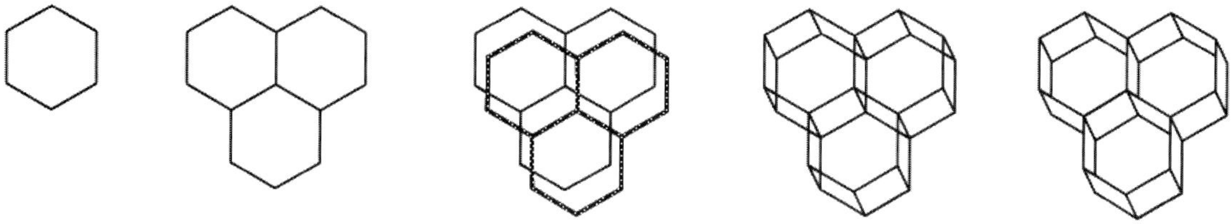

FIGURE 1.54 Create a honeycomb in five easy steps.

Pencil Tool

Drawing freehand with the Pencil tool has its advantages in letting you draw lines and shapes. This tool has three drawing options, which let you set how you want the line to flow, as shown in Figure 1.55. Straighten gives you straight lines and conversion approximations of common geometric shapes. Smooth lets you draw smooth, curved lines. Ink lets you draw freehand lines with no modification applied. Holding down the Shift key as you draw with the Pencil tool will produce constrained lines that are vertical or horizontal. This tool comes in handy for sketching your ideas or if you need to draw a curvy line. Although the Pencil tool may seem like the best tool to use to draw, it produces lines that are neither optimized nor precise as you draw them. For more optimized and precise line creation, use the Line and Selection tools. Try it by selecting the Pencil tool and practicing drawing lines similar to those shown in Figure 1.55.

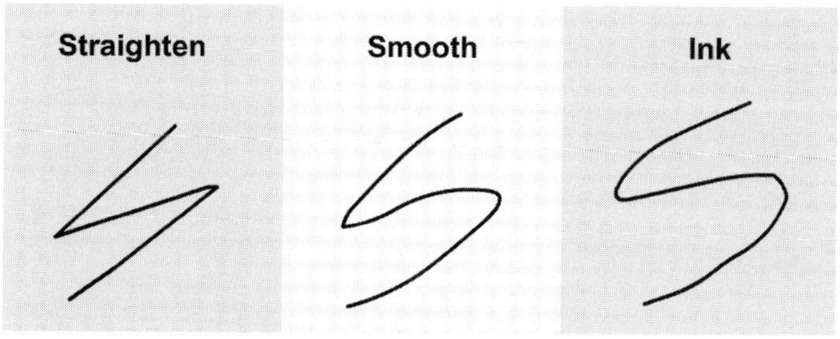

FIGURE 1.55 The different types of line flow.

Paint Bucket Tool

The Paint Bucket tool lets you apply a new fill to a closed or semiclosed stroke, or edit the color of an already existing fill. A semiclosed stroke can be filled, thanks to the Gap Size modifier. The Paint Bucket tool is often used to apply fills and gradients to already drawn outlines.

Gap Size Modifier

The Gap Size modifier lets you add a fill even if your circle is not closed. Figure 1.56 shows the four different Gap Size modifiers. Use the Paint Bucket tool to apply a solid fill to each broken circle in the file. Change the Gap Size modifier to experience how each works.

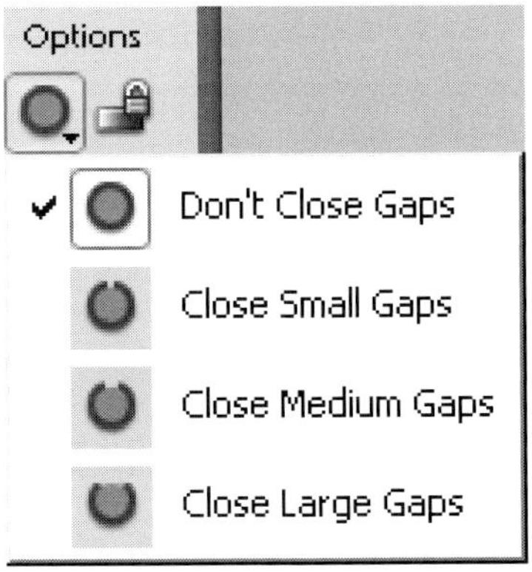

FIGURE 1.56 Identify the four Gap Size modifiers.

Lock Fill

The Lock Fill feature lets you take an existing gradient grabbed with the Eyedropper and paint it anywhere with the same gradient, with the same placement and scale.

Gradient Transform Tool

Another most commonly used tool is the Fill Transform tool. Once you have applied a gradient, it is hardly ever exactly how you want it. This tool lets you position, rotate, and scale the size of the gradient and how it is displayed. Modifiers will appear once the tool is activated, as shown in Figure 1.57. To create a radial gradient, click on the Fill Color swatch in the Tool panel and select one of the premade gradient swatches. Select the Rectangle tool and create a square. The chosen radial gradient should

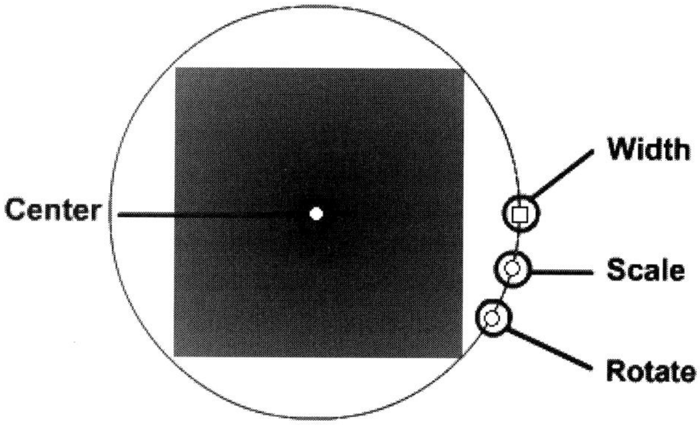

FIGURE 1.57 Identify the Fill Transform modifiers.

appear as the fill for the square you just created. Switch to the Fill Transform tool, click on the radial gradient square, and the modifiers will appear. Interact with the modifiers to get a feel for how they act and affect the gradient.

Once you mouse over any of these modifiers, your cursor will change, confirming what action will occur once you start to click and drag with your mouse. There are four modifiers, and their changing cursors are shown in Figure 1.58.

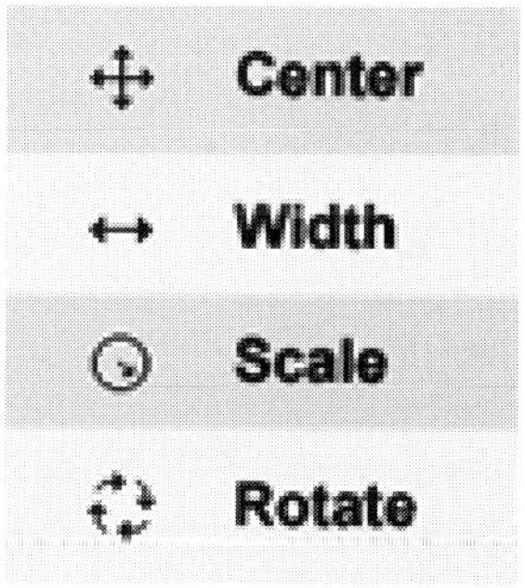

FIGURE 1.58 Identify the Fill Transform modifier cursors.

The plus-shaped modifier lets you edit the placement of the gradient. The minus-shaped modifier lets you edit the scaling on a single axis. The circle with the angled arrow lets you edit the entire scaling of the gradient. The last modifier, which has four arrows pointing in a circle, lets you edit the rotation of the gradient. Other than editing gradient fills, you can also edit the bitmap on a broken-down imported raster graphic. This tool is not used often to edit bitmaps, because raster graphic preparations are usually done in a raster program such as Fireworks or Photoshop.

Free Transform Tool

Ever since the Transform tool was introduced, editing graphics and objects has become simple to do. Using the shortcut key to turn on the Free Transform tool on the selected objects, you have the ability to modify scale, rotation, and skew. Although this tool is flexible in how you can edit objects, if you are looking for precise edits, we recommend that you use the Transform panel. By selecting the Free Transform tool, which is set at default with the rotate, skew, and scale modifiers, you can then click on the transform options in the Tool panel to switch between rotate and skew, scale, distort, or envelope modifiers, as shown in Figure 1.59. Practice with the Free Transform tool; select the Rectangle tool and create a perfect square. Switch to the Free Transform tool, click on the Distort button in the Tool panel, and click and drag the modifiers to deform the shape of the square.

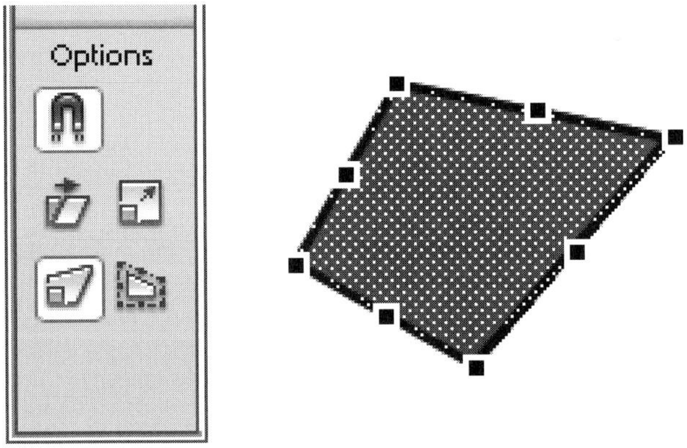

FIGURE 1.59 Using the Transform tool to change the shape of the square.

Hand Tool

The Hand tool is used to move the stage around, and is especially effective when zoomed at a high magnification.

Zoom Tool

The Zoom tool lets you modify the resolution you are viewing by clicking anywhere on the stage or work area. When illustrating in Macromedia Flash, this tool is used quite a bit, especially when drawing varied amounts of detail or editing graphics. If the Zoom tool default is set at zooming in and you would like to zoom out, just hold down the Alt key and the tool will switch to zooming out. If your Zoom tool default is set at zooming out, do the same to zoom in. The tool can be dragged on the stage and a bounding box is created; unclick, and the view will zoom in according to the size of the bounding box you made, as in Figure 1.60.

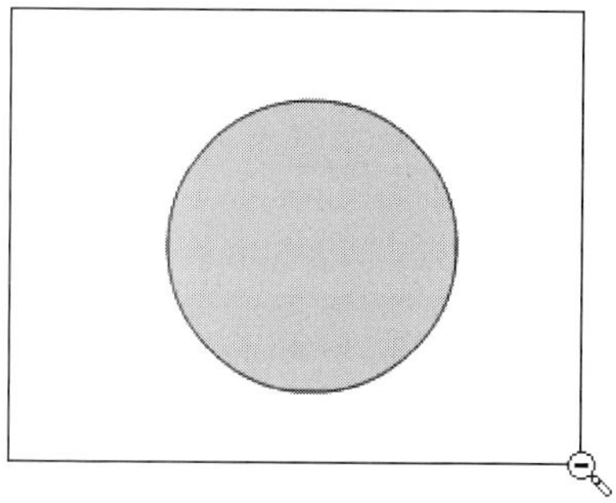

FIGURE 1.60 Create a bounding box to zoom into an area on the stage.

Timeline Panel

The Timeline panel is the linear timeline located at the top of the program, and is used extensively when creating animations. When illustrating in Flash, create multiple layers in the Timeline panel to help you organize your graphics; place your graphic detail on the highest layer and your basic shapes on the lower layer. Figure 1.61 shows the most-used features in the Timeline panel.

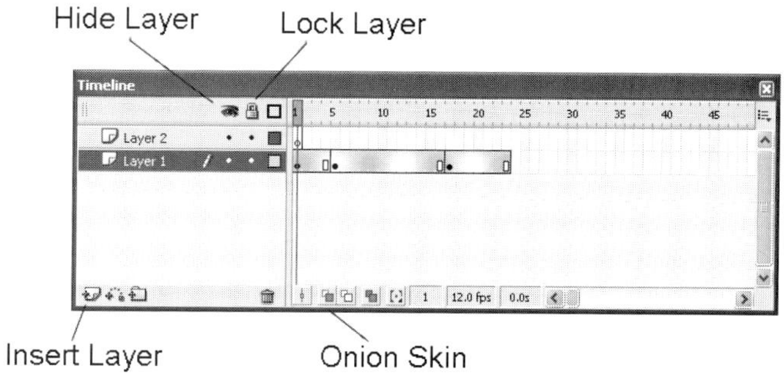

FIGURE 1.61 The Timeline panel and the most-used buttons.

Properties Panel

The Properties panel is located at the bottom of the program. When you select an object, the properties of that item will show up there. Properties of an object such as dimensions are commonly modified here. When you are using a certain tool, more options for that tool will show up there. For example, when you are using the Line tool, you can edit the style of line the tool will make in the Properties panel, as in Figure 1.62.

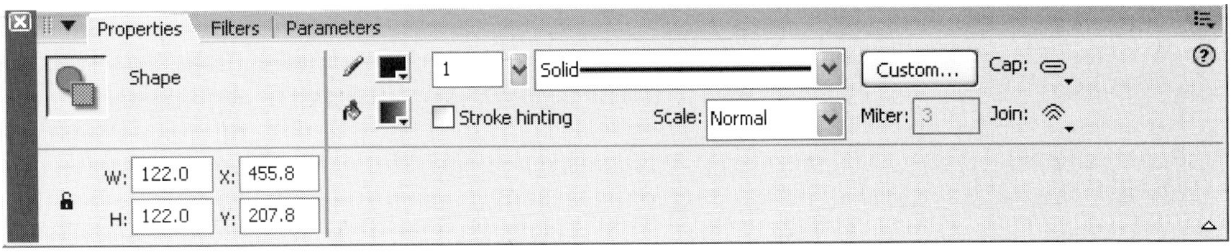

FIGURE 1.62 Properties panel and the other options it holds.

Scale and Rotate Panel

When you are working on your graphic and need to scale it a certain percentage quickly, the Scale and Rotate panel does the trick. In a matter of seconds, what you have selected can be scaled at 50% or 200%. Select the graphic or object you wish to scale, and execute the keyboard shortcut to bring up the Scale and Rotate panel. The text field to modify scale is already active, so you do not have to click on it to make it active, as in Figure 1.63. Enter the amount you wish to scale at and press the Enter key on your keyboard. The Enter key is already active to the OK button. In a matter of three quick steps, you can scale a graphic, unlike using the Transform panel, which requires extra mouse clicking.

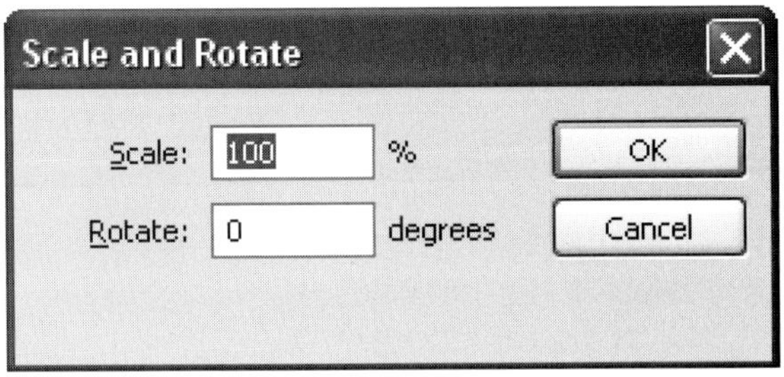

FIGURE 1.63 The simple and efficient Scale and Rotate panel.

Color Mixer Panel

The Color Mixer panel is used a lot when in the coloring phase of illustrating. This is where you choose your color swatches and construct your gradients, as shown in Figure 1.64. The Eyedropper tool is built into the Color Mixer panel and color swatches in the Tool panel. Just click once on any color swatch and the color grid will pop up, and your cursor will turn into the Eyedropper tool, as in Figure 1.65. The next color you click on will set the color swatch you previously clicked on. Use this feature to acquire colors from previous drawn vector graphics and raster graphics imported in Flash.

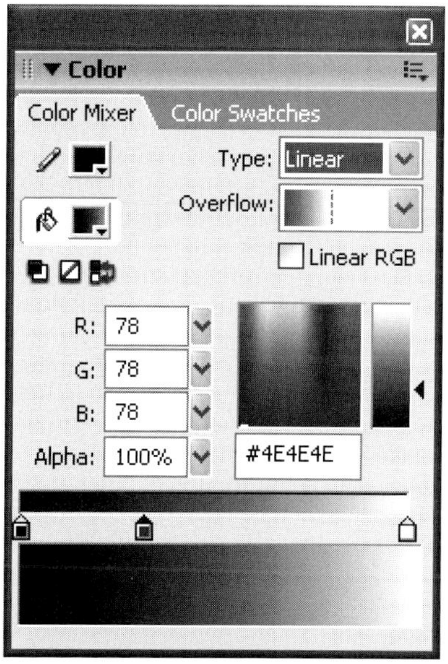

FIGURE 1.64 The Color Mixer panel.

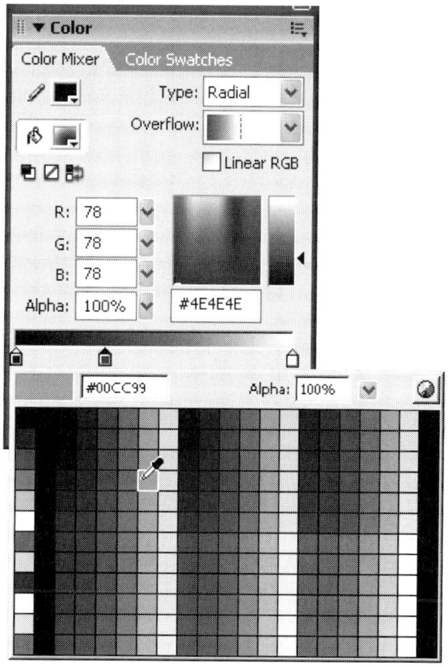

FIGURE 1.65 The color grid is brought up by clicking on a color swatch.

Macromedia Flash Professional 8 New Features

New features that will affect the way you illustrate and produce graphics and improve your efficiency have been added to the latest version of Macromedia Flash. Many improvements and enhancements have been implemented. The new feature that intrigues us the most is the Gradient Effect Filters, which will have a huge impact on illustrating. Although these filters are quite simple, if used in innovative ways you can achieve intricate light and shadow effects. Most of these filter effects can be reproduced in Flash by using linear and radial gradients. With all these new additions, you are sure to become more efficient in the developing environment.

Real-Time Disable Snap to Objects

Hail to Macromedia for bringing back a critical feature we have not seen since Flash 4. Turning off the Snap to Objects feature while using the Arrow tool and Line tool is essential if you want to have complete control over where you position your vector points, as shown in Figure 1.66. Without it, turning Snap to Objects off or on required you to stop what you were doing, click the Snap to Objects button in the Tool panel, or use the keyboard shortcut. For an in-depth explanation on how to use this feature, refer to the section Selection Tool in this chapter.

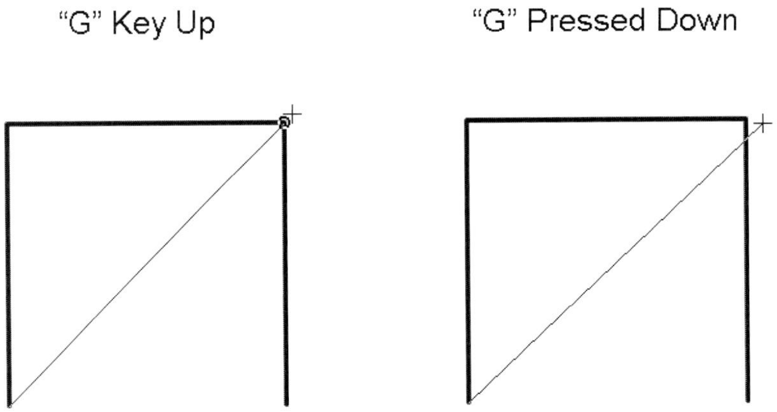

FIGURE 1.66 Results when holding down the G key.

Improved Preferences

Preferences throughout the program have been improved. Now, you can set how you want Flash to launch—start with no document, new document, last documents open, or that lovely start page we have grown to love, as in Figure 1.67. Although this may seem trivial, consider what you do every time you launch Flash. With even small projects lasting over a couple of days, the On Launch, Last Documents Open option could save you two to four minutes every time the program is launched. Preferences in the Properties panel have been improved and centralized. For example, when using the Text tool you have more quality options, and if you are using the Line tool, you can further customize how your line is rendered.

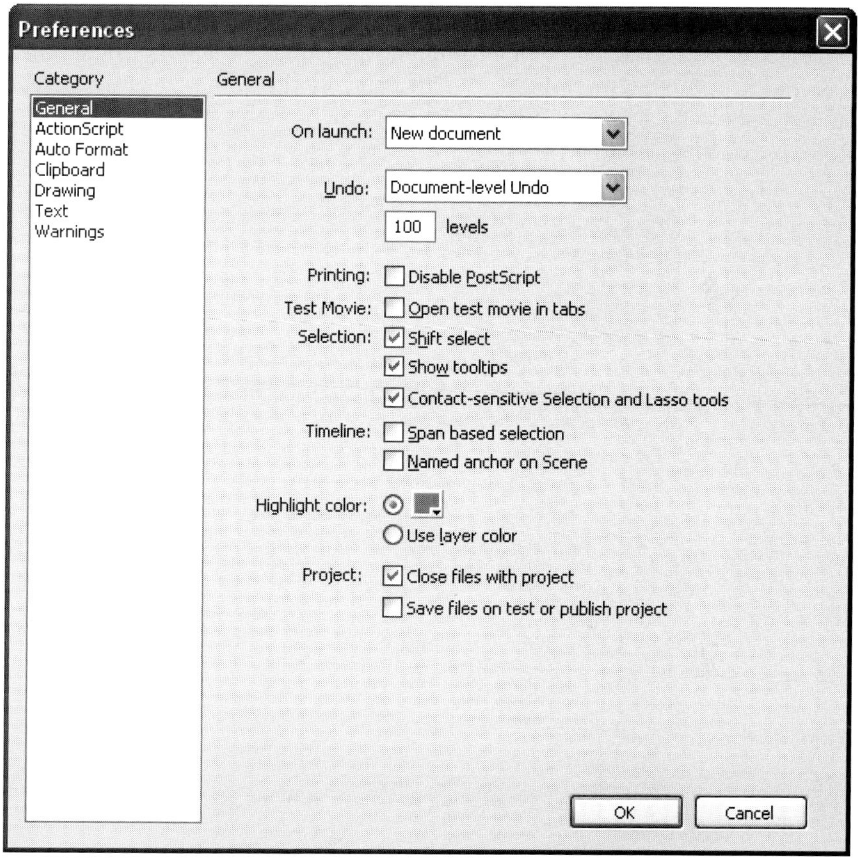

FIGURE 1.67 The Preferences panel.

Object-Level Undo and Redo Commands

The more options you have, the more you can customize something to meet your needs. In previous versions of Flash, preferences were limited, and when major features changed, learning the new way could frustrate even veteran users. With Flash Professional 8, that trend seems to be changing, as you can set how you want the Undo feature to work. You can choose to work at either Object-level or Document-level Undo and Redo. Flash has always worked at Object-level Undo until the previous version of Flash, when it was switched to Document-level Undo. For illustrating purposes, we recommend that you set your Undo setting to Object-level Undo.

Object-Level Undo

Object-level Undo means that for everything that has a timeline in your document, Flash will store the history of each separately, as shown in Figure 1.68. For example, if you realized an edit you made 10 edits ago messed up some graphic in your movie clip, you do not have to undo through the previous nine edits; you just go into the movie clip with the edit and execute the keyboard shortcut to undo. This way, you do not lose your progress from previous edits.

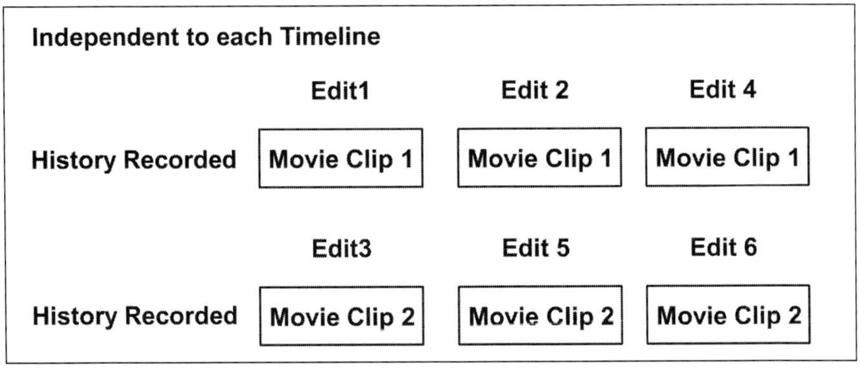

FIGURE 1.68 Diagram of Object-level Undo.

Document-Level Undo

Document-level Undo is where Flash keeps track of everything you do in a linear fashion, even though you are moving between different timelines, as shown in Figure 1.69. The problem with this is that if an edit you made 10 steps ago was incorrect, you have to undo 10 times, erasing those nine other edits. Undoing in this fashion can become quite confusing and disorienting, because it involves flipping through different timelines. This style of undoing was introduced in the previous version to easily keep track of the user's history for the new History panel.

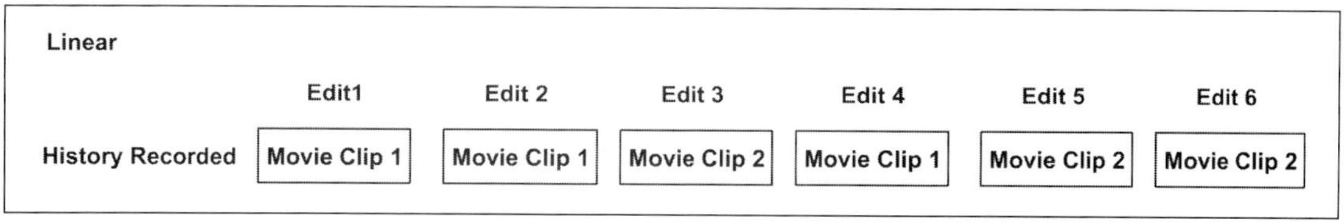

FIGURE 1.69 Diagram of Document-level Undo.

Bitmap Smoothing

Bitmap images now look much better on the stage when greatly enlarged or reduced, as shown in Figure 1.70. The appearance of these bitmaps in the Flash authoring tool and in Flash Player is now consistent—an issue with the Flash developing environment dating back several versions of the program. The fact that it is finally addressed will make many illustrators and animators very happy. If you were to trace over a raster image at a magnification of 200% and then zoom out to a magnification of 100%, the graphics you drew would look like they have shifted. The real problem was that the redrawing of the raster image you were tracing had moved.

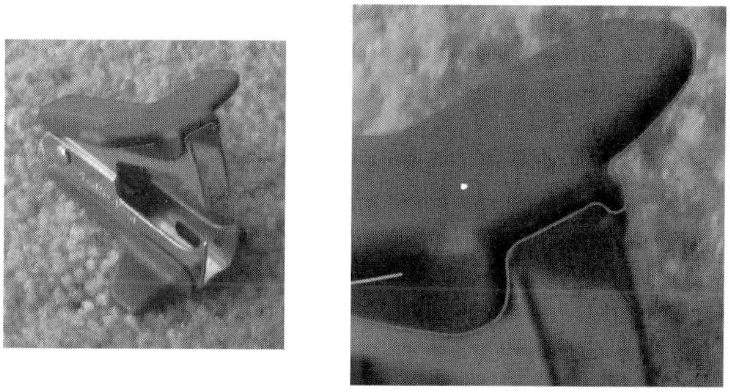

FIGURE 1.70 Bitmaps do not move at different resolutions.

Object Drawing

Object Drawing is a feature that if turned on will create shapes directly on the stage as a group. For example, if you take the Pencil tool and draw around on the stage, the moment you stop, that line shape will be converted into a group, as shown in Figure 1.71. Of course, when turned into a group, it will not interfere with other shapes on the stage. Although this feature is interesting, having your vectors all in separate groups will only slow you down if you have to edit them. Moreover, a layer with many grouped objects on top of each other is very difficult to manage. If you want to separate graphics so they do not interfere with each other, place them on difference layers. Layers are easier to manage with the Hide, Lock, and Outline features in the Timeline panel. However, keep the number of layers to a minimum when illustrating in Flash.

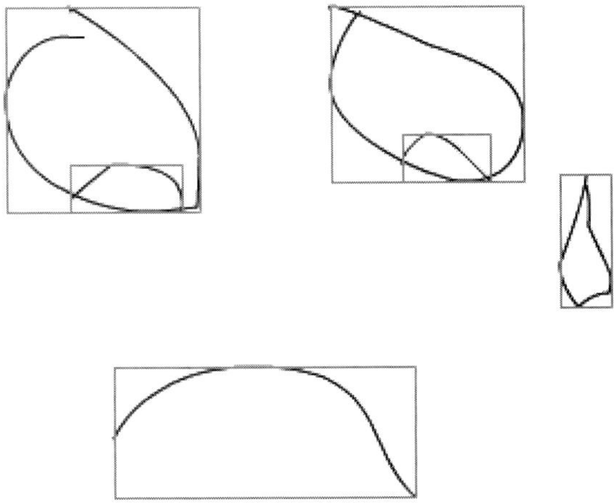

FIGURE 1.71 Line drawing with the Object Drawing feature on.

The only reason we can think of why this feature was implemented was to cater to PowerPoint® users who are new to Flash. With PowerPoint, all elements are separated, although PowerPoint does not have physical layers for the users to separate their content. Similar items have been introduced to Flash that cater to users of other programs, such as the Subselection tool and Pen tool, which are exact copies of vector drafting tools found in programs such as Illustrator and Freehand.

Enhanced Strokes

When using the Line and Pencil tools, new settings for the type of line rendered are available for you to edit in the Properties panel. The new settings are Cap, Join, Miter, Scale, Stroke hinting, and Smoothing, as shown in Figure 1.72.

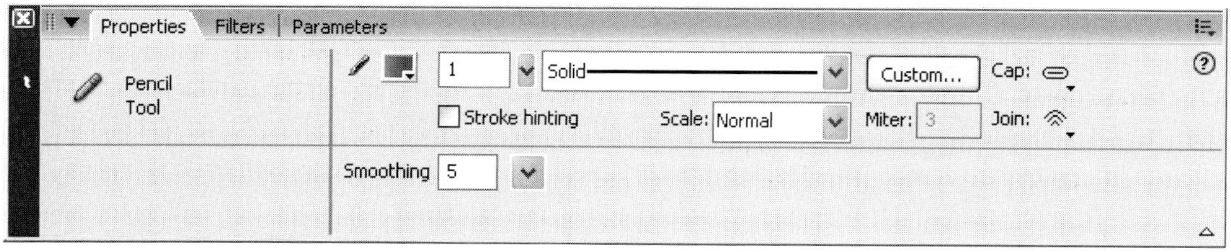

FIGURE 1.72 In the Properties panel, Strokes now have more options.

Cap

Cap is how the end of the line looks. If set to None or Square, the end of the line will be flat. If set to Round, the edge will be round as in previous versions of Flash.

Join

The Join option defines how two path segments meet: Miter, Round, or Bevel. To change the corners in an open or closed path, select a path and select another Join option.

Miter

To avoid beveling a Miter join, enter a Miter limit. Line lengths exceeding this value are squared off instead of pointed. For example, a Miter limit of 2 for a 3-point stroke means that when the length of the point is twice the stroke weight, Flash removes the limit point.

Scale

Scale constrains stroke scaling in the Flash Player.

Stroke Hinting

Select the Stroke Hinting checkbox to enable Stroke hinting. Stroke hinting adjusts line and curve anchors on full pixels, preventing blurry vertical or horizontal lines.

Smoothing

If you are drawing lines using the Pencil or Brush tools with the drawing mode set to Smooth, you can specify the degree to which Flash smoothes the lines using the Smoothing pop-up slider. By default, the Smoothing value is set to 5, but you can specify a value from 0 to 10. The greater the smoothing value, the smoother the resulting line. Note: when the drawing mode is set to Straighten or Ink, the Smoothing pop-up slider is disabled.

Color Mixer Enhancements

The Color Mixer panel has been slightly redesigned. A new setting, Overflow, lets you control how the gradient repeats outside the original color swatch layout. You can now add up to 15 color swatches on the gradient layout as shown in Figure 1.73, as opposed to the previous version's limited of 8 swatches. This means more complicated gradients can be achieved with ease.

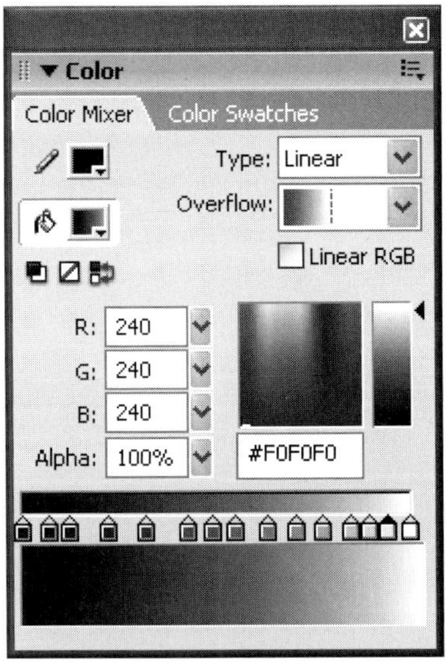

FIGURE 1.73 A linear gradient with 15 color swatches.

Gradient Effect Filters

You can apply graphics filters to any symbol. These are called filters because they pass the image data of the object through an algorithm that filters the data in a specific way. With these filters, you can make objects glow, add drop shadows, and apply many other effects and combinations of effects. These filter settings can be modified with a tween and can be animated. To apply a filter to your symbol, click on the symbol, click on the Filter tab in the Properties panel, click on the + symbol, and select from a filter from the dropdown, as shown in Figure 1.74.

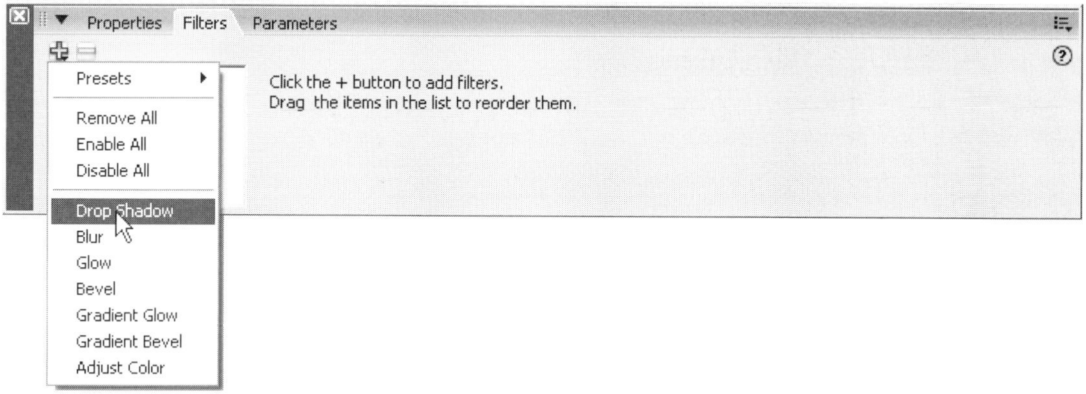

FIGURE 1.74 Use the Transform tool to change the shape of the square.

Select Drop Shadow and you have several settings to choose from, as shown in Figure 1.75.

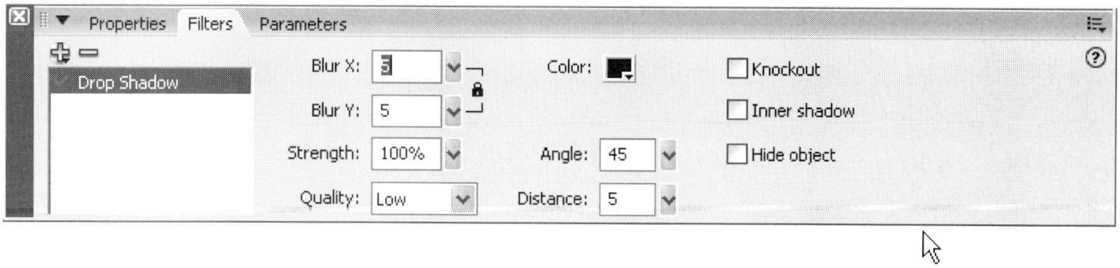

FIGURE 1.75 Drop Shadow filter settings.

DIFFERENCES IN OPERATING SYSTEMS

When following along with this book and using Macromedia Flash on a Windows or Macintosh operating system, there is one difference of which you should be aware. Although Macromedia has done a great job of keeping the two different versions of the software identical (other than the operating system user interface look and feel), there remains a peripheral difference on the keyboards of these two operating systems: the naming of two keys. For example, on a Windows keyboard, you have the Ctrl key, while on a Macintosh keyboard, you instead use the Command key. On a Windows keyboard, you execute a shortcut key command with the Alt key; on a Macintosh, you use the Option key. All shortcut key commands can be modified as of Macromedia Flash 5 and later. Choose Edit > Keyboard Shortcuts to open the Keyboard Shortcuts dialog.

SUMMARY

- Macromedia Flash and its drawing tools enable you to produce optimized, photorealistic-looking graphics at a smaller file size than when using raster graphics.
- Trace features that convert raster images to vector graphics result in unoptimized, poor graphic quality.
- The new features of Macromedia Flash Professional 8—such as real-time disable snap to objects, improved preferences, and object level undo and redo commands—will increase your productivity.
- You will need a scanner if you want to import your sketches into Macromedia Flash. If you want better control over the vectors you draw, a graphics tablet is recommended.
- Learn the shortcut key commands, and find a hand position that works for you.
- You should have a basic understanding of all the drawing tools in Macromedia Flash.

EXERCISES

1. Customize your keyboard shortcuts to improve efficiency in your workflow. Then, print out a list of the Tool panel commands and place it beside your keyboard for quick reference until you have them memorized.

2. Draw the shape in Figure 1.76 using only the Line and Arrow tools.
3. Draw the shape in Figure 1.77 using only the Oval, Line, and Arrow tools.

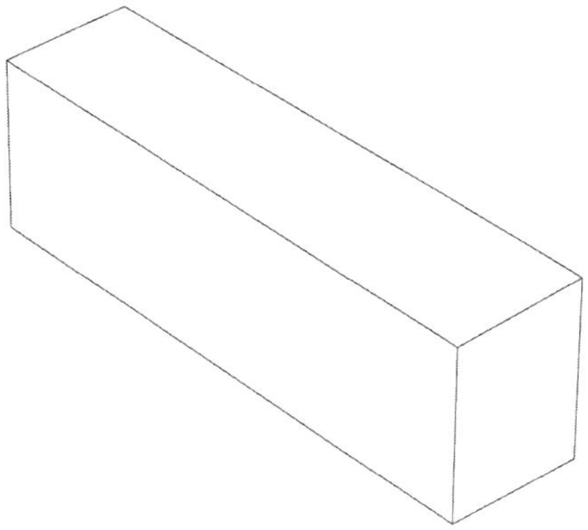

FIGURE 1.76 Using the Transform tool to change the shape of the square.

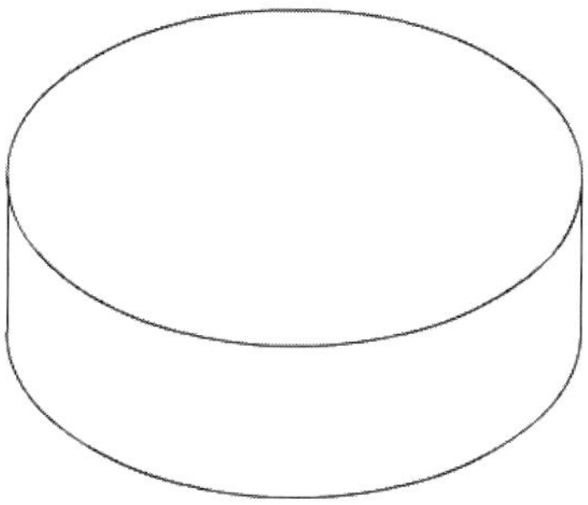

FIGURE 1.77 Using the Transform tool to change the shape of the square.

4. Using the Arrow tool, assemble the shapes from Exercises 2 and 3 to make the object shown in Figure 1.78.
5. Create a linear gradient and a radial gradient, and apply them to the shape created in Exercise 4, as shown in Figure 1.79.

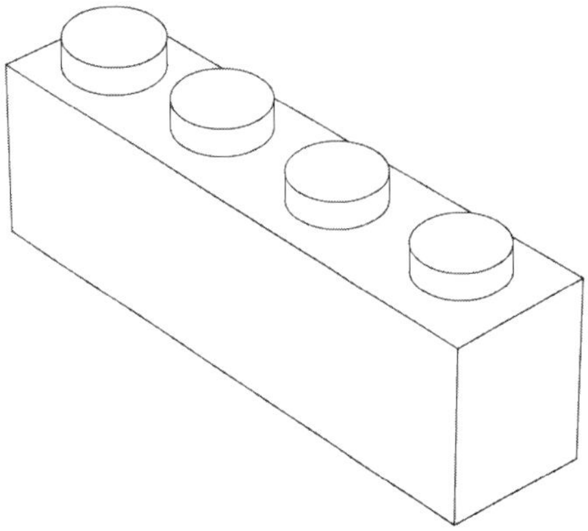

FIGURE 1.78 Using the Transform tool to change the shape of the square.

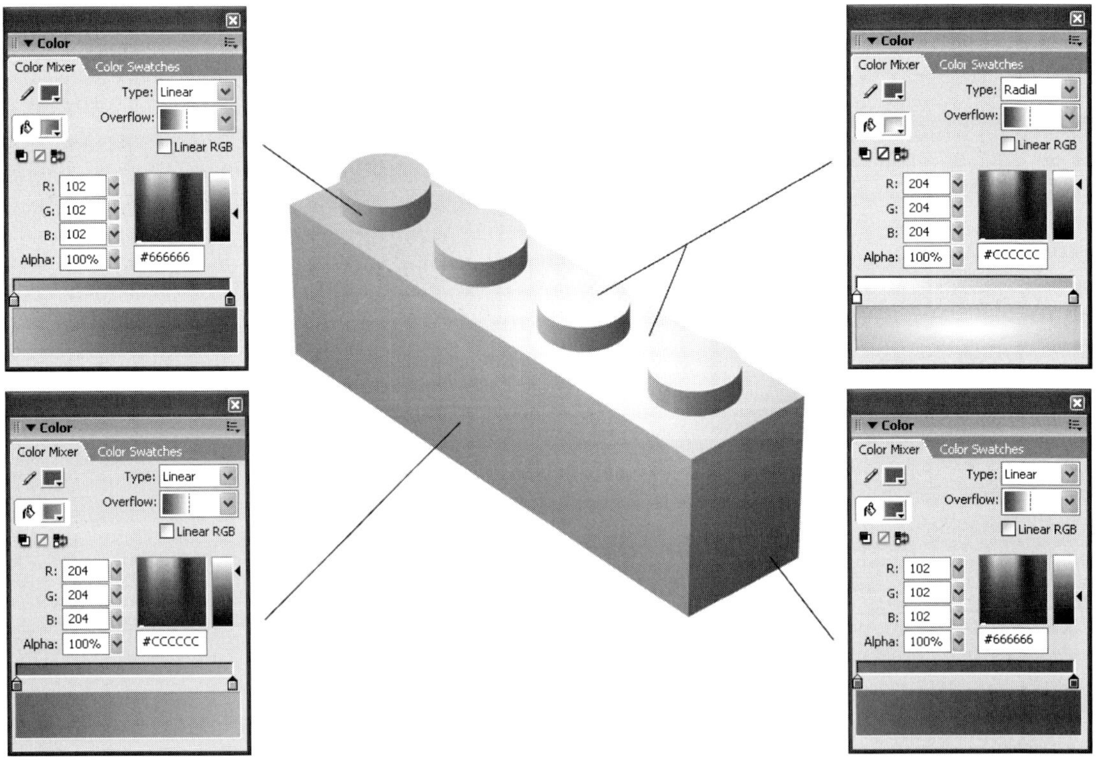

FIGURE 1.79 Using the Transform tool to change the shape of the square.

CHAPTER

2 ILLUSTRATION CONCEPTS

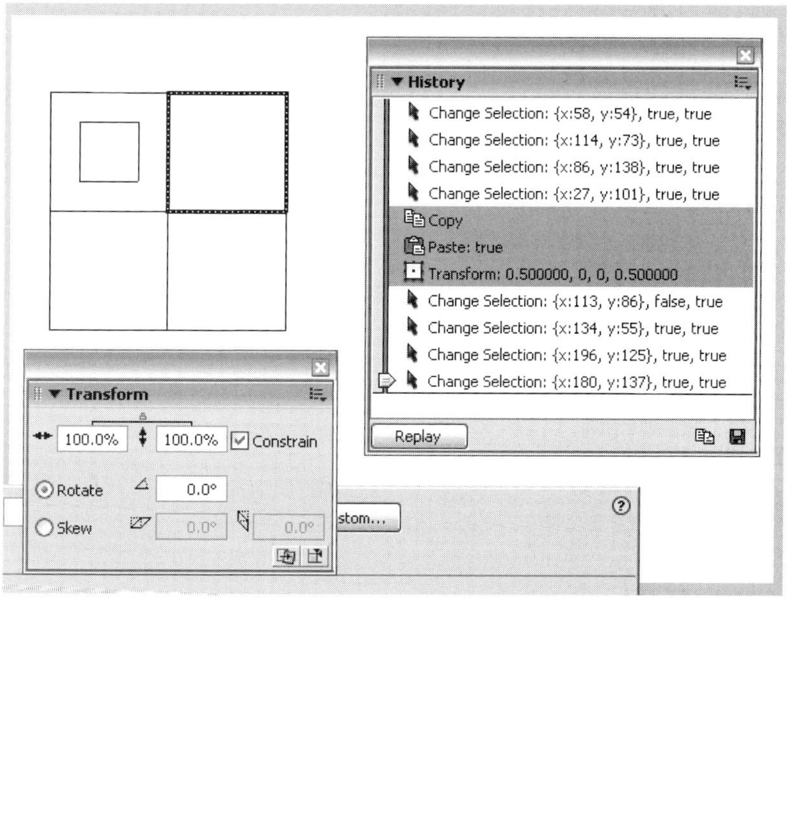

Macromedia Flash provides you with many drawing tools to get your job done. The tools seem straightforward, but when it comes to actually using them to illustrate a user interface, edit a series of vector graphics, or perform whatever your specific task may be, you must understand how they can be used most efficiently to get the job done quickly. For those who don't want to spend hours trying to figure everything out, you're in luck. Through the author's countless hours of experience using Macromedia Flash, the following concepts were derived. To better familiarize yourself with them, they are organized into four categories: viewing, editing, creating, and coloring.

VIEWING

Viewing the graphics and necessary panels to get your work done may seem easy, and not the most important task to worry about at first. With the ever-recurring trend of tasks and small features being consolidated into easy-to-use panels, we are more dependent on them—and they take up more of our

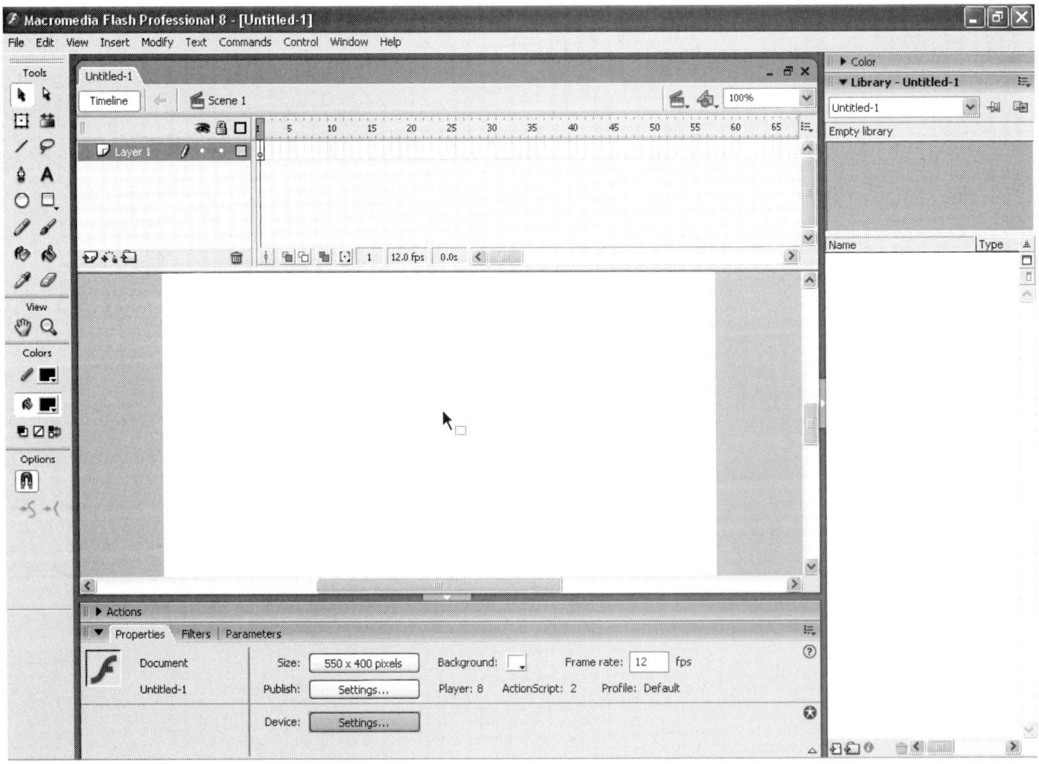

FIGURE 2.1 Default user interface layout.

work area. This section reviews how you can manage your panels and master the viewing tools so you can focus more on creating content.

Managing Panels

When you first launched Macromedia Flash, how much space was left in your workspace? To refresh your memory, review Figure 2.1.

By now, you have done one of three things with your Macromedia Flash interface. One, you are working with a computer with two monitors, with the program running on one and your panels on the other. Of course, this is the way to go, but not everyone has the money to purchase another monitor, nor enough desk space. Two, you have detached all the panels and only view the ones you use the most. Three, you do not want to bother with configuring them, nor do you like viewing them, and you have left them close to their default location. With Macromedia Flash, there are approximately 28 panels, which if all displayed would leave you very little room to work, as shown in Figure 2.2.

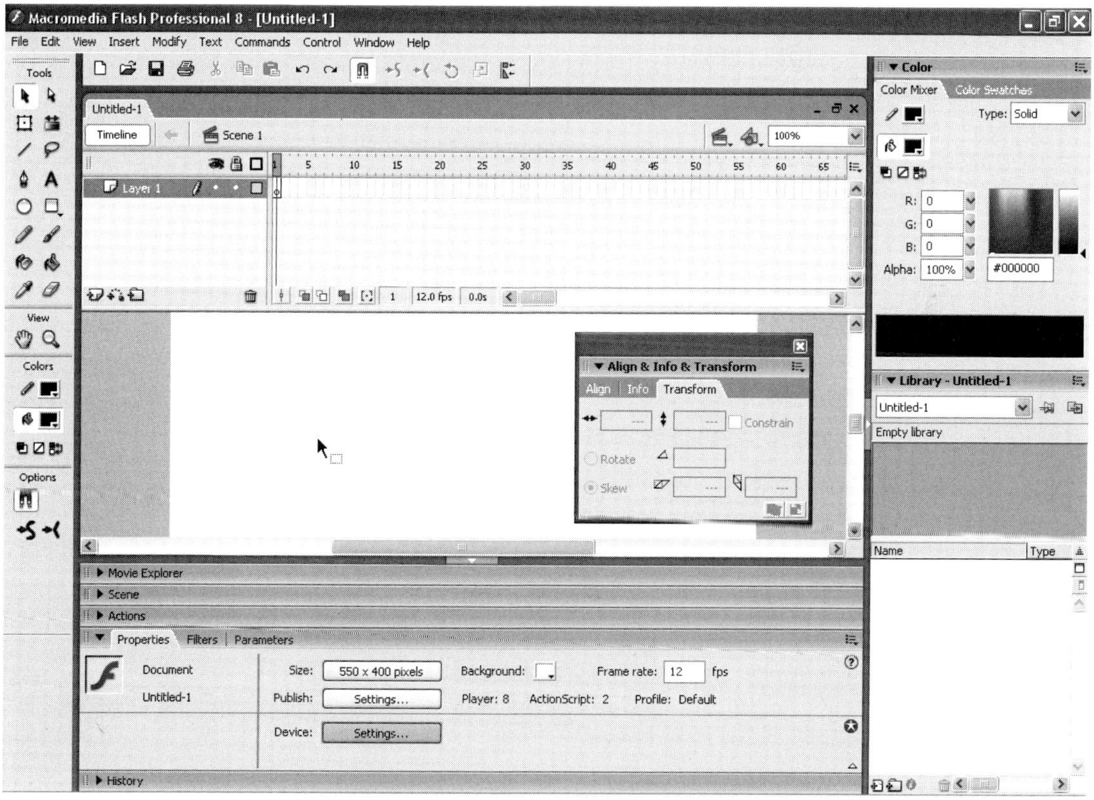

FIGURE 2.2 You would see something like this if you were to display all the panels.

The solution, if you are not working with two monitors, is to get rid of all the panels on the right and the Main panel. Leave the Tools panel in its default position, detach the Properties panel, and arrange it as shown in Figure 2.3. If you need to use any other panels such as Color Mixer or Actions, open and close them with shortcut key commands, and make sure they are not docked to your user interface or they will be hard to control. To save your layout configuration, go to Window > Workspace Layout > Save Current and type in your desired panel name. To recall your saved layout, go to Window > Workspace Layout > Panel Name.

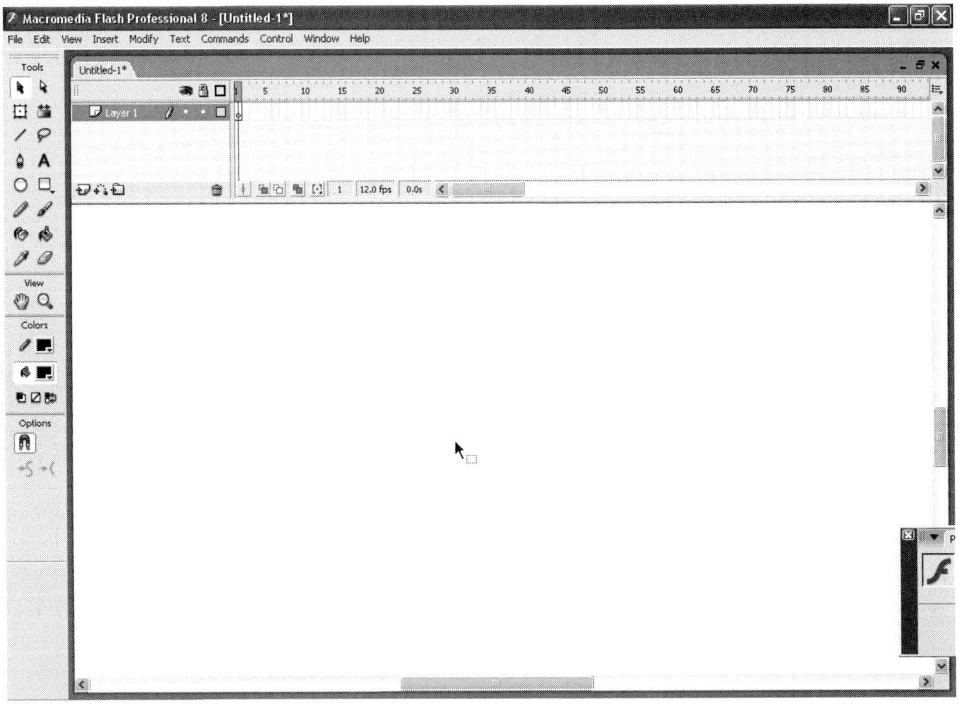

FIGURE 2.3 Display only the panels you need.

Placing them in this fashion and executing the shortcut key commands to open or save a document or launch a panel is the best use of the program's user interface. When illustrating in Macromedia Flash, we mostly rely on the drawing tools, and those can be accessed via shortcut keys. However, we cannot get rid of the Tools panel because it contains key elements that cannot be accessed from any other panel, such as the Colors and Options area. The Main panel consists of buttons that can be executed with shortcut keys, and the other buttons—Snap to Objects, Smooth, Straighten, or Scale and Rotate—can all be accessed in the Tools panel, depending on which drawing tool you are using. The Align button just opens the Align panel, which can be opened with a shortcut key. The most important thing to remember is to make more room for your work area and exploit the shortcut key commands as much as you can, so you will spend less time interacting with the user interface and more time creating content.

If you want to maximize your developing environment, the best way to do so is to have two monitors. You will need a video card that supports dual monitors. Flash will launch on your main monitor, and you can position all the panels on your secondary monitor, as shown in Figure 2.4.

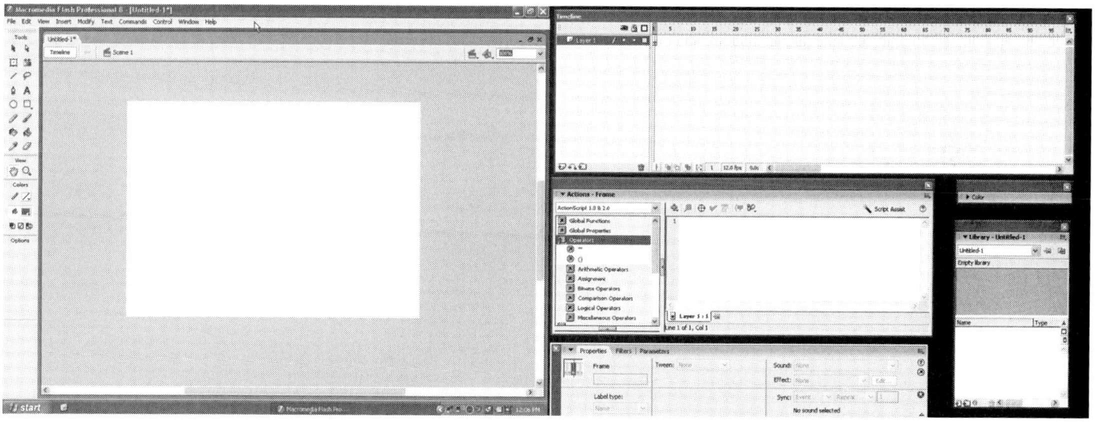

FIGURE 2.4 Flash using two monitors to expand the developing environment.

Magnification and the Brush Tool

When using the Brush tool set at a certain brush size, viewing the stage at different magnifications will make the brush size vary. For example, set your brush size to the third size from the top in the Brush Size drop-down menu and draw a z-shaped stroke in three magnifications: 100%, 50%, and 25%, as shown in Figure 2.5. The brush size remains the same, but the width of the stroke is different.

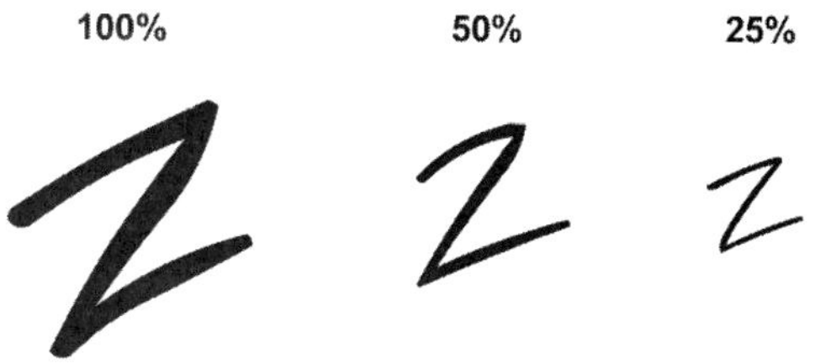

FIGURE 2.5 Brush stroke varies at different magnifications.

This occurs because Flash is making sure that at whatever resolution you are drawing, it maintains the brush size you set it at. When illustrating with the Brush tool, the stroke of your line most likely needs to be consistent across your entire drawing, so keep in mind the magnification you are using, and if you zoom out to view the entire drawing, you need to zoom back to the created magnification to resume drawing.

Magnification and the Zoom Tool

While editing your vectors or adding detail, it is important to view your work closely to make sure your edits or additions are precise. A good approach to using the Zoom tool is using the Click and Drag feature, which creates a bounding box to zoom in, and setting the Zoom tool to Reduce to zoom out if you want to back out, as shown in Figure 2.6. If for some reason you want to zoom in but your Zoom tool is set to Reduce, you can hold down the Shift key on your keyboard to switch to Enlarge. Once you release the Shift key, the Zoom tool will go back to its default setting; in our case, Reduce. This works the opposite way if Enlarge is your default.

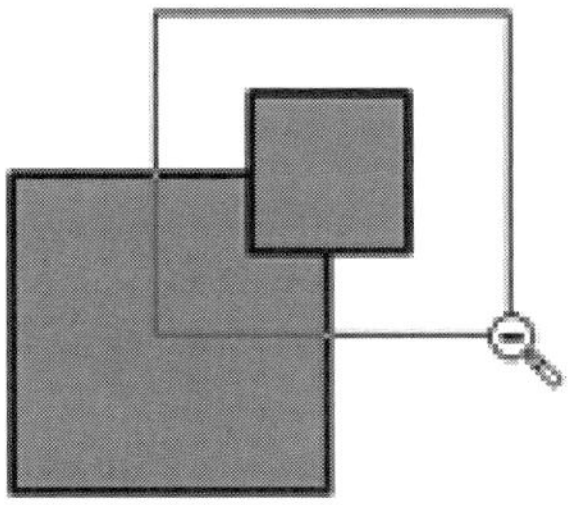

FIGURE 2.6 Use the Click and Drag feature of the Zoom tool to zoom in.

Using the shortcut key commands to switch to a certain magnification is a quick way to zoom in and out. These commands can be accessed under View > Magnification. Another quick feature is if you double-click on the Zoom tool icon in the Tools panel, it will reset the magnification to 100%. When judging whether your graphics need any edits, you should rely on viewing at 100% magnification, since that is what the user will be viewing. Of course, there are exceptions, such as if you are going to scale up your work. The bottom line is to draw your vector graphics for the magnification at which your users will be viewing it. Extra detail just adds to your file size and can slow the speed at which your animation plays because there are more vectors to move.

EDITING

A great deal of editing is involved when it comes to illustrating in Macromedia Flash, and the key to creating more elaborate, optimized, and professional-looking graphics is to practice concepts developed from the author's experience with the program. These concepts mostly involve the two main editing tools: the Selection tool and the Lasso tool. We will also review several new features of Flash that help automate the editing process and will save you hours of production time.

Mastering the Selection Tool

It is important that the graphic we will be editing is not scaled by the Free Transform tool, because using that tool will not maintain the radius of the rounded corners. Where the Selection tool comes in handy is the ability to easily select what we do not want and reposition what we do want. If you click and drag your mouse with the Selection tool, a bounding box is formed, and upon release whatever is in that bounding box is selected. As shown in Figure 2.7, click and drag to select a center portion of the graphic.

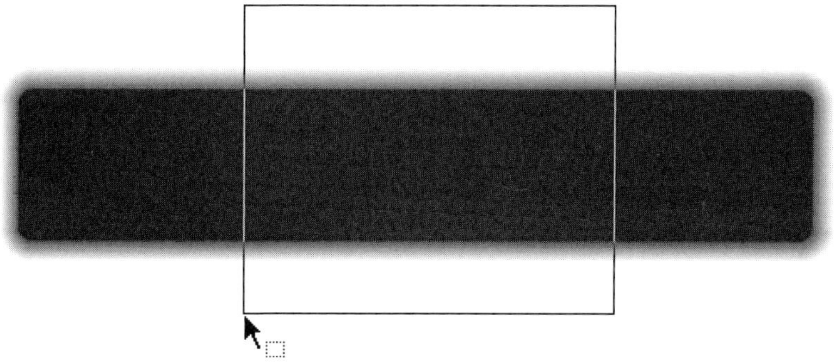

FIGURE 2.7 With the Selection tool, click and drag; notice the bounding box where the selection will be made.

Once you are happy with the area you have marked, release your mouse button and the area will be selected as shown in Figure 2.8.

Now, delete the selected area using the Cut shortcut key command. With the Selection tool, click and drag to select the right side of the graphic, as shown in Figure 2.9.

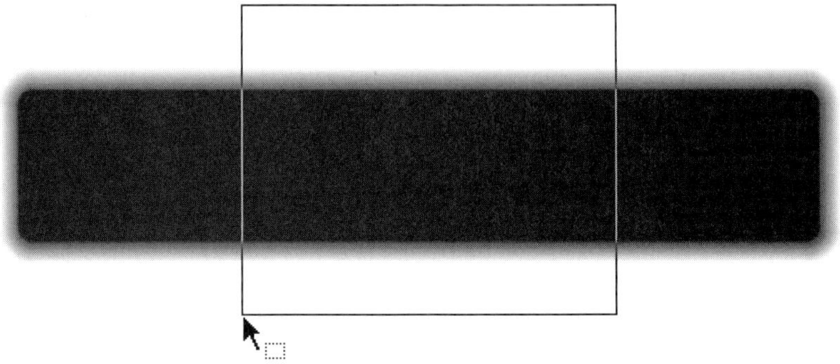

FIGURE 2.8 On release, the selection is made.

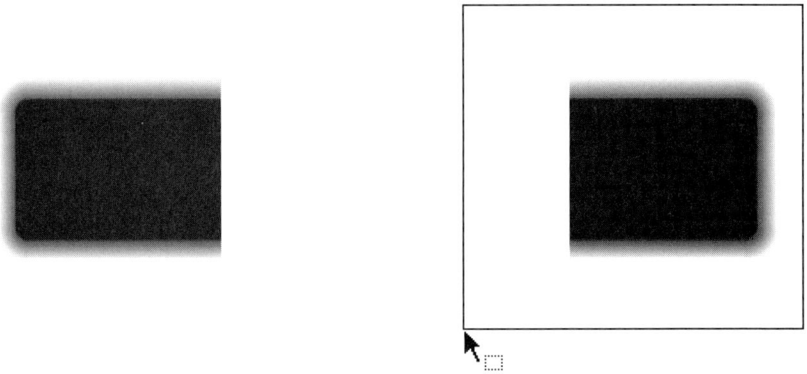

FIGURE 2.9 Delete selected portion and select the right piece.

Now that the right side is selected, with Snap to Objects on, click and drag from the top-left corner to begin to drag the graphic. Drag and snap it to the top-right corner of the left graphic, as shown in Figure 2.10.

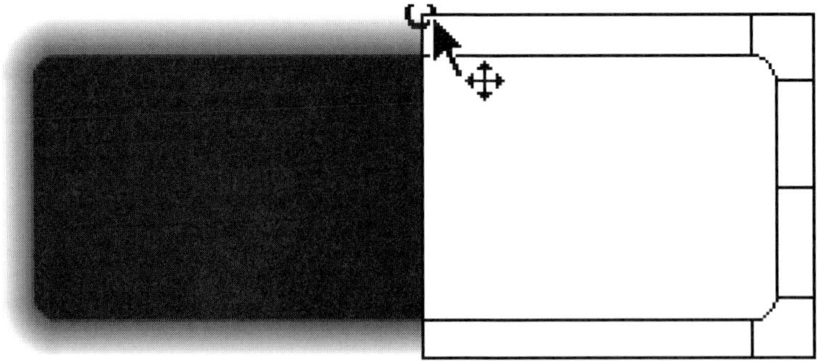

FIGURE 2.10 With the right piece selected, snap it to the left side.

Now, to make the graphic longer, vertically click and drag to select the bottom portion of the graphic, as shown in Figure 2.11.

FIGURE 2.11 With the Selection tool, select the bottom half of the graphic.

Once selected, hold down the Shift key and use the down arrow key, both on your keyboard, to move the bottom part of the graphic down, as shown in Figure 2.12. Moving graphics with the arrow keys and the help of the Shift key to advance farther will give you precise graphic placement.

FIGURE 2.12 Move the selected piece down with the down arrow key.

Select the top half of the bottom graphic and execute the shortcut key to use the Free Transform tool, as shown in Figure 2.13.

FIGURE 2.13 Using the Selection tool, select a top portion of the bottom piece.

Scale the selected graphic vertically by using the top center transform modifier, as shown in Figure 2.14, and connect it to the bottom of the top graphic.

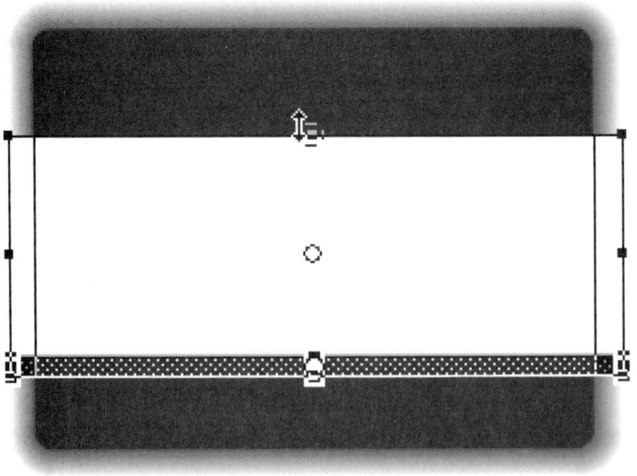

FIGURE 2.14 Use the Free Transform tool and scale vertically.

The graphic now has a new shape with the radius of the corners untouched, as shown in Figure 2.15.

FIGURE 2.15 The graphic now has a new shape.

With the Rectangle tool, create a square, and with the Selection tool, select a square portion of the top-right corner of the square, as shown in Figure 2.16.

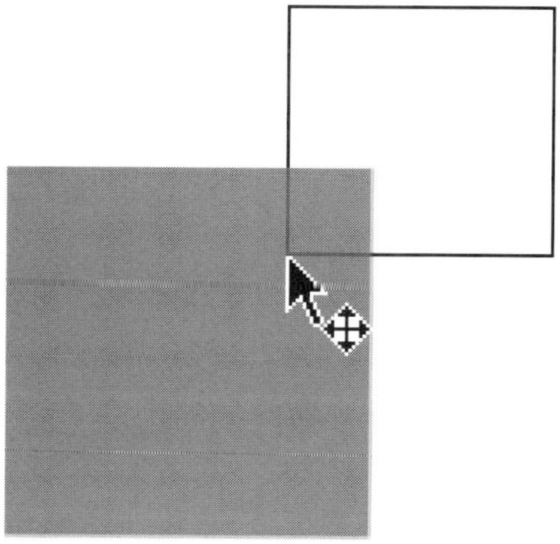

FIGURE 2.16 Create a square and select the top-right corner with the Selection tool.

Delete the selected corner, grab the bottom-right vector point of the deleted area, and snap it to the top-left vector of the deleted area, as shown in Figure 2.17.

FIGURE 2.17 Delete the selected corner, grab the vector point, and snap it to the vector point above it.

Grab the line that looks like the flattened corner of the square, and your cursor should display a curved line. That is when you know you will be editing the curve of the line and not a vector point. As shown in Figure 2.18, click and drag it up and to the right until you find a nice curve so the corner of the square will be rounded.

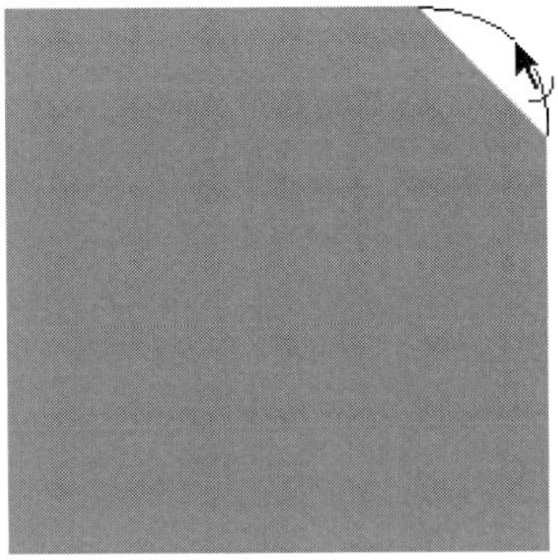

FIGURE 2.18 Grab the center of the line and pull it out to give it a curve.

With the Selection tool, select a rectangular portion at the lower area of the square, as shown in Figure 2.19.

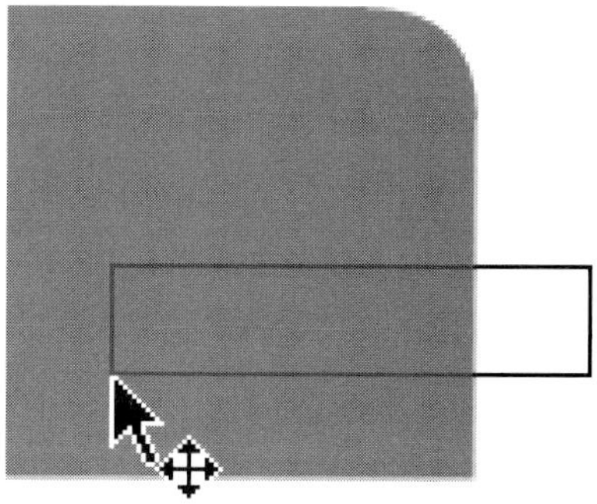

FIGURE 2.19 Select and delete a rectangle shape from the lower part of the shape.

Delete the selected area, and select and delete two more areas from the corners of the rectangle-shaped area, as shown in Figure 2.20. We are deleting these areas to change the shape of the square so we can add some curves going through it.

FIGURE 2.20 Select and delete the corners.

To flatten out these corners, grab the middle vector point and connect it to one of the points next to it, as shown in Figure 2.21.

FIGURE 2.21 Grab the corner vector and snap it to one of the edges.

Grab the flattened lines and make them round, as shown in Figure 2.22.

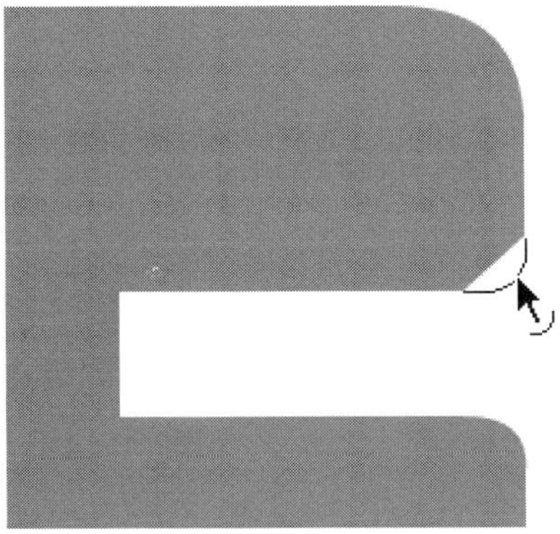

FIGURE 2.22 Grab the line and pull it out to make it round.

Grab the top-left vector point of the cut out rectangle and bring it to the middle point between the two vector points on the left side, as shown in Figure 2.23.

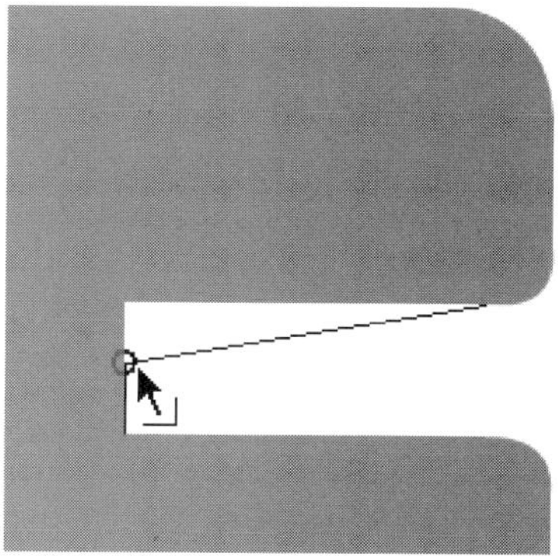

FIGURE 2.23 Move the top-left vector point to the middle.

Grab the bottom-left vector point of the cut out rectangle and snap it to the recently moved vector point above it, as shown in Figure 2.24.

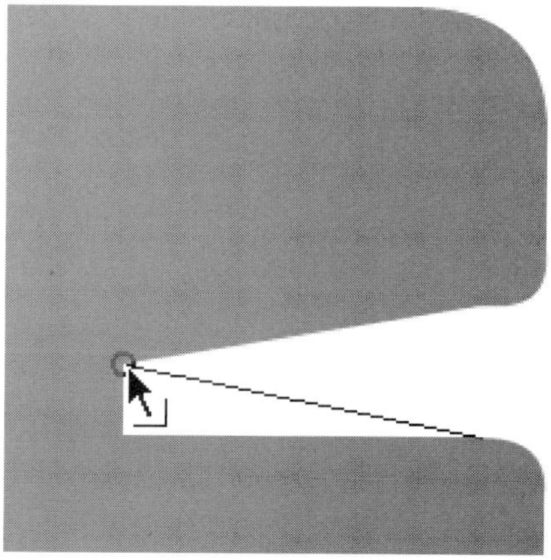

FIGURE 2.24 Snap the bottom left vector point to the point above it.

Still using the Selection tool, grab the top line and pull it up to give it a nice arch, as shown in Figure 2.25.

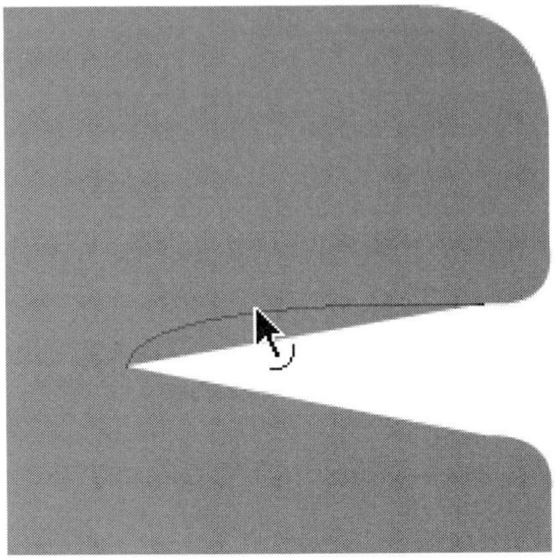

FIGURE 2.25 Grab the top line and curve it out.

Grab the bottom line and pull it down to give it a nice arch mirroring the top arch, as shown in Figure 2.26.

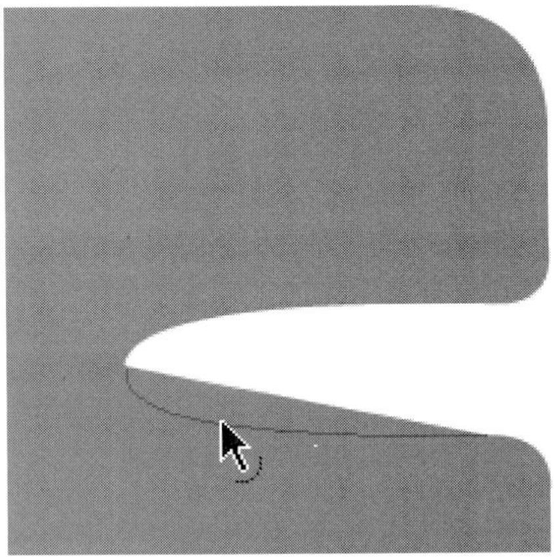

FIGURE 2.26 Grab the bottom line and curve it out.

Made entirely from the Selection tool, this complex shape shows you the potential of its editing capability, as shown in Figure 2.27.

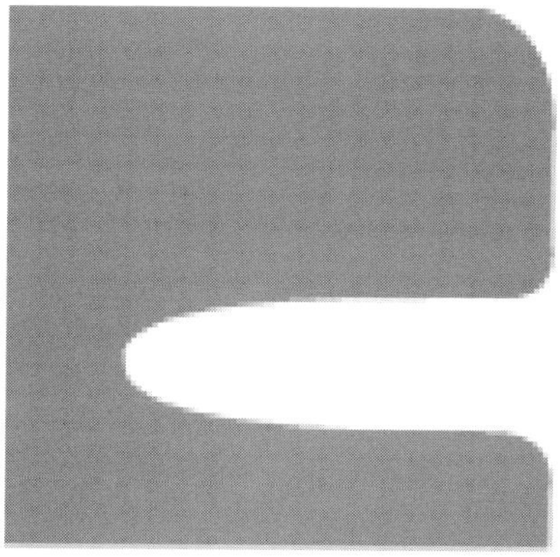

FIGURE 2.27 Final shape made by editing with the Selection tool.

Mastering the Lasso Tool

By using the Lasso tool in Polygon mode while selecting certain areas of a vector shape, you can create complex shapes that could not be created by any other tool, as shown in Figure 2.28.

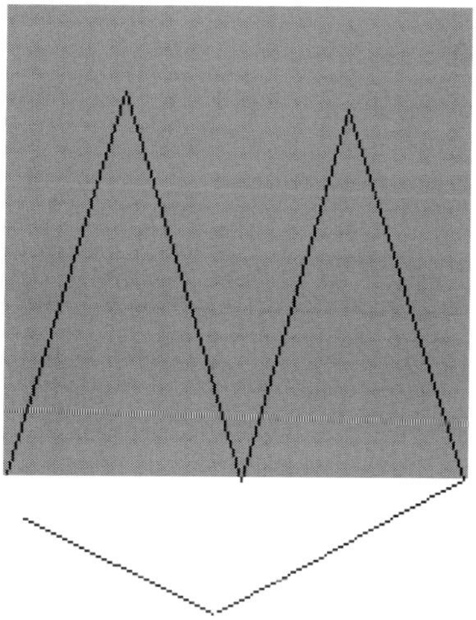

FIGURE 2.28 Using the Lasso tool in Polygon mode to select.

Delete the selected shape and begin to plot your points with the Lasso tool to select the area on top, as shown in Figure 2.29.

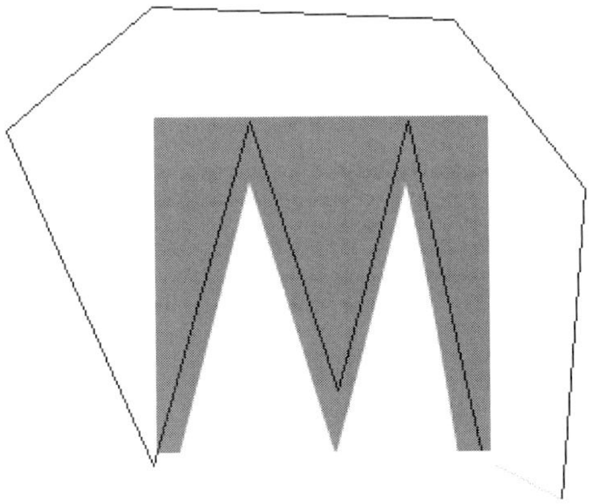

FIGURE 2.29 Delete the selected shape and lay out a new shape to select.

Delete the selected shape and notice the shape that has been made with the Lasso tool, as shown in Figure 2.30. Try using this tool to create other complicated shapes.

FIGURE 2.30 M-looking fill shape.

As shown in Figure 2.31, the shape we are about to make might be extreme, but shows the potential of this tool and how intricate you can get.

FIGURE 2.31 Use the Lasso tool to select complicated shapes.

Once you close the lasso line, you should have something similar to Figure 2.32.

FIGURE 2.32 Once the lasso shape is closed, the area will be selected.

Delete the selected shape to reveal the shape we have left, as shown in Figure 2.33.

FIGURE 2.33 Delete the selected shape to reveal the final shape.

Copy and Paste in Place

Copy and Paste in Place is used a lot when illustrating with Macromedia Flash, because shapes are often needed more than once and in specific positions in relation to other shapes. Create a perfect circle with the Oval tool by holding down the Shift key on your keyboard as you draw the circle. Give it a black outline and a gray solid fill. Select the black outline and scale it down to 95% with the Scale and Rotate panel, as shown in Figure 2.34.

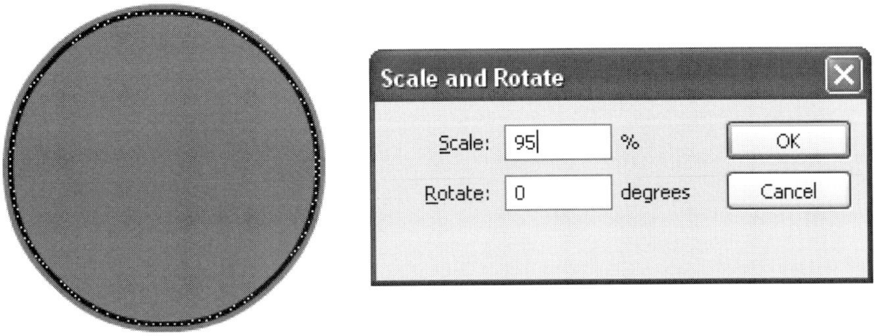

FIGURE 2.34 Create a circle and scale the outline down to 95%.

Execute the shortcut key to Copy and Paste in Place the black outline, and with the Scale and Rotate panel, scale it down to 90%, as shown in Figure 2.35.

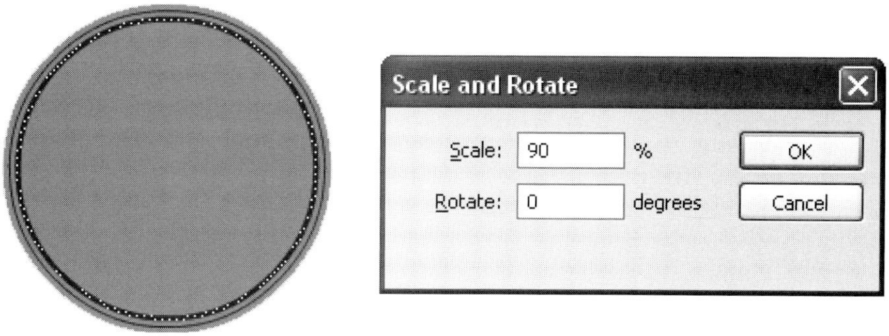

FIGURE 2.35 Copy and Paste in Place and scale down to 90%.

Moving Graphics Precisely

Create a rectangle with the Rectangle tool and select the top line with the Selection tool, as shown in Figure 2.36.

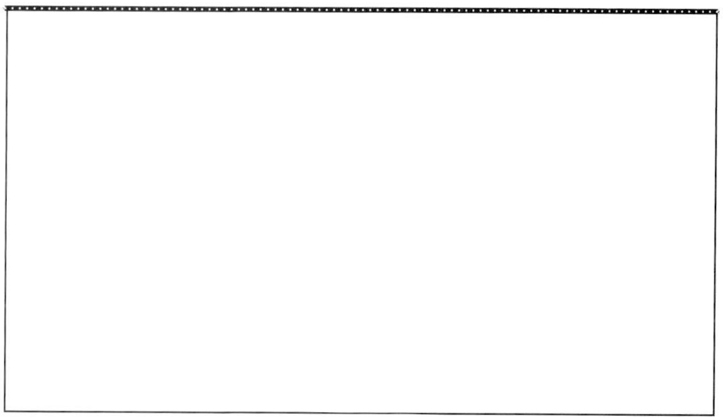

FIGURE 2.36 Create a rectangle-shaped outline and select the top line.

Execute the shortcut keys to Copy and Paste in Place a new line, and use the down arrow key to move the line down twice with the Shift key held down, as shown in Figure 2.37.

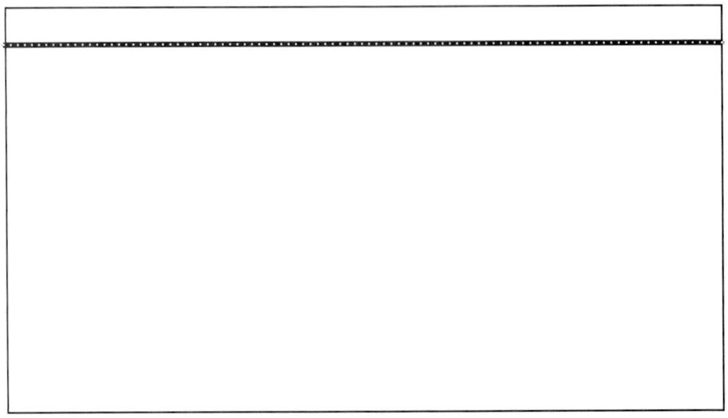

FIGURE 2.37 Copy and Paste in Place, and move the line down two down-arrow clicks while holding down the Shift key.

Paste in Place another line and click the down arrow while holding down the Shift key to create a third line evenly spaced with the first two lines. Paste in Place a fourth line and move it down as shown in Figure 2.38.

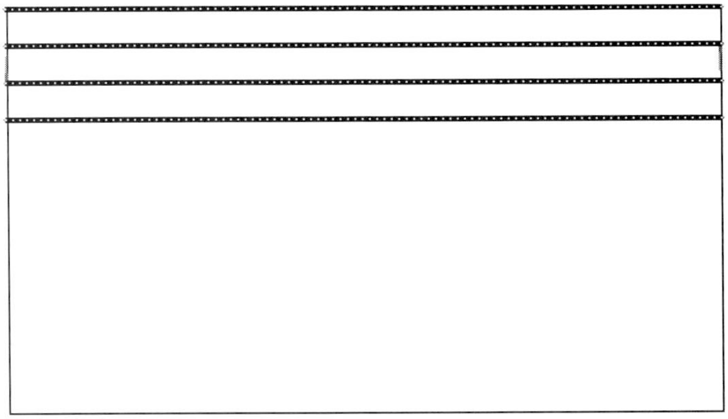

FIGURE 2.38 Repeat previous step two more times.

With the Selection tool, select the four lines and duplicate them by executing the shortcut key to duplicate the graphic, as shown in Figure 2.39.

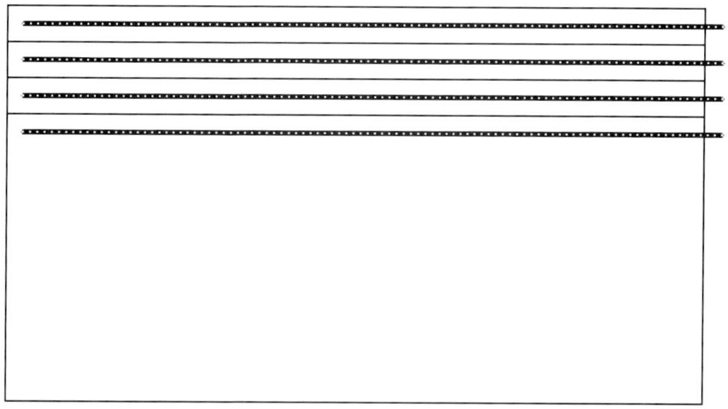

FIGURE 2.39 Select the four lines and duplicate them.

With the Selection tool, grab the top-left line and snap it to the bottom-left line as shown in Figure 2.40.

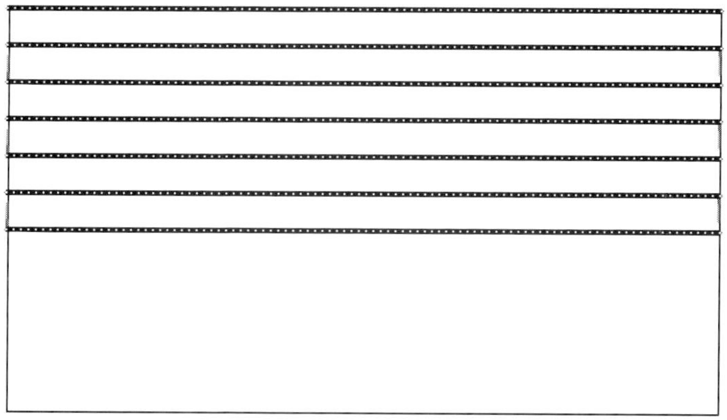

FIGURE 2.40 Grab the top-left line of the selected graphics and snap it to the bottom-left line.

Selecting and Deselecting

We would like to select the complicated shape shown in Figure 2.41, but because it is made up of eight triangular shapes, there is a quicker way to do so without having to select them individually.

FIGURE 2.41 A complicated shape.

With the Selection tool, start to select the center part of the graphic, selecting the eight triangles and part of the square, as shown in Figure 2.42.

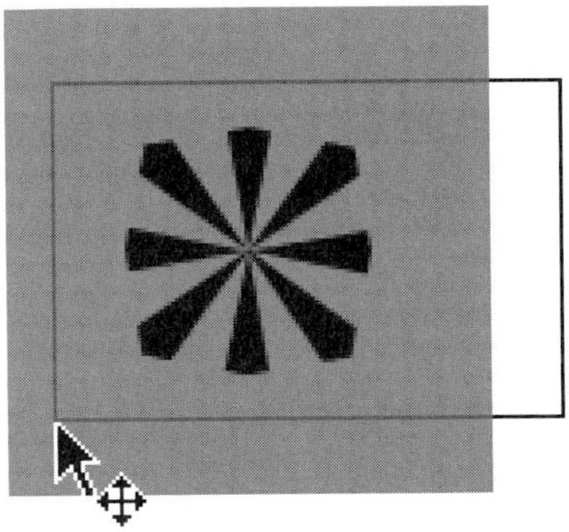

FIGURE 2.42 With the Selection tool, select the complex shape.

By holding down the Shift key as you select the square with your Selection tool, the square fill should deselect, as shown in Figure 2.43.

Execute the shortcut key to delete the selected shapes, as shown in Figure 2.44.

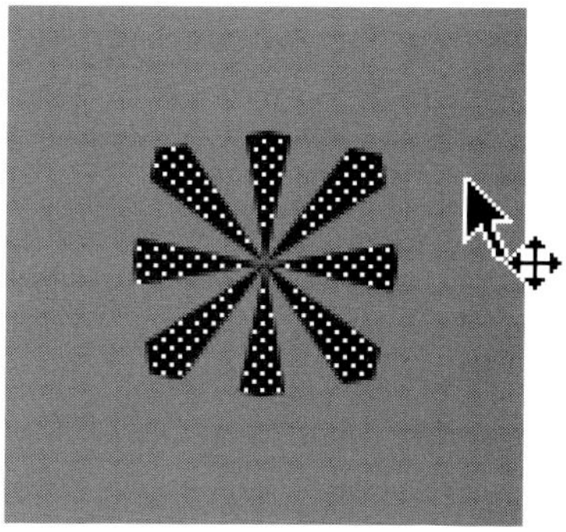

FIGURE 2.43 Deselect the background by holding down the Shift key and clicking the background.

FIGURE 2.44 Delete the selected complicated shape.

Optimize Your Vectors

It is important when illustrating in Macromedia Flash that you optimize your vectors when using the Pencil and Paint Brush tools, since these tools produce unoptimized lines and shapes. With the Pencil tool set at Smooth mode, draw a crazy line with plenty of curves, as shown in Figure 2.45.

Execute the shortcut keys to launch the Optimize Curves window, and set the slider to None. You will find this feature under Modify > Shape > Optimize. Make sure both checkboxes are selected as shown in Figure 2.46, and click OK when you are ready.

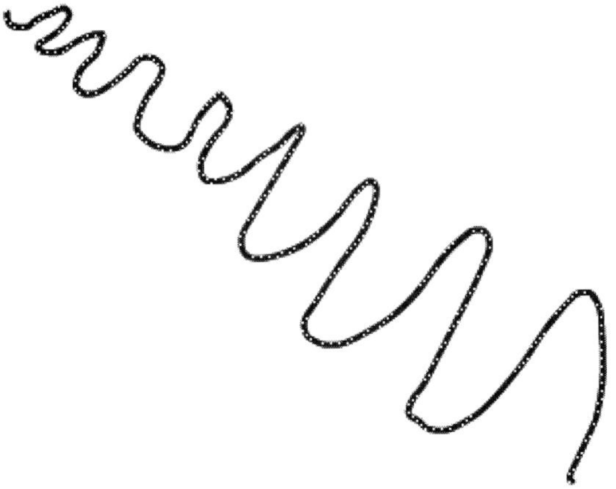

FIGURE 2.45 Draw a line with the Pencil tool in Smooth mode.

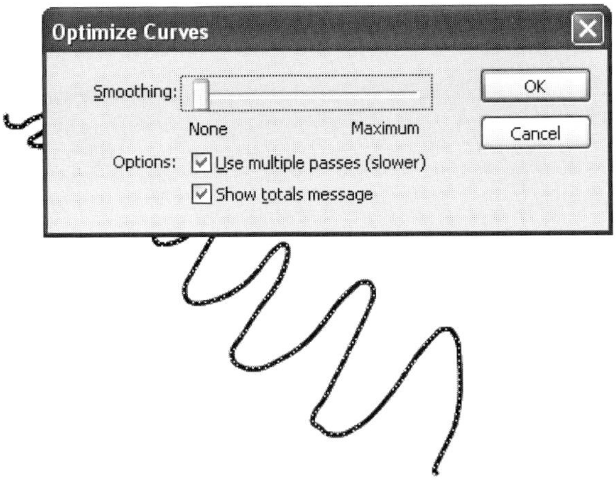

FIGURE 2.46 Open the Optimize Curves pop up and set the slider to None.

A results window is displayed with the number of curves it originally had, how many curves it has after the optimization, and the percentage of how much was optimized, as shown in Figure 2.47.

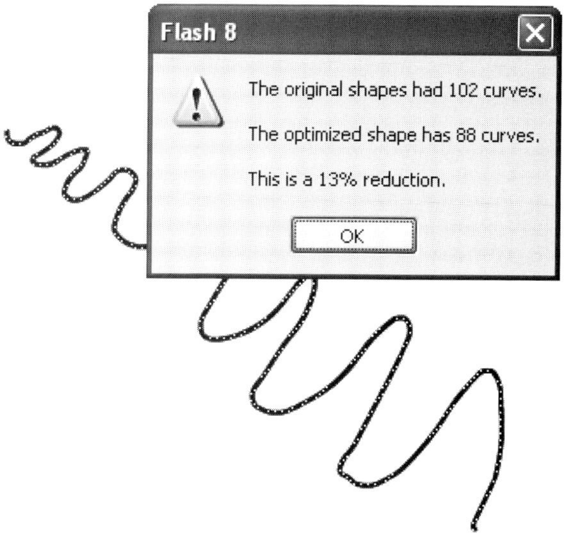

FIGURE 2.47 Click OK and the results of the optimization are shown.

This is great—the line has been optimized by 13%. Feel free to try it again but with different settings to see how low you can get it without changing the look of the line. As shown in Figure 2.48, the optimization did not seem to change the line much.

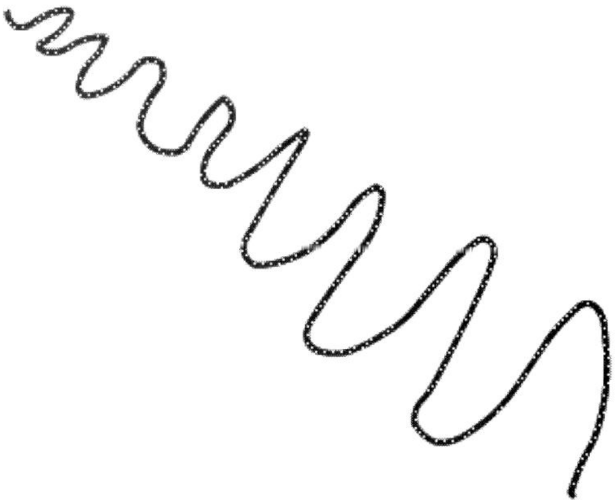

FIGURE 2.48 The result of optimization.

History Panel

The History panel can save you time by automating previous tasks. In this scenario, we will create a square, divide it into four halves, and select the top-left square, as shown in Figure 2.49. To open the History panel, go to Window > Other Panels > History.

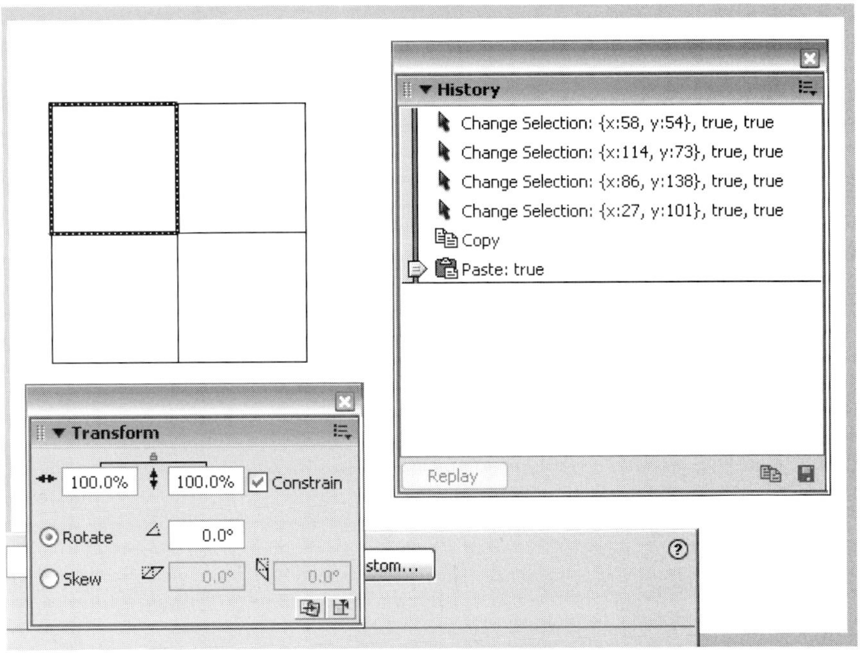

FIGURE 2.49 Create a square, divide it into four halves, and select the top-left square.

With the square selected, copy it, paste it in place, and scale it down to 50%. Notice how the History panel is tracking everything you are doing, as shown in Figure 2.50. Make sure you do not click somewhere on the stage or mistakenly click the wrong line, because the History panel will record that.

With the Selection tool, select the square on the top right and select the History to Copy, Paste, and Transform, as shown in Figure 2.51.

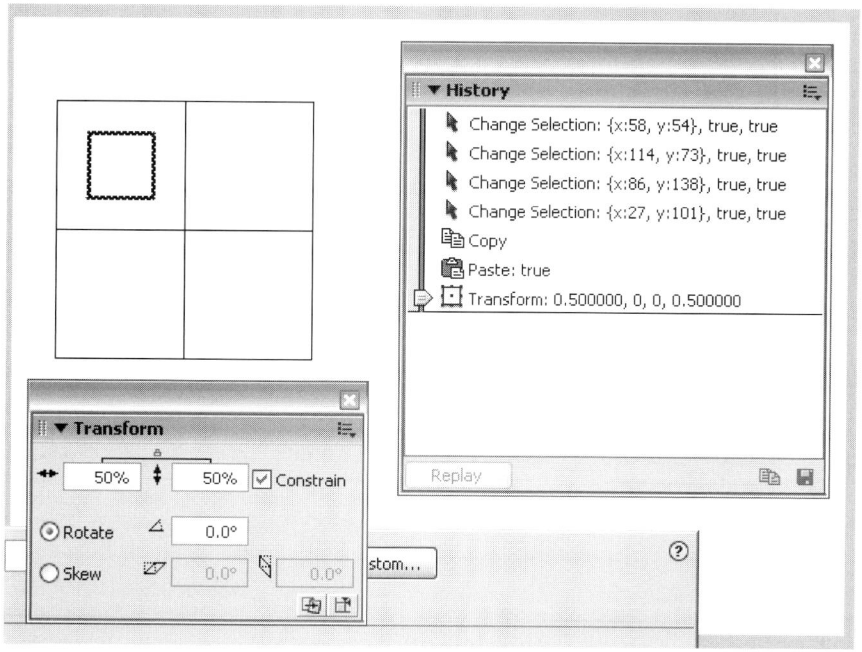

FIGURE 2.50 Copy, Paste in Place, and scale down to 50%.

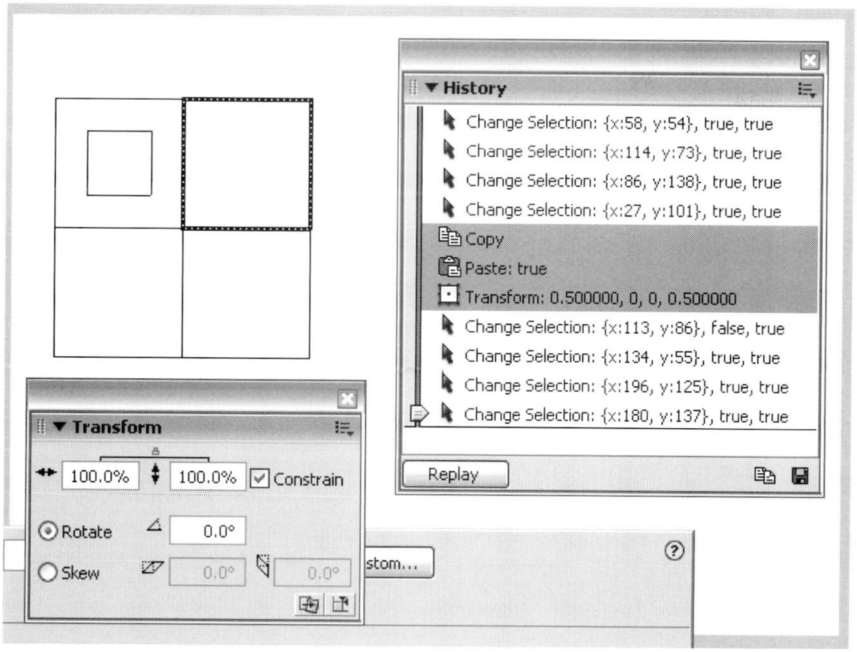

FIGURE 2.51 Select the other square and History of Copy, Paste, and Transform.

Click the Replay button to watch the selected history executed on the selected graphic, as shown in Figure 2.52. Once you replay several tasks, the History panel will display the Replay as one item, called Replay Steps.

Select the bottom-left square and execute the Replay Steps as shown in Figure 2.53.

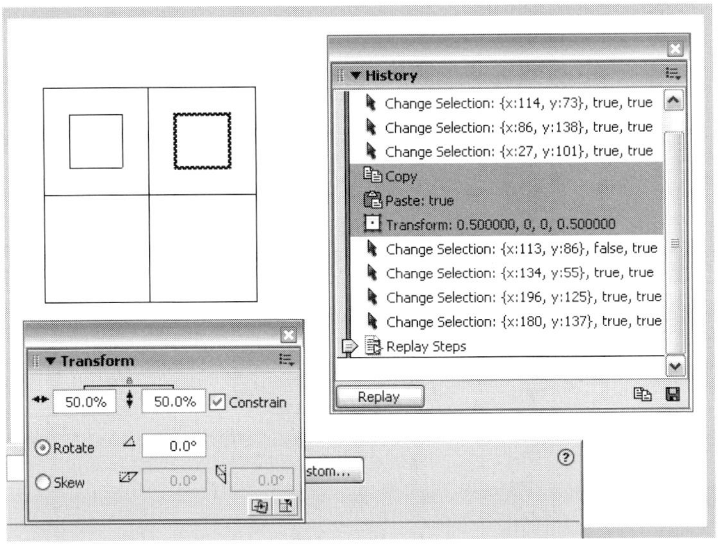

FIGURE 2.52 Click the Replay button in the History panel and watch the tasks replayed.

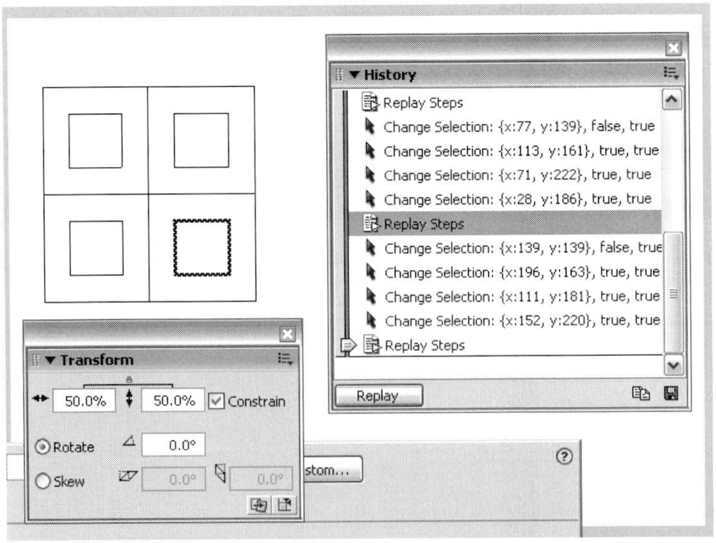

FIGURE 2.53 Repeat the previous step on the last two squares.

Check Spelling

Check Spelling is a very useful new feature when working with a file with quite a bit of content, as it saves you from having to manually check for spelling mistakes. As shown in Figure 2.54, many settings can be modified. To bring up this panel, access Text > Spelling Setup.

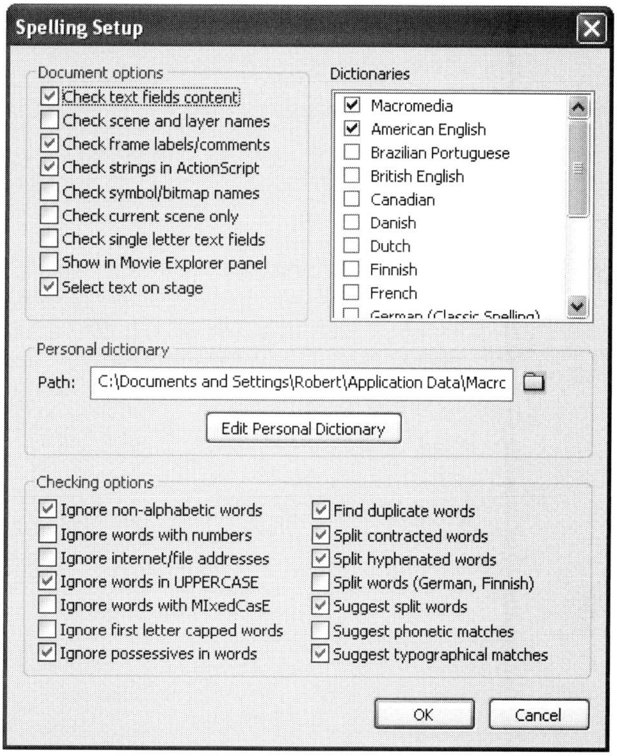

FIGURE 2.54 Review the Spelling Setup window.

Once you run the feature, the display box shown in Figure 2.55 appears, telling you what word is misspelled and providing a place where you can type in the correct spelling. To bring up this panel, access Text > Check Spelling.

FIGURE 2.55 Check Spelling found a misspelled word; type in the correct spelling.

Find and Replace

As with any Find and Replace feature, the program searches for a certain type of content and will replace it with your requested content. The useful part about this feature is that you can find and replace solid fills. As shown in Figure 2.56, the window is set to replace the color red with blue.

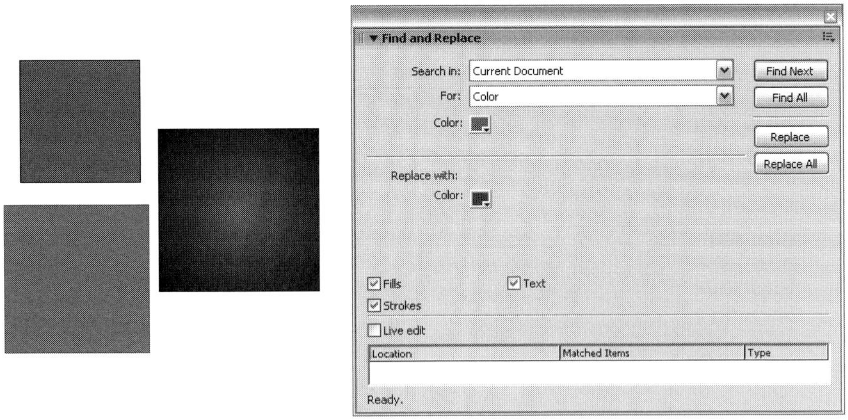

FIGURE 2.56 Use the Find and Replace feature to change solid colors.

Once it is done searching, it displays how many items it found. After the Replace All button is clicked, it switches the colors, as shown in Figure 2.57. Notice the red color in the radial gradient did not change, only the solid fills. The other attributes you can search for are Text, Font, Color, Symbol, Sound, Video, and Bitmap.

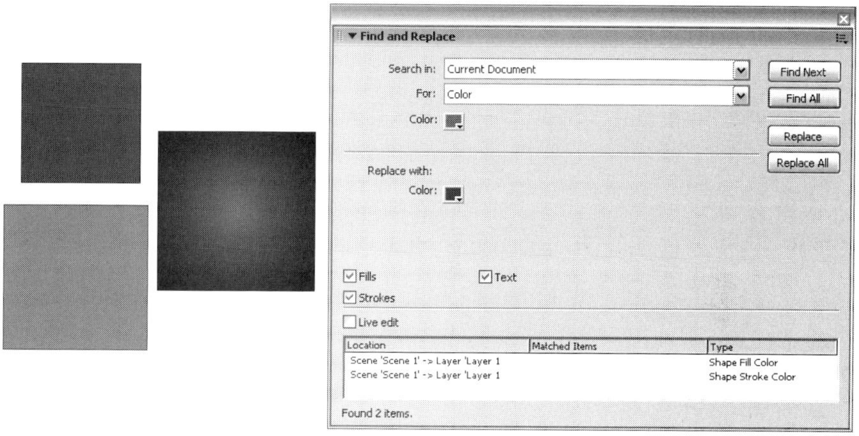

FIGURE 2.57 Only the solid colors change.

CREATING

Macromedia Flash has a nice assortment of basic drawing tools, which by themselves let you create and edit rectangles, ovals, lines, fills, and much more. At first glance, this may not seem like much, but further analysis of these tools and how they are used together to produce optimum results will show their true potential. In this section, we will review the big part the Line tool plays in creating graphics, and how a tool as simple as the Rectangle tool can help you create complex shapes and grids.

Simple Shapes

With the Rectangle tool, create a square and draw a line connected to the top-right corner to the bottom-left corner, as shown in Figure 2.58.

Switch to the Paint Bucket tool and apply a solid fill to the top triangle-shaped outline, as shown in Figure 2.59.

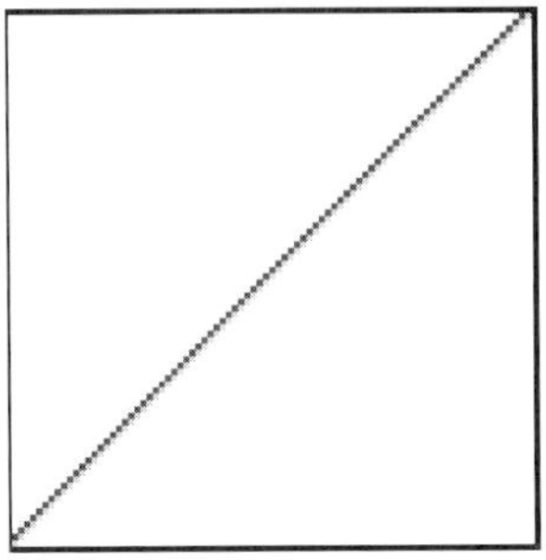

FIGURE 2.58 Create a square and draw a line connecting the top-right corner to the bottom-left corner.

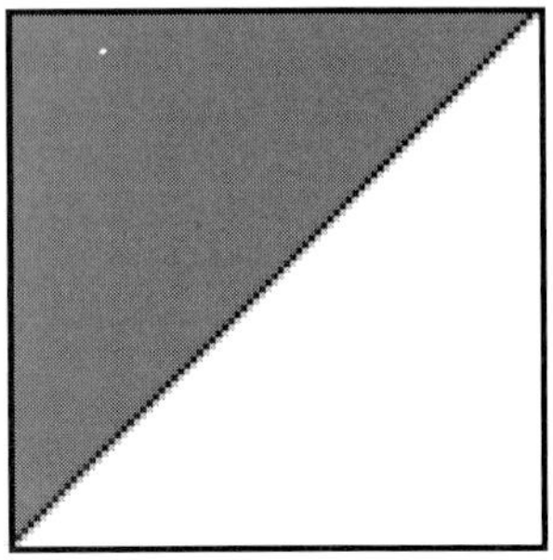

FIGURE 2.59 Apply a solid fill to the top triangle.

With the Selection tool, double-click anywhere on the outline to select all of it, and delete it. Select the remaining triangle shape, open the Transform panel, and rotate it by 45°, as shown in Figure 2.60.

FIGURE 2.60 Rotate the triangle by 45°.

With the Rectangle tool, create a square, and with the Line tool, divide it into four equal pieces diagonally, as shown in Figure 2.61.

Using the Line tool, divide the square into eight equal pieces vertically and horizontally, as shown in Figure 2.62.

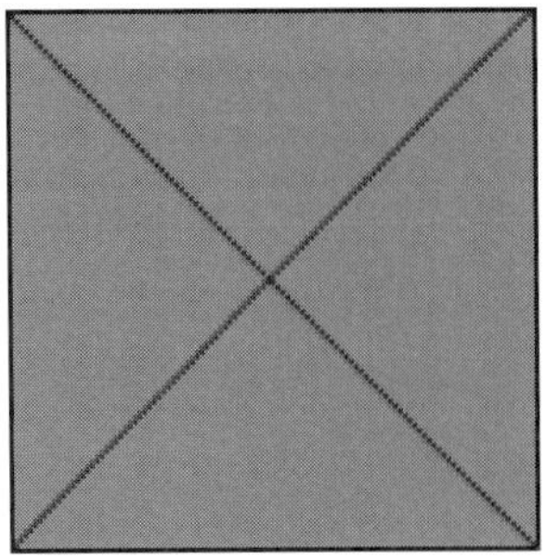

FIGURE 2.61 Create a square and divide it in four equal pieces diagonally.

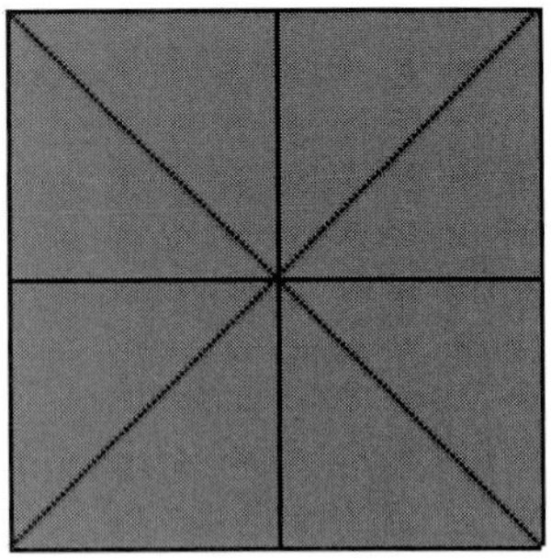

FIGURE 2.62 Divide the square into eighths.

Select the diagonal lines and delete them. Create a new layer by going to Insert > Timeline > Layer. On the new layer, create a circle outline by snapping it from the top-left corner of the square to the bottom-right corner of the square, as shown in Figure 2.63. The circle is initially created on a different layer but snapped to align with the square so the circle does not collapse with the square.

Select the vertical and horizontal lines on the original layer, and delete and paste them in place on the new layer, dividing the circle into four equal pieces. Now Select the two bottom pieces of the circle and delete them so you will have half of a circle, as shown in Figure 2.64.

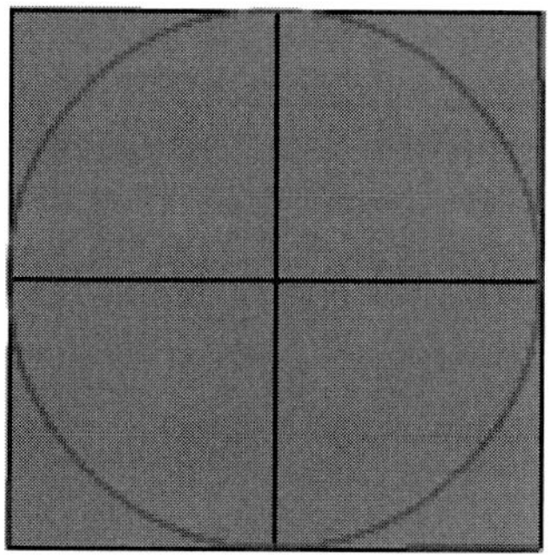

FIGURE 2.63 Delete diagonal lines and draw a circle, snapping it to the top-left and bottom-right corners of the square on a new layer above the square.

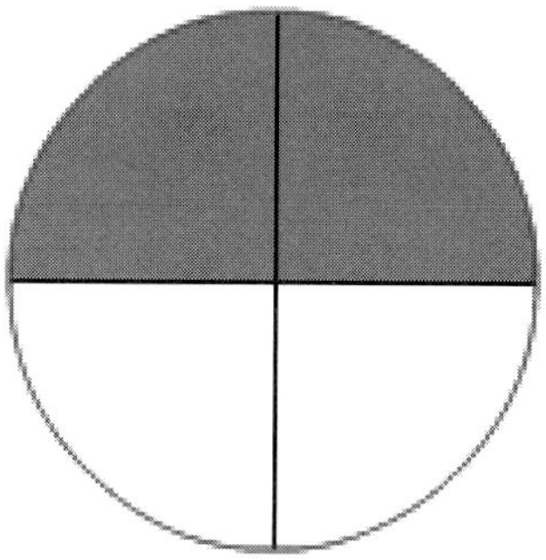

FIGURE 2.64 Copy the circle and Paste in Place on the layer with the square. Delete the fill outside of the circle and the two bottom pie-shaped pieces.

Select all the outlines and delete them to reveal a precisely divided circle, as shown in Figure 2.65.

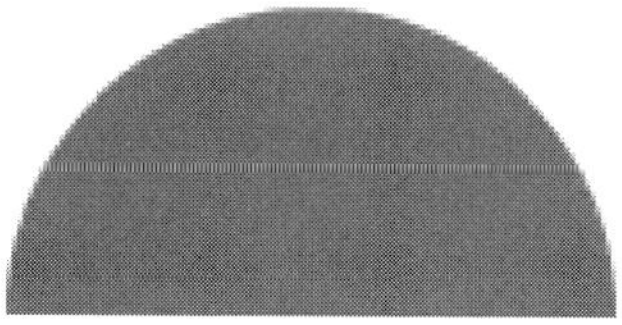

FIGURE 2.65 Delete the outlines.

Advanced Shapes

With the Rectangle tool, create a square, and with the Line tool, divide it into eight pieces diagonally, and then vertically and horizontally, as shown in Figure 2.66.

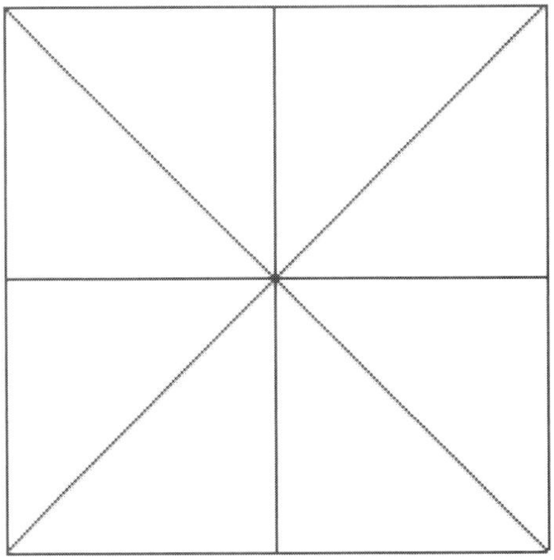

FIGURE 2.66 Create a square and divide it into eight equal parts.

Create a new layer by going to Insert > Timeline > Layer. On the new layer, create a circle outline by snapping it from the top-left corner of the square to the bottom-right corner of the square. Select the circle outline, copy it, Paste in Place, and scale it down to 90%, as shown in Figure 2.67.

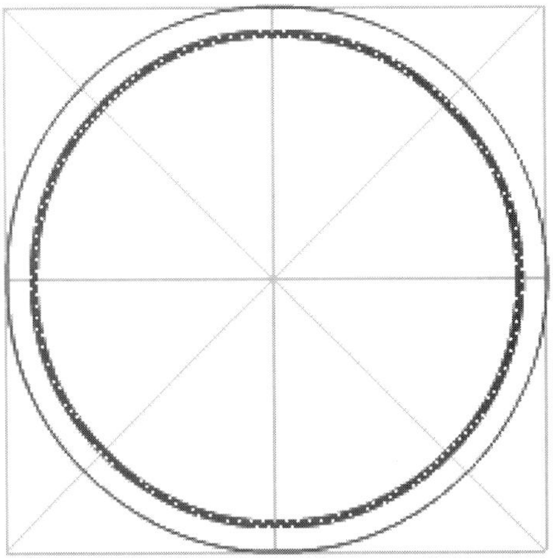

FIGURE 2.67 On a new layer above the square, draw a circle, snapping it to the top-left corner and the bottom-right corner. Copy and Paste in Place the circle outline and scale it down to 90%.

Hide the new layer with the circle outlines on it by clicking on the Show/Hide Layer dot in the Timeline panel. With the Selection tool, select the square outline and delete it, leaving the diagonal, vertical, and horizontal lines, as shown in Figure 2.68.

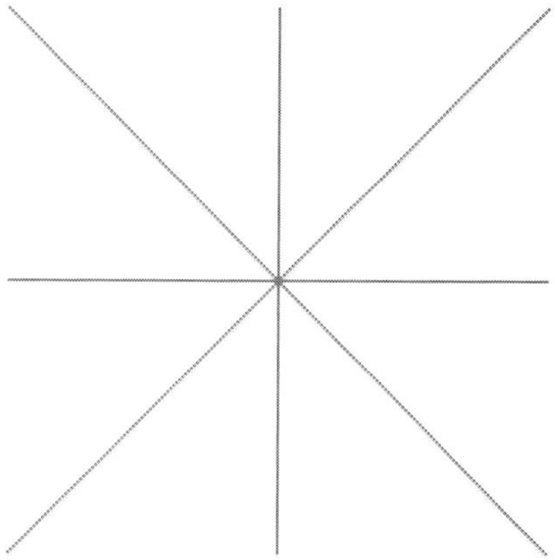

FIGURE 2.68 Hide the layer that holds the circles. Delete the square outline.

Select all the lines by double-clicking on them with the Selection tool. Copy and paste them in place. With the Scale and Rotate panel, rotate the new lines by 22.5°, as shown in Figure 2.69.

Execute the shortcut key to Paste in Place, which will paste the original lines, and rotate them by 11.25°, as shown in Figure 2.70.

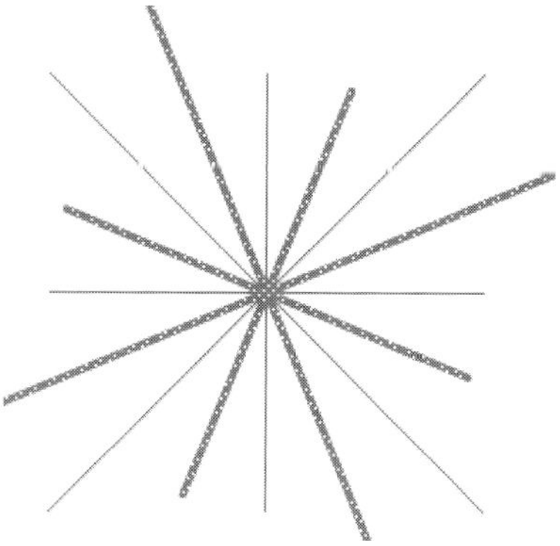

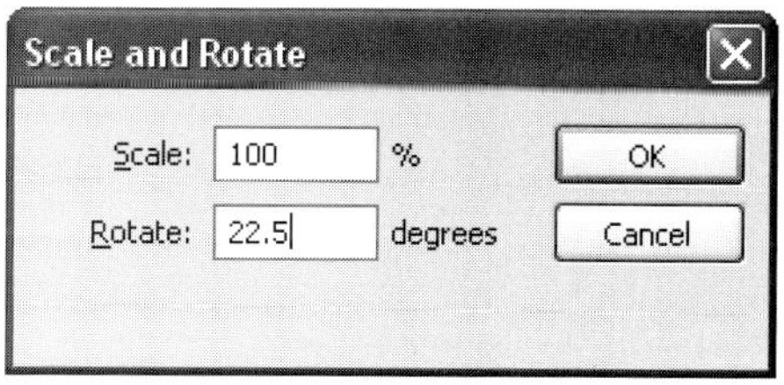

FIGURE 2.69 Copy and Paste in Place the eight lines, and rotate the new lines by 22.5°.

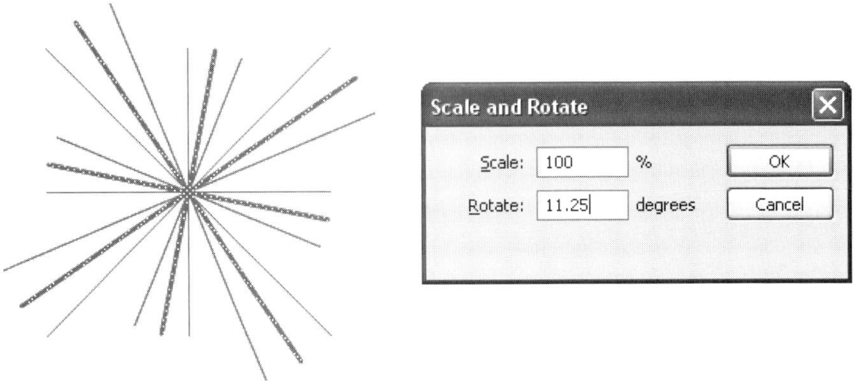

FIGURE 2.70 Paste in Place the new eight lines and rotate by 11.25°.

Paste in Place again and rotate the lines by –11.25°, as shown in Figure 2.71.

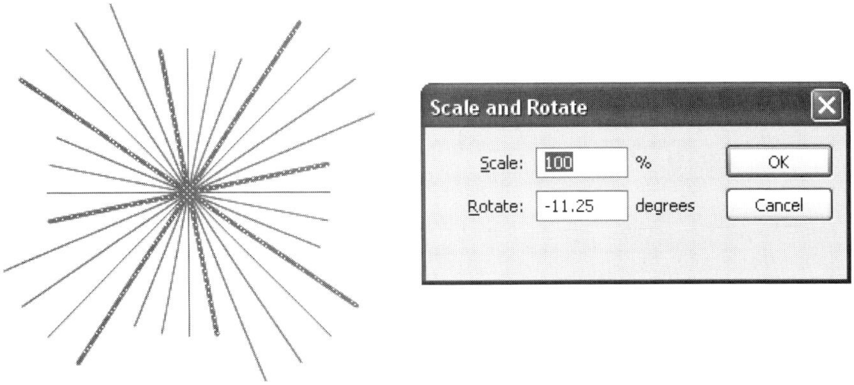

FIGURE 2.71 Paste in Place the new eight lines and rotate by –11.25°.

Unhide the top layer that contains the two circles, and select, delete, and paste them in place on the bottom layer with all the lines, as shown in Figure 2.72. Once on the same layer, all the lines (assuming they are the same color and line width) will collapse together.

Using the Paint Bucket tool, apply solid fills in the areas shown in Figure 2.73.

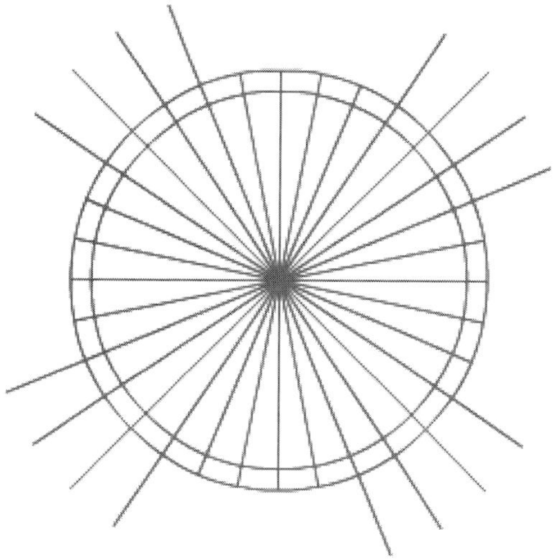

FIGURE 2.72 Place the two circles on the top layer and paste them in place on the lower layer with all the lines.

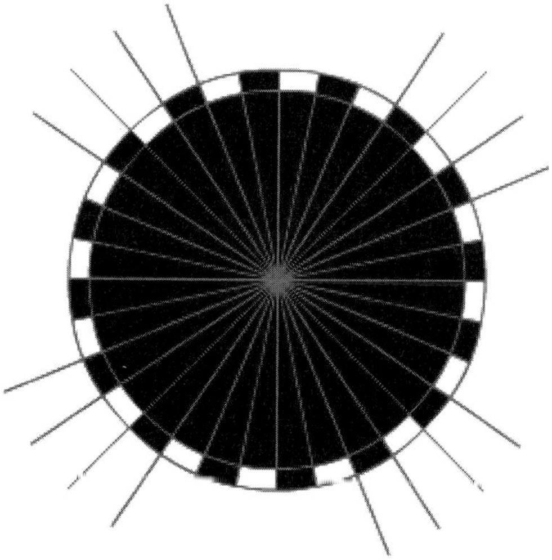

FIGURE 2.73 Apply solid fills to the areas shown here.

With the Selection tool, double-click anywhere on the outlines to select all the outlines and delete them, as shown in Figure 2.74.

FIGURE 2.74 Delete the outlines.

Create a square with the Rectangle tool and divide it into equal pieces diagonally, vertically, and horizontally with the Line tool. Use the PolyStar tool and set the tool to Polygon, with 16 sides and .25 star point size (which will not matter since we are making a polygon). Create a small polygon with these settings off to the side, as shown in Figure 2.75.

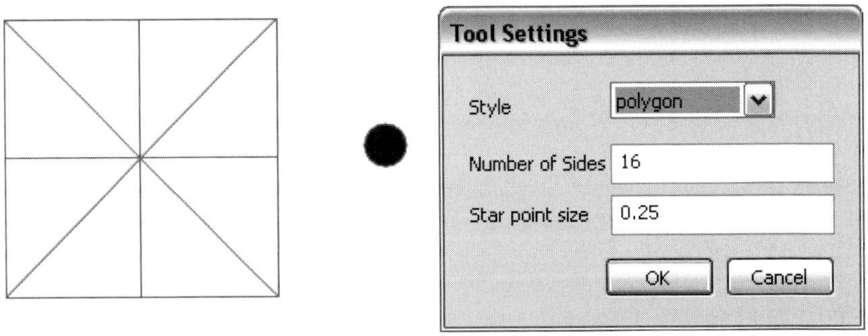

FIGURE 2.75 Create a square divided into eight equal pieces. Create a polygon with the displayed settings.

Draw a vertical and horizontal line dividing the polygon into four equal pieces, use the Selection tool to select the center where the two lines meet, and snap it to the center of the square. Using the Oval tool, draw a perfect circle on top of the square, as shown in Figure 2.76.

With the Line tool, draw lines that connect from the outer radius of the circle to the inner radius of the small polygon outline, forming a star-like shape, as shown in Figure 2.77. Make sure when creating the lines that you are snapping to specific vector points so your line placement will be precise.

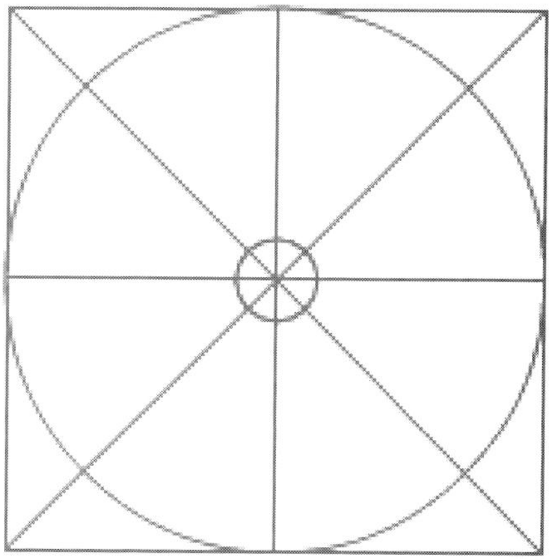

FIGURE 2.76 Snap the polygon to the center of the square.

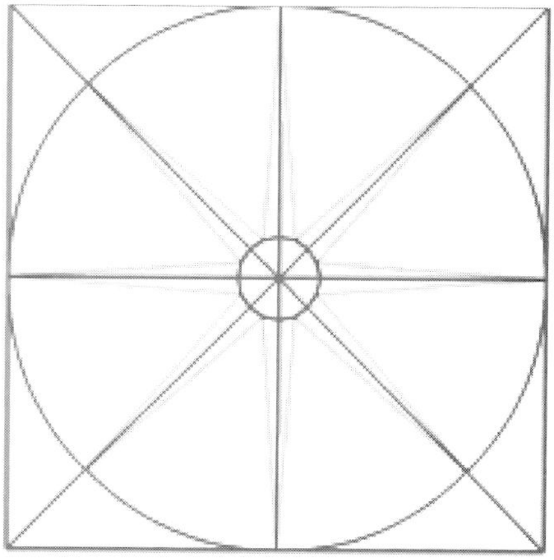

FIGURE 2.77 Connect a line to the outer part of the circle to the inner polygon.

With the Paint Bucket tool, apply a solid fill to the inner outline of the star shape, as shown in Figure 2.78. Make sure the Paint Bucket tool is set to Don't Close Gaps, found in the Options area in the Tools panel. That way, the paint will fill in completely.

Select all the outlines with the Selection tool and delete them to reveal the final shape, as shown in Figure 2.79. To compare optimization of number of curves, if you create the same star shape with the PolyStar tool, you should end up with a star with the same number of curves, 16.

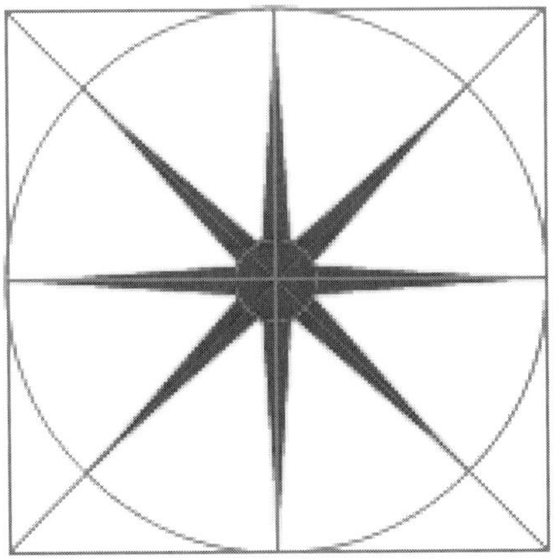

FIGURE 2.78 Apply solid fills to the inner star outline.

FIGURE 2.79 Delete all the lines.

Grids and Evenly Spaced Content

With the Rectangle tool, create a rectangle, and with the Line tool, divide it into four, as shown in Figure 2.80.

Apply two different solid fills to the four areas, alternating colors with the Paint Bucket tool. Delete the side lines, select the top and bottom lines, and change their stroke to black, as shown in Figure 2.81.

FIGURE 2.80 Create a long rectangle and divide it into four areas.

FIGURE 2.81 Fill in the areas with solid fills, delete the side lines, and change the color of the top and bottom lines.

With the Selection tool, select the entire graphic and execute the shortcut key to duplicate it. Snap the new graphic's top-left corner to the bottom-left corner of the original and you should have something like that shown in Figure 2.82.

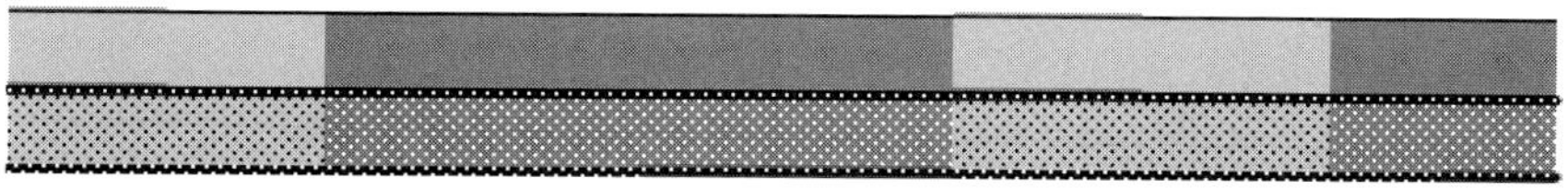

FIGURE 2.82 Select the entire graphic, duplicate it, and snap it to the bottom of the original.

Repeat the previous task once more to double the rows one last time. Select the two rows, duplicate them, and attach them under the original, as shown in Figure 2.83.

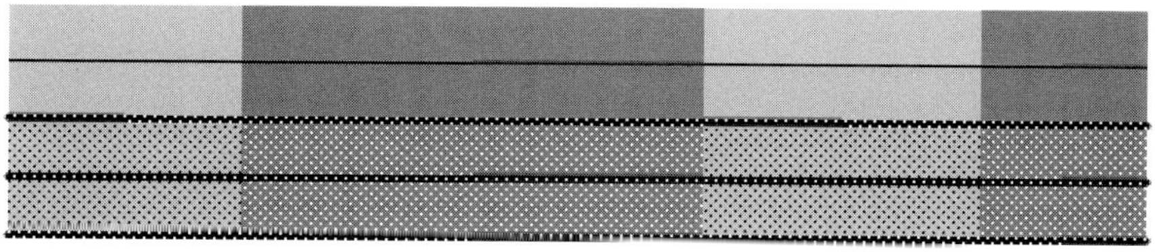

FIGURE 2.83 Select the entire graphic, duplicate it, and snap it to the bottom of the original.

Select all the lines, apply a white stroke to them, and change the solid fills to colors, so they resemble a grid. You can see the grid with the text added in Figure 2.84.

Name	Description	Subject	Date

FIGURE 2.84 Add text to the top row, and modify the colors as you desire.

Perspective

Before drawing an object, visualize at what angle you want it displayed. The figures in this section show you the thought behind visualizing the angle. The angle at which a figure is displayed is also known as the camera angle, since the view it is seen at can be considered a camera view. Depending on how the object is seen, the camera view can set a feeling or emotion on how the object is perceived. For example, if the camera is looking down on the object, the object can be perceived as inferior. If the camera is looking up at the object, the object can be perceived as bigger than it really is. As shown in Figure 2.85, we are looking at the scene from a side view, and we can see the camera angle and position of our object, the book.

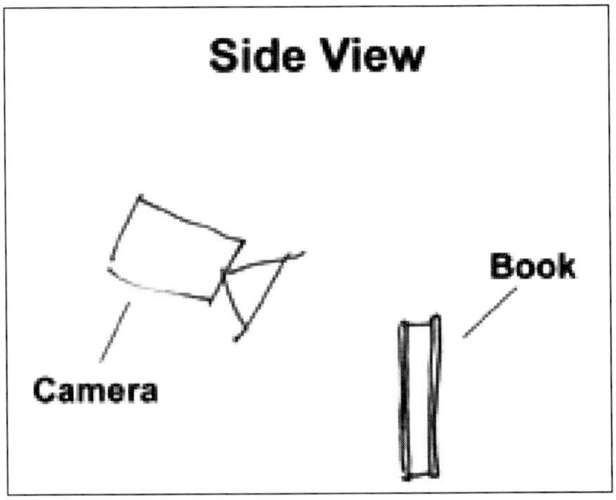

FIGURE 2.85 Side view of camera and object.

As shown in Figure 2.86, we are looking from a top view the angle and position of the book.

It is important to analyze your scene from three angles so you can fully understand the position and angles at which all the elements are placed. A perspective view is shown in Figure 2.87, where the camera angle and the position of the book seem to be consistent with the previous two figures.

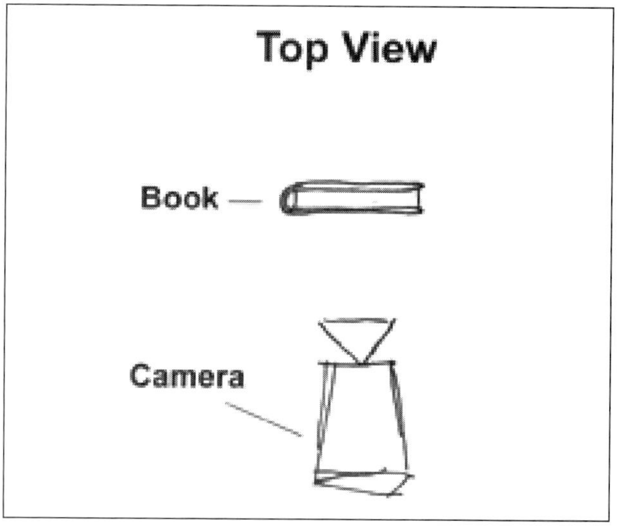

FIGURE 2.86 Top view of camera and object.

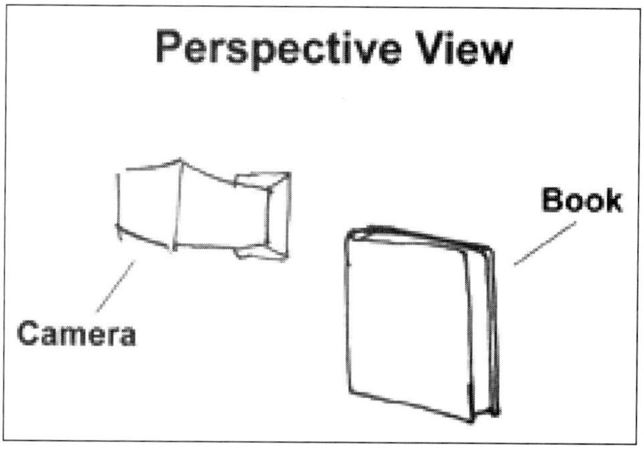

FIGURE 2.87 Perspective view of camera and object.

As shown in Figure 2.88, we are looking through the camera and see how the book will look.

Finding the Perfect Font

A quick way to browse through your different types of fonts is to type a word. Select the entire word in the text box and click once in the Font type selection field, as shown in Figure 2.89.

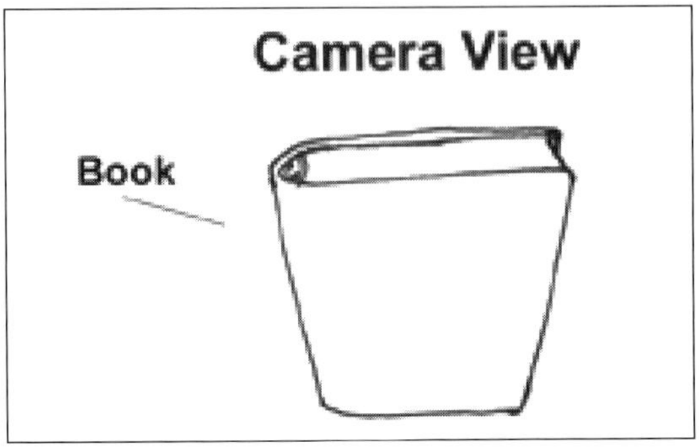

FIGURE 2.88 View through the camera.

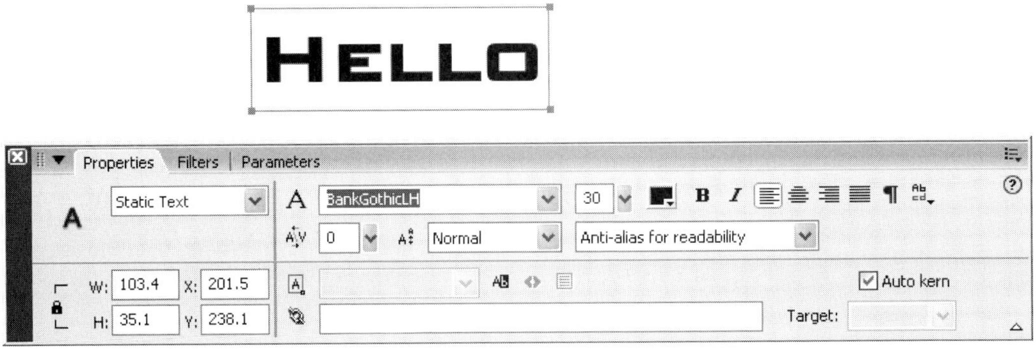

FIGURE 2.89 Preview fonts by using the arrow keys instead of going through the font drop-down field.

Once the cursor is in the Font type field use your up or down arrow keys on your keyboard to browse through all your fonts and watch the text field with your selected text change to the next font type, as shown in Figure 2.90.

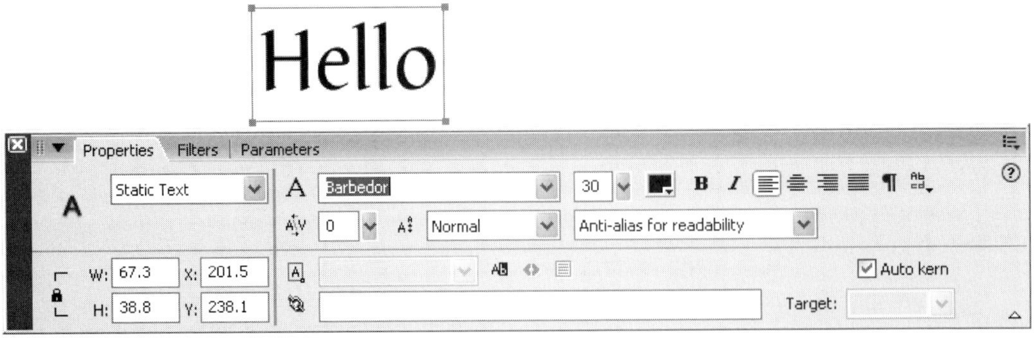

FIGURE 2.90 Pressing the down arrow will select the next font and change the look of the text in the text field.

COLORING

Color can ultimately change the way your object will look, depending on how it is applied. Consider the environment your object is in and the light cast upon it. We will also review how to choose your colors and gradients. From there, we will go into detail on how linear and radial gradients can be connected.

Light Source

Everything you see has some type of light source, whether natural sunlight or artificial light. If you can understand the role light plays in setting the color of your object, coloring your object will become much easier. Figure 2.91 shows a sketch of three objects and how light could possibly affect the look of each. Remember, if light is hitting your object, a shadow will be cast, and that must be taken into consideration. For example, if you have a ball and the main light source is shining down from the top left, the ball will be brighter from the top left and a shadow will be cast to the right of the ball.

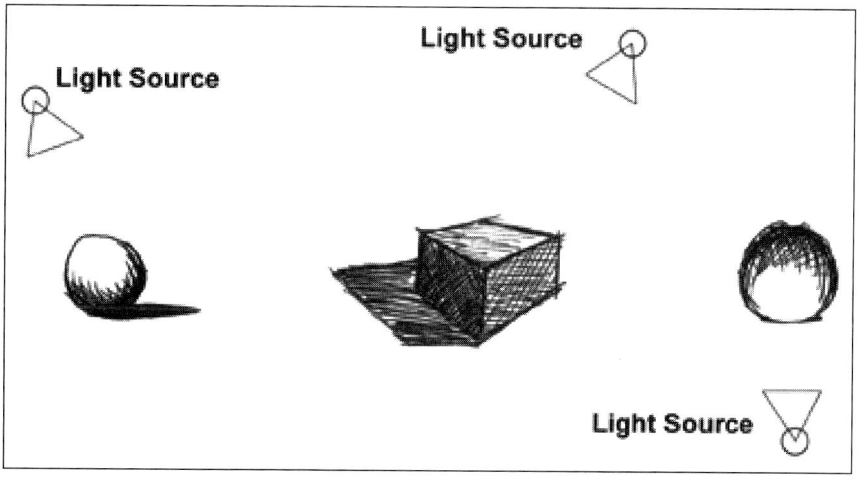

FIGURE 2.91 Light source and how it affects the color of an object.

Choosing Colors

The Color Swatches panel is the place where all the default swatches and personally created swatches can be found, as shown in Figure 2.92. You will also have access to the types of colors available for you to work with. For instance, you can choose to work only with Web-safe colors, and save, load, or reset the colors. Although the Color Swatches panel is needed for its color settings, the Color Mixer panel is the more important panel when it comes to choosing and creating solid fills, and linear and radial gradients. To bring up this panel, access Window > Color Mixer.

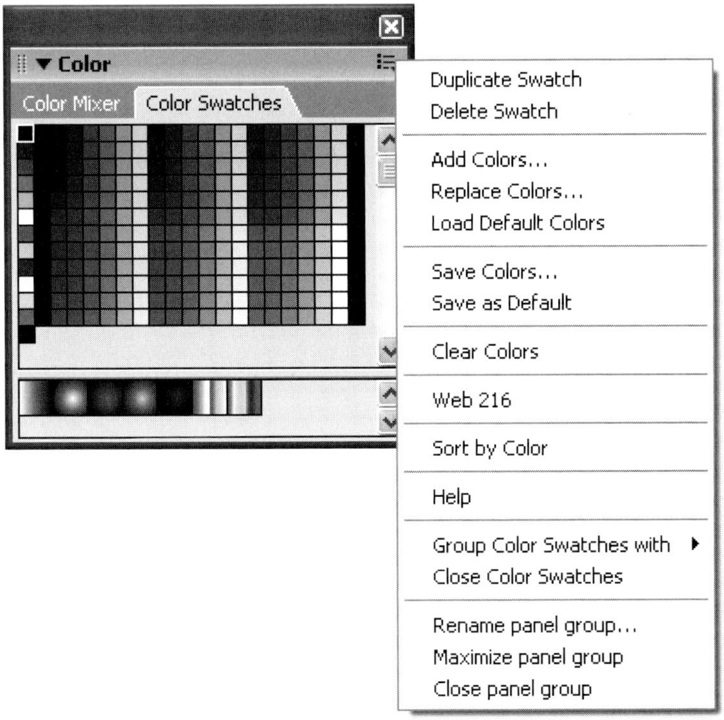

FIGURE 2.92 Color Swatches panel and its options.

Open the Color Mixer panel and click on the solid stroke swatch that has a Pencil icon next to it to access a drop-down menu with all the solid fill swatches to choose from, as shown in Figure 2.93.

By moving the crosshairs in the color field, you can change the solid color of the solid fill, as shown in Figure 2.94. You will notice the R, G, and B numbers will change based on the position of the crosshairs.

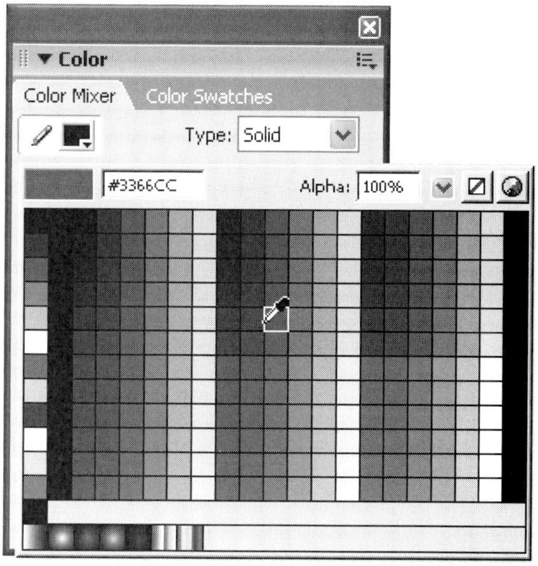

FIGURE 2.93 Color Swatches pop up accessed from the Color Mixer.

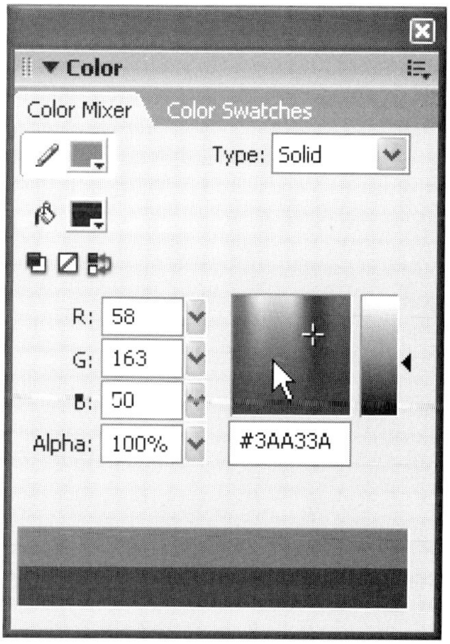

FIGURE 2.94 Editing the crosshairs in the color field to change the color of the fill or stroke swatch.

If you switch the Color Mixer to edit a radial gradient, Gradient Pointers will show up underneath a colored line. This defines the way your gradient will look, and more Gradient Pointers can be added by clicking underneath the colored line, as shown in Figure 2.95. To add the swatch to your Color Swatches panel, click on the Options drop-down field and select Add Swatch. The R, G, B, and alpha text fields state the settings of the selected color swatch on the colored line located in the center of the Color Mixer panel. More settings of the selected color swatch are under the color line showing where the color is located on the color grid in the lower right corner of the Color Mixer panel. When describing a gradient in this book, all the color swatches are written out for your reference, since the Color Mixer panel can only display the HEX value for one of the swatches in the color line.

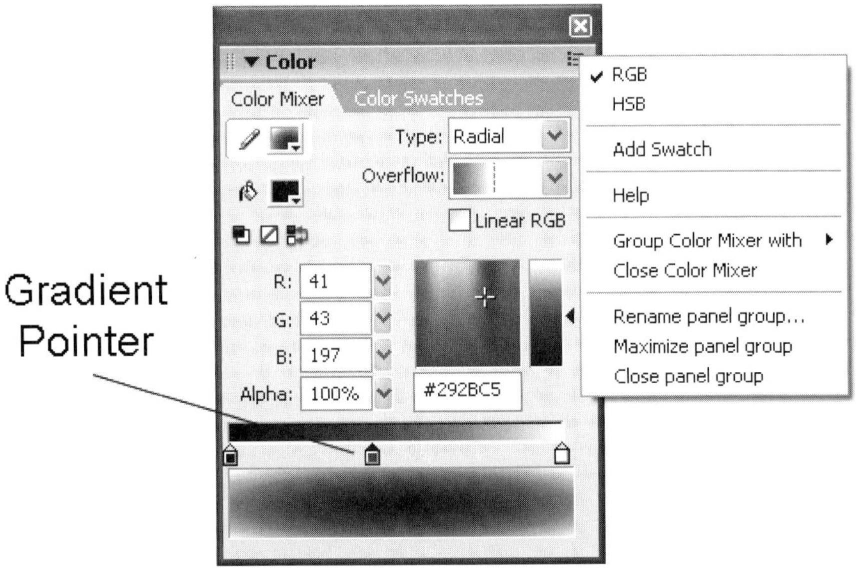

FIGURE 2.95 Gradient Pointers define gradients and the menu to Add Swatch.

Switching Colors

Select any solid fills and lines, and you can switch their colors with the Swap Colors button in the Color Mixer, as shown in Figure 2.96.

Click the Swap Colors button and watch the colors being swapped, as shown in Figure 2.97.

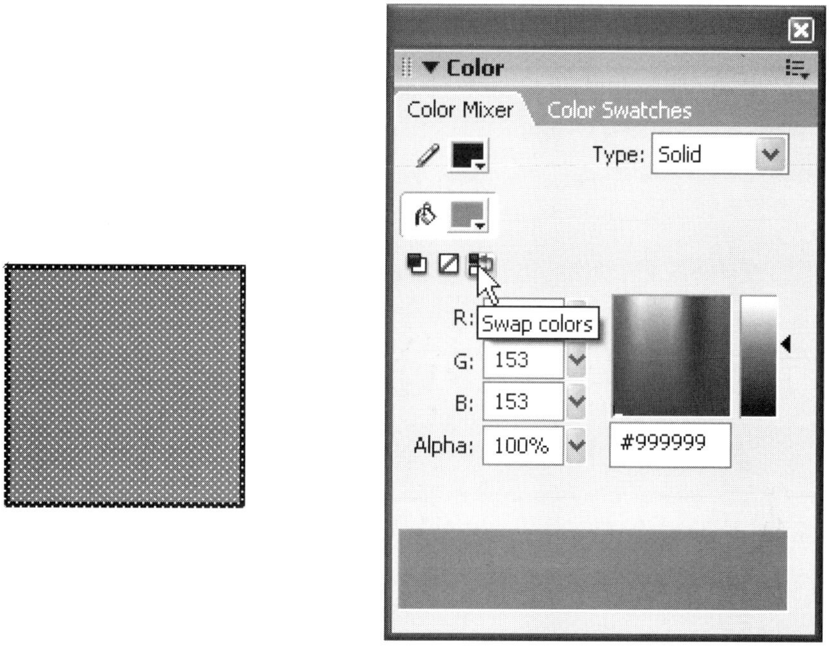

FIGURE 2.96 Select solid fills and lines, and switch their colors with the Swap Colors button in the Color Mixer.

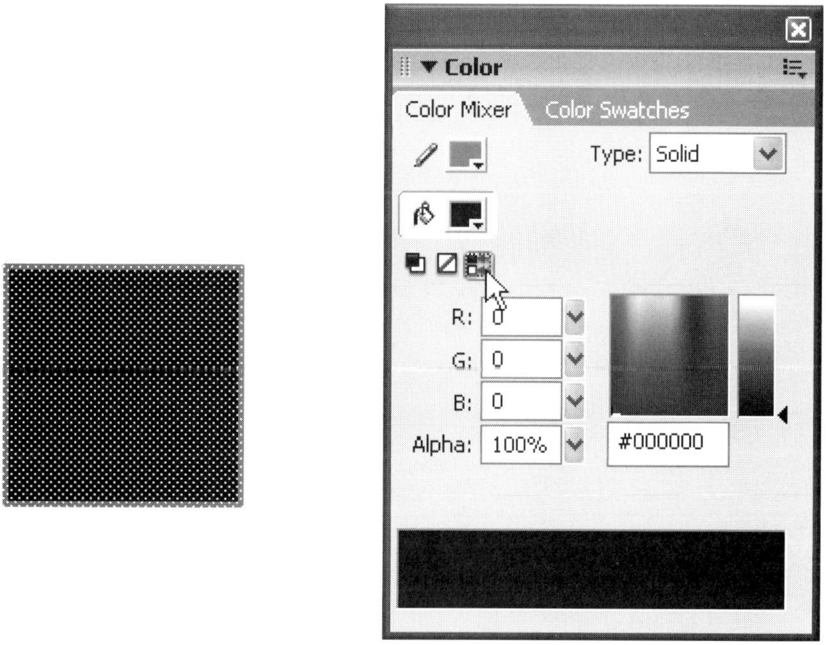

FIGURE 2.97 The colors are swapped.

What if you have two different-colored fills next to each other and you want to swap their colors? If you apply one of the colors to the opposite fill, the two fills will become one fill, which you don't want. The solution is to apply a stroke line between the two fills, so when you apply the same color to the opposite fill, they will not blend. As shown in Figure 2.98, apply a stroke line between the two fills and draw a solid fill of the color you are going to change first so you have it for reference.

With the Eyedropper tool, grab the center color and apply it to the outer color, as shown in Figure 2.99. Now the graphic is all one color, but the lines are separating the two fills.

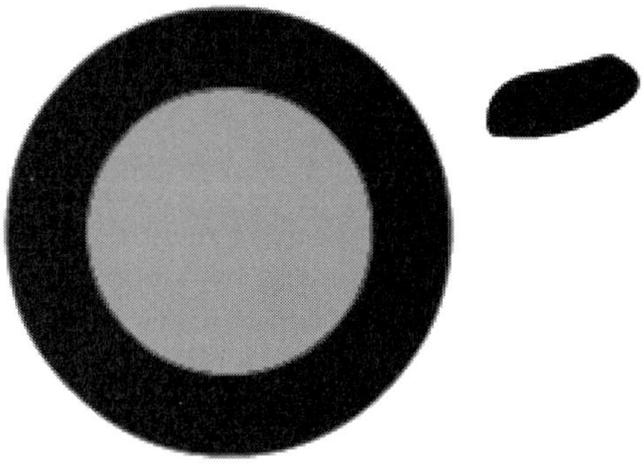

FIGURE 2.98 Swap two solid fills: draw one color on the stage, and apply a stroke between the two colors.

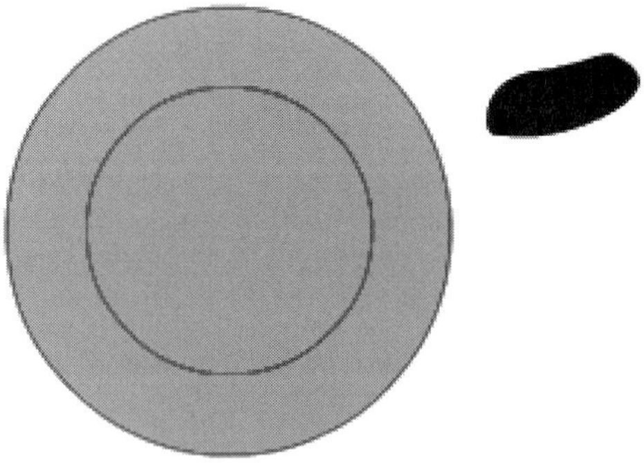

FIGURE 2.99 Apply the center color to the outer area.

Use the Eyedropper tool to grab the drawn fill color and apply it to the center fill. Delete the drawn fill and the lines once you are done, as shown in Figure 2.100.

FIGURE 2.100 Apply the drawn color on the stage to the center fill, and delete the drawn fill from the stage.

Creating the Right Gradient

To create a linear gradient, open your Color Mixer panel and choose Linear from the Fill Style drop-down field. Click on the Gradient Pointer to the left and set its HEX value to #000066. Click on the Gradient Pointer to the right and set its HEX value to #0099FF, as shown in Figure 2.101.

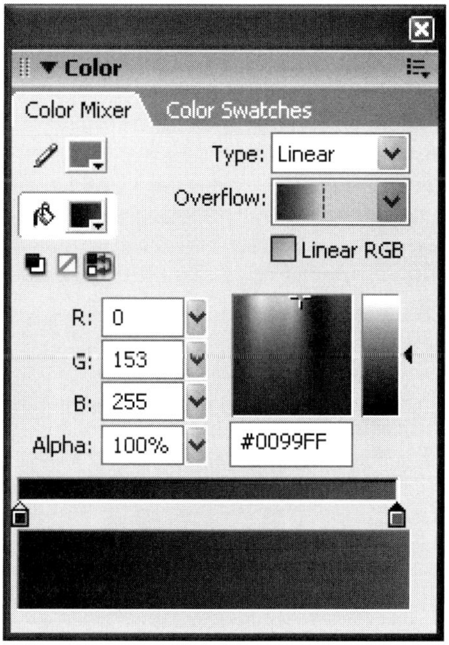

FIGURE 2.101 Create a linear gradient.

Position the left Gradient Pointer toward the center and add a new Gradient Pointer to the right, as shown in Figure 2.102.

Add a Gradient Pointer on the left side of the color bar, as shown in Figure 2.103.

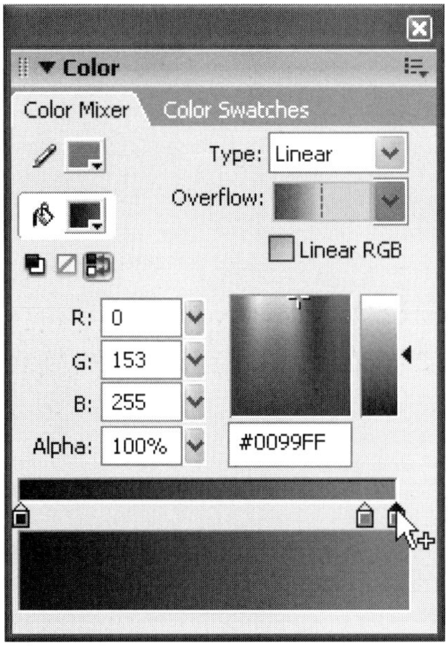

FIGURE 2.102 Move and add a Gradient Pointer.

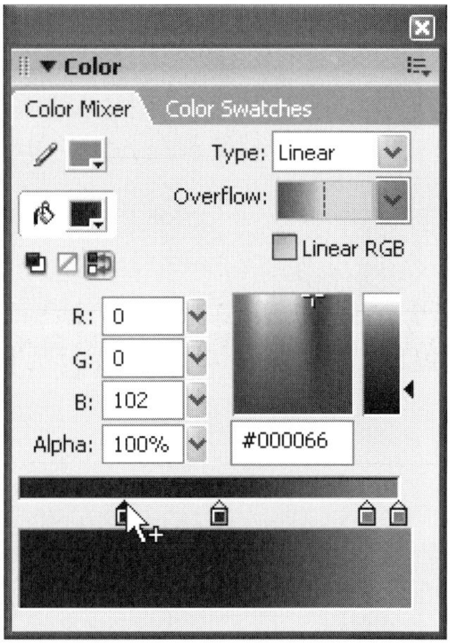

FIGURE 2.103 Add a gradient point.

Reposition the right Gradient Pointer to the far left, and move the two center Gradient Pointers so they are centered, as shown in Figure 2.104.

Add the swatch to your Color Swatches panel by clicking on the Add Swatch button in the options drop-down field.

To create a radial gradient version of the linear gradient, select Radial from the Fill Type drop-down field and the linear gradient will be converted to radial, as shown in Figure 2.105. To add it, click the Add Swatch button in the Options panel.

Connecting Gradients

Connecting linear gradients with radial gradients requires some thought as to whether the two will match up. The key thing to remember is that if you want two gradients to match, make sure the two gradients are using the same colors. Create a rectangle with the linear gradient we first made, as shown in Figure 2.106.

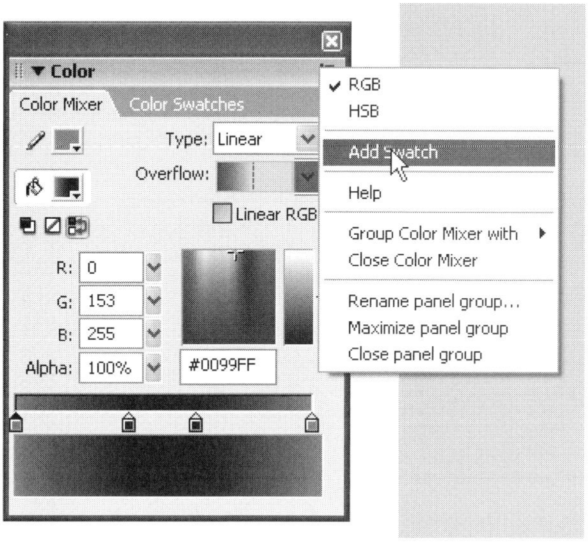

FIGURE 2.104 Reposition the Gradient Pointers and Add Swatch.

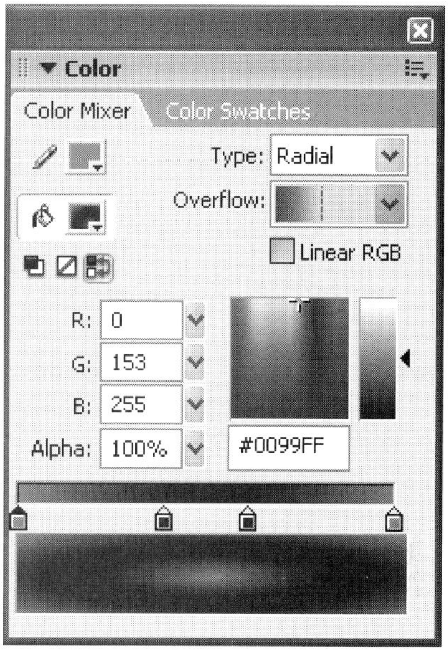

FIGURE 2.105 Create a radial gradient.

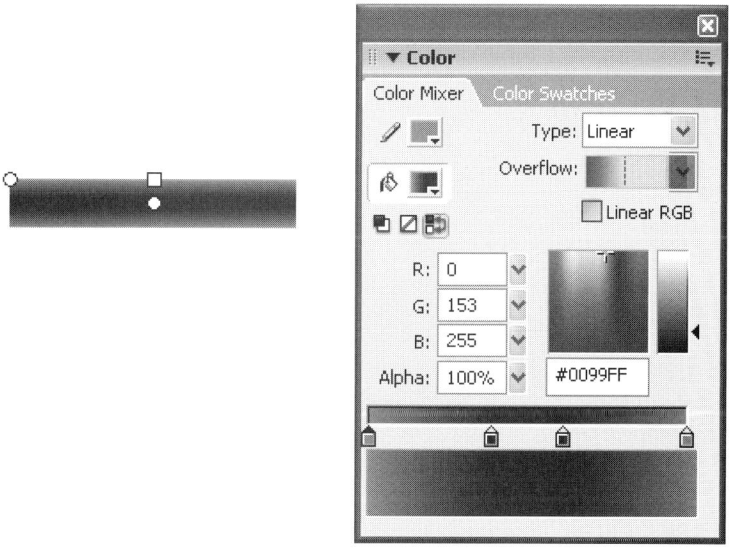

FIGURE 2.106 Create a rectangle with the linear gradient we made.

Duplicate the rectangle, rotate it 90%, and snap the corners together, as shown in Figure 2.107. With the Line and Selection tools, draw a curved line to form the bend of the graphic.

FIGURE 2.107 Duplicate and position the second rectangle and draw a line joining them.

Draw the inner curve that will complete the bending look, as shown in Figure 2.108.

Take the radial gradient we created and apply it to the bend area, as shown in Figure 2.109. Make sure the center of the radial gradient is snapped at the point where the two rectangles were snapped, and that the radius of the gradient matches the shape of the bend. Delete all the lines when you are finished.

FIGURE 2.108 Draw the inner curve.

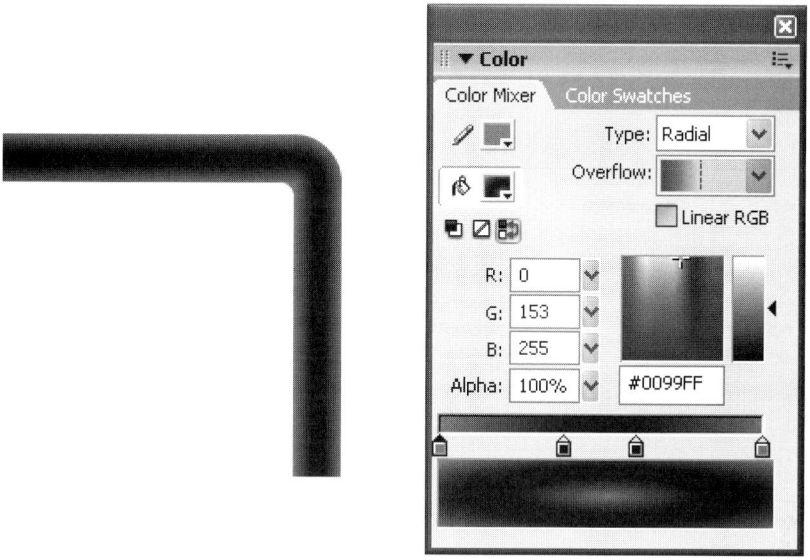

FIGURE 2.109 Apply the radial gradient and delete all the lines.

SUMMARY

- Familiarize yourself with how the Brush tool is affected when you use it at different magnifications, and learn how to use the Zoom tool to its full potential.
- Understand the basic concepts of how to efficiently edit your vector graphics with the Selection tool, Lasso tool, and optimizing tasks.
- Use lines to create simple and advanced shapes to give you the most optimized vector shape.
- Know how to create swatches and gradients with the Color Mixer.
- Connect gradients to create more complicated gradient shapes.

EXERCISES

ON THE CD The files for the following exercises are on the companion CD-ROM in the folders cited.

1. To set up your workspace, position your panels so you maximize the amount of work area. Once you have a configuration you like, save it for future use.

2. With the Arrow tool, take the four cylinders and space them evenly with the lines provided, as shown in Figure 2.110. The Flash file is located on the companion CD-ROM in Chapter_2/Exercises/2-110.fla.

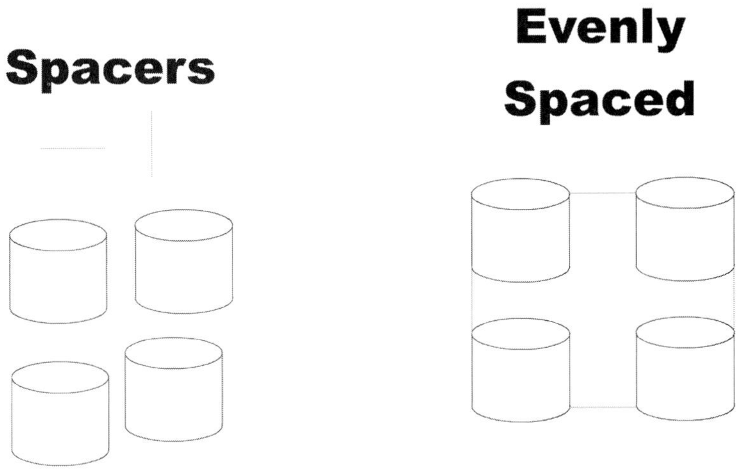

FIGURE 2.110 Before and after of the cylinders and spacer lines.

3. Using the Lasso and Arrow tools, delete the main part of the fish's fin, as shown in Figure 2.111. The Flash file is located on the companion CD-ROM in Chapter_2/Exercises/2-111.fla.

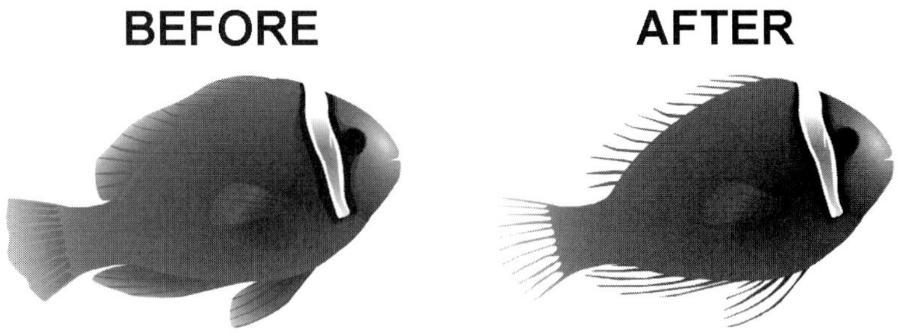

FIGURE 2.111 Before and after of removing the fins.

4. Complicated graphics like the ice cube shown in Figure 2.112 require more optimizing than normal to make sure you have the smallest file size without jeopardizing image quality. The Flash file is located on the companion CD-ROM in Chapter_2/Exercises/2-112.fla.

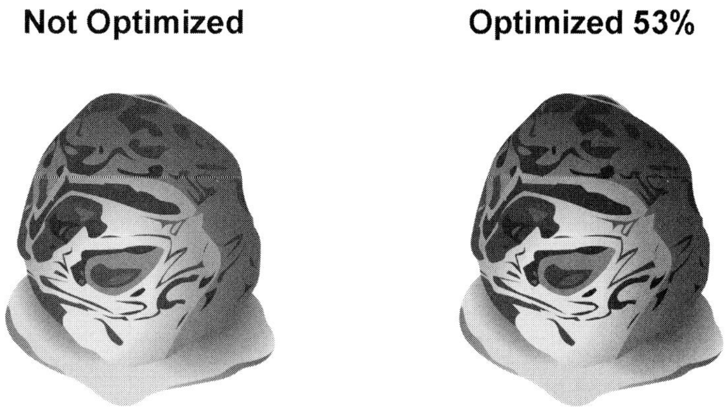

FIGURE 2.112 Before and after of optimized graphic with visually no quality loss.

5. Using the Polystar, Free Transform, and Line tools, create the pyramid shown in Figure 2.113. Create the bottom shape first, duplicate it, and scale it down to create other two smaller versions stacked on top.

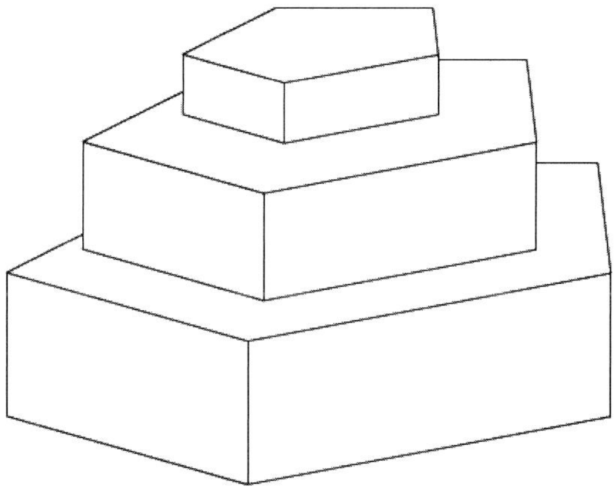

FIGURE 2.113 Line drawing of a basic pyramid.

6. With the Rectangle and Line tools, create the open box shown in Figure 2.114.
7. Create a skinny cylinder with the Oval and Line tools, as shown in Figure 2.115.

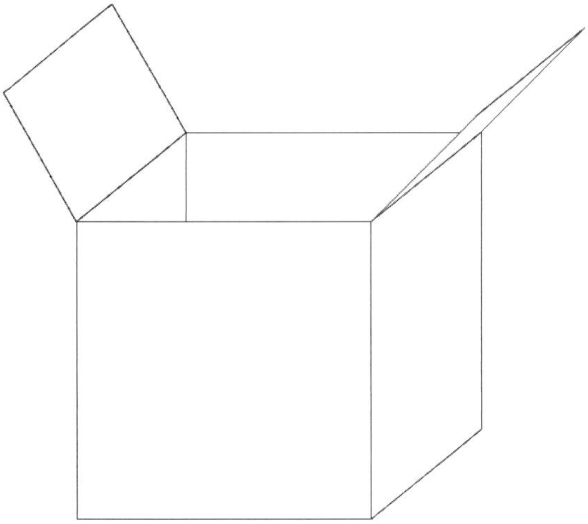

FIGURE 2.114 Line drawing of an open box.

FIGURE 2.115 Line drawing of a skinny cylinder.

8. Using the pyramid you created in Exercise 5, apply a solid fill color to it, as shown in Figure 2.116. Delete the lines when you are done applying color.

FIGURE 2.116 Solid fill pyramid.

9. Using the open box you created in Exercise 6, apply the same radial gradient throughout the object. Use the Fill Transform tool to position and scale the gradients differently to give the effect shown in Figure 2.117.

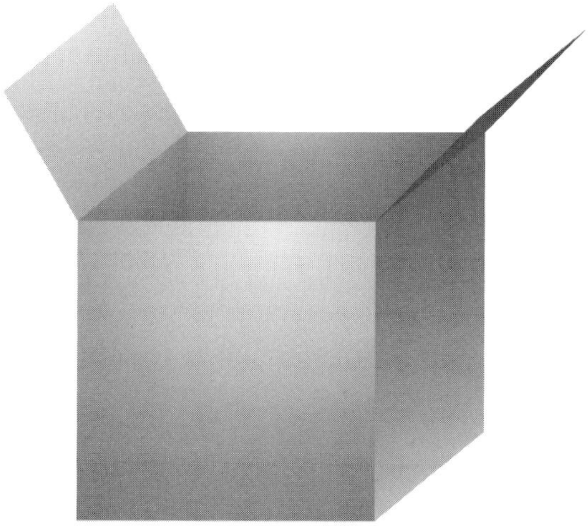

FIGURE 2.117 Radial gradients applied to the open box.

10. Using the skinny cylinder you created in Exercise 7, apply linear gradients throughout the object. Use the Color Mixer to modify one linear gradient darker and lighter to give the effect shown in Figure 2.118.

FIGURE 2.118 Linear gradients applied to the skinny cylinder.

CHAPTER

3 ILLUSTRATION APPROACH

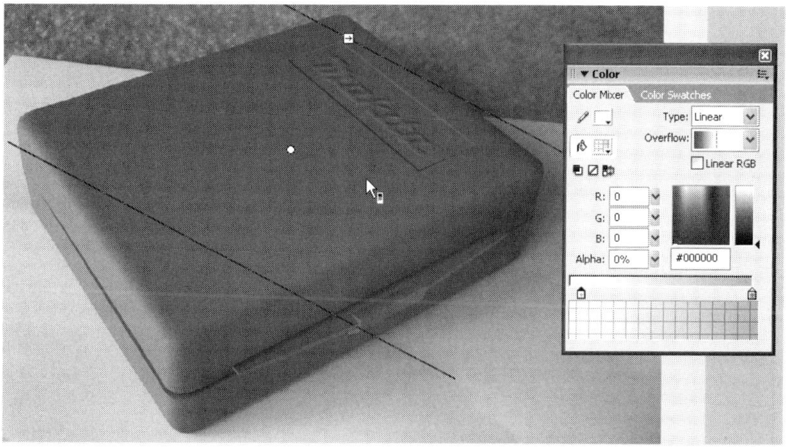

You can illustrate many things with Macromedia Flash. Thanks to its nice assortment of drawing tools, the possibilities are not limited to illustrating cartoons or flat, colored graphics as most people may think. In Chapter 1, "Getting Started," you were shown the true potential of Flash as an illustration tool. To create professional-looking graphics, you cannot start drawing with the Brush tool and expect to get outstanding results; you have to know what you want to draw, start with the basics, and leave the details until the end. Figure out what you want to draw and find your inspiration. Once that is established, an outline is drawn, basic shapes are applied, and final detail is added. This approach is very efficient because it keeps your vectors optimized and the amount of detail limited.

What Do You Want to Illustrate?

First things first, what do you want to illustrate? For this explanation, we are going to assume you want to draw a toolbox. This item's shape and detail are simple, and a great first project. Since this will be all vectors, the user can zoom in to see the detail without a loss of quality. To do the same with a bitmap would require a high-resolution image, which would make the file size too big and increase loading time. You should always illustrate your object at the resolution at which you want your audience to view it. When illustrating in Macromedia Flash, you should only be worried about how your graphic looks at 100%, not 200% or 400%. This way, detail that needs to be drawn is limited to what the audience is capable of viewing.

So, you have decided to illustrate the toolbox, which is a great idea. It is a perfect object to illustrate in Flash because it has many simple linear gradients making up a dynamic-looking object.

Find Your Inspiration

You can get inspiration for an object you wish to draw in several ways. The most important is to use your imagination, and sketch with pencil and paper any ideas you may already have. Look around you. Do you have a toolbox you could look at? If you happen to have one in front of you, set it up next to your computer and use it as a visual reference. Search in books, magazines, or online sites for any pictures of toolboxes that work for you. Although this may pertain more if you wish to animate a toolbox, video clips of a toolbox could be a great source of inspiration, too.

Still Life

Still-life drawing is using an object as visual reference by looking at it from a specific angle and illustrating the lines or shapes, which mimic what you are seeing. Having the object in front of you can be very beneficial, since you can examine it at any angle and from any distance. With the object in front of you, it is also possible to control the environment it is in by setting up the lighting and surroundings around the object. The most common lighting used to accentuate the object's detail is to place a spotlight above and off to the side of the object. By experimenting with more than one light, their positions, and the color of your lights, you'll see the impact lighting has at bringing out the detail in your object or creating a certain mood. To make sure the area around your object does not affect the way your object looks, you should have a backdrop underneath and behind your object—a blanket or large piece of paper will work fine. Choose the color of your backdrop carefully, because it will affect the way your object looks, especially if your object is transparent or has reflective surfaces.

Images

If you have an image of what you wish to draw, whether it is a scanned drawing or photograph, you can import the image into Flash. Once the image is in the program, you can do several things with it: you can use it for visual reference, or trace over the image. Using the image as visual reference within the program can help you illustrate the object to its correct proportions. Using the Eyedropper tool, you are able to acquire the exact colors from the image. Illustrating your ideas on paper first, and scanning and tracing the image in Flash is a recommended approach and something with which everyone is familiar. Finalize your ideas on paper, and then use Flash as the coloring and animation tool.

Video

In a similar way that images are used for reference, video clips are a great source of inspiration and not limited to illustrating. A video clip of a man walking or a tree branch swaying is great material to reference from, assuming you are curious as to how certain objects move. This is a great medium to reference because video clips can be analyzed frame by frame to truly understand how a certain effect is achieved or how to make something move a certain way.

OUTLINES

ON THE CD

Since we are focusing on learning how to use the drawing tools correctly, we will be tracing the toolbox from a raster image imported into Flash. Start with a new document in Flash, execute the quick key to Import to Stage, or access File > Import > Import to Stage. The image to import is located on the companion CD-ROM in the directory Chapter_3/-1.fla. Once the image is placed on the stage, position it as you like, and then lock that layer so the image will not be disturbed. To lock the layer, click on the Lock icon in the Timeline panel, as shown in Figure 3.1. Create a new layer above the previous one, which is where you will start drawing your outlines. To add a new layer, click on the New Layer icon in the Timeline panel, as shown in Figure 3.1.

FIGURE 3.1 The Lock Layer and New Layer buttons.

The first stage in drawing any object is to create the outlines defining the shape of your object. To illustrate a vector graphic with as few vector points and curves as possible, outlines (also known as guidelines) should be used. Outlines are vector lines, which you draw with the Line tool; their job is to precisely set, in an organized fashion, where your solid fills and gradients will be placed. Since the outlines are drawn with the Line tool, using a mouse peripheral device will not be a problem. Outlines are placed on the stage and snapped together with the Selection tool, as shown in Figure 3.2. Notice that more points are used where a curve or round corner is needed. This first step is important, because it defines the base of how many vectors your object is going to consist of. Remember, the more vector points your object contains, the larger the file size.

Connect the lines with another line, as shown in Figure 3.3. This will be where the curves will be defined.

FIGURE 3.2 Lines are created defining the basic shape of the object.

FIGURE 3.3 Bridging the first lines you made.

Once your lines are in the correct position, begin to define the shape of your outline by giving your lines curves, as shown in Figure 3.4. To apply a curve to a straight line, use your Selection tool and grab between two points; your cursor will display a curved line when you are hovering over the correct part of the line.

Repeat the previous steps with the bottom part of the toolbox. Define the basic shape with the Line tool, as shown in Figure 3.5.

FIGURE 3.4 Define the shape of your outline on the corners.

FIGURE 3.5 Lines are created defining the bottom part.

Draw lines connecting the corners, and use the Arrow tool to apply a curve shape, as shown in Figure 3.6.

Now, define more detail by adding the basic shape of the label on the top and lock detail on the side, as shown in Figure 3.7. Since this is a smaller area, use the G key to turn off Snap to Objects to align lines in tight positions with other lines.

FIGURE 3.6 Define the shape of your outline at the corners.

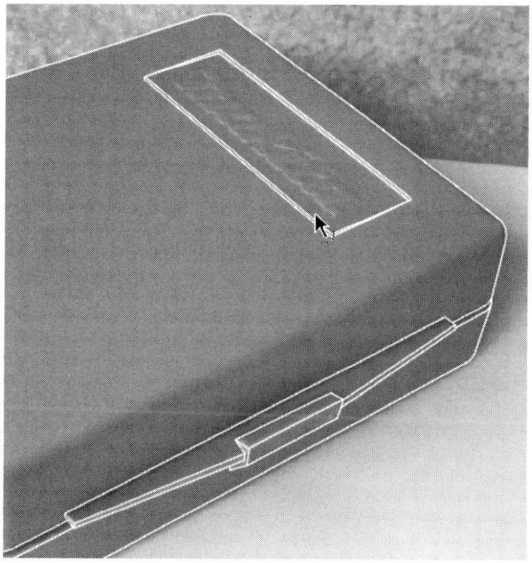

FIGURE 3.7 Define detail on the toolbox.

To re-create the logo on the top of the box, lay down horizontal and vertical lines to define the basic shape of the lettering, as shown in Figure 3.8.

ON THE CD

Now that you have the basic shape, it is time to zoom in more with the Zoom tool and add more lines where curves in the lettering are needed, as shown in Figure 3.9. Once all the lines are placed, delete the unnecessary lines that could block spreading of the fill when you start coloring.

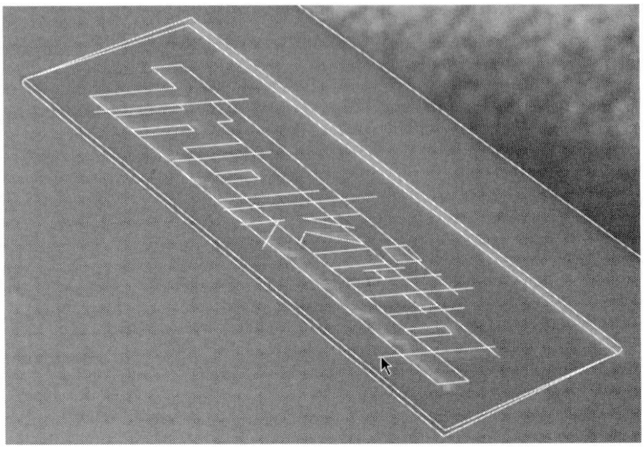

FIGURE 3.8 Define the basic shape of the logo.

FIGURE 3.9 Adding the curve shape to the logo.

Now that the basic shape is defined, our object is starting to resemble a toolbox. It is time to add outlines defining where our different gradients will be placed, as shown in Figure 3.10. To know where the dividing outlines should be placed, analyze how the light and shadows form on the object. Knowing that Flash can create linear and radial gradients, visualize how it might be accomplished, and then apply the outlines.

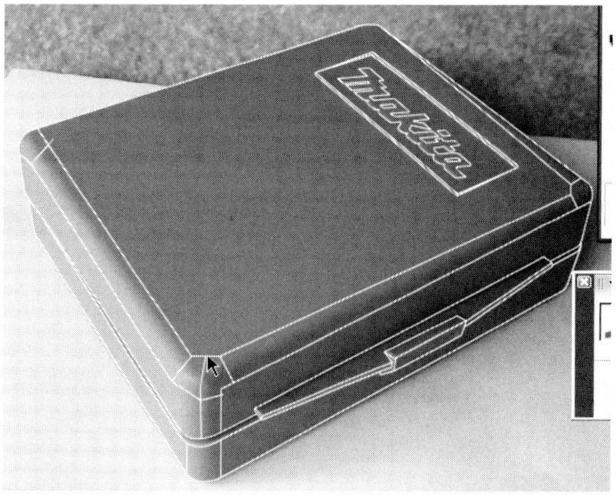

FIGURE 3.10 Adding more outlines to define where gradients will be placed.

Basic Colors Defined

ON THE CD

Swatches of solid color and gradients must be made before we can start coloring the object. Swatches are made with the Color Mixer panel. This section reviews the process of how several gradients are chosen and how they are applied to our object. Many colors and gradients are applied to these outlines. However, we will only be covering the major ones here, so feel free to refer to the source file on the companion CD-ROM in Chapter_3/3-1.fla. We will start by choosing the basic colors we will be using. Since we are tracing the item and the exact colors of the item can be extracted, bring up the Color Mixer panel found under Windows > Color Mixer. Open the Color Mixer and click on the Fill Color swatch, which will bring up the Eyedropper tool, as shown in Figure 3.11. Click on the raster image where you would like to extract a color; you should have a color swatch with a Hex value of #0088A2. You are now ready to apply that color with the Paint Bucket tool, which should already be active.

The left side of the toolbox is made up of one linear gradient. In the Color Mixer panel, choose Linear in the Type drop-down. Notice at the bottom of the Color Mixer panel a linear gradient with two color Gradient Pointers, one at each end defining the color change of the linear gradient. By using the same technique of extracting colors, double-click on one of the gradient pointers and extract a color from the bitmap image. You should have a similar linear gradient of #37C4E2 to #0088A2. Use the Paint Bucket tool to apply it to the outline, and use the Fill Transform tool to position it as shown in Figure 3.12.

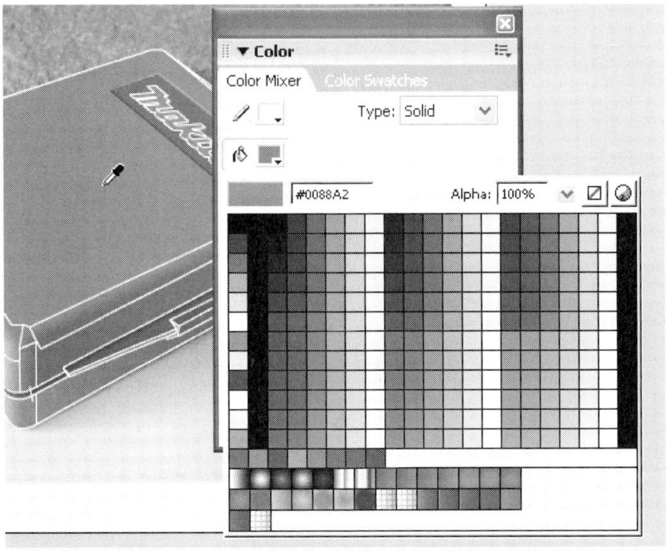

FIGURE 3.11 Extracting the base color of the toolbox and applying it to your guideline.

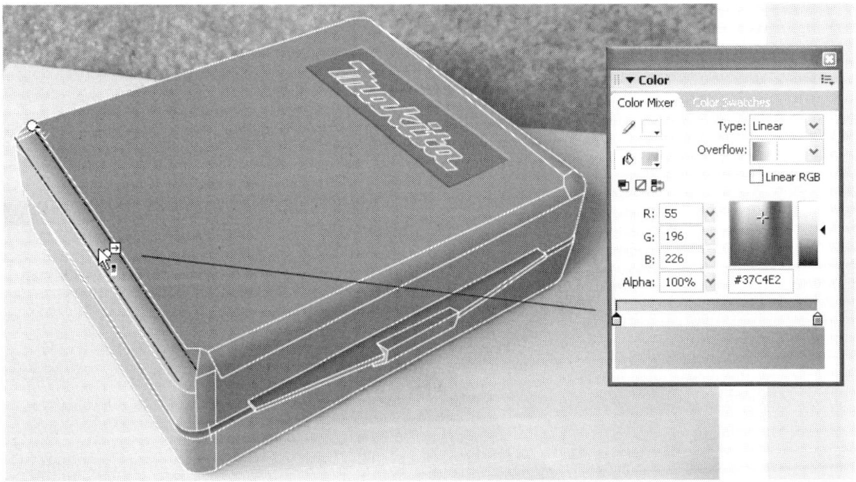

FIGURE 3.12 Extracting and applying the left-side gradient.

Similar steps are used to create and apply the linear and radial gradients on the right side of the toolbox, as shown in Figure 3.13. You should have a similar linear gradient of #167281 to #0088A2. Notice that both gradients had the same Gradient Pointer as the first color we extracted for the top of the toolbox; this is to make sure all the gradients meet seamlessly.

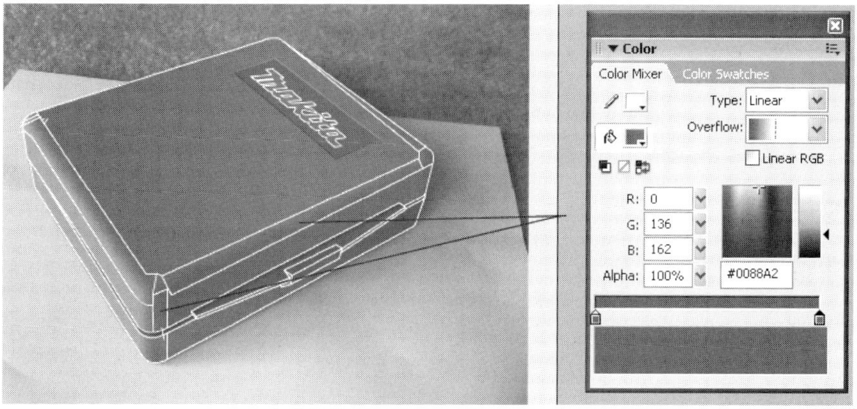

FIGURE 3.13 Extracting and applying the right-side gradient.

DETAIL

When adding detail to your graphic, in most cases it is beneficial to place your detail on a new layer positioned above the basic color graphics. Create a new layer by clicking on the Insert Layer button, which is located in the lower left corner of the Timeline panel. Place the new layer above the current layer if it is not already in that position.

The logo on the top of the toolbox has a slight bevel to it, and is a perfect example for using the new filters. First, however, we must select the logo, delete it, and paste it in place on the top new layer you just created, as shown in Figure 3.14.

FIGURE 3.14 Preparing the logo to be filtered.

With the logo still selected, convert it to a symbol by accessing Modify > Convert to Symbol. A Convert to Symbol dialog box will appear. Choose any name, Movie clip and default registration point. Once it is a symbol, the logo is ready to have a filter applied to it. Select the symbol, and in the Properties panel, click on the Filters tab, click the + icon, and select Bevel. Use the settings shown in Figure 3.15.

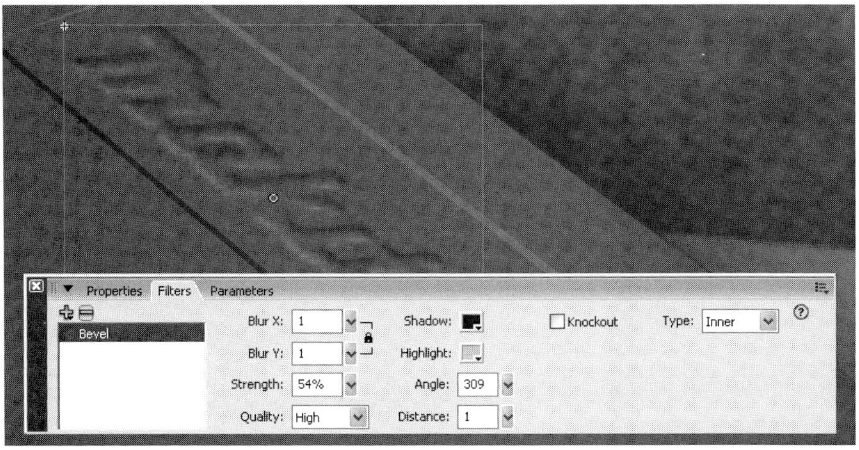

FIGURE 3.15 Applying a Bevel filter to the logo.

The final details we will be adding are two linear gradients on top of the base color in the new layer. This will define a darker shadow throughout the object and a small shadow created by the lock on the side of the toolbox.

To create the darker shadow, select all the graphics on the base layer and copy them. Go to the top layer and paste them in place, and while they are still selected, turn all of those graphics into one big fill by selecting a fill color from the Color Mixer panel. Choose Linear in the Type drop-down and set the linear gradient as follows: on one end, have a Gradient Pointer of #000000 with 0% alpha, and on the other end of the linear gradient, a Gradient Pointer of #000000 with 25% alpha. Apply this new linear gradient as shown in Figure 3.16.

ON THE CD

For the second shadow, create a new layer so it will not interfere with the first shadow graphics we just made. Use the Line tool to create an outline in the shape above the lock on the box. Apply the last linear gradient to this outline and delete the lines. Position the linear gradient at a slight angle, as shown in Figure 1.17.

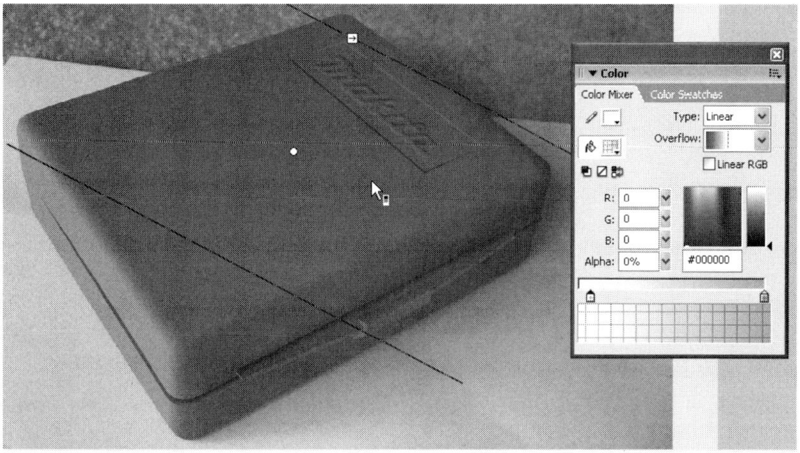

FIGURE 3.16 Applying a shadow to the entire object.

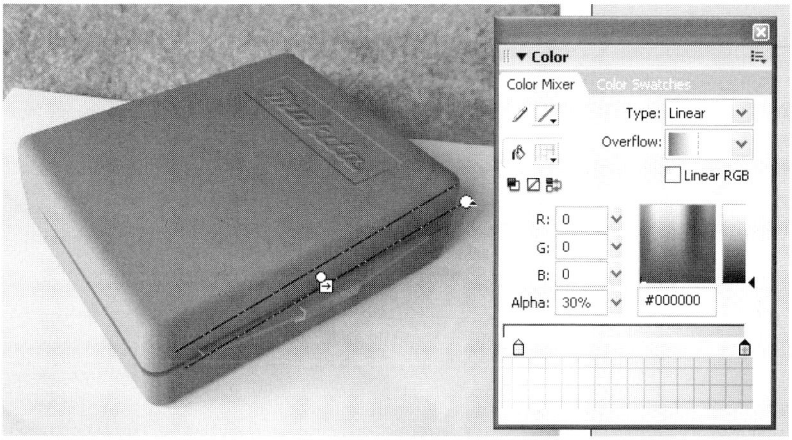

FIGURE 3.17 Applying a new shadow graphic on a new layer.

The last shadow will be the drop shadow the entire toolbox will cast on the ground. Simply create a new layer and place it at the bottom of all the previous layers. Go to the layer with the basic graphics of the toolbox, copy them, and paste them on the bottom layer. Use the Color Mixer panel to change all the fill graphics to one color fill, and convert it to a symbol. Select the symbol, click on the Filters tab in the Properties panel, and choose Drop Shadow. Use the settings shown in Figure 3.18, and use the Free Transform tool to reposition this symbol to cast the shadow in a certain direction.

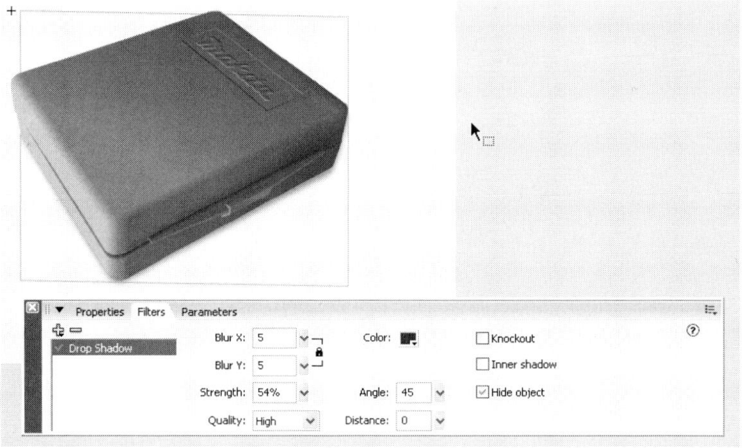

FIGURE 3.18 Creating a drop shadow for the toolbox.

With the toolbox finished as shown in Figure 3.19, you can see how linear and radial gradients can go a long way in replicating a photorealistic object. One of the most important lessons learned in this chapter is the full process of how to start with an idea of what you want to illustrate and find the inspiration you need to get your ideas into Macromedia Flash. The approach of creating outlines, defining the basic shape of your object, and adding the needed detail will have you on your way to creating optimized and professional-looking vector graphics.

FIGURE 3.19 Final rendering of the toolbox.

SUMMARY

- Get inspired about what you are drawing. Use still life, images, or video for reference.
- Create outlines of your object to give you a great foundation to color from and produce optimized vector graphics.
- Use solid and gradient fills on the same layer to define the basic shape of your object.
- Create details like extra highlights and deeper shadows on a new layer above all other layers with alpha gradients.

EXERCISES

ON THE CD

The files for the following exercises are on the companion CD-ROM in the folders cited.

1. Illustrate a simple tube-shaped film canister, as shown in Figure 3.20. Use the approach of creating outlines, defining basic colors, and adding final detail. You should us the Line tool, Arrow tool, Color Mixer panel, Paint Bucket tool, and Fill Transform tool. The image to import is on the companion CD-ROM in the directory Chapter_3/Exercises/filmtube.jpg.
2. Illustrate a simple dog toy ball, as shown in Figure 3.21. Use the Oval tool to create the shape of the ball. The image to import is on the companion CD-ROM in the directory Chapter_3/Exercises/dogball.jpg.

FIGURE 3.20 A film canister.

FIGURE 3.21 A dog toy ball.

3. Illustrate a simple mp3 player, as shown in Figure 3.22. The image to import is located on the companion CD-ROM in the directory Chapter_3/Exercises/mp3device.jpg.

FIGURE 3.22 An mp3 player.

CHAPTER

4

ILLUSTRATION TECHNIQUES

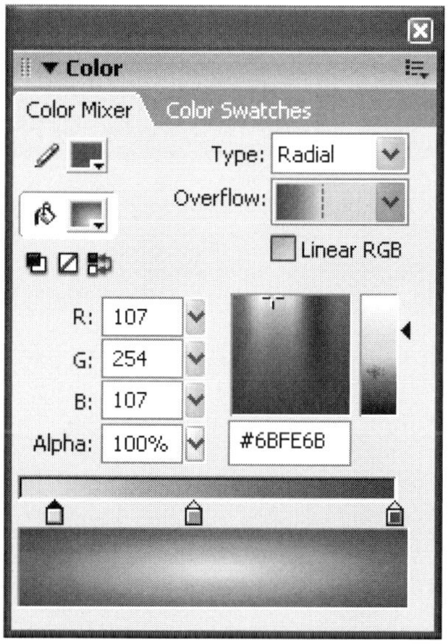

Many Web projects require user interfaces, navigation controls, and buttons. Normally, these graphics would be drawn outside Macromedia Flash to give that drop shadow effect or certain lighting. Unfortunately, importing vector graphics from another program can be a hassle to optimize, and if it is a raster graphic, it will increase your file size. By using several drawing tools together, we can create simple yet effective effects, all in Macromedia Flash. By exercising these techniques, you will be able to create clean, crisp vector graphics with a fraction of the file size.

BLUR

Giving the illusion that your graphic is blurred is simple to do, and depending on what you want to blur, several approaches can be applied. In this section, you will learn how to create blurred text, a blurred square with solid fills, a blurred square with gradient fills, and a blurred object. Creating a blurred effect with vector lines is possible, but will result in a larger file size. In addition, lines do not animate well if scaled. New to Flash Professional 8 is the Blur filter, which will blur any symbol, movie clip, button, or graphic. The Blur filter is a quick way to blur any graphic, but making a simple object look blurry manually is still an essential technique to know.

Blur Text

Select your Text tool and click anywhere on the stage to activate a text field. Type the words *Blur Text,* and set your Properties panel to Arial, bold, size 32, as shown in Figure 4.1.

FIGURE 4.1 With the Text tool, type Blur Text.

With your Selection tool, select the text field you just created. Execute your shortcut key commands to Copy the text field and Paste in Place. You should now have two of the same text field, one on top of the other. Press your right arrow key twice, moving the text field over to the right two spaces. Open your Color Mixer panel and bring the alpha of the black fill color down to 50%, as shown in Figure 4.2.

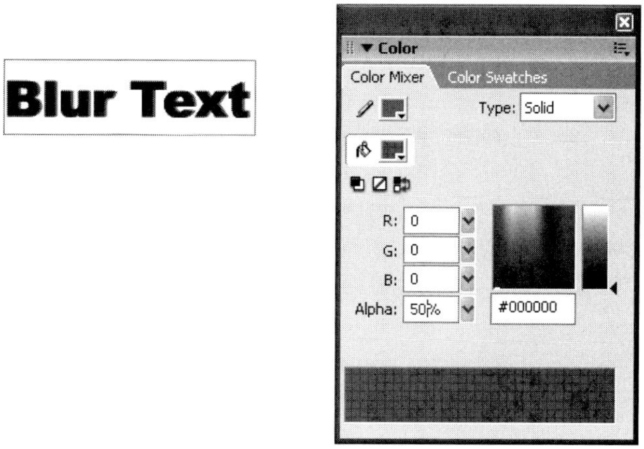

FIGURE 4.2 Color Mixer with fill of black, 50% alpha.

To make the other side blur, select the first text field you made, the one that is 100% alpha, and execute your shortcut key commands, Copy and Paste in Place. Press your left arrow key twice to move the text field over to the left two spaces. Open your Color Mixer panel and bring the alpha of the black fill color down to 50%, as seen in Figure 4.3.

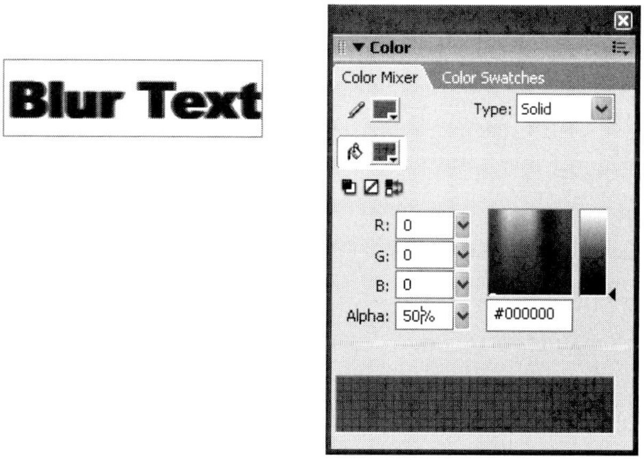

FIGURE 4.3 Color Mixer with fill of black, 50% alpha.

Although you do not get a perfect blur all the way around your text, if viewed at a medium or small resolution the human eye cannot tell the difference. In most cases, this technique is smaller in file size versus importing a raster image with the text blurred.

Blur a Square—Solid Fills

Making an object looked blurred with solid fills is one way to blur a square, and if applied to more complex shapes can achieve a blurred look. Normal linear and radial gradients cannot achieve this. Before drawing your rectangle, set your line to the color red and at line width hairline in the Properties panel; that way, you can see and edit your lines better. Choose the fill color #666666, which will be our base color for the rectangle. This can also be edited in the Properties panel. With your Rectangle tool selected and the Shift key depressed, click and drag down and diagonally to create a square, and then release your mouse button. You should have a shape similar to Figure 4.4.

Double-click on the outline of the square to select the entire line on all four sides, as shown in Figure 4.5.

FIGURE 4.4 Create a square with the Rectangle tool.

FIGURE 4.5 Square line and fill with the line selected.

Open the Scale and Rotate panel, enter 104%, and press Enter on your keyboard, as shown in Figure 4.6.

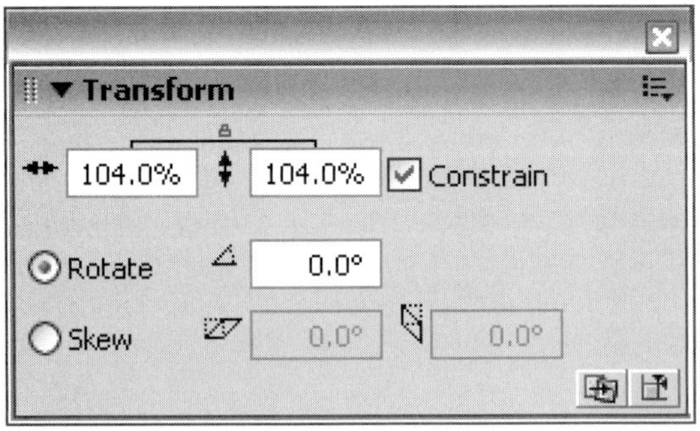

FIGURE 4.6 Scaling by 104%.

The Scale and Rotate panel is simple and efficient to use. What makes this panel more efficient is that once it pops up, you can begin typing directly in the Scale text field. After entering your selection, press the Enter key on your keyboard and the scale and/or rotate will be executed.

You should now have a square fill with a square line around it as shown in Figure 4.7.

FIGURE 4.7 Square-shaped fill and outline.

With your Color Mixer, create a fill the same color as your square fill, but change the alpha to 35%. Use the Paint Bucket tool to fill the area between the square fill and the line, as in Figure 4.8.

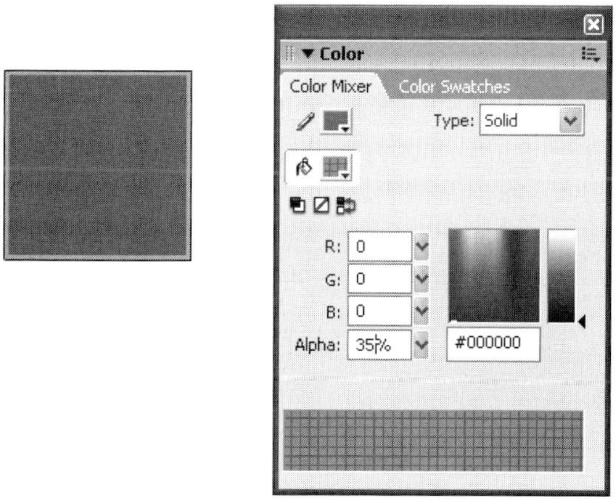

FIGURE 4.8 Modify fill and apply it.

To make the second fill, take your Selection tool and double-click on the square-shaped line to select it. Open the Scale and Rotate panel, type 104% in the text field, and press Enter on your keyboard. With your Color Mixer, create a fill the same color as your square fill, but change the alpha to 25%. Use the Paint Bucket tool to fill the area between the square fills and the line, as shown in Figure 4.9.

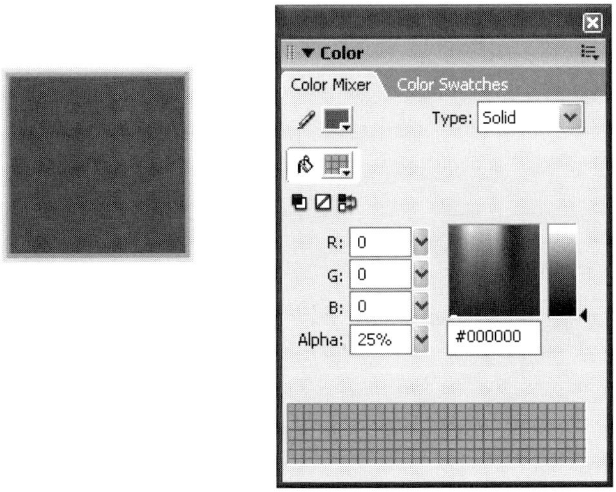

FIGURE 4.9 Modifying gradient and applying.

To make the final fill, take your Selection tool and double-click on the square-shaped line to select it. Open the Scale and Rotate panel, type 104% in the text field, and press Enter on your keyboard. With your Color Mixer, create a fill the same color as your square fill, but change the alpha to 15%. Use the Paint Bucket tool to fill the area between the square fills and the line, as shown in Figure 4.10.

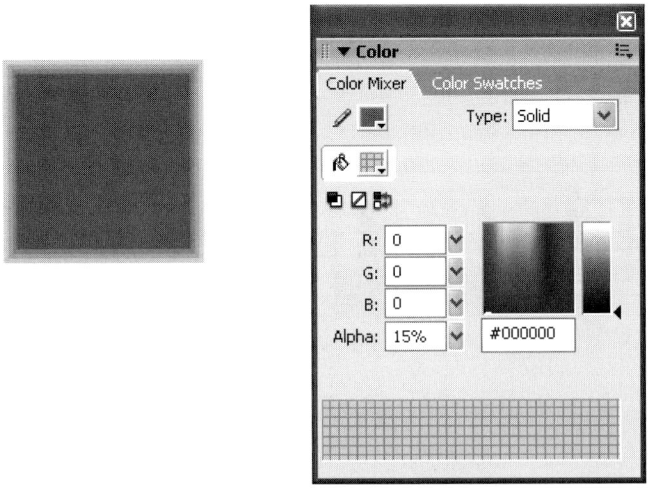

FIGURE 4.10 Modifying gradient and applying.

To see your results, zoom out to 100% by double-clicking on the Zoom tool. Up close, what you have just made may not look like a blur, but at a small resolution, your viewer will not be able to tell. The more outlines of alpha square fills you have, the blurrier your object will look.

Blur a Square—Gradient Fills

Set your line to the color red and at hairline line width in the Properties panel. Choose a fill color #666666, which will be our base color for the rectangle. This can also be edited in the Properties panel. With your Rectangle tool selected, click and drag diagonally to create a square, and then release your mouse button. You should have a shape similar to Figure 4.11. If you hold down the Shift key while creating the square, it will be constrained to a perfect square.

FIGURE 4.11 Create a square.

With your Selection tool, double-click on the red line, selecting the outline of the square. Open the Scale and Rotate panel, type 120% in the text field, and press Enter on your keyboard. You should have something similar to Figure 4.12.

FIGURE 4.12 Scaling outline.

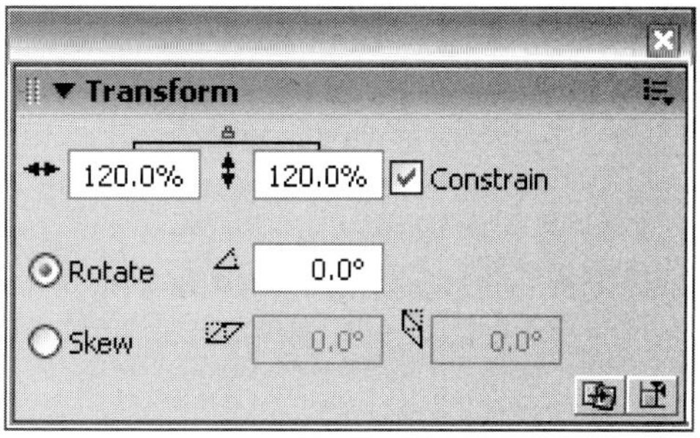

Now we are going to divide the space between the square fill and the square outline so we have areas to fill with a gradient. Select your Line tool, make sure Snap to Objects is on, and set to color red, hairline width. Start your line at the upper right corner of the grey square fill and connect it to the adjacent upper right corner square outline, as shown in Figure 4.13.

With the Line tool, connect the other three corners of the square fill to their adjacent square outline corners, as shown in Figure 4.14.

FIGURE 4.13 Creating a line.

FIGURE 4.14 Creating three lines.

Now our guidelines are set and ready for coloring. First, however, we must create the linear gradients with the Color Mixer. Open the Color Mixer and select Linear from the drop-down menu. At one end of the gradient, select the little colored square, type #666666 in the text field toward the bottom left, and press Enter, setting the value. Select the other little colored square at the other end of the gradient, type #666666 in the text field, and press Enter. Then, set the alpha to 0%. To save the linear gradient you just created, click on the icon in the upper right, below the Close button, and click Add Swatch.

Select your Paint Bucket tool and make sure you have it set to the gradient you just created. Once you have the Paint Bucket tool selected, click on the fill setting under the Color area in the toolbar. Click on the fill setting and choose the fill you want to create; it is located to the left of the Fill Type drop-down menu. Solid fills are organized at the top, and linear and gradient fills are located at the bottom.

Before you apply your linear gradient, make sure the Lock Fill in the Toolbar is turned off; leaving it on causes the Paint Bucket to apply the fill based on the entire movie size. Consequently, when you try to modify it with the Fill Transform tool, the modifiers may not show up. However, if you just applied a fill and want to apply it exactly the same way, you would want Lock Fill on.

Now that Lock Fill is off and you have your fill set to the one you created, apply the fill in the four empty areas, as shown in Figure 4.15.

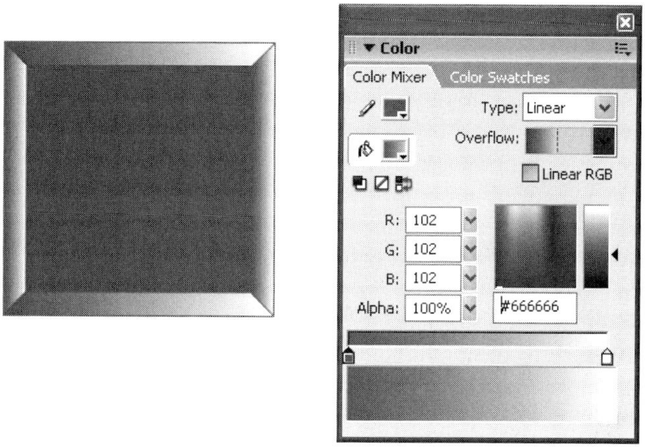

FIGURE 4.15 Apply gradient.

Select your Fill Transform tool and click on the top linear gradient. Grab the rotation modifier and rotate it so the white end of the gradient is facing up. Grab the square modifier toward the center of the gradient to change the length, making sure the entire gradient appears in the fill, as shown in Figure 4.16.

Do the same for the other three linear gradients: first, rotate the gradient with the circle modifier at the end, and scale the gradient with the square modifier toward the center.

With the Selection tool, double-click on any part of the red line and all of it should be selected, as in Figure 4.17.

Once selected, execute the shortcut key command to delete them. To view the result, double-click on the Zoom tool to see it at 100%.

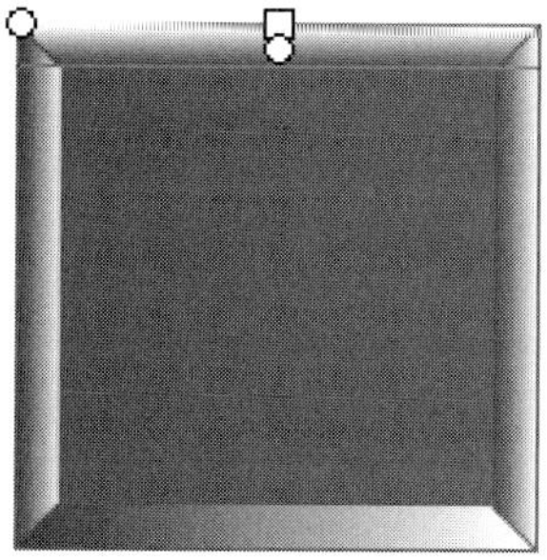

FIGURE 4.16 Modifying gradient.

FIGURE 4.17 Select all the red lines.

Blur a Square—Filter

To blur a graphic with a Filter, your graphic must first be a symbol. Create a square with the Rectangle tool and select it with the Selection tool. Once selected, convert it to a symbol. As a symbol, select it and open the Properties panel. Click on the Filter tab and click on the + icon, which will bring up a drop-down as shown in Figure 4.18.

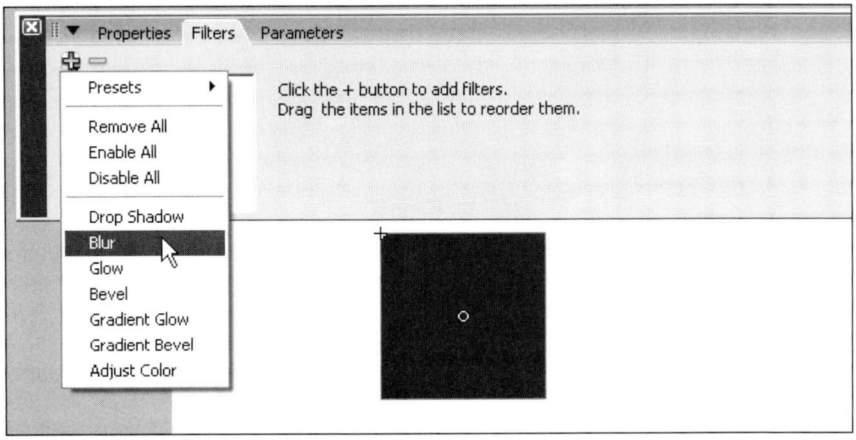

FIGURE 4.18 Filter drop-down.

Select Blur in the drop-down and notice the options you have, as shown in Figure 4.19.

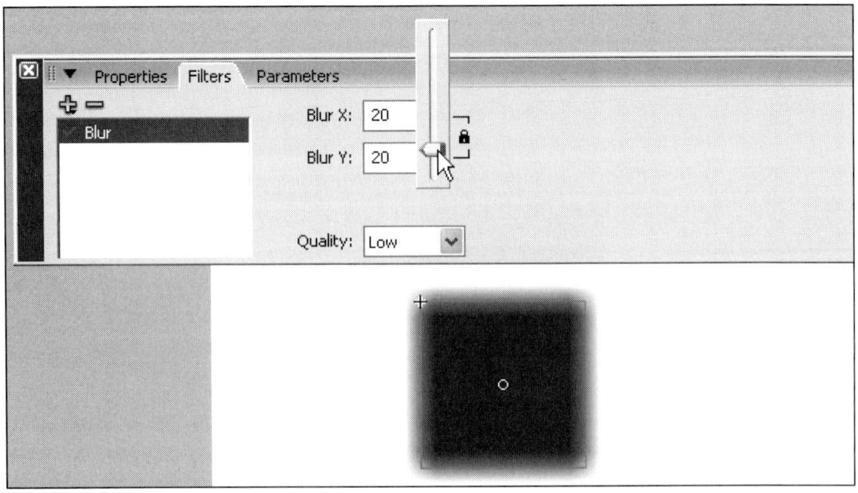

FIGURE 4.19 Blur filter and the options.

Blur a Graphic Object

To make a graphic look blurred is easy. We will be using the same technique we used with the blurred text, but with a few modifications.

Your graphic can be comprised of lines, fills, groups of vectors, or symbols. Select the assets you would like to blur and make them into a symbol, either by executing the shortcut key command for creating a new symbol or going to Insert > New Symbol.

Once your graphic is a symbol, select it with your Selection tool. Execute the shortcut key command for Copy and Paste in Place. While it is still selected, use your right arrow key and press it twice to move it to the right two spaces. Open the Properties panel, click on the Color drop-down menu, select alpha, and set it to 50% as shown in Figure 4.20.

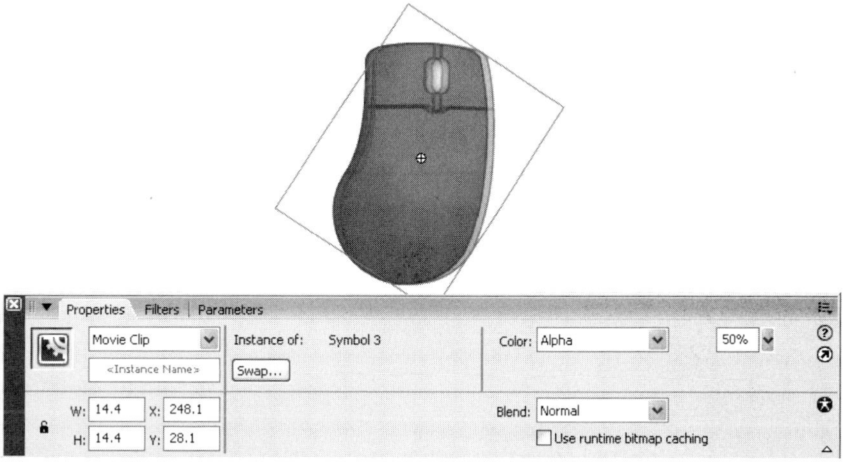

FIGURE 4.20 Apply alpha setting.

With your Selection tool, select the first symbol and repeat the previous step, but instead of moving it two spaces to the right, you are going to move it two spaces to the left and set the Color to alpha 50%. Set your view to 100% by double-clicking on the Zoom tool. You should have something similar to Figure 4.21.

If it is not looking blurred enough, try playing with how far the symbols are from each other or try different alpha settings. Also try using more symbols for the graphic; the more you use, the more motion can be portrayed.

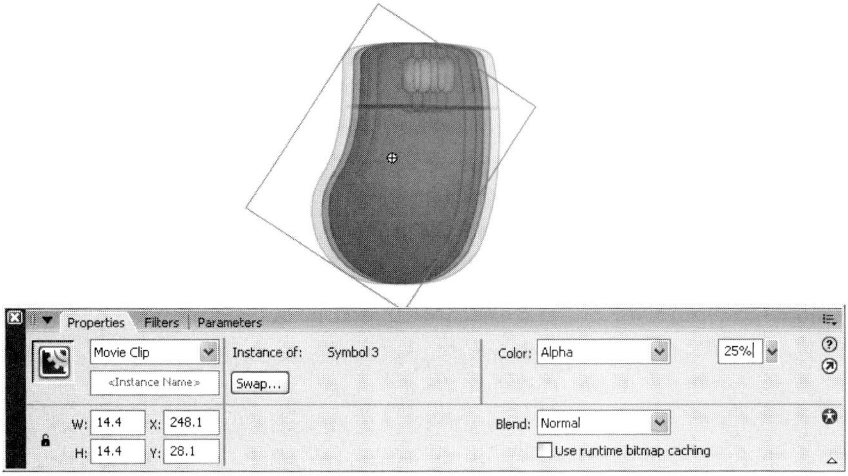

FIGURE 4.21 Create two symbols to the left and apply alpha settings.

HIGHLIGHTS

Highlights are the effect of sunlight or artificial light (from light bulbs) casting on an object. In Macromedia Flash, highlights can be reproduced with solid fills, and linear or radial gradients. Using linear and radial gradients together can achieve any type of highlight shape.

In this section, we show you how to create a highlight on a basic circle and combine linear and radial gradients to add highlights to a beveled square.

Circle

There is more to adding a radial gradient to a circle than most Macromedia Flash illustrators think. You can tweak several attributes to give you a more realistic look that a light is really shining down on your circle. To do so, select your Oval tool in the toolbar. Set the line color to red and the fill color to green, at #006600, as shown in Figure 4.22.

To create the radial gradient we will be working with, open the Color Mixer. Make sure you have three color swatches in the gradient color line. The color swatch to the left is the color that will show up in the center of the radial gradient. The color swatch to the right is the color that will show up in the outer part of the radial gradient. Pick a light green for your color swatch on the left, and a dark green for the color swatch on the right. As for the middle color swatch, choose a more vibrant green. Play around with the position of the color swatches; moving the light green swatch farther to the right will give the effect that the light source is closer to your circle, as shown in Figure 4.23.

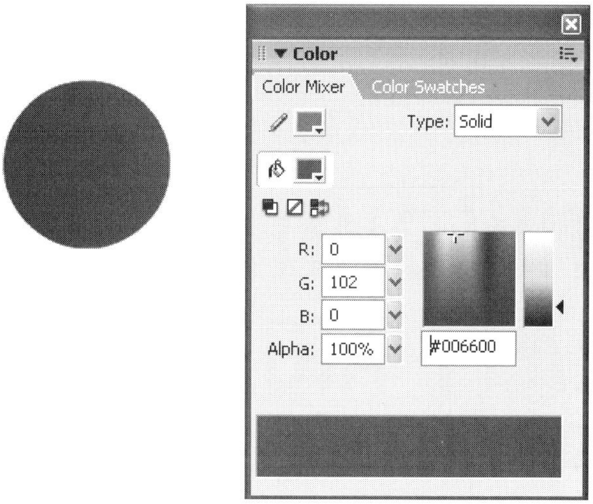

FIGURE 4.22 Create a circle.

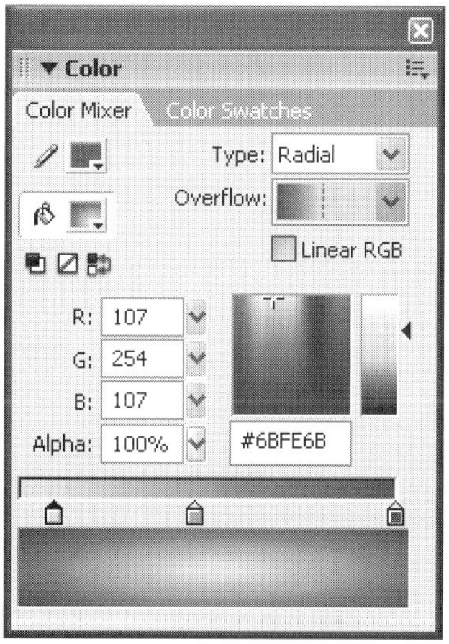

FIGURE 4.23 Create a gradient.

Once you have the Paint Bucket tool selected, click on the fill setting under the Color area in the toolbar. Make sure the Lock Fill in the toolbar is turned off. Click on the fill setting and choose the fill you just created. Apply the radial gradient fill anywhere in the circle as shown in Figure 4.24.

Now that you have the radial gradient applied to the circle, it will need to be edited slightly. Select the Fill Transform tool and press on the gradient to activate the modifier. Grab the center of the radial gradient and place the center light where you would like the light shining on your circle. Use the outer scale circle modifier to adjust the size of the gradient. You should have something similar to Figure 4.25. Delete the red outline and zoom to 100% to view the finished circle.

FIGURE 4.25 Modifying gradient.

FIGURE 4.24 Apply radial gradient.

Square

By combining linear and radial gradients, it is possible to give a curved-corner square an outer highlight.

Select the Rectangle tool and set the corner radius to 10. Make sure the line is red and set to hairline width, and the fill is set to #666666 gray. While holding down the Shift key, click and drag to a perfect square, as shown in Figure 4.26.

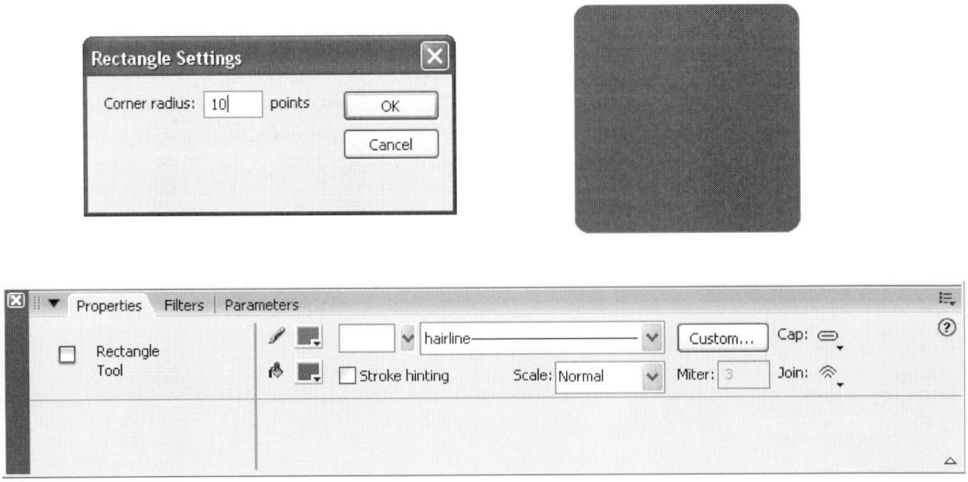

FIGURE 4.26 Create a square with round corners.

Now that the square is built, we need to create the outline with lines that will be our guide when we have to fill in our highlight gradients.

Select the Line tool, and set Snap to Objects on. From where the curved corner line meets and connects with a horizontal line, start the first point of the line and draw it straight down and past the lower line, as shown in Figure 4.27. To make the line you just made stick out on both ends, select the line with the Selection tool and scale it by 110% in the Transform panel.

Do the same for the other three corners, as shown in Figure 4.28.

FIGURE 4.27 Create a line to outline the highlight area.

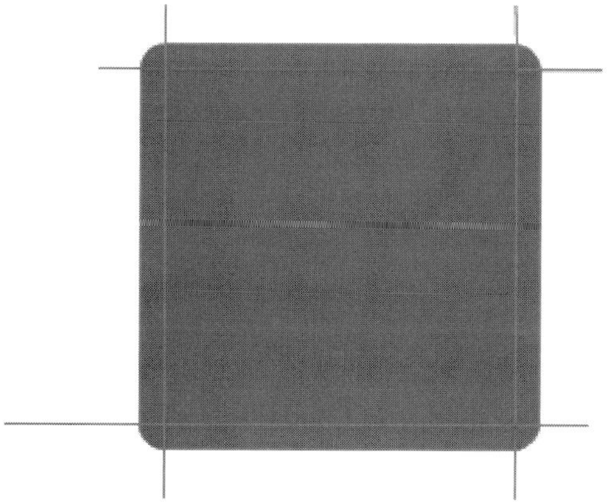

FIGURE 4.28 Create three more lines to outline the highlight area.

Now that the guidelines have been plotted, it is time to create the gradients we will be working with. Open the Color Mixer and create a linear gradient from #666666 to #CCCCCC, as shown in Figure 4.29. To save the gradient you just made, click on the icon in the upper right, below the Close button, and click Add Swatch.

To make a radial gradient out of the linear gradient, click on the drop-down menu and select Radial, as shown in Figure 4.30. To save it, click on the icon in the upper right, below the Close button, and click Add Swatch.

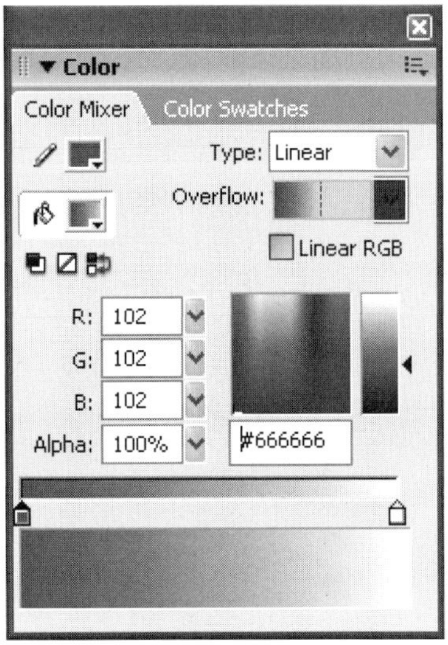

FIGURE 4.29 Create a linear gradient.

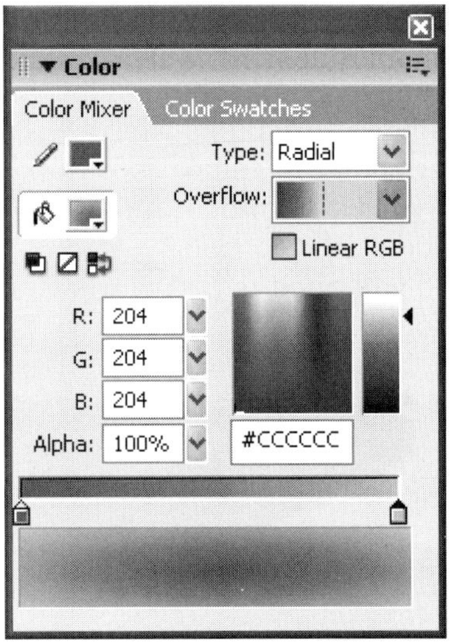

FIGURE 4.30 Create a radial gradient.

Now that the gradients are made, we are ready to apply them. Make sure the Lock Fill feature in the toolbar is turned off; it is located in the Tool panel in the Options area. Select your Paint Bucket tool and set the fill it will apply to the linear gradient you just created. Apply it to the horizontal and vertical areas. Set the fill on the Paint Bucket tool to the radial gradient you just created, and apply it to the corner areas as shown in Figure 4.31.

Once the fills are applied, they will have to be modified with the Gradient Transform tool. Make sure Snap to Objects is on so editing the gradient will be more precise. Select the Gradient Transform tool and click on the radial gradient in the upper right corner. First, snap the center modifier to the interceding red lines, as shown in Figure 4.32. Since the center of the radial gradient is the solid color of the square, that would be the most optimal place for it.

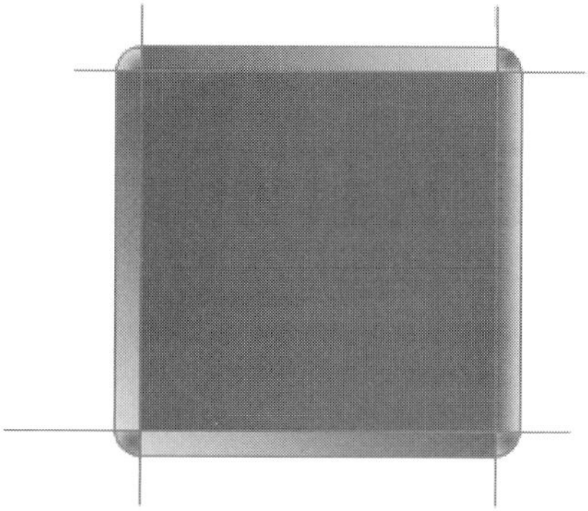

FIGURE 4.31 Apply gradient.

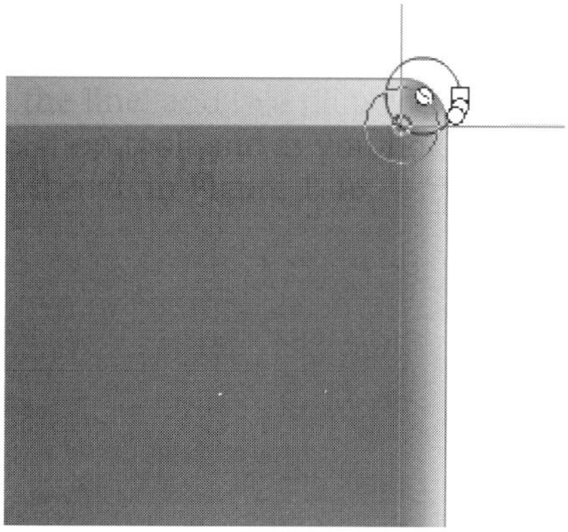

FIGURE 4.32 Modify the position of the gradient.

Now, edit the scaling of the radial gradient by grabbing the outer circle modifier and snapping it where the vertical line meets with the top horizontal line, as seen in Figure 4.33. By doing this, we are making sure that the vertical colors from dark gray to white of the radial gradient are meeting perfectly, with the dark gray square to the white background.

To make sure the horizontal colors of the radial gradient are set correctly, grab the square modifier and snap it to where the horizontal line meets with the far right vertical line, as shown in Figure 4.34.

If you wish to check your job to see how precisely you edited the radial gradient, double-click on the red line to select all the red guidelines, copy them so they are in memory in case you need to paste them in place later, and delete them. This way, you can see how the colors meet and make final adjustments with the Gradient Transform tool. If you are looking to do minor tweaks, turn off Snap to Objects.

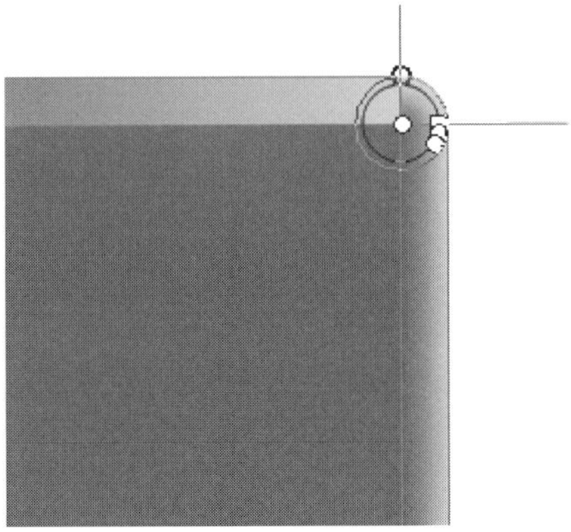

FIGURE 4.33 Modify scaling of gradient.

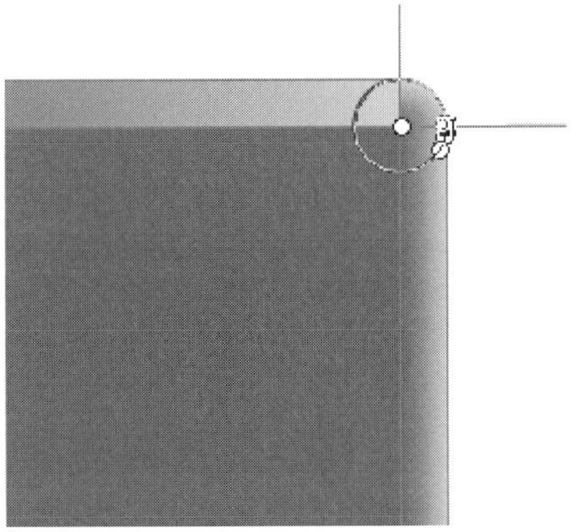

FIGURE 4.34 Modify gradient horizontally.

To continue with the next step, make sure you Paste in Place the red guidelines.

To edit the linear gradient, select the Gradient Transform tool and click on the top linear gradient. First, grab the square modifier at the end of the gradient and scale it closer to the center, as shown in Figure 4.35.

With the circle modifier located at the corner of the gradient, rotate the gradient so the white end is facing toward the white background. Make further adjustments to the gradient, making sure the white end of the gradient is touching the white background, and the dark gray end of the gradient is touching the dark gray square. Now, edit the other three sides and three corners so your image appears as shown in Figure 4.36.

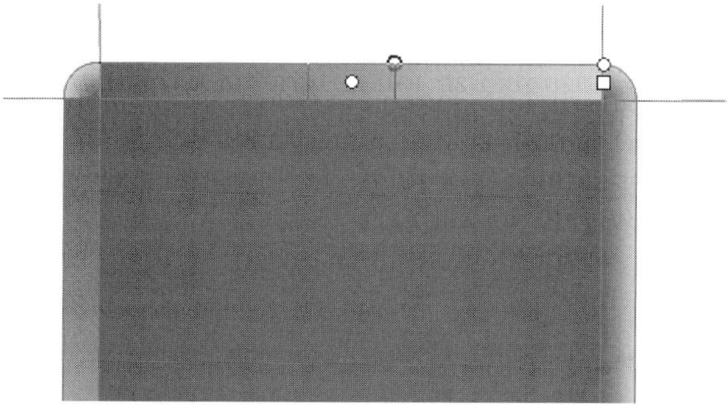

FIGURE 4.35 Scale gradient.

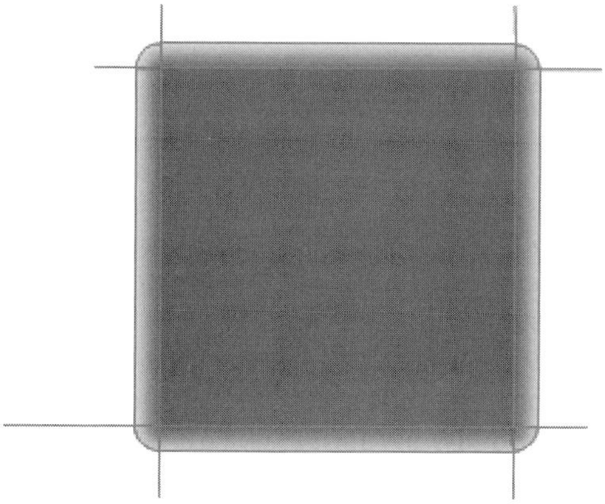

FIGURE 4.36 Modify rotation of gradient.

To delete all the red guidelines in two easy steps, double-click on any part of the red lines, which should select all the red guidelines. Once all are selected, execute the shortcut key command to delete them. Your round corner square with highlights should look like the one in Figure 4.37.

Square Bevel—Filter

Create a square and convert it to a symbol. Apply a Bevel filter to it and notice the options available, as shown in Figure 4.38.

FIGURE 4.37 Delete unnecessary lines and view at 100%.

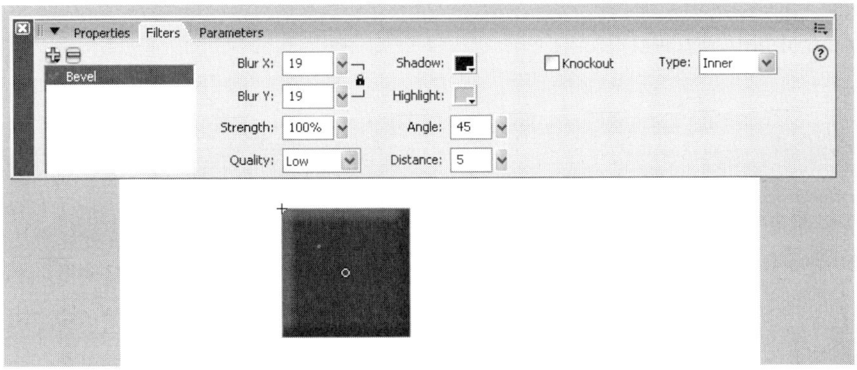

FIGURE 4.38 Applying a Bevel filter.

DROP SHADOWS

Creating a drop shadow is very simple. Using the Line, Selection, Paint Bucket, and Fill Transform tools together you can create a drop shadow for just about anything.

Shadow Create with Solid Fills

Select the Rectangle tool and set the corner radius to 5 points, the line to red, width to hairline, and fill color to #666666. Create a rectangle shape similar to that shown in Figure 4.39.

To create the solid fills, we will be plotting guidelines to give us areas to fill. Double-click on the red outline of the rectangle you just created to select it. Bring up the Transform panel, making sure the Constrain checkbox is unchecked, and enter 102% for horizontal, 104% for vertical, and press Enter. You should have something similar to Figure 4.40.

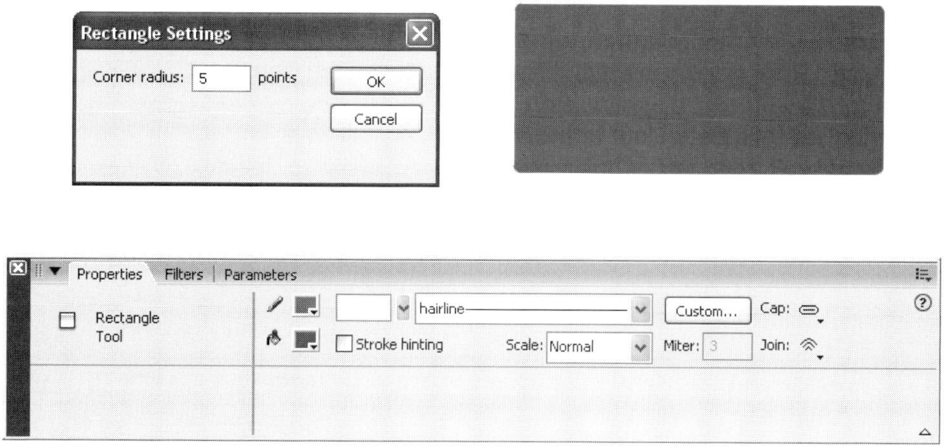

FIGURE 4.39 Create a rectangle with rounded corners.

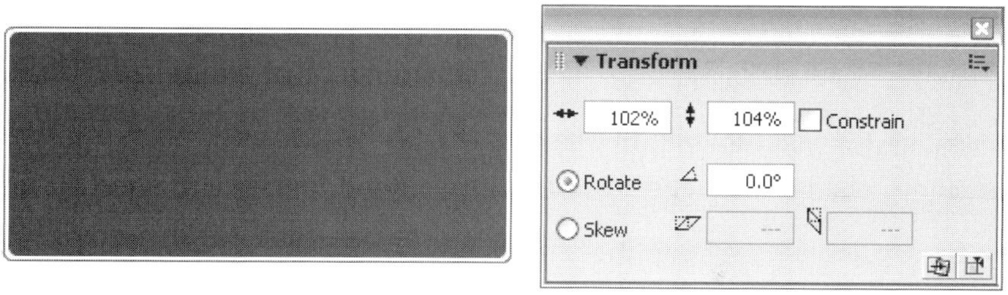

FIGURE 4.40 Scale outline to create an area to fill.

It will need one more of these outlines, so double-click on the outline and execute the shortcut key command to Copy and Paste in Place. With it still selected, open the Transform panel, again making sure the Constrain checkbox is unchecked, and enter 102% for horizontal, 104% for vertical, and press Enter. You should have something similar to Figure 4.41.

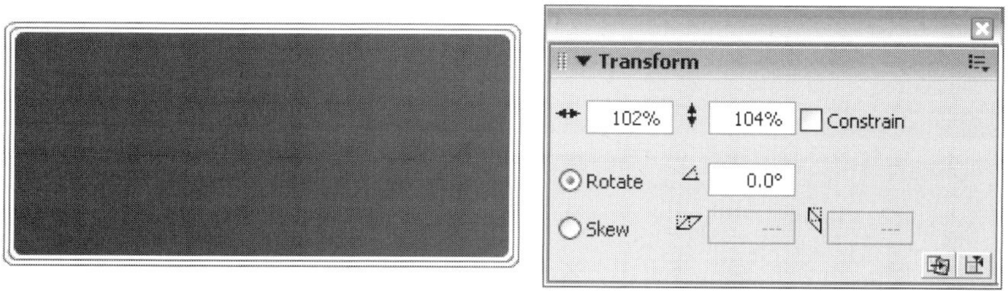

FIGURE 4.41 Create another outline and scale it.

Select the Zoom tool and zoom in on one of the corners. Next, we will be adding the fills between the outlines. Select the Paint Bucket tool, set the fill to #000000 with 30% alpha, and apply it between the dark gray rectangle and the first red line, as shown in Figure 4.42.

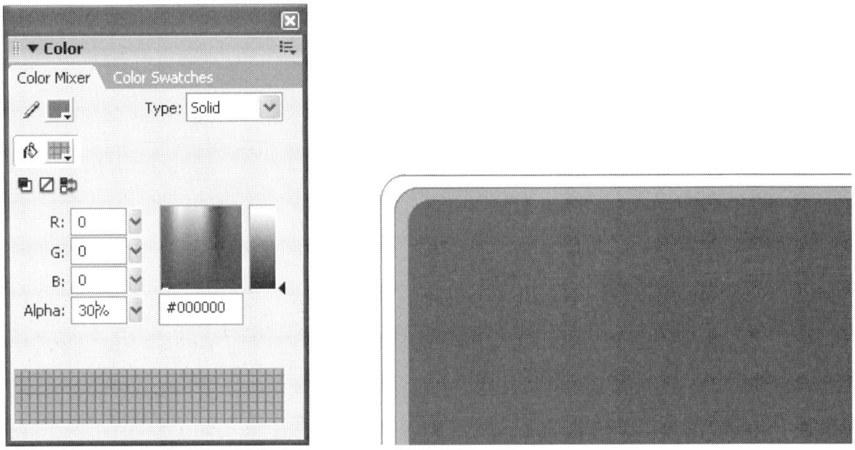

FIGURE 4.42 Zoom in and apply fill.

With the Paint Bucket tool, set the fill to #000000 with 15% alpha and apply it to the last area, as shown in Figure 4.43.

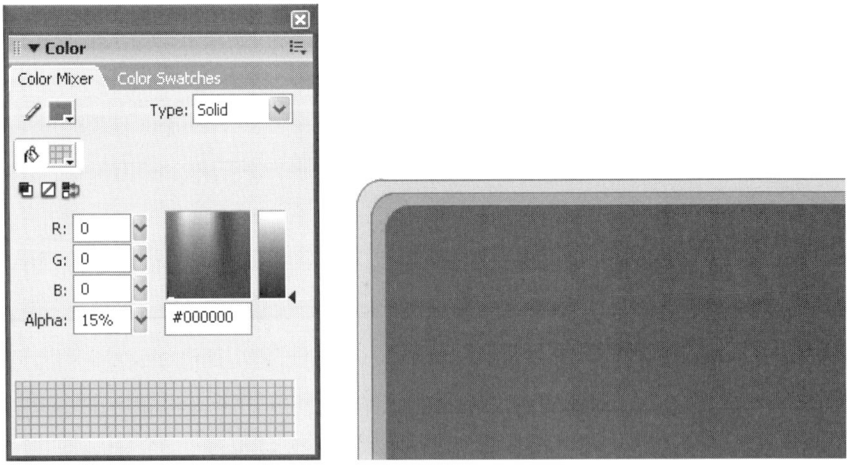

FIGURE 4.43 Apply modified fill.

The fills have been applied, and now it is time to see how it looks at 100%. We need to delete the guidelines we created with square outlines. Select the Line tool and draw a line touching both of the square outlines, as shown in Figure 4.44. With the Selection tool, double-click on any part of the red lines to select all the red lines. If for some reason all the lines are touching but everything is not selected, make sure the lines are all the same width and color. To do so, use the Eyedropper tool to grab the width and color from the existing lines.

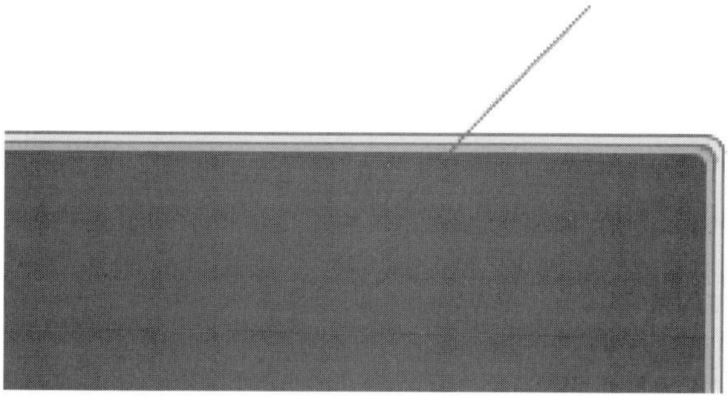

FIGURE 4.44 Apply a line striking through existing outlines.

Once all the lines are selected, execute the shortcut key command to delete. Set your view to 100% to see exactly how it will look when published, as shown in Figure 4.45. If you can see the fills at 100%, the drop shadow is not smooth, so you might want to try making more levels of fills. However, remember that the more fills you add, the bigger your file size is going to be. If you are looking for a more realistic drop shadow, try the next technique, with gradient fills.

FIGURE 4.45 Delete all red lines and view at 100%.

Shadow Create with Gradient Fills

Select the Rectangle tool and set your corner radius to 5, as shown in Figure 4.46. The button to edit the corner radius is located on the Options panel on the toolbar.

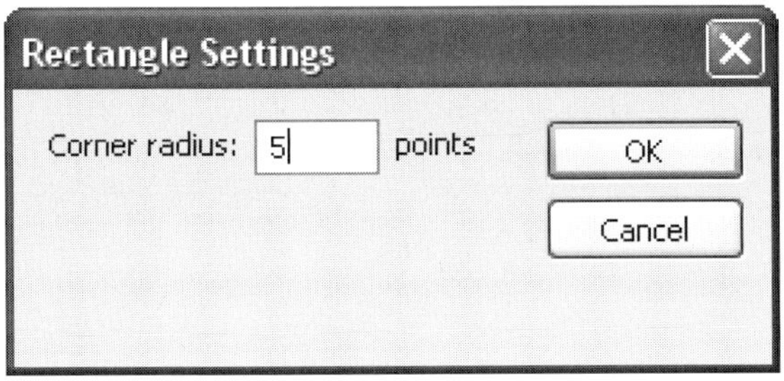

FIGURE 4.46 Set corner radius to 5.

Before drawing your rectangle, set your line to the color red and at line width hairline in the Properties panel; that way, you can see and edit your lines better. Choose a fill color of #666666, which will be our base color for the rectangle. This can also be edited in the Properties panel.

With your Rectangle tool selected, click down and drag diagonally to create a rectangle. Once you have a shape you like, release your mouse button. You should have a shape similar to that in Figure 4.47.

FIGURE 4.47 Create a rectangle.

To create gradient fills exactly where we need them, it is necessary to create guidelines out of vector lines, similar to a coloring book where all we have to do is fill in color between the lines. To start, select your Line tool, make sure it is set to hairline width, and choose a bright color that stands out, like red. To plot the guidelines, we will need to connect lines to where a line intersects with the curved line. Because we are attaching these lines to existing points, we are not creating new points, which saves in file size and makes for a cleaner graphic. With the Snap to Objects feature on, take the Line tool and start from one point to the other side, as shown in Figure 4.48.

Continue this task until each point has lines intersecting, as shown in Figure 4.49.

FIGURE 4.48 Create a line starting an outline where a gradient will be applied.

FIGURE 4.49 Create three more lines completing the inner outline.

To close the guidelines, we need to create a box around the rectangle. You can use the Rectangle tool set to No Fill, or use the Line tool and plot one line at a time, as shown in Figure 4.50. Plotting lines can be more precise because you have control over each line and where it lies.

Duplicating a line and using its double for the other side is a shortcut to create the lines, and one side will be identical to the other. Just select the first line you created, execute the shortcut keys to Copy and Paste in Place, and move it to the other side quickly by holding down the Shift key as you press the direction arrow key, as shown in Figure 4.51. If you are looking for more precise movement, do not hold down the Shift key.

FIGURE 4.50 Create a line starting the outer outline.

FIGURE 4.51 Create three more lines closing the area where gradients will be applied.

To create the gradients, we will be working with the Color Mixer panel, as shown in Figure 4.52. Starting with the linear gradient, set the drop-down menu to Linear, and make the first color square #000000, alpha 50%, and set the last color square #000000, alpha 0%. To save the gradient you just made, in the Color Mixer panel click on the icon in the upper right corner and click Add Swatch.

To create the radial gradient, we will be slightly editing the linear gradient. Take the first color swatch, #000000 alpha 50%, and move it closer to the center as shown in Figure 4.53. If the position of this swatch is not correct, it can be modified later. To save the gradient you just made, in the Color Mixer panel click on the icon in the upper right corner and click Add Swatch.

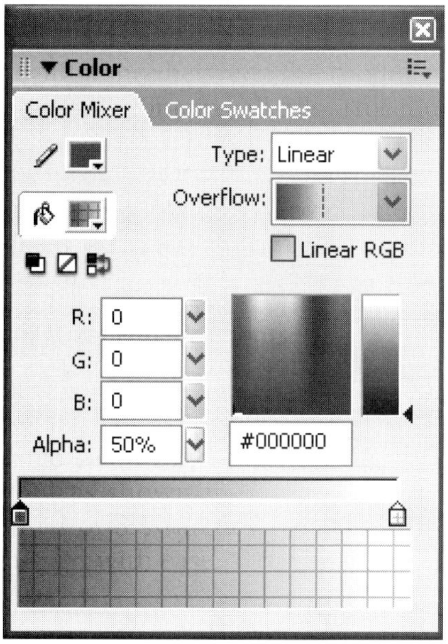

FIGURE 4.52 Create a linear gradient.

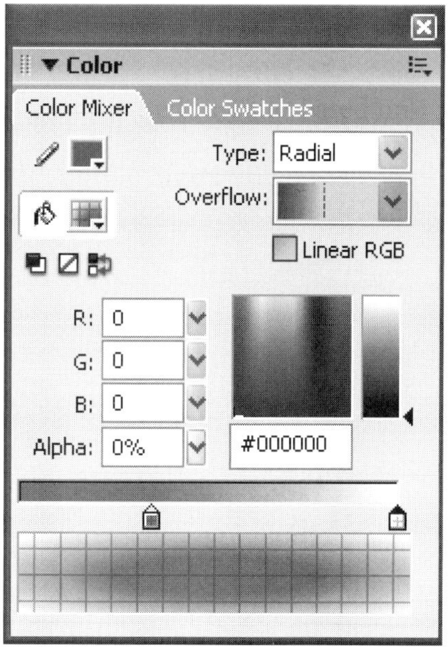

FIGURE 4.53 Create a radial gradient.

Select the Paint Bucket tool, and click on the fill setting under the Color area in the toolbar. Make sure the Lock Fill in the toolbar is turned off. Click on the fill setting and choose the linear gradient you just created. Apply the linear gradient fill to the horizontal and vertical areas as shown in Figure 4.54. Choose the radial gradient you just created and apply it to the corner areas as shown in Figure 4.54.

FIGURE 4.54 Apply linear and radial gradients.

To modify the gradients so they are positioned to show the correct colors, select the Gradient Transform tool. Similar to the previous gradients you edited, modify the center point, scale the gradient to fit your use, and rotate the gradient in the correct direction. Review Figures 4.55 through 4.57 for further detail.

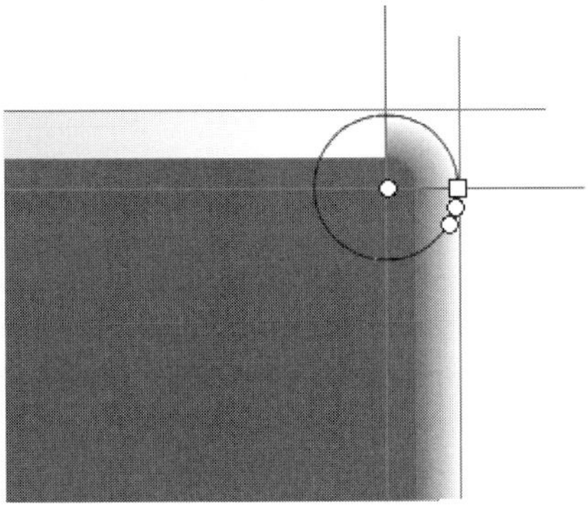

FIGURE 4.55 Position center point where the two lines intersect.

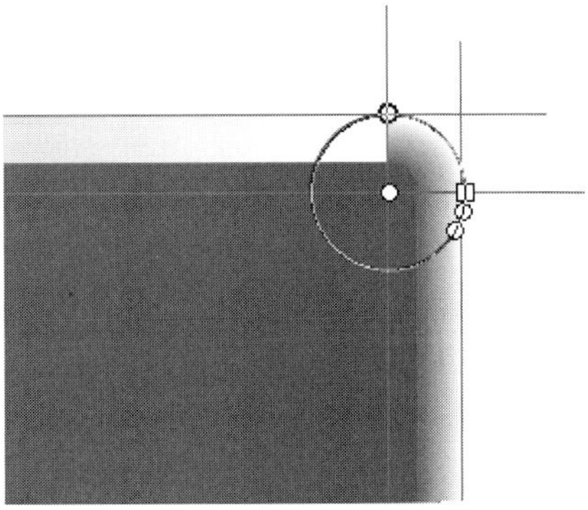

FIGURE 4.56 Snap the scale modifier to the top point.

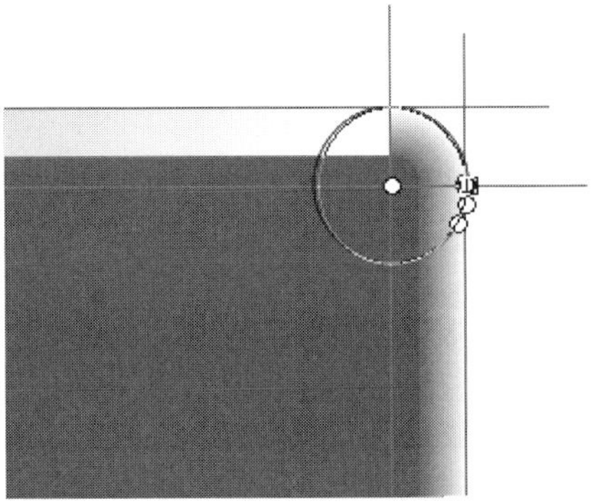

FIGURE 4.57 Snap the scale modifier horizontally to match the radial gradient with the vertical linear gradient.

Repeat the previous steps so all the gradients link up color-wise to the gradients next to each other. For a final check to see how well each gradient runs into each other, remove the red guidelines. To select them, double-click on any part of the red lines with the Selection tool and execute the shortcut key command to delete, as shown in Figure 4.58.

FIGURE 4.58 Delete the outlines and view at 100%.

Shadow Create with Filter

Create a square and convert it to a symbol. Apply a Drop Shadow filter to it and notice the options available, as shown in Figure 4.59.

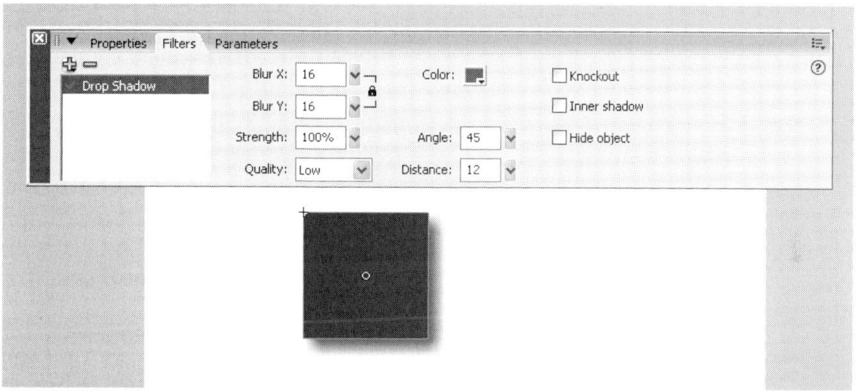

FIGURE 4.59 Apply a Drop Shadow filter.

GLOW

Glow effects are most commonly created in Photoshop, but can be easily created in Macromedia Flash with linear and radial gradients. This technique is very similar to creating a drop shadow with gradient fills, except we are using the color associated with the object for which the glow is being created. This technique focuses more on how this process can be accelerated, so make sure you read the section *Shadow Create with Gradient Fills*.

Button Glow

To follow along with this lesson, your button should resemble a square or rectangle, with or without curved corners. For a circle or oval-shaped button, use a radial gradient.

To start, we need to create our guidelines so we have a grid in which to apply our gradients. Using your Line tool, lay down lines where the curve in the button shape meets the straight part of the button shape, as shown in Figure 4.60. If your button does not have rounded corners, the lines will be drawn at the edge of the square or rectangle.

FIGURE 4.60 Draw four lines creating inner guidelines.

FIGURE 4.61 Draw four lines creating outer guidelines.

To create the lines that close the grid, use the Rectangle tool, but make sure the Snap to Objects feature is off, or your rectangle might snap to places you do not want it to. Your result should look similar to Figure 4.61.

Create the two gradients we will be working with, using settings Linear gradient: #00FF00 50% swatch located in the center, #00FF00 0% swatch located on the far right, as shown in Figure 4.62.

Radial gradient: #00FF00 50% swatch located in the center, #00FF00 0% swatch located on the far right, as shown in Figure 4.63.

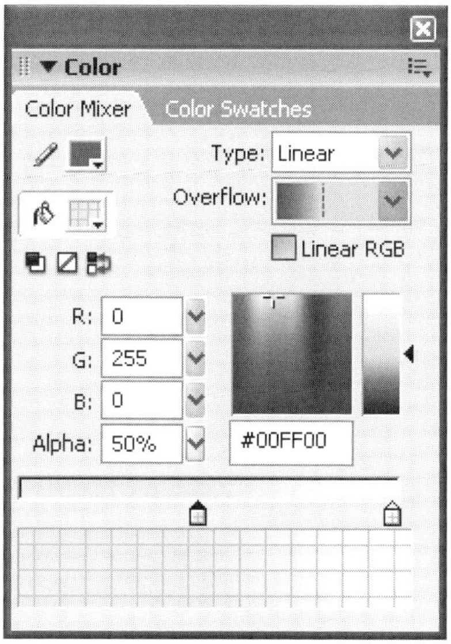

FIGURE 4.62 Create linear gradient.

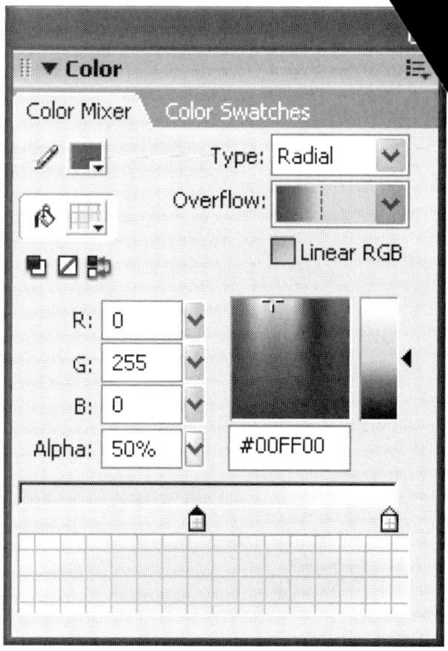

FIGURE 4.63 Create radial gradient.

Apply the gradients in the particular areas as shown in Figure 4.64.

FIGURE 4.64 Apply gradients.

Modify the gradients so they are positioned as you like with the Gradient Transform tool as shown in Figure 4.65.

Once you feel you are ready to check your work, with the Selection tool double-click on any part of the guidelines to select all of them and execute the shortcut key command to cut them from the stage. You should have something similar to Figure 4.66.

FIGURE 4.65 Modify gradients with the Gradient Transform tool.

FIGURE 4.66 Delete guidelines and view at 100%.

Ball Glow

In this lesson, we will use three techniques: applying highlights to a circle, creating a drop shadow with solid fills, and giving an object a glow.

Select the Oval tool, set it to No Fill and red hairline width, and draw a perfect circle by holding down the Shift key as you click and drag, creating a circle similar to Figure 4.67.

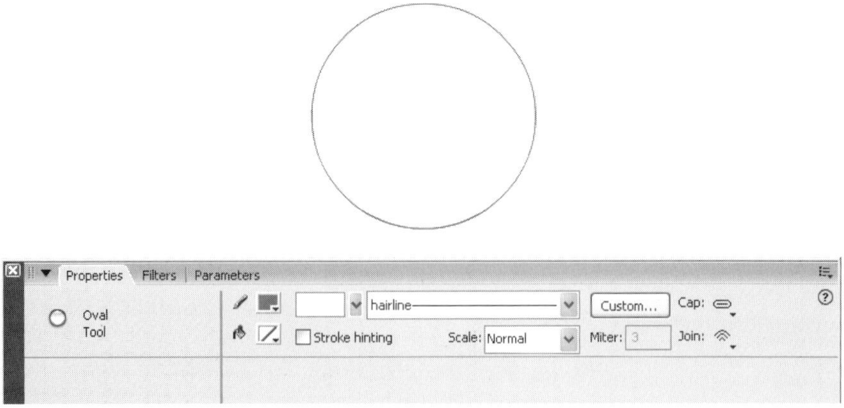

FIGURE 4.67 Create a circle.

Open the Color Mixer panel and create a radial gradient similar to Figure 4.68. We are using several color swatches; the one on the far left is for the main light source, and the light one to the right, in between the two purple swatches, is the light reflecting off the surface the ball is sitting on. Once you are done editing your gradient, save it by clicking Add Swatch. Select your Paint Bucket tool and apply it to the circle.

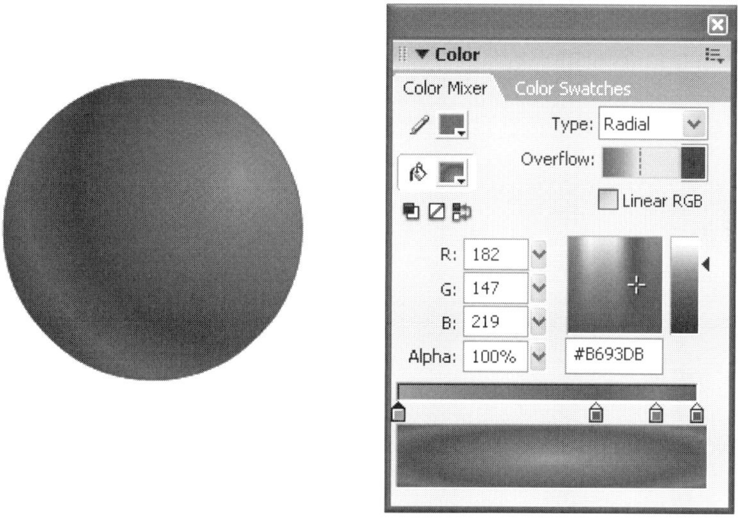

FIGURE 4.68 Create a radial gradient and apply it.

Select the Gradient Transform tool and edit how the radial gradient is placed on the circle. Position the gradient in a way similar to Figure 4.69. Notice where the main light is shining and how the reflection slightly shows on the bottom right of the circle.

Once you are satisfied with the placement of the gradient, lock the layer it is on by clicking on the black dot below the Lock icon in the Timeline panel. Clicking it once will lock all objects on that layer, and clicking it again will unlock all objects on that layer. This circle needs to be locked so that when we create new graphics on new layers, our edits will not interfere with previous graphics.

Now that the circle on that layer is locked, create a new layer by clicking on the Insert New Layer icon located in the bottom left-hand corner of the Timeline panel. Select the Oval tool and set the fill color to No Fill and the line to red hairline width. Draw an oval similar to that in Figure 4.70. Make sure the oval you just drew works with the actual circle, so it is possible that the ball could cast a shadow similar to the shape of the oval you just drew.

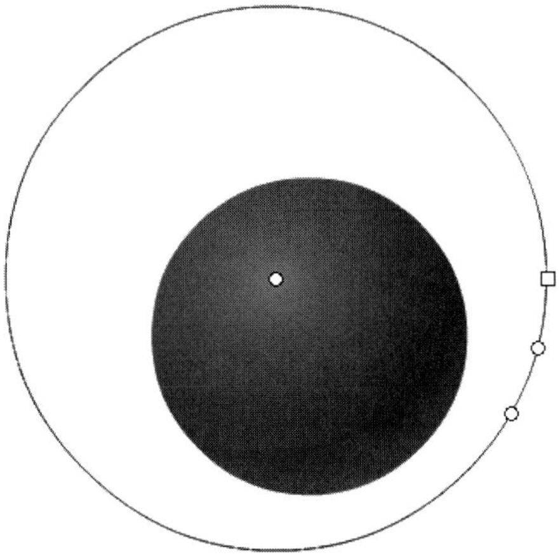

FIGURE 4.69 Modify placement of gradient.

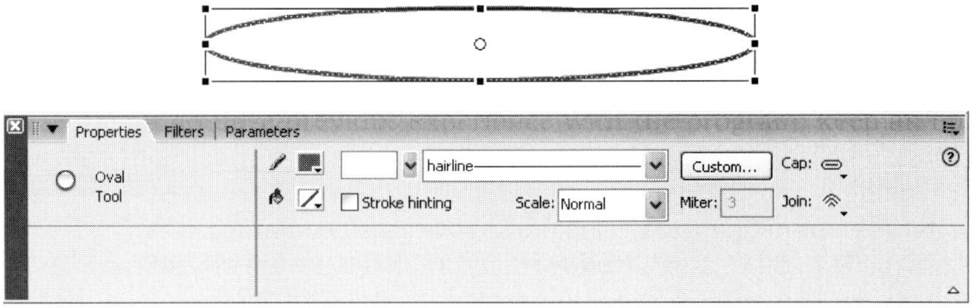

FIGURE 4.70 Create an oval on a new layer.

Once you have the initial shadow shape, Copy, Paste in Place, and Scale up a new oval, as shown in Figure 4.71. Making two more of these will work to hold the other fills, making the shadow look as if it is fading out.

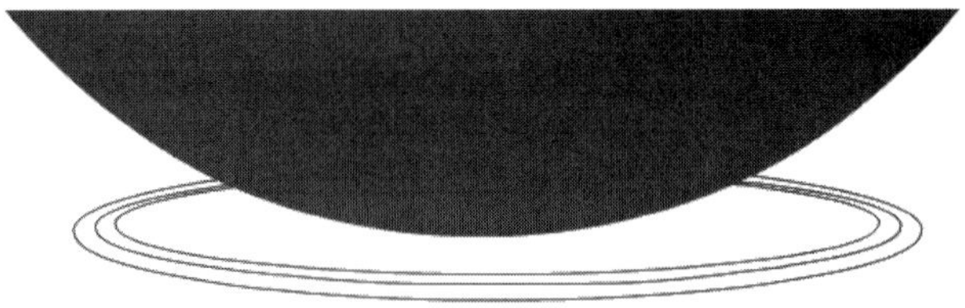

FIGURE 4.71 Create two more oval lines, scaling each larger than the previous.

Fill in between the oval lines with the following settings and as shown in Figure 4.72:

- For the center circle, use a fill of #000000.
- For the area between the first and second oval lines, use a fill of #000000, alpha 50%.
- For the area between the second and last oval lines, use a fill of #000000, alpha 15%.

FIGURE 4.72 Apply fills between the oval lines that were created.

An alpha of 10% or lower is not used because if your graphics are viewed at a low resolution or on most laptop displays, an alpha of that percentage most often cannot be seen.

To give the ball more depth, another layer should be added of shadow on the ball with a radial gradient. To make the guideline you will be applying the radial gradient in, select the Ink Bottle tool and apply it to the original radial gradient. With the Selection tool, double-click on the circle-shaped line you just created, Copy and Delete it, create a new layer, and Paste in Place on the new layer as shown in Figure 4.73.

FIGURE 4.73 Create an outline from existing radial gradient and place it on a new layer.

Create a radial gradient: #4A2570 0% swatch located in the center, and #4A2570 100% located on the right. Select the Paint Bucket tool and apply a radial gradient with the settings shown in Figure 4.74.

To adjust the position of the radial gradient, use the Gradient Transform tool, as shown in Figure 4.75.

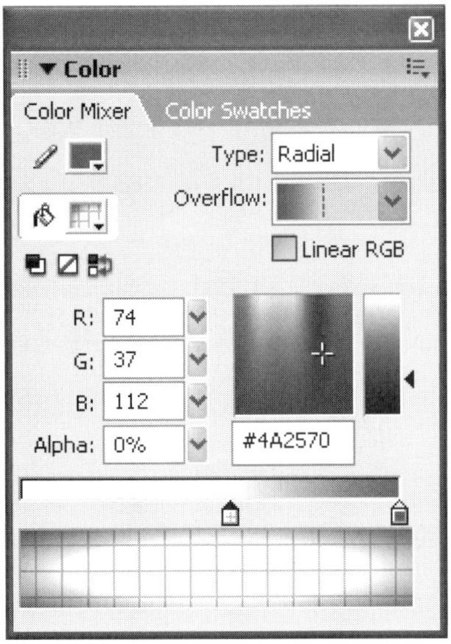

FIGURE 4.74 Create radial gradient.

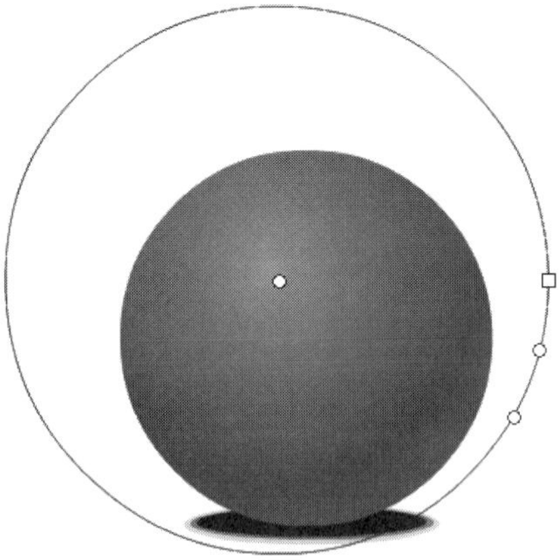

FIGURE 4.75 Apply radial gradient to outline.

With the previous steps completed for applying the highlight and shadow for the ball, now we will begin creating the glow for the ball. To give us a guideline where the glow will emanate from, select the Oval tool and draw a circle around the ball, as shown in Figure 4.76.

If the ball were to glow for real, there would have to be two glows drawn, one for the initial ball glow, and is the other for the reflection of the glow appearing on the ground. The next guidelines to plot are used to crop the initial ball glow. Use the Line tool to plot the initial guideline, and use the Ink Bottle tool to apply the lines around the shadow of the ball, as shown in Figure 4.77.

FIGURE 4.76 Create an outline around the circle, and scale another outline defining how big the glow will be.

FIGURE 4.77 Create lines defining where the glow hits the ground.

With the Selection tool, click and select the bottom curve and delete it, since it will not be needed, as shown in Figure 4.78.

FIGURE 4.78 Delete line.

With the Paint Bucket tool, apply the following radial gradient to the area outside the ball: swatch placed in the mid-right #6600FF alpha 50%, and swatch placed on the far right #0066FF alpha 0%, as shown in Figure 4.79. To edit the gradient in real time, have the fill selected as you edit it in the Color Mixer panel. Doing so will save you time having to reapply the gradient.

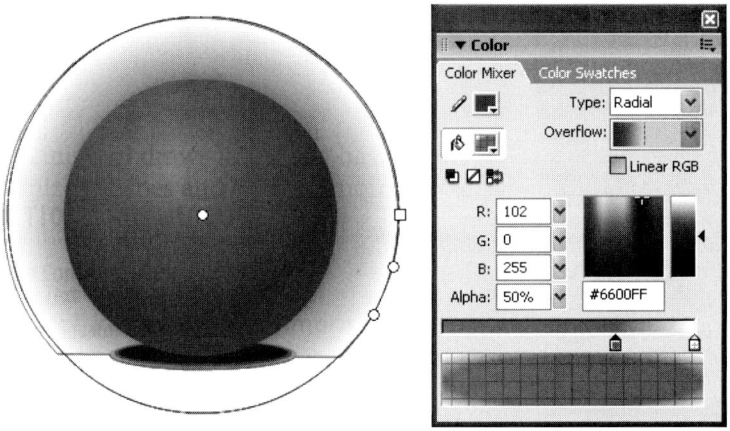

FIGURE 4.79 Create and apply gradient.

To create the reflection for the glow on the ground, we will be reusing the outer glow gradient. Select the Rectangle tool, set it to No Line, and set the fill to the previous radial gradient but move the center color all the way to the left. To make sure the rectangle you just drew does not interfere with the other graphics, create it on a new layer, or create it off to the side and group and position it in the correct place, as shown in Figure 4.80.

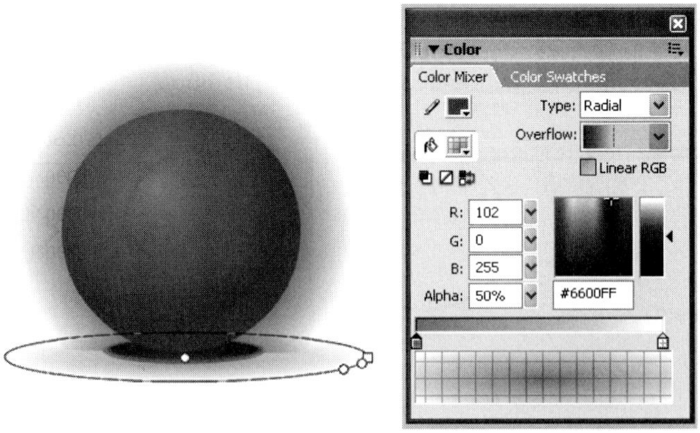

FIGURE 4.80 Create glow on the ground.

Once you have finalized the position of the gradient with the Gradient Transform tool, the guidelines can be removed. View the graphic at 100% to make sure enough detail is added or to see if any gradients need minor tweaks. Your result should look something similar to Figure 4.81.

FIGURE 4.81 Delete red lines and view at 100%.

Button Glow—Filter

Grab the Submit button we were working with earlier, but without the glow gradients. Convert it to a symbol if it is not already, apply a Glow filter to it, and notice the options available, as shown in Figure 4.82.

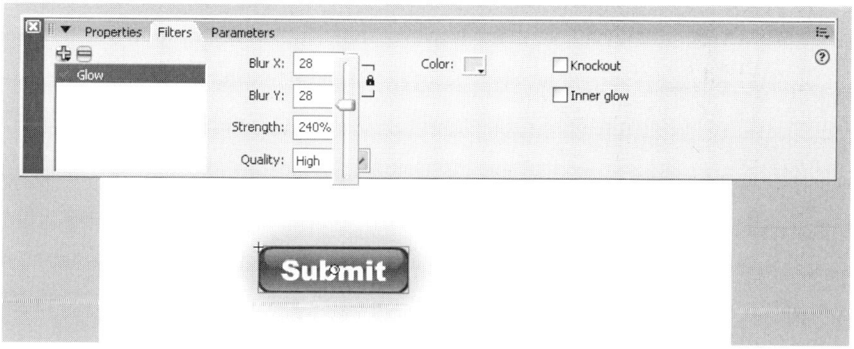

FIGURE 4.82 Apply a Glow filter effect.

DRAWING IN PERSPECTIVE

Drawing in perspective in Macromedia Flash is simple, assuming you know three techniques. In this section, we review how you can use 1-point perspective, 2-point perspective, and 3-point perspective to create 3D cubes. These techniques can also be used to create 3D text and 3D buildings.

1-Point Perspective

1-point perspective involves the use of one vanishing point where lines are drawn to define perspective in an object. The point plotted is the horizon line in the world in which your object lives.

Select the Rectangle tool and create a perfect square. Plot a point off to the lower right of the square you just drew, as shown in Figure 4.83.

Select the Selection tool and make sure Snap to Objects is on. Drag one of the lines from the point you just created and snap it to the bottom-right corner of the square, as shown in Figure 4.84.

Grab another line, and drag it and snap it to the bottom-left corner of the square, as shown in Figure 4.85.

Grab another line and snap it to the top-right corner of the square, as shown in Figure 4.86.

FIGURE 4.83 Create a square and plot a vanishing point.

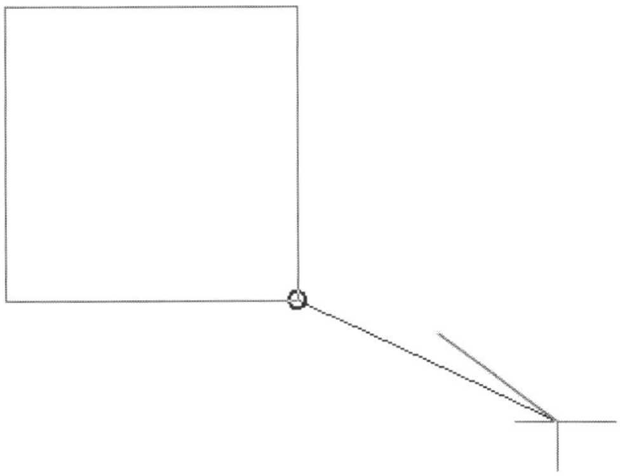

FIGURE 4.84 Connect the vanishing point with the lower right corner of the square.

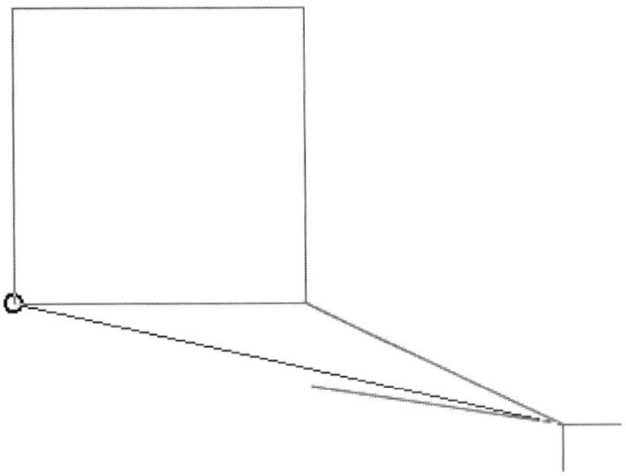

FIGURE 4.85 Connect the vanishing point with the lower left corner of the square.

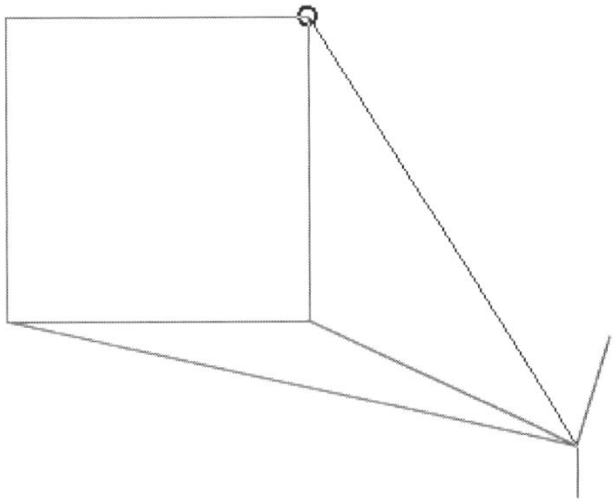

FIGURE 4.86 Connect the vanishing point with the upper right corner of the square.

Now we are going to define how deep the 3D square is by drawing a vertical and a horizontal line with the Line tool. Draw the straight vertical line first, and make sure it runs through the line connecting to the lower right point of the square, as shown in Figure 4.87.

Start drawing the horizontal line by connecting it to the point where the vertical line connects to the lower right diagonal line, and draw a straight horizontal line running through the lower left diagonal line, as shown in Figure 4.88.

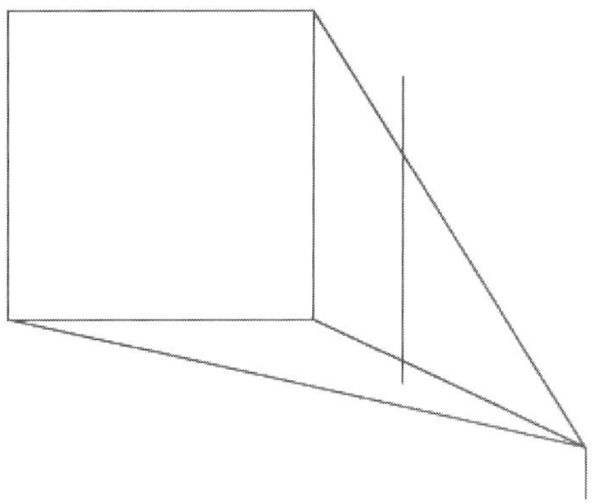

FIGURE 4.87 Draw a vertical line defining the depth of the square.

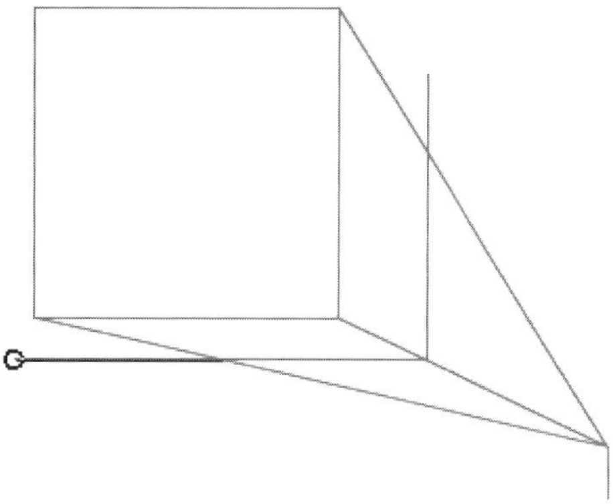

FIGURE 4.88 Draw a horizontal line defining the depth of the square.

Select and delete the unnecessary lines, as shown in Figure 4.89.

Now the 3D square is ready to be colored. Open the Color Mixer and choose three colors of the same hue: one for the highlight color (#003399), another the base color (#000066), and another the shadow color (#000033), as shown in Figure 4.90. Apply these colors based on where you feel the sunlight is coming from. In this instance, the sun is located directly above the cube.

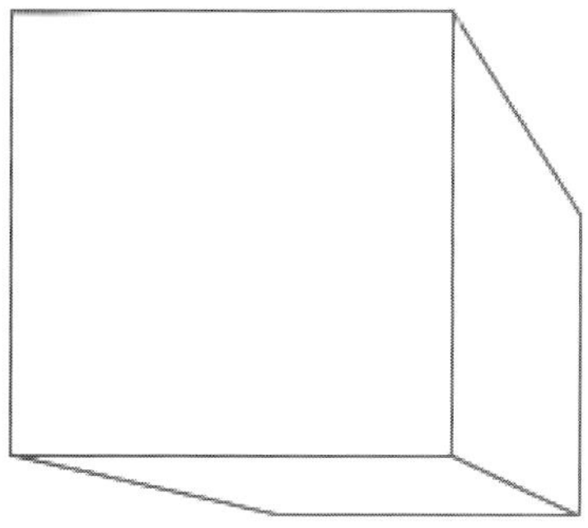

FIGURE 4.89 Delete unnecessary lines.

FIGURE 4.90 Choose and apply fills to the outlined 3D square depending on where your light is coming from.

2-Point Perspective

2-point perspective involves the use of two vanishing points where lines are drawn to define perspective in an object. The two points are plotted on a horizon line, similar to 1-point perspective, except there are two points to plot.

Plot two points on the same horizontal line; this invisible horizontal line is called the horizon. Use the Line tool and draw a cross to signify the point. That way, you can pull the arms of the cross for the lines, as shown in Figure 4.91.

As we are doing this, try to visualize the top of the 3D box. With the Selection tool, grab one of the arms of the cross and drag it out to the left, as shown in Figure 4.92.

FIGURE 4.91 Draw two vanishing points.

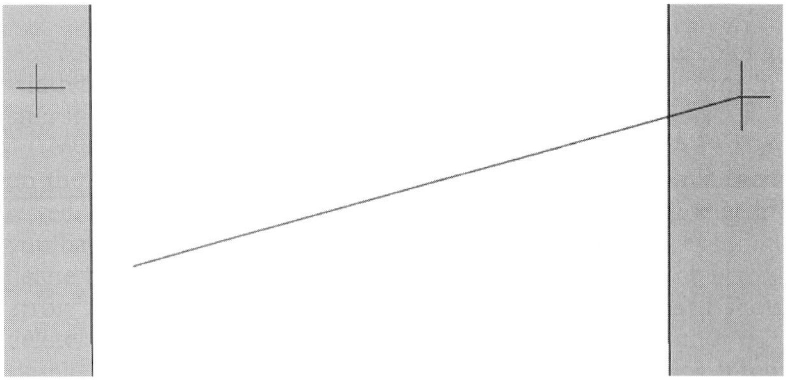

FIGURE 4.92 Draw a line coming out from the right vanishing point.

Grab one of the arms of the cross on the left and pull the point out to the right, as shown in Figure 4.93.

Grab one of the arms on the cross to the right and pull the point out to the left above the first one, as shown in Figure 4.94.

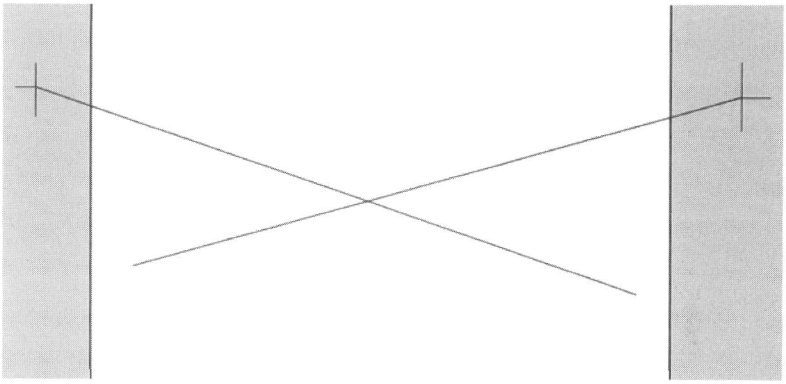

FIGURE 4.93 Draw a line coming out from the left vanishing point.

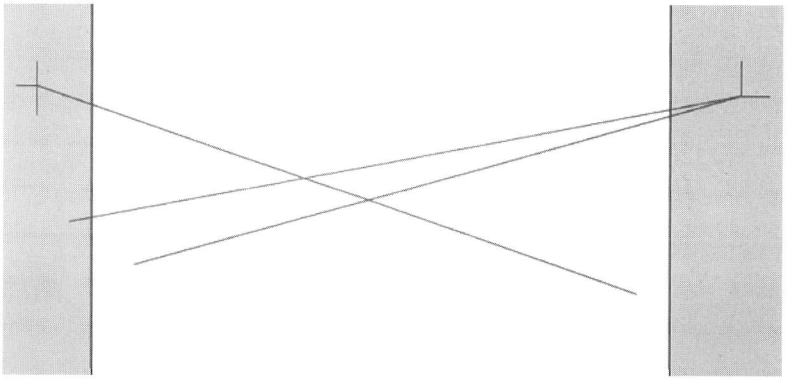

FIGURE 4.94 Draw a line coming out from the right vanishing point defining the back side of the box.

Grab one of the arms on the cross to the left and pull the point out to the right above the first one, as shown in Figure 4.95.

The sides of the box must now be set. Take the Line tool and draw vertical lines from the points shown in Figure 4.96.

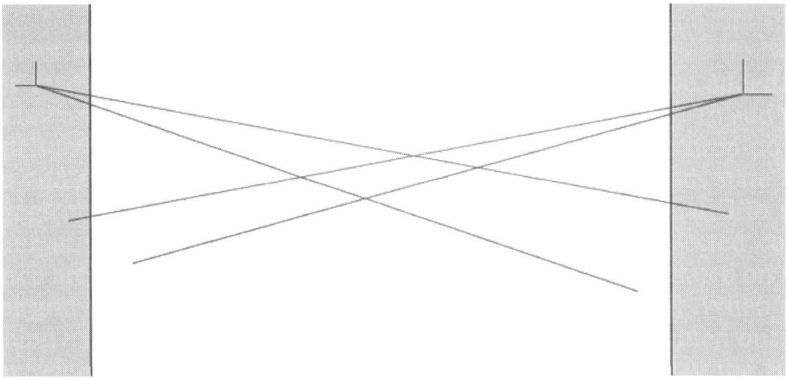

FIGURE 4.95 Draw a line coming out from the left vanishing point defining the backside of the box.

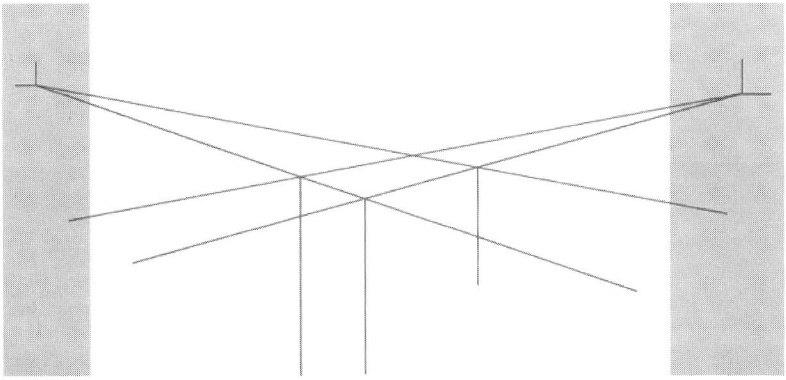

FIGURE 4.96 Draw vertical lines defining the sides of the box.

Now, the nex we will be pulling out will make up the side of the 3D box. Grab the arms on the cross to the right and pull the point out to the left, snapping it to the vertical line drawn, as shown in Figure 4.97.

With the Line tool, draw the far-left vertical line defining the second side of the 3D box, as shown in Figure 4.98.

Now the 3D box is ready to be colored. Open the Color Mixer and choose three colors of the same hue: one for the highlight color (#003399), another the base color (#000066), and another the shadow color (#000033), as shown in Figure 4.99. Apply these colors based on where you feel the sun coming from. In this instance, the sun is above the cube and off to the right.

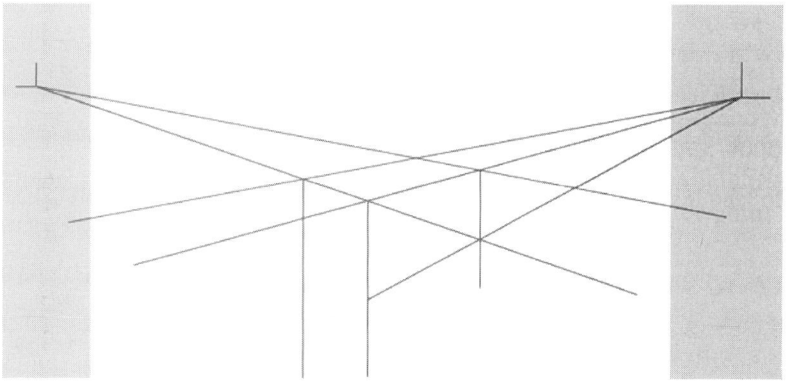

FIGURE 4.97 Draw a line coming out from the right vanishing point defining the bottom side of the box.

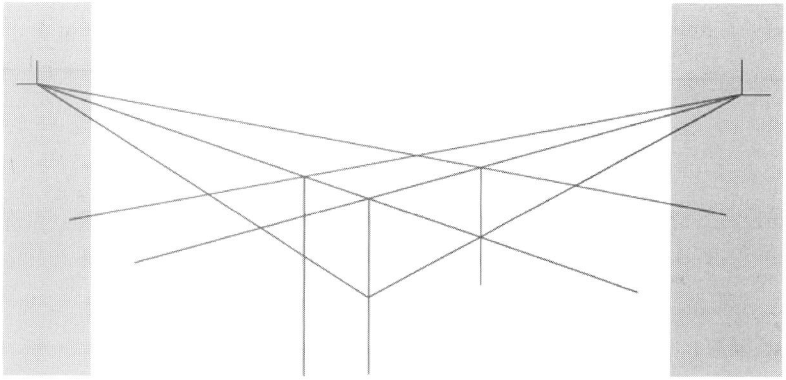

FIGURE 4.98 Draw a line coming out from the left vanishing point defining the bottom side of the box.

FIGURE 4.99 Choose and apply fills to the outlined 3D square depending on where your light is coming from.

3-Point Perspective

3-point perspective involves the use of three vanishing points where lines are drawn to define perspective in an object. Two of the vanishing points connected together create the horizon line. The third vanishing point adds further depth to an object.

Start by plotting three vanishing points and begin pulling the point of the crosses out, as shown in Figure 4.100. This starts similar to the 2-point perspective lesson.

Once you have pulled out the two top lines, connect the third bottom line to where the top two meet, as shown in Figure 4.101.

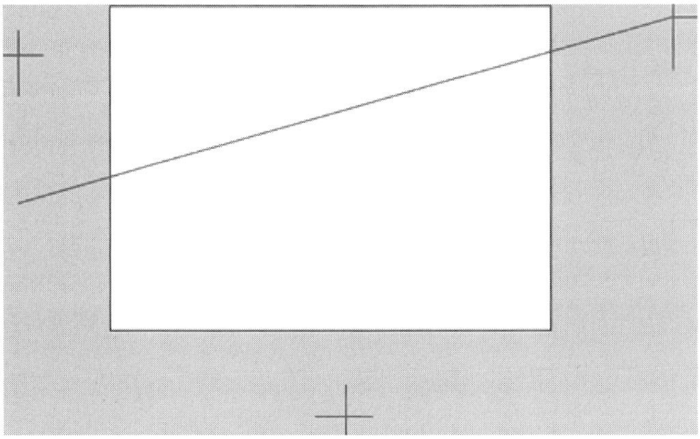

FIGURE 4.100 Create three vanishing points and draw a line coming out from the right vanishing point.

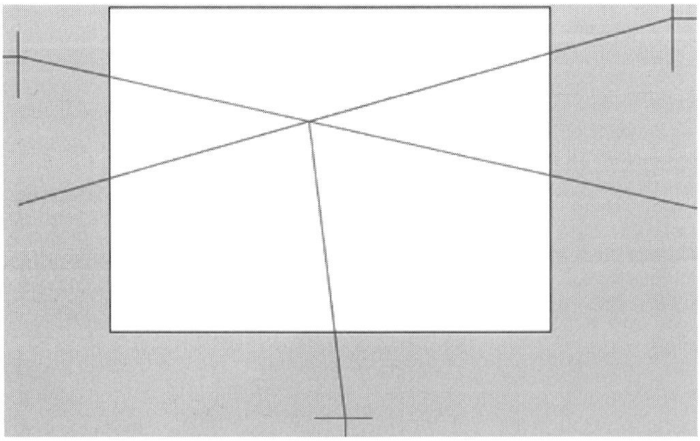

FIGURE 4.101 Draw a line coming out from the left vanishing point, bring a line coming from the bottom vanishing point, and connect it to the meeting left and right lines.

To start drawing the side of the box, grab one of the arms of the cross and pull it out to the left, as shown in Figure 4.102.

Do the same for the left vanishing point: grab one of the arms of the cross, pull it out to the right, and snap it to the intersection of the right line and bottom line, as shown in Figure 4.103.

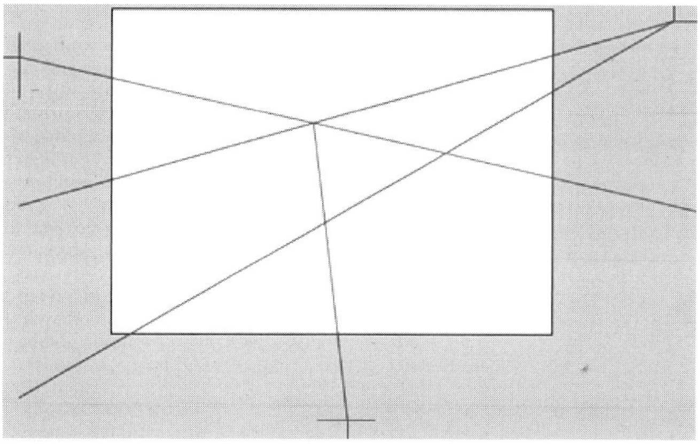

FIGURE 4.102 Draw a line coming out from the right vanishing point defining the bottom side of the box.

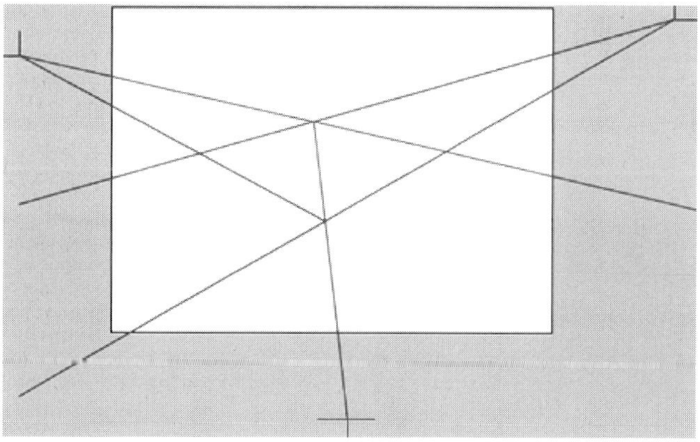

FIGURE 4.103 Draw a line coming out from the left vanishing point defining the bottom side of the box.

From the bottom vanishing point, drag up two lines, both defining the left and right side of the box, as shown in Figure 4.104.

To close off the top of the 3D box, bring a vanishing point from the right and snap it to the intersection of a line from the left and bottom, as shown in Figure 4.105.

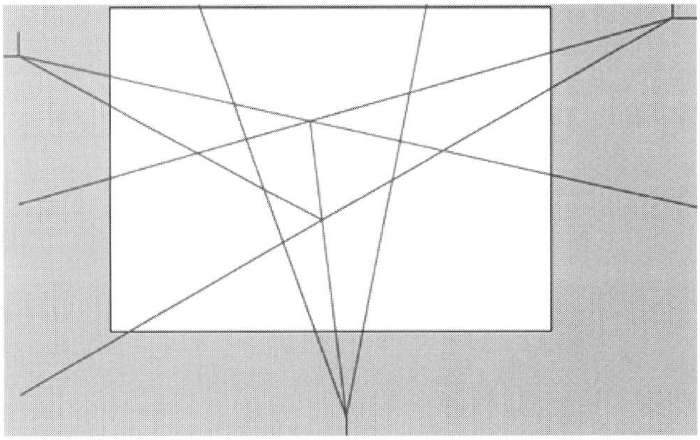

FIGURE 4.104 Draw two lines coming from the bottom vanishing point defining the sides of the box.

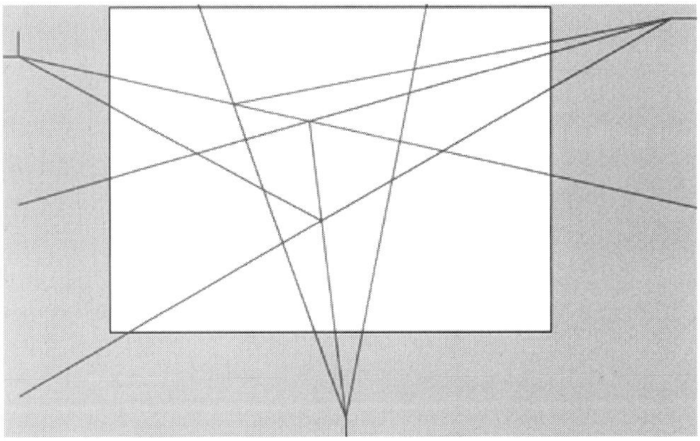

FIGURE 4.105 Draw a line coming out from the right vanishing point defining the top of the box.

Do the same for the left vanishing point. Drag a line from the left and snap it to the intersection of a line from the right and bottom, as shown in Figure 4.106.

Now the 3D box is ready to be colored. Open the Color Mixer and choose three colors of the same hue: one for the highlight color (#003399), another the base color (#000066), and another the shadow color (#000033), as shown in Figure 4.107. Apply these colors based on where you feel the sun is coming from. In this instance, the sun is located above the cube and off to the left.

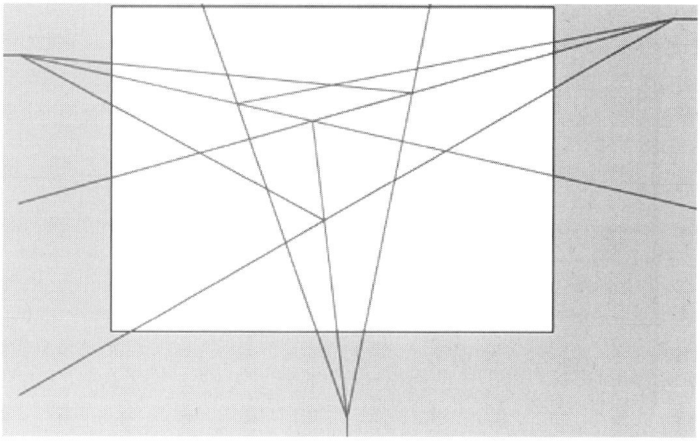

FIGURE 4.106 Draw a line coming out from the left vanishing point defining the top of the box.

FIGURE 4.107 Delete the unnecessary lines and apply fills to the outlined 3D square depending on where your light is coming from.

SUMMARY

- Effects like blur, highlights, drop shadows, and glows can all be done in Macromedia Flash.
- Filters in Macromedia Flash enable you to achieve effects quicker and more efficiently.
- Use any of the three perspective techniques in Macromedia Flash to create 3D text and objects.

EXERCISES

ON THE CD

The files for the following exercises are on the companion CD-ROM in the folders cited.

1. Blur the graphic with filter effect, as shown in Figure 4.108. The Flash file is on the companion CD-ROM in Chapter_4/Exercises/4-108.fla.

FIGURE 4.108 The graphic, before and after.

2. Create highlights on a square manually done with linear gradients, as shown in Figure 4.109.

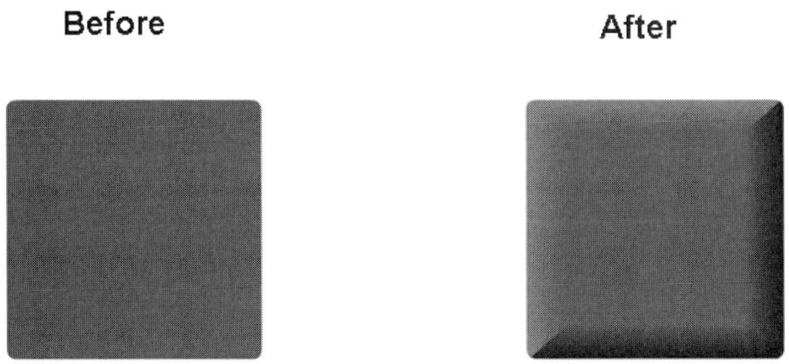

FIGURE 4.109 Before and after of a square with highlights.

3. Add a bevel filter effect to a basic circle graphic, as shown in Figure 4.110.
4. Add a drop shadow to the cylinder graphic made from one radial gradient, as shown in Figure 4.111. The Flash file is on the companion CD-ROM in Chapter_4/Exercises/4-111.fla.
6. Add a drop shadow filter effect to the pyramid graphic, as shown in Figure 4.112. The Flash file is on the companion CD-ROM in Chapter_4/Exercises/4-112.fla.

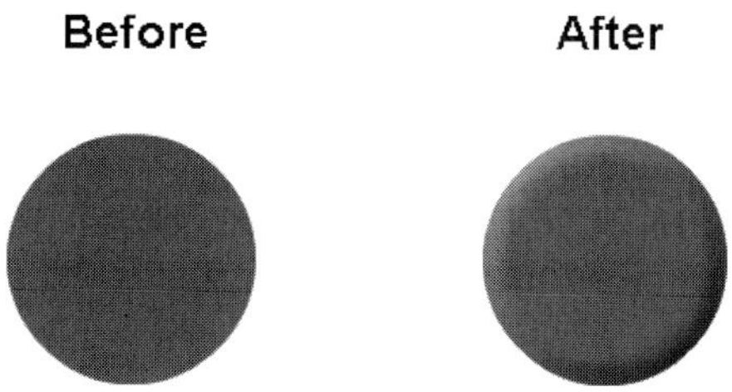

FIGURE 4.110 Applying the bevel filter effect.

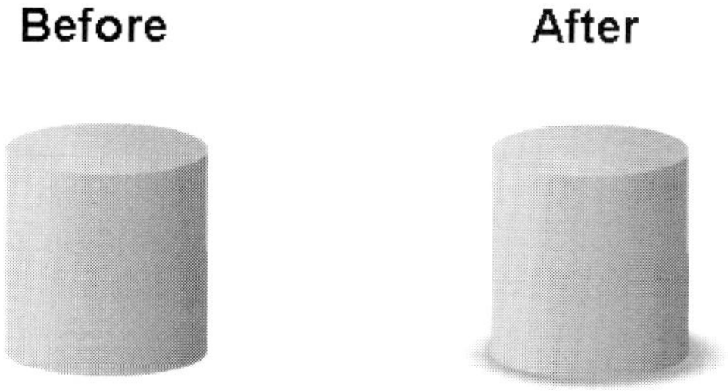

FIGURE 4.111 Add a drop shadow to the cylinder.

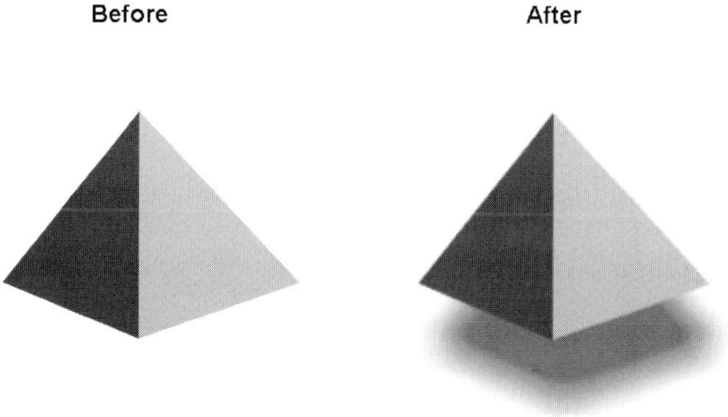

FIGURE 4.112 Before and after of a drop shadow effect.

7. Create a glow effect manually with linear and radial gradients, as shown in Figure 4.113. The Flash file is on the companion CD-ROM in Chapter_4/Exercises/4-113.fla.
8. Add a glow filter effect, as shown in Figure 4.114. The Flash file is located on the companion CD-ROM in Chapter_4/Exercises/4-114.fla.

FIGURE 4.113 Create a glow effect on a button.

FIGURE 4.114 Apply a glow effect to the ghost graphic.

9. Create a 1-point perspective object, as shown in Figure 4.115.
10. Create a 2-point perspective object, as shown in Figure 4.116.
11. Create a 3-point perspective object, as shown in Figure 4.117.

FIGURE 4.115 1-point perspective square.

FIGURE 4.116 2-point perspective square.

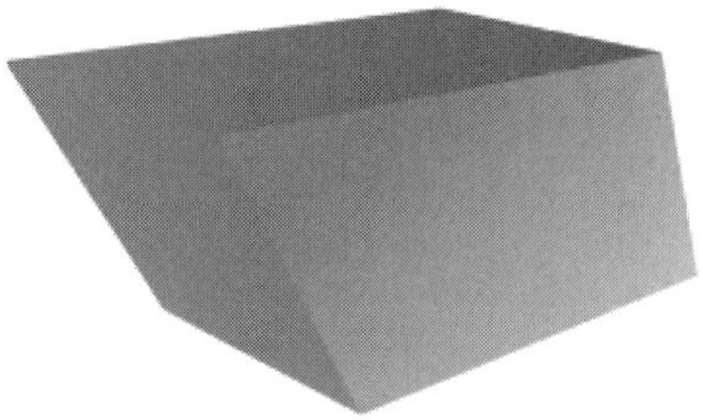

FIGURE 4.117 3-point perspective square.

CHAPTER

5

DESIGN TECHNIQUES

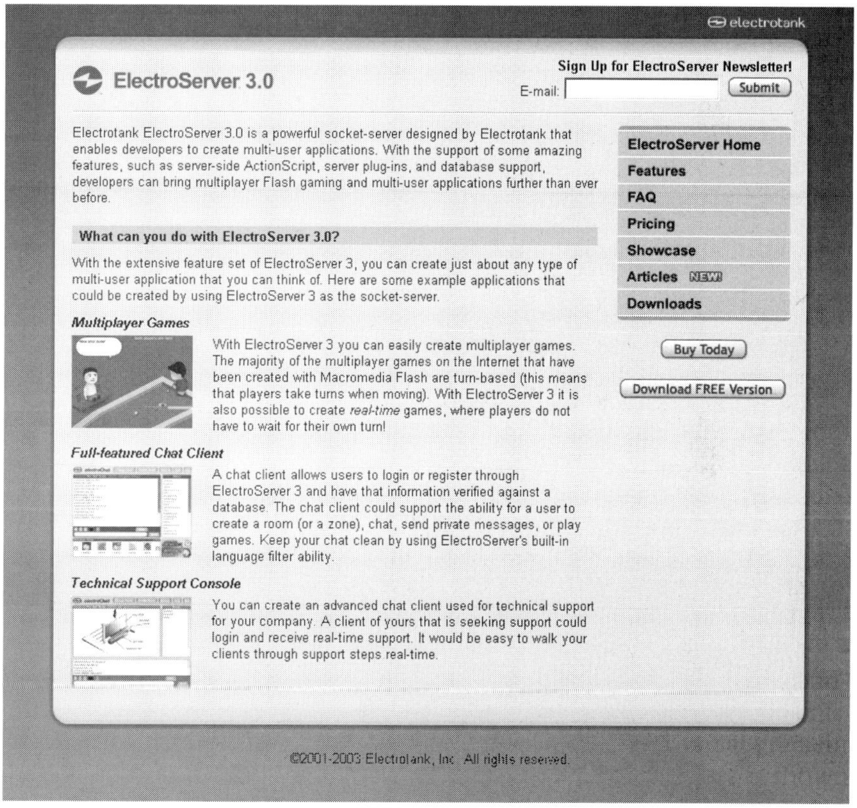

A great designer has the ability to produce exceptional designs that communicate the client's needs and speak to the target audience or users. Professional designers do not let their personal preferences sway them from meeting the client's and target audience's or user's needs. For instance, if you were designing a Web site for a baby clothing store, you would not want to use black, red, and sharp corners in the user interface; instead, you might want to use soft, light colors, and perhaps white, with beveled corners and a soft look. Many designers specialize just in content layout, user navigation, or logo design, to name a few. We could cover many areas on the topic of design, although this chapter focuses on particular design techniques that can be applied with Macromedia Flash and Web site creation—creating logos, user interfaces, and content layout. The examples here will show you the possibilities of using Flash as your primary design tool, saving you production time and making you more efficient in your design creation.

CONTENT LAYOUT

When designing a Web site, large or small, you want to design the content so it is easy to read and arranged in order of importance. Users viewing your Web site start at one point on the page and move in a certain direction depending on how the content is laid out and displayed. Knowing that, you can design your Web page so the user views the most important content first, then continues to the second most important content, and so on. Naturally, users view from left to right and top to bottom because that is how they are used to reading content. There are some exceptions, such as Asian cultures that read from back to front and top to bottom. That doesn't mean you should go out and design two sites catering to both styles; the standard for the Web seems to be left to right and top to bottom. Even though Web site navigation is in a small area of your Web page, it is the most critical part. An effective user navigation design is organized in a way that users can find whatever content they are looking for without getting lost or confused. By using Macromedia Flash, you can easily organize your Web site content and prepare Web page layout designs quickly and efficiently.

Site Architecture

Knowing how your Web pages will be organized and how a user will get to all of them can be frustrating, especially if you have trouble visualizing everything. Flash can make this job much easier; by using its drawing tools, one can mock up a simple diagram of all the pages and navigation paths, as shown in Figure 5.1. Similar to how family trees are visualized, each box with text in the center is a Web page. The user starts in the center where you see the word *Home*, which signifies the home page. From there, Web pages are created to organize all the pages the client requires.

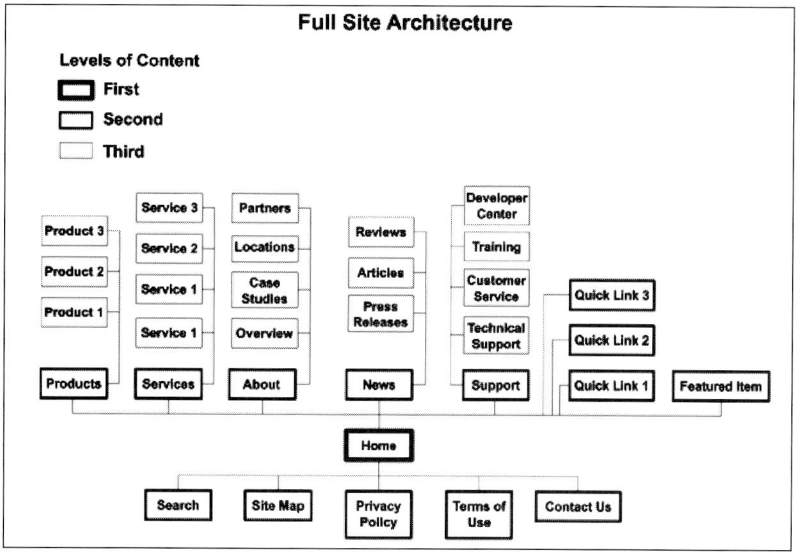

FIGURE 5.1 All the Web pages and their architecture.

Notice the key in the top-left corner that shows the difference in line width, which communicates the depth levels of Web pages.

To analyze a single Web page, a similar diagram can be created as shown in Figure 5.2, which focuses on the links on the page and which content is more important for the user to see.

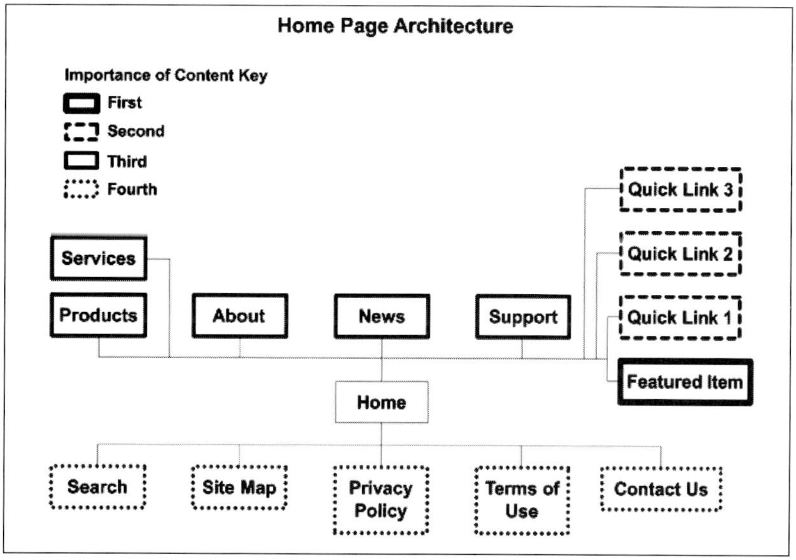

FIGURE 5.2 A home page and the importance of the content.

Working with Macromedia Flash in this way gives you a bird's-eye view of your Web site content, and therefore gives you more control to produce better designs. Since the drawing tools are very easy to use, one can make these diagrams quickly, giving you more time to focus on designing the site architecture and navigation.

Navigation

The navigation bar on a Web page is designed in two traditional ways. The most common approach is with the main navigation bar displayed running across the top of the Web page from left to right, as shown in Figure 5.3. This approach is often seen in search portal sites like *Yahoo.com* and *Google.com*, and online store sites like *Amazon.com* and *eBay.com*. Having the navigation bar at the top works well for these types of sites because they have so much content to display and need the extra room.

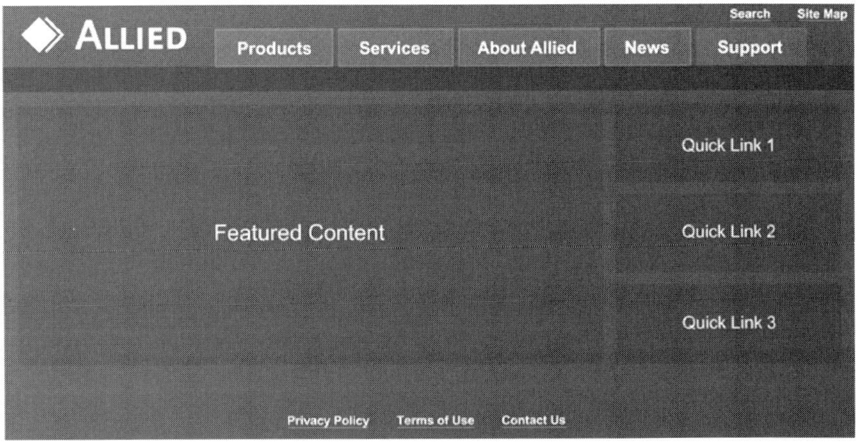

FIGURE 5.3 A home page with the navigation on the top.

To understand how the user will access the content a level deeper, review Figure 5.4. Notice how another horizontal row is added to display the next level of links.

Having the navigation bar on the left is the second most common place to put it, as shown in Figure 5.5. This approach is often seen in corporate Web sites like *Microsoft.com* or *PeopleSoft.com*. It is more formal than having the navigation on the top and leaves less room horizontally for content. Users are quite familiar with this style because it mimics the folder design your operating systems use.

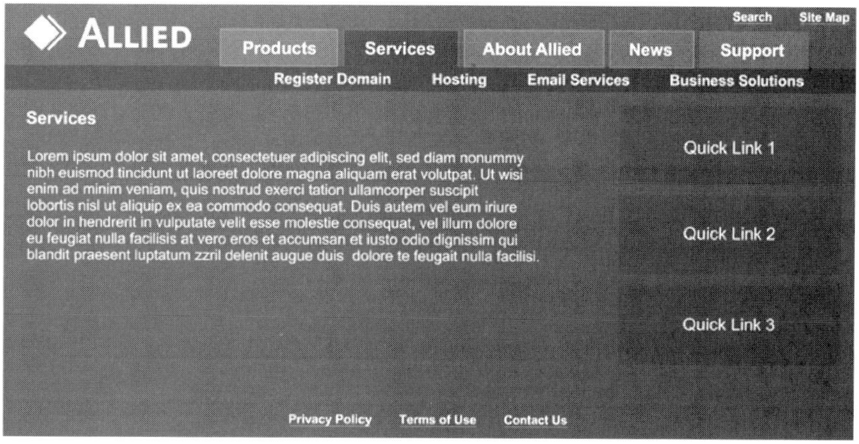

FIGURE 5.4 The top navigation displaying another level of links.

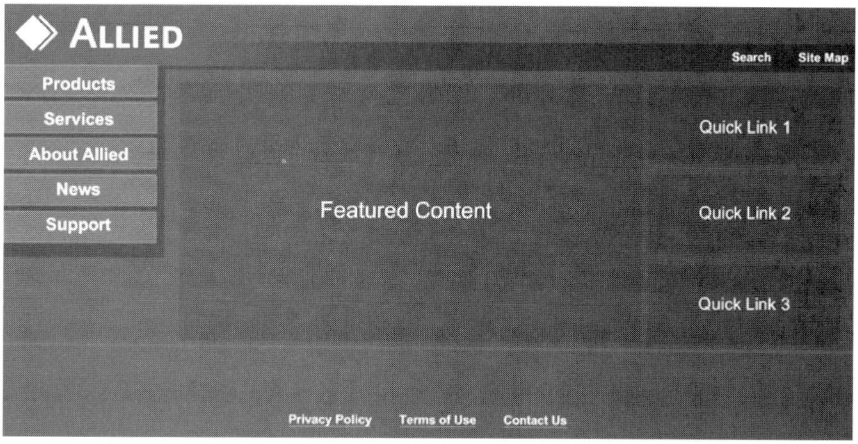

FIGURE 5.5 A home page with the navigation on the left.

To understand how the user will access the content a level deeper, review Figure 5.6. Notice how the lower part of the navigation moves down to make room for the next level of links.

From browsing the Web and analyzing many different Web sites, it seems most navigation bars are at the top, yet every site seems to place them slightly differently or use a combination of the two styles, meaning traditional approaches are being practiced less. You will find that the more creative the company may be, the higher the odds its navigation will not be traditional.

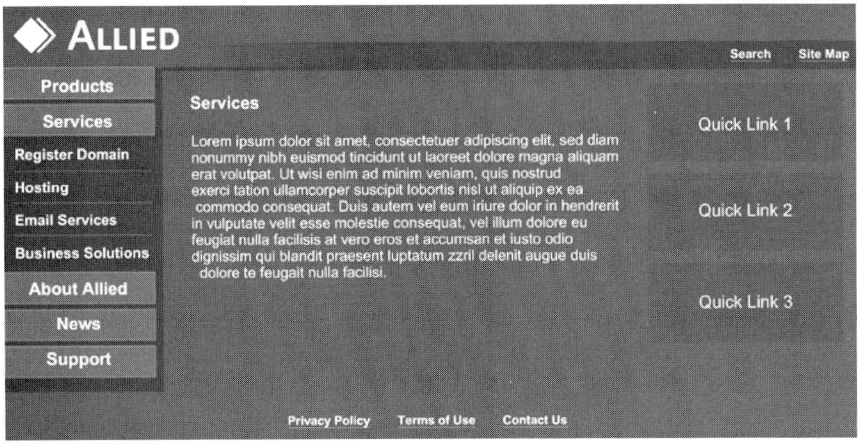

FIGURE 5.6 The side navigation displaying another level of links.

LOGOS

All company or product logos are created in a vector-based drawing program; that way, at whatever resolution they need it, the graphic can be scaled and will not lose its quality. Logos are any type of graphic that symbolizes a company's brand or product. Other terms you might hear are *icon,* which is a symbol with no text, and *font type,* which is text with no icons. Often, icons and font types are put together to form a company's logo. Knowing this, Macromedia Flash is a perfect illustration tool to create logos, since it is a vector-based program with strong drawing tools.

Icons

Here, we review the steps it took to create the ElectroServer™ icon for the company Electrotank, Inc. This icon was used as part of their branding for a popular socket-server, which enables their customers to create multiuser applications. As shown in Figure 5.7, the icon is only part of the entire logo. Next to the icon is a font type, which spells the product name. Although the icon may look simple, to get the precision of the lighting bolt in the center took some work.

FIGURE 5.7 ElectroServer logo. Courtesy of Electrotank, Inc.

With the Rectangle tool, draw a perfect square, as shown in Figure 5.8. To lock the tool into producing a perfect square, hold down the Shift key while dragging your cursor to create the square.

Now, divide the square into eight different pie shapes. Start by connecting lines from each corner of the square forming an X. Then, draw lines that divide the square horizontally and vertically from the center point of the X, as seen in Figure 5.9.

FIGURE 5.8 Square line drawing.

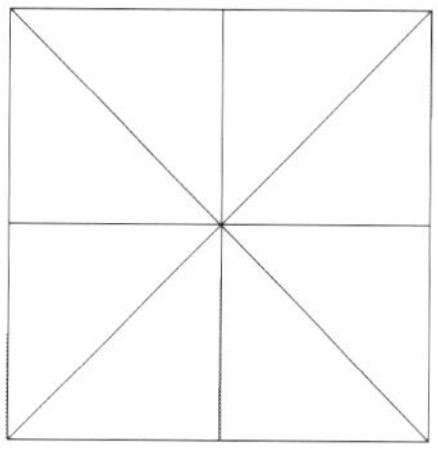

FIGURE 5.9 Square line drawing divided into eight pie shapes.

Delete the X-shaped lines first drawn. Select the horizontal line, copy it, and paste it in place, moving it up by two to three up arrow keystrokes. With the new line selected and repositioned, copy it, paste it in place, and move it down twice the amount you moved the first line up. For example, if we moved the first line three up arrow keystrokes, and then move the newly created line down six down arrow keystrokes, you should have something like that shown in Figure 5.10.

FIGURE 5.10 Certain lines are added and deleted.

Now we are going to create the angled line, which will make up the center of the lightning bolt. Select the vertical line in the middle of the square with the Selection tool, and open your Transform panel. Click the Rotate button and enter 15 in the Rotate text box, as shown in Figure 5.11.

Next, press the Enter key on your keyboard to execute the transformation and you should have a result as shown in Figure 5.12.

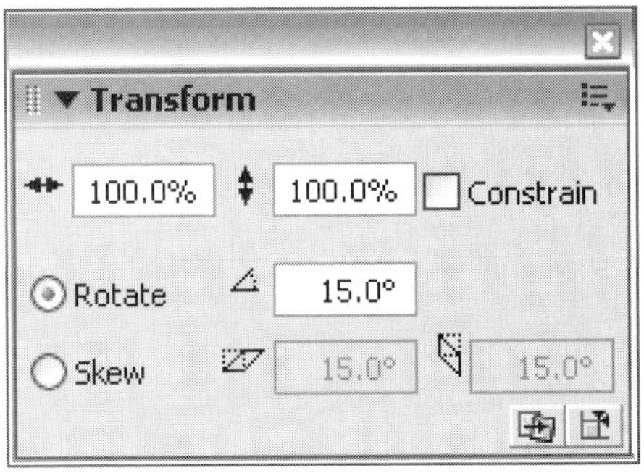

FIGURE 5.11 Rotate the center line by 15%.

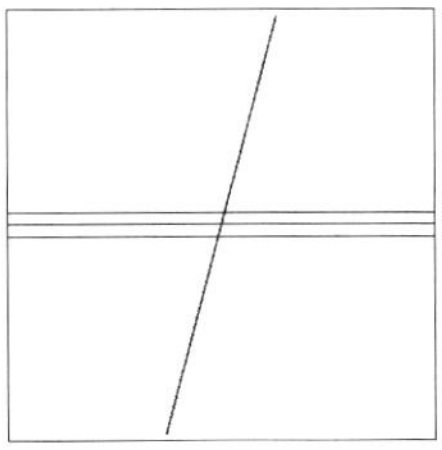

FIGURE 5.12 Center line is rotated and displayed at an angle.

The diagonal line is quite long and will need to be trimmed. Each lightning bolt will protrude halfway into each half of the square. To make sure the diagonal line is the perfect length, we will divide the two horizontal halves of the square in half. To do that by using the Line tool, draw an X shape within the two horizontal halves, as shown in Figure 5.13. Draw a horizontal line where the two lines meet forming the X shape. This is where the tip of the lightning bolt will stop.

Delete all unnecessary lines, leaving you with the outer square, diagonal line, and the two equally spaced horizontal lines that will define the horizontal center of the lightning bolt, as shown in Figure 5.14.

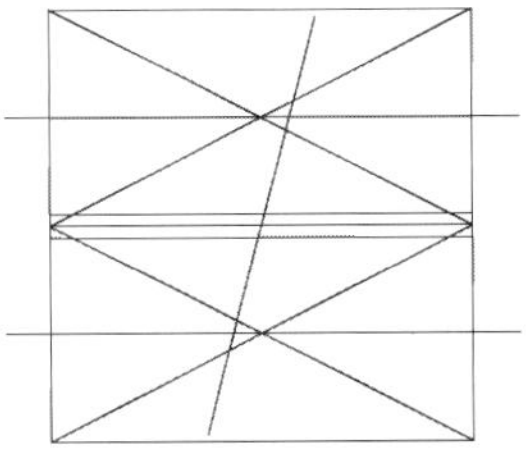

FIGURE 5.13 Creating guidelines to find the center points of the two halves of the square.

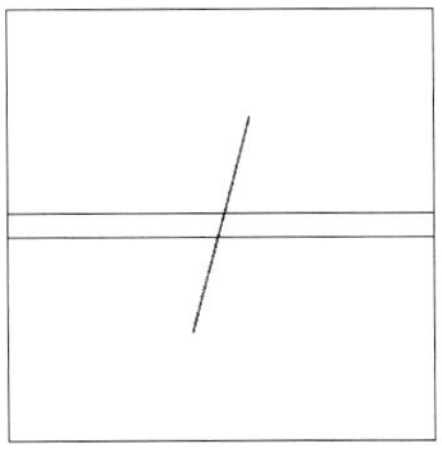

FIGURE 5.14 Delete all unwanted lines.

With the Line tool, draw two lines, each creating the horizontal diagonal line forming the top and bottom of the lightning bolt, as shown in Figure 5.15.

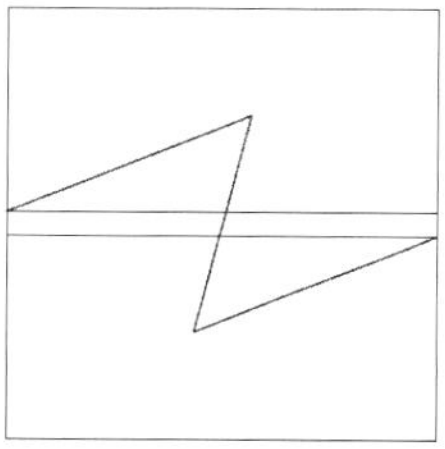

FIGURE 5.15 Draw two angled lines forming the shape of the lightning bolt.

To create the outer circle of the icon and to make sure it will not conflict with other lines already drawn, we want to initially draw it on a new layer. Therefore, create a new layer and place it on top of the first one we have been working on. Lock the first layer and execute the shortcut key to switch to the Oval tool. Focus on the new layer and draw a perfect circle, as shown in Figure 5.16. To make sure the perfect circle is drawn over the existing square, have the Snap to Objects feature on and hold the Shift key down as you are drawing the circle.

Now, to make sure there is a perfect composite of both the lightning line drawing and the circle line drawing, you must unlock the lower layer and delete the square line shape, so all you are left with is the lightning shape. Then, select the perfect circle on the top layer with the Selection tool and delete it. Focus on the lower layer with the lightning line drawing, and Paste in Place the perfect circle, as shown in Figure 5.17.

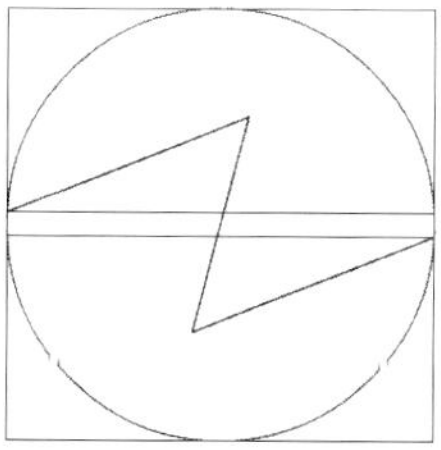

FIGURE 5.16 Create the outer circle shape of the logo.

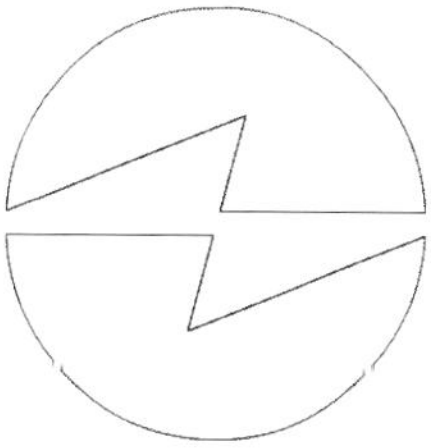

FIGURE 5.17 Delete any unwanted lines. Courtesy of Electrotank, Inc.

With your Color Mixer panel, create a solid fill with a HEX value of #2762C2. Execute the shortcut key to switch to the Paint Bucket tool, select the newly created color swatch, apply it to the outline of the icon, and delete the outlines, as shown in Figure 5.18. By using this approach, you should have an optimized icon of 16 curves, which is very small.

FIGURE 5.18 Fill area within the lines and delete the unwanted lines to complete the icon.
Courtesy of Electrotank, Inc.

Font Type

Font types are often used to create text of varying styles, but many times just using a special font is not enough. Especially for online games or a flashy product line, an elaborate illustrated font type is needed, as shown in Figure 5.19. This particular font-type logo was created for an online puzzle game for Electrotank, Inc. Contrary to some people's first impression, the logo was illustrated entirely in Macromedia Flash. For the next dozen figures, we will be focusing on the letter F and how the highlights and outer strokes were created.

FIGURE 5.19 Fruit Smash game logo. Courtesy of Electrotank, Inc.

The font type used in this logo is a modification of an already existing font type and cannot be distributed, but if you wish to follow along with this exercise, any font type will work. With the Text tool, type the capital letter F with a font size of about 120 points and in black, as shown in Figure 5.20.

Break the font down by executing the shortcut key to break apart the text. With the Ink Bottle tool, apply a solid stroke style with a stroke height of 8 to the broken letter F, as shown in Figure 5.21.

With the Selection tool, select the red line, delete it, paste it in place on a new layer below the black F, and convert line to fill, as shown in Figure 5.22. To access this function, go to Modify > Shape > Convert Lines to Fills. This is important to do because later we will be adding a stroke on the converted line and changing its color.

FIGURE 5.20 Type the letter F. Courtesy of Electrotank, Inc.

FIGURE 5.21 Add a stroke around the fill shape F. Courtesy of Electrotank, Inc.

FIGURE 5.22 Convert the stroke to a fill. Courtesy of Electrotank, Inc.

Go back to the first layer with the black F on it and add another stroke, this time applying a green solid stroke style with a stroke height of 5. Select this new line, delete it, and paste it in place on a new layer above all the other layers we have created. Once on its own layer, convert the line into a fill, as shown in Figure 5.23.

Execute the shortcut key to switch to the Ink Bottle tool, and apply a red hairline stroke around the green fill, as shown in Figure 5.24.

Select the green fill with the Selection tool and delete it, as shown in Figure 5.25. We will no longer need it.

With the Selection tool, select the outer line, delete it, and paste it in place on the same layer that contains the red outline fill. Switch to the Line

FIGURE 5.23 Add another stroke to the fill-shaped F. Courtesy of Electrotank, Inc.

FIGURE 5.24 Convert the stroke to a fill and add strokes to the inner and outer part of the fill. Courtesy of Electrotank, Inc.

FIGURE 5.25 Delete the fill. Courtesy of Electrotank, Inc.

tool and edit the outline as shown in Figure 5.26. These newly shaped lines will give us an outline to give dimension to the letter.

Switch to the Paint Bucket tool, apply a dark red color to the areas shown in Figure 5.27, and delete the lines used.

Go to the top layer, and with the Selection tool, select the inner line. Copy it and paste it in place. At 100% view, use your arrow keys to move the line down two down arrow clicks and left three left arrow clicks. Once positioned, deselect the line by executing the shortcut key to Deselect All graphics, as shown in Figure 5.28.

Execute the shortcut key to switch to the Selection tool, select the unwanted lines, and delete them, as shown in Figure 5.29.

FIGURE 5.26 Modify the outer line. Courtesy of Electrotank, Inc.

FIGURE 5.27 Apply a fill to the modified line area and delete the lines. Courtesy of Electrotank, Inc.

FIGURE 5.28 Select the inner line, duplicate it, and position it. Courtesy of Electrotank, Inc.

Execute the shortcut key to open the Color Mixer, and create and save the following color swatch. Create a solid fill with a HEX value of #FFFFFF, and an alpha value of 90%. To add the swatch to your Color Swatches panel, click on the menu drop-down button in the upper right corner of the Color Mixer panel and click the Add Swatch button. It is recommended that all specially made fills or gradient fills are saved in this manner to be accessed quickly in any of the Color Swatches found in Flash. Once saved, execute the shortcut key to switch to the Paint Bucket tool, and select the new color swatch you just created by selecting the Fill Color menu item in the Color area of your Tools panel. Apply the color to the outline areas as shown in Figure 5.30 and delete the outlines.

Hide the top layer, which should contain the highlight we just finished. Go to the center layer, which should contain the black fill of the letter F. Execute the shortcut key to switch to the Pencil tool, and in the Tools panel, make sure the line style is set to Smooth. Draw two curved lines, as shown in Figure 5.31, with the Pencil tool. Another way to draw these lines is with the Line tool. By plotting straight lines and switching to the Selection tool, grab the center of the lines and drag down to apply a curve to them. Using the Line tool in this way will give you a more optimized curve versus using the Pencil tool.

Now that the letter F fill is divided into three pieces, execute the shortcut key to open the Color Mixer panel to start creating linear gradients to fill in these areas. The first linear gradient we will be creating will be placed in the top fill. In the Color Mixer, set the Fill Style to Linear with the settings Swatch #1 to the left, #FF6900, and Swatch #2 to the right, #FF9F00, both with an alpha of 100%, as shown in Figure 5.32. Once you are satisfied with the gradient, click the Add Swatch menu item to save it.

FIGURE 5.29 Delete the unwanted lines to show the areas where we will apply the highlight fills. Courtesy of Electrotank, Inc.

FIGURE 5.30 Apply a fill to the outlined area and delete the lines. Courtesy of Electrotank, Inc.

FIGURE 5.31 Draw the curved lines that will set the three areas to fill. Courtesy of Electrotank, Inc.

The second linear gradient will be placed in the middle fill. Keep the Fill Style at Linear with the settings Swatch #1 to the left, #FF8E00, and Swatch #2 to the right, #FEC023, both with an alpha of 100%, as shown in Figure 5.33. Once you are satisfied with the gradient, click the Add Swatch menu item to save it.

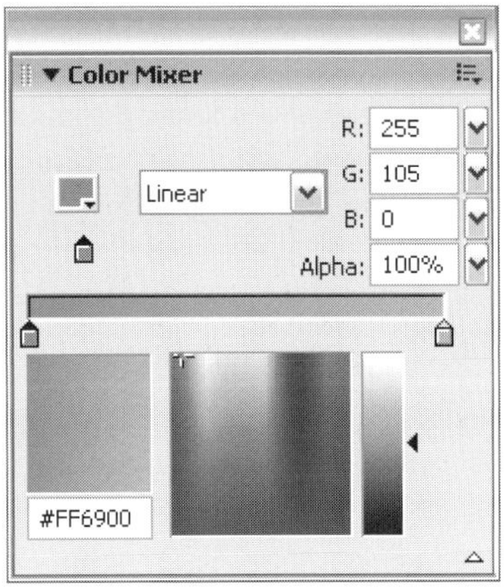

FIGURE 5.32 Create a linear gradient that will be applied in the top fill graphic.

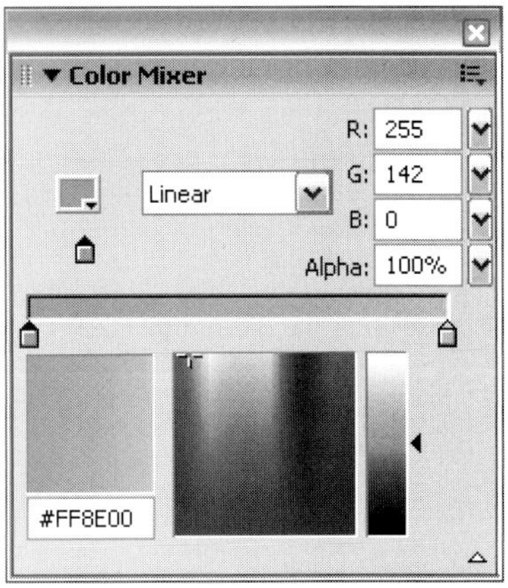

FIGURE 5.33 Create another linear gradient that will be applied in the center fill graphic.

The last linear gradient will be placed in the bottom fill. Keep the Fill Style to Linear with the settings Swatch #1 to the left, #FED21C, and Swatch #2 to the right, #FFFFB5, both with an alpha of 100%, as shown in Figure 5.34. Once you are satisfied with the gradient, click the Add Swatch menu item to save it.

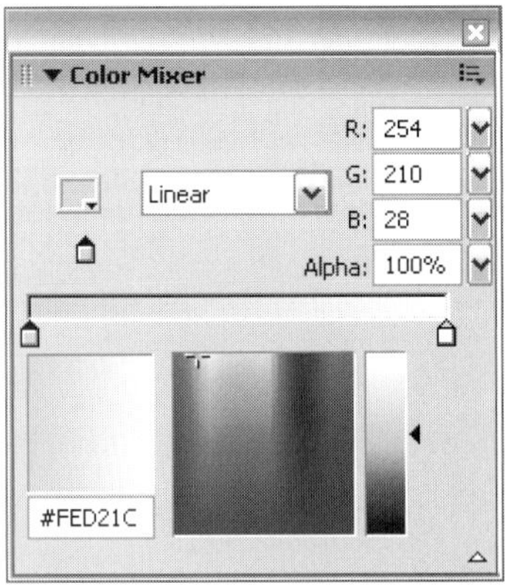

FIGURE 5.34 Create another linear gradient that will be applied in the bottom fill graphic.

Now that all the linear gradients have been created and saved, execute the shortcut key to switch to your Paint Bucket tool. Select the color swatches you just created by selecting the Fill Color menu item in the Color area of your Tools panel, and apply them in their designated fills, as stated in the previous steps and as shown in Figure 5.35. If you need to adjust the placement or scale of the linear gradients, use the Fill Transform tool. After applying the linear fills, delete the two curved lines used to divide the F-shaped fill.

FIGURE 5.35 The final rendering of the graphic with all three linear gradients applied. Courtesy of Electrotank, Inc.

USER INTERFACES

Every Web page has some idea or story behind it as to why it was designed a certain way and how certain elements were achieved. Here, we will review two different Web pages and analyze why and how certain things were done. You will learn several different approaches to getting down your initial design. Ultimately, this exercise will open your mind to the many ways Macromedia Flash plays a part in creating professional-looking designs and innovative interactive Web pages.

ElectroServer Web Site

A Web site to market server software will most likely not contain abstract designs or crazy Flash animations. In fact, the ElectroServer Web site's main purpose is to be informative and very descriptive on the software's special features and overall capabilities. With the idea that this site must convey a lot of information in the short amount of time the user will be looking at the site, the content has to be displayed in a traditional and straightforward manner—which leads to the first sketch of the home page, as shown in Figure 5.36. Notice how the main content is at the top left. It is important that the user read the brief description of the product, and then the three selling points listed below. Then, off to the left is the user navigation. Assuming users are still interested after reading the brief description, they will find the user navigation useful to direct them to more in-depth information about the product. Sketching out your initial designs is a great way to get your ideas down on paper first and visualize which design approach will work best. It is also a great way to focus on content layout and plan the flow of how a user might read your content.

FIGURE 5.36 Sketch of the ElectroServer home page. Courtesy of Electrotank, Inc.

ON THE CD

Figure 5.37 shows the finished design look of the home page. Notice how the design is simple, which lets the user focus on the text content. The colors used went along with the company's original branding colors. The images do a great job of drawing attention to the three selling points.

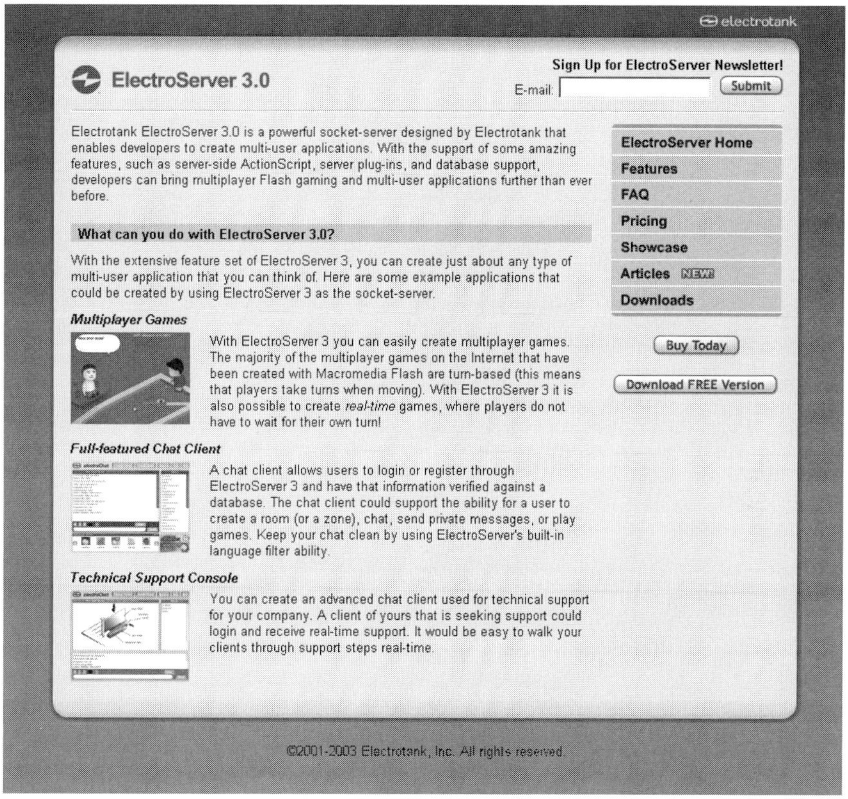

FIGURE 5.37 Final design of the ElectroServer home page. Courtesy of Electrotank, Inc.

Electro Air Hockey Web Site

In contrast to the ElectroServer Web site, the Electro Air Hockey Web site contains outrageous design and Flash animations. This particular Web site's purpose is to market an air hockey computer game that contains game features, character information, screen shots, and extra downloads. As you may know, air hockey is an aggressive game, and therefore justifies the radical design and look and feel. In the sketch shown in Figure 5.38, notice how the angled lines and large character graphics help convey that feel.

As shown in Figure 5.39, you can see how the top graphics, logo, and user navigation contain great motion, moving the user's eyes across the Web page. Then, the lower side character graphic brings the user's eye down to the body content. Marketing a product that contains characters or themes can be easier to design because you have many more design elements to work into your design. Use Flash to make some mockups of

FIGURE 5.38 Sketch of the Electro Air Hockey home page.
Courtesy of Electrotank, Inc.

FIGURE 5.39 Final design of the Electro Air Hockey home page. Courtesy of Electrotank, Inc.

how ambient animations can play a part in making your Web page feel more alive and interactive. In this instance, a quick animation was created in Flash to visualize how the animation would enhance the user experience. Sometimes, doing a mockup is a quick way to help you understand that a particular idea will not work and you can move on to the next idea.

INCORPORATE VIDEO

ON THE CD

Video can make a static, boring Web page come alive with motion and action. There are many ways to bring video into your Flash project, and many require knowledge of ActionScript and server programming. For this example, we will be importing video into Flash the basic way, which is to embed it into your project. Flash supports the video formats mov, avid, mpeg, wavy, and flu. On the companion CD-ROM is a mov file for you to work with located in Chapter_5/intro_fs.mov. Start a new document in Flash, and to import a video, access File > Import > Import Video. A window will pop up asking where the video file is, as shown in Figure 5.40. Click the Browse button and find the intro_fs.mov file. Once you have located the file, click the Next button at the bottom of the window.

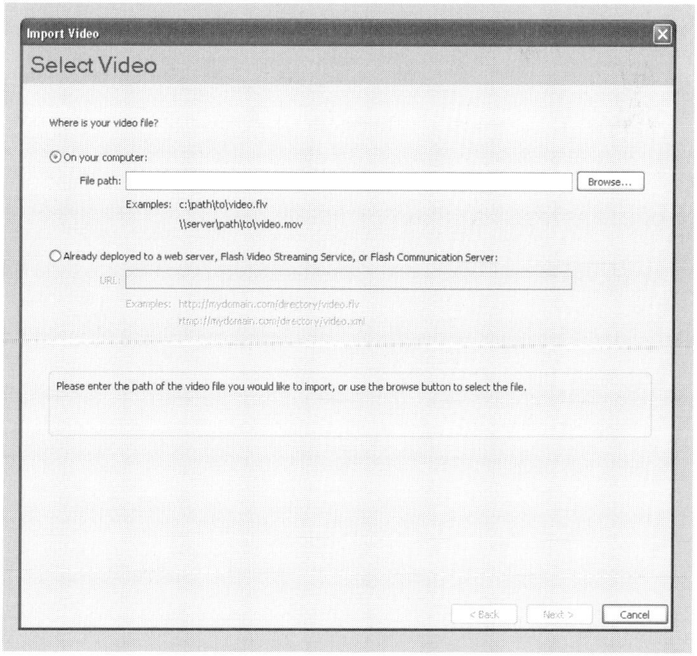

FIGURE 5.40 Locating the mov file.

The next screen will ask you how you want to deploy the video. Click the radio button to have the video embedded into the SWF and play in the timeline, as shown in Figure 5.41. Click the Next button to continue.

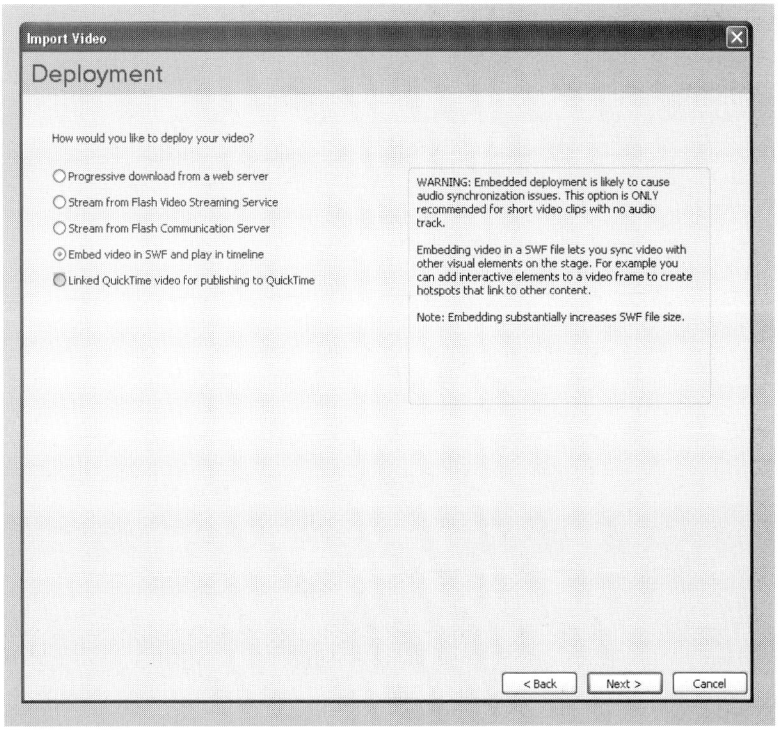

FIGURE 5.41 Choose how to deploy the video.

The next screen asks you how you would like to embed the video, as shown in Figure 5.42. For this example, let us keep the settings at default and click the Next button to continue.

The next screen wants to know how you want the video encoded or compressed, as shown in Figure 5.43. There are a couple of quality levels to choose from; the lower the quality, the more grain and chunky pixels in your movie. It is recommended to compress your movie prior to importing it into Flash, and programs like Sorenson Squeeze for Flash can give you smaller video file sizes and still maintain high-quality video. Choose Flash 8 – Medium Quality (400kps) for this example, and click the Next button to continue. Next, Flash will embed the video on the main timeline.

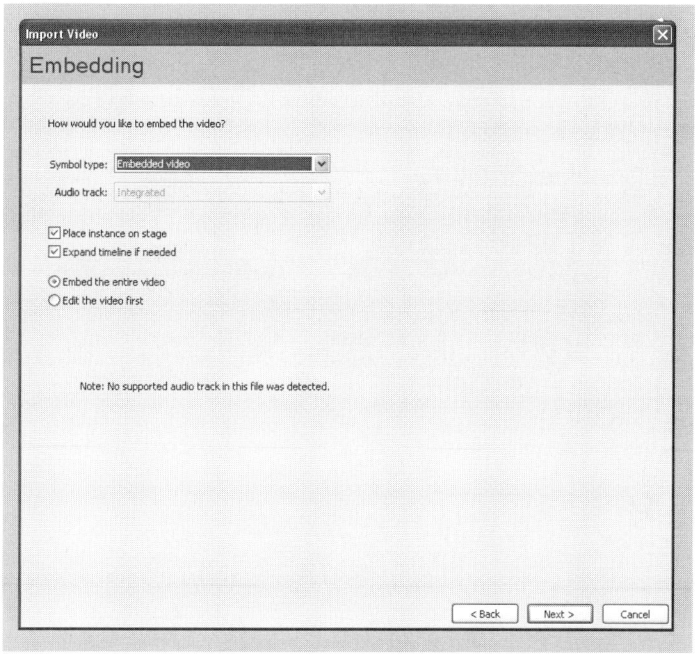

FIGURE 5.42 Choose how to embed the video.

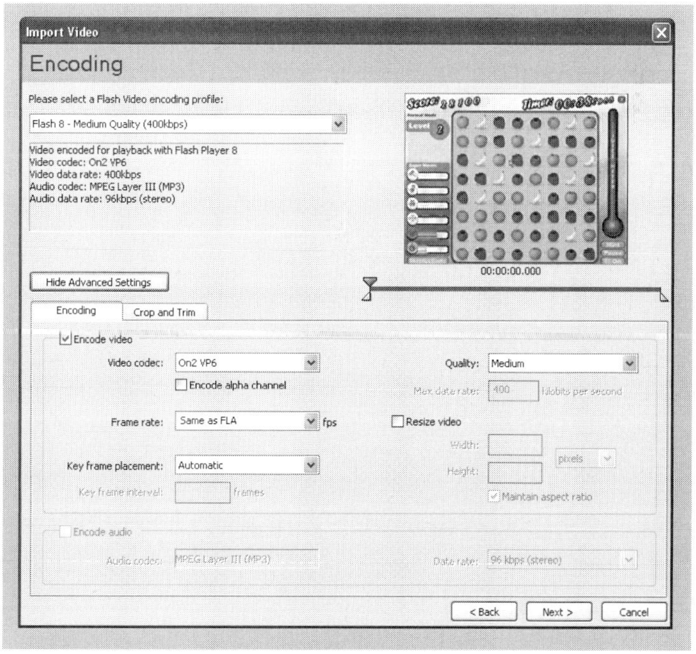

FIGURE 5.43 Choose video encoding.

Adding Code

Create two new layers in the Timeline panel. Create a Keyframe on the last frame of the new layers you created, as shown in Figure 5.44. Select the last frame, and to make it a Keyframe, access Insert > Timeline > Keyframe. On the top layer, select the keyframe and open the Actions panel by accessing Window > Actions. The main programming window should be active with your cursor, so type

```
Stop();
```

which means that when the movie gets to this frame, it will be told to stop, not start over.

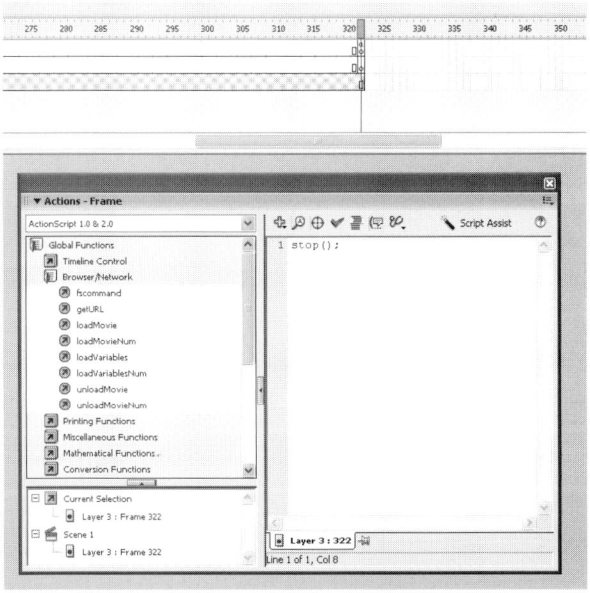

FIGURE 5.44 Adding a stop action to the end of the timeline.

Select the other blank keyframe you created. Get the Rectangle tool, create a square covering the video, select the square, and convert it to a symbol. Click the radio button for Button, and click OK. Double-click on the button you just made, going inside it. Select the frame with the graphic in it, which should be on frame 1, and drag and drop it on frame 4. Frames 1 through 3 should be blank now. Return to the main timeline by accessing View > Go to > First. Select the button, and with the Actions panel still open, click the Script Assist button at the top of the user interface in the Actions panel, as shown in Figure 5.45. This will simplify the act of writing code. Notice the left-side user interface, and click on Global Functions > Browser/Network > getURL. This should place the following code in the main programming window:

```
getURL("");
```

In the URL text box, type *http://www.fruit-smash.com/purchase.asp*. In the Window drop-down, select _blank.

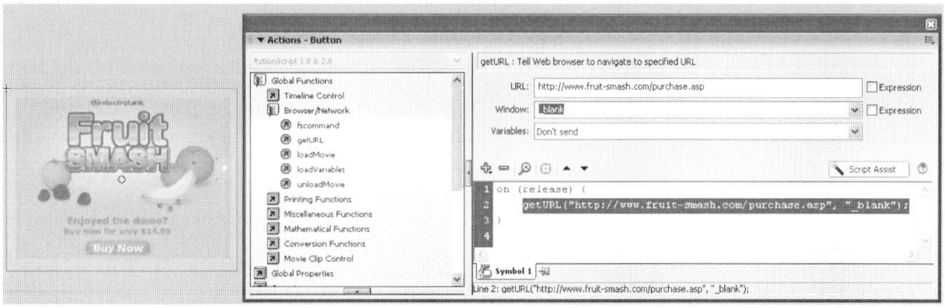

FIGURE 5.45 Create a button and add a link to it.

ON THE CD

To publish what you have, access File > Publish. To show you how the video will look on a Web page, see the file Chapter_5/intro_fs.mov on the companion CD-ROM and Figure 5.46.

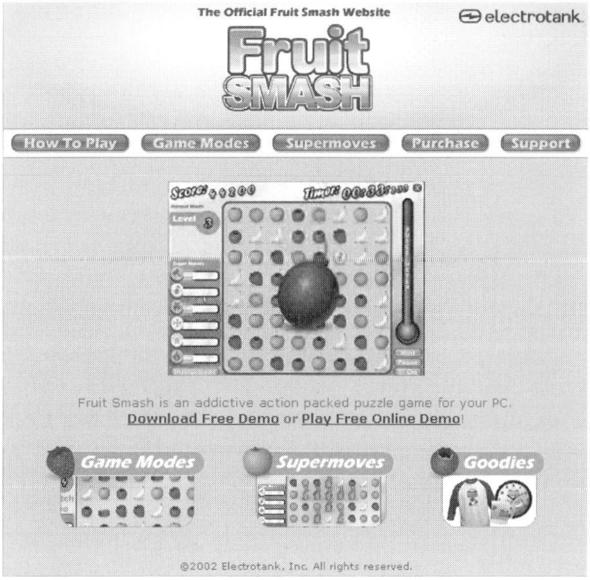

FIGURE 5.46 The SWF with embedded video placed in a Web page.

Summary

- Use Macromedia Flash to design Web site architecture and navigation.
- Since Macromedia Flash is a vector-based program, and graphics can be exported at any dpi, you can use the program to design company logos or any other print designs.
- Use different line width settings to create borders of color around your graphics.
- Understand who your target audience is to develop a design with which they will be able to connect.
- Decide the order in which you want your audience to view certain content on your Web site, and lay out your content accordingly.

Exercises

Design is everywhere, and anything you see had to be designed at some time—from the look of the computer that Flash is on to the user interface in Flash. For the following exercises, we will be helping a small neighborhood bakery with its online presence—its logo, site architecture, and Web site design. This bakery is called Teresa's Bakery, which specializes in an assortment of Italian breads. When you walk past the store, you can smell the pungent aroma of their delicious breads, and they want to capture that essence in their brand. They need a Web site to sell their breads online globally, let people know who they are and what they do, and report investor information. The owners like the colors red and orange, symbolizing harvest season. All these exercises can and should be executed in Flash with the drawing tools.

1. Create a logo from the following information we know. The logo should be about 50 × 50 pixels in size and one color. Remember, logos should be simple in shape and communicate what the company does. Figure 5.47 shows a variety of logos.
2. Create site architecture for the home page of the bakery's Web site. This should include what Web pages the site consists of, and the content included on the home page. Before we start designing the page, we have to know what content will be on it. In most cases, you should ask the client if they have any content to start with. In our case, we know what they want to do with their site—sell different kinds of bread, tell people who they are and what they do, and report investor information.
3. Create the design for the main page of the Web site. With the site architecture done, you now know what content is needed on the home page and what links to other pages are necessary in the main navigation. You have designed the company logo, and that needs to be incorporated into your home page design.

FIGURE 5.47 Examples of other logos. Courtesy of Electrotank, Inc.

CHAPTER

6 ANIMATION TECHNIQUES

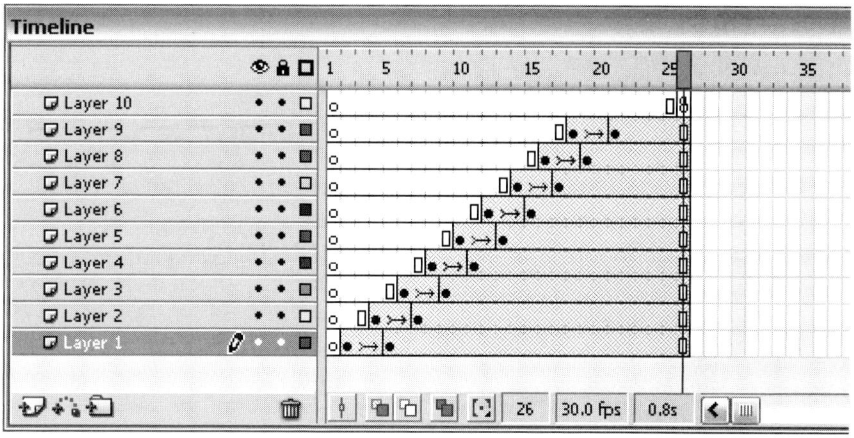

Traditional animations are created by displaying a series of images one by one, which makes it look like an object is moving. Since Macromedia Flash's animations are primarily streamed over the Internet for viewing, including a series of images for every frame of animation would give you a file too big to stream to your viewer. To create optimized animations of minimal file size, several techniques can be used. The most popular is the motion tween feature in Macromedia Flash. Architecting a movie clip inside a movie clip, both containing motion tweens, can achieve dynamic motion and a small file size, thanks to Flash's animation features.

CREATE LOOPING ANIMATIONS

Creating a motion tween is quite simple, and with the motion tween properties available—Ease, Rotate, Orient to Path, Sync, and Snap—much more complicated animations can be achieved. With Flash 8, you now have the enhancements Custom Ease In/Out, Rotate Clockwise/Counter Clockwise, and Blend with Shape tweens. To begin, we will focus on the basic idea of how motion tweens work and how they can be used to their full potential. A motion tween is comprised of two keyframes that contain the same movie clip graphic but in different positions, rotation, color, filter, or blend settings. Since a movie clip contains its own timeline, it could contain its own motion tween. Knowing this, imagine we need to animate a bee flying in the air. As shown in Figure 6.1, two things need to be animated, the bee moving up and down and the wings rotating. Analyzing the figure, you can see that the animation of the bee moving up and down could hold the animation of the wings flapping. Set your movie's frame rate to 30 frames per second (fps) by accessing the document properties. The standard frame rate

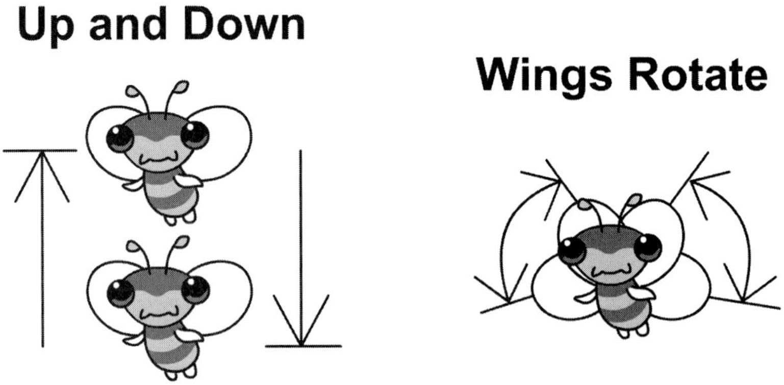

FIGURE 6.1 The two key animations involved in portraying flying animation.
Courtesy of Electrotank, Inc.

for Web animations is 15 fps, and the standard frame rate for game animations is 30 fps. Although this may be different from what your in-house production uses, it is mostly a personal preference depending on how optimized or fluid you need your animations to be. Web animations can use a lower frame rate because optimization is more important, while frame rate in games needs to be higher for smoother game play. The lower the frame rate, the fewer keyframes you need to portray a motion.

Take a closer look at how the animation of the bee is set up. As shown in Figure 6.2, the animation is comprised of three keyframes, which are symbolized in the timeline as black dots. Each keyframe contains the same movie clip graphic but in a different position. To get Flash to animate the frames between two keyframes, you have to select a keyframe, open the Properties panel, click on the Tween drop-down menu, and choose Motion. This should change the color of the keyframe to a light purple and will display an arrow in the keyframe where the motion tween was applied. Note that the first keyframe and the second keyframe in your motion tween must contain the same movie clip. If other graphics or movie clips are in either of the keyframes, the motion tween may not work properly and will display a dashed line instead of an arrow. In addition, if you modify the center point of the movie clip in one of the keyframes, the motion tween will animate strangely. Make sure to set the center point before duplicating the movie clip or keyframe.

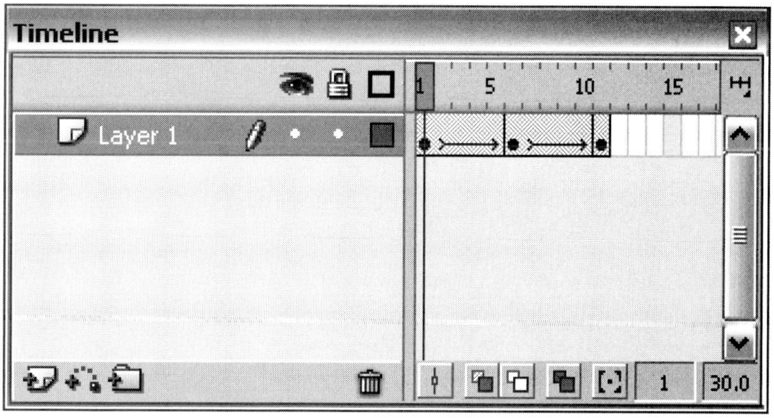

FIGURE 6.2 Timeline of the motion tween that makes the bee move up and down.

Look at the position of the bee movie clips placed next to each other. The first keyframe and the last keyframe are the same, as shown in Figure 6.3. Keyframe 2 contains the same movie clip, but at a lower Y position than the movie clips on keyframes 1 and 3.

FIGURE 6.3 The position of the bee movie clips in the three keyframes of the motion tween. Courtesy of Electrotank, Inc.

The bee movie clip contains a still graphic of the bee and an animation of the wings flapping. As shown in Figure 6.4, this animation is comprised of three layers. The body layer contains the still graphic of the bee without wings. The left wing layer contains a motion tween of the wing rotating facing left. The right wing layer contains a duplicate animation of the wing rotating facing to the left, but the animation was flipped horizontally to make it look like it is rotating facing to the right.

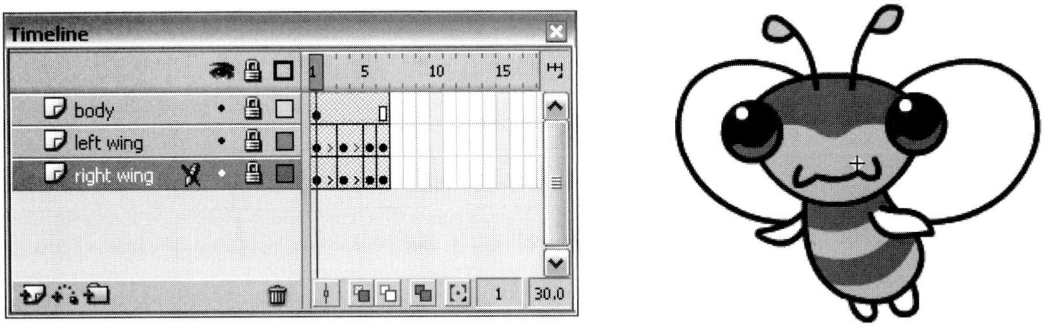

FIGURE 6.4 Timeline of the motion tweens that make the wings rotate up and down. Courtesy of Electrotank, Inc.

Taking a closer look at the first frame, in the left wing layer you will notice that the center point is in the center of the wing, as shown in Figure 6.5. The center point will need to be adjusted so the wing can rotate around a point more accurate to that of a real bee.

To change the center point location of the wing movie clip, select it with the Selection tool and execute the shortcut key to switch to the Free Transform tool. With your cursor, grab the center point and reposition it as shown in Figure 6.6.

On the second keyframe located on frame three, execute the shortcut key to switch to the Free Transform tool and rotate the wing down as shown in Figure 6.7.

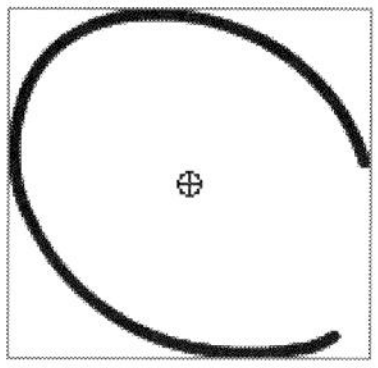

FIGURE 6.5 First keyframe of the motion tween of the left wing rotating.

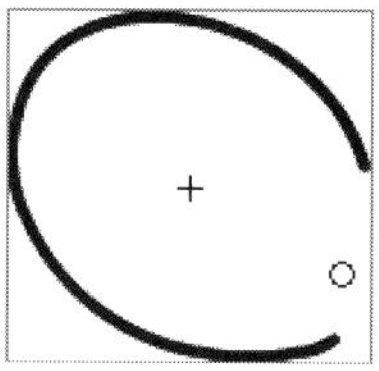

FIGURE 6.6 Modifying the center point of the left wing.

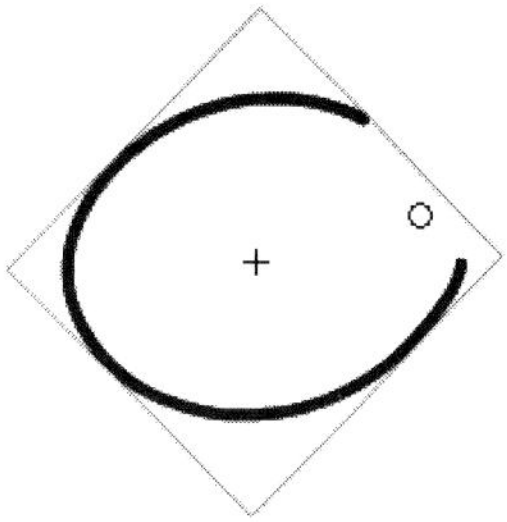

FIGURE 6.7 Second keyframe of the motion tween of the left wing rotating.

On the third keyframe located on frame five with the Free Transform tool still applied, rotate the wing up as shown in Figure 6.8.

On the fourth keyframe located on frame six with the Free Transform tool still applied, rotate the wing down in a position between the rotated positions of the wings in frames one and five, as shown in Figure 6.9. This way, when the wing animation loops it will repeat without the viewer noticing it has started over.

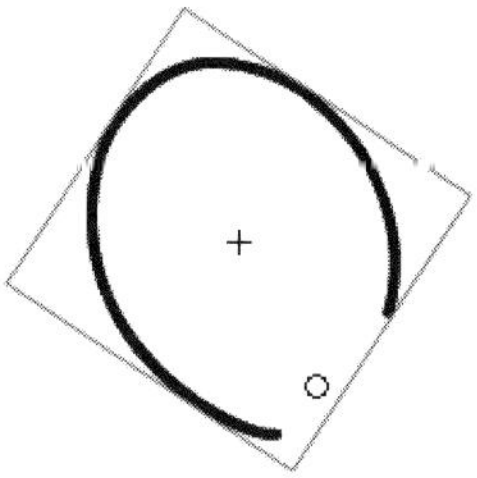

FIGURE 6.8 Third keyframe of the motion tween of the left wing rotating.

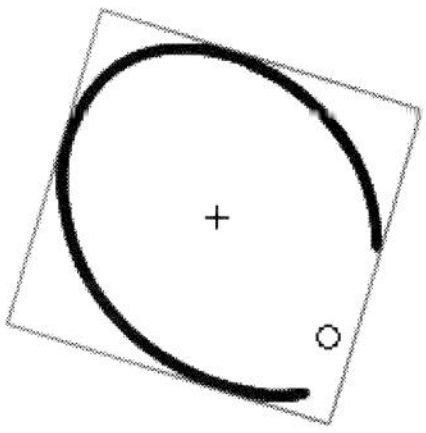

FIGURE 6.9 Fourth keyframe of the motion tween of the left wing rotating.

Now that the left wing animation is complete, it is time to copy it and duplicate it on a new layer. With your cursor, select all the frames, as shown in Figure 6.10. Once selected, execute the shortcut key to copy selected frames. To access the command in the menu, click on Edit > Timeline > Copy Frames.

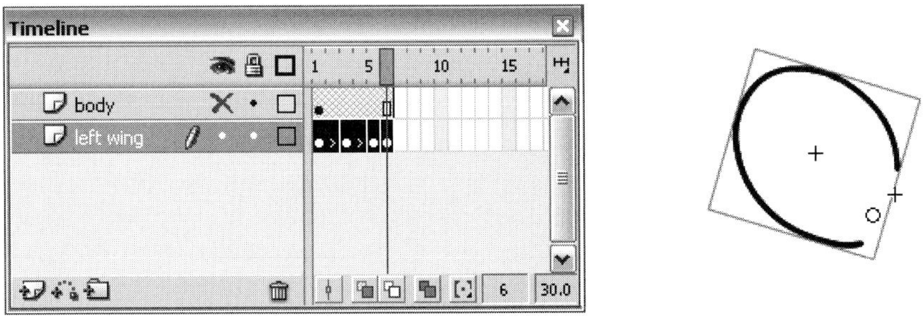

FIGURE 6.10 Select and copy all the frames in the left wing layer.

Create a new layer by clicking on the Insert Layer icon located in the Timeline panel in the bottom-left corner. To access the command in the menu, click on the Insert > Timeline > Layer. Rename the layer by double-clicking on the layer name and typing in "right wing," as shown in Figure 6.11.

To paste the copied frames in the new layer, click and drag your cursor over the blank keyframes to select the blank frames, and execute the shortcut key to paste frames, as shown in Figure 6.12. To access the command in the menu, click on Edit > Timeline > Paste Frames.

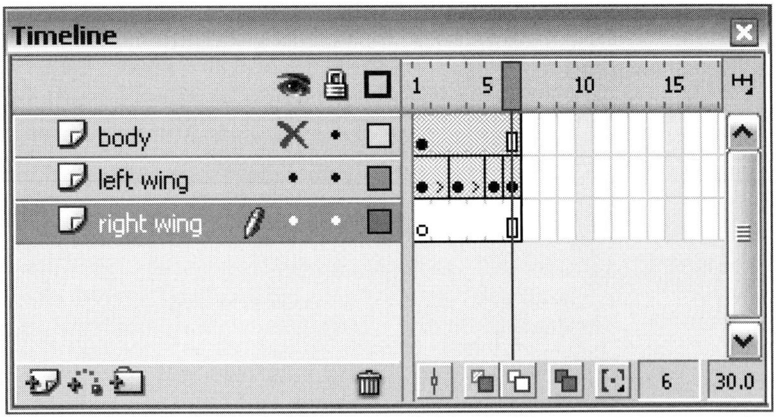

FIGURE 6.11 Create a new layer.

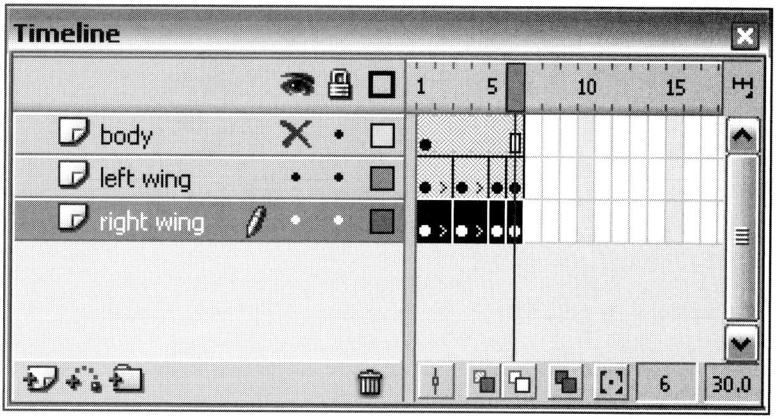

FIGURE 6.12 Paste the copied frames into the new layer.

After pasting the frames, they should remain selected. If for some reason they aren't, select them again. Once selected, to horizontally flip the wings so they are facing to the right, we have to turn on the Onion Skin Outlines and Edit Multiple Frames buttons located at the bottom of the Timeline panel, as shown in Figure 6.13. Make sure the Start Onion Skin point and End Onion Skin point span across the entire animation in the Timeline. The Onion Skin Start and End points are located on the frame number line on the top area of the Timeline panel. Make sure the body and left wing layers are locked so those graphics are not manipulated.

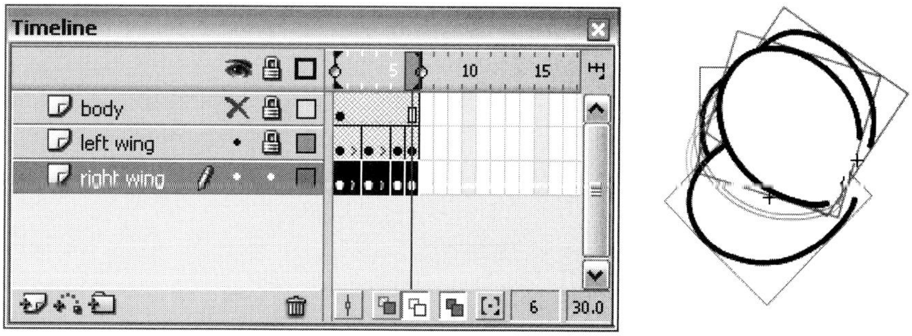

FIGURE 6.13 Turn on Onion Skin Outlines and Edit Multiple Frames, and position Start Onion Skin point and End Onion Skin point spanning the entire animation in the Timeline.

Select all the wing graphics. Once the Onion Skin Outlines and Edit Multiple Frames buttons are pressed and the Onion Skin Start and End points are set, execute the Select All shortcut key to select all the graphics on the right wing layer.

Once all the graphics on the right wing layer are selected, it is time to flip them horizontally. To do so, access the menu items Modify > Transform > Flip Horizontal, as shown in Figure 6.14.

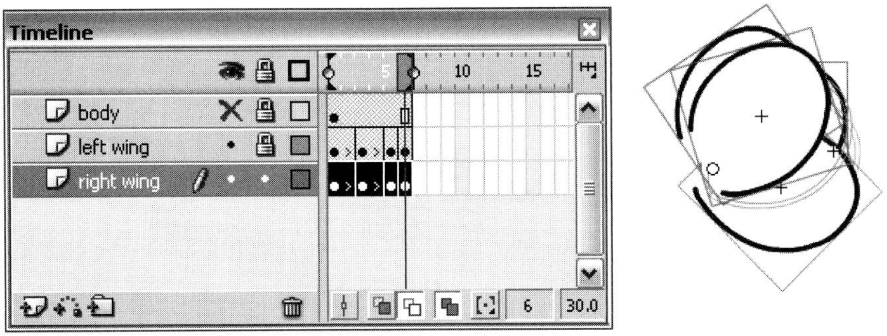

FIGURE 6.14 Flip all the wing graphics horizontally.

While the graphics are still selected, use your right arrow key on your keyboard to position the wings to the right side of the bee, as shown in Figure 6.15. Unhide the body or left wing layer to see exactly where the wings need to be positioned. Make sure you reposition all the wings as instructed for more precise positioning, and do not position them individually. Once you are done positioning the right wings, make sure you unclick the Onion Skin Outlines and Edit Multiple Frames buttons in the Timeline. Feel free to execute the shortcut key to Test Movie to view the animation of the bee flying up and down. To test the movie, access Control > Test Movie.

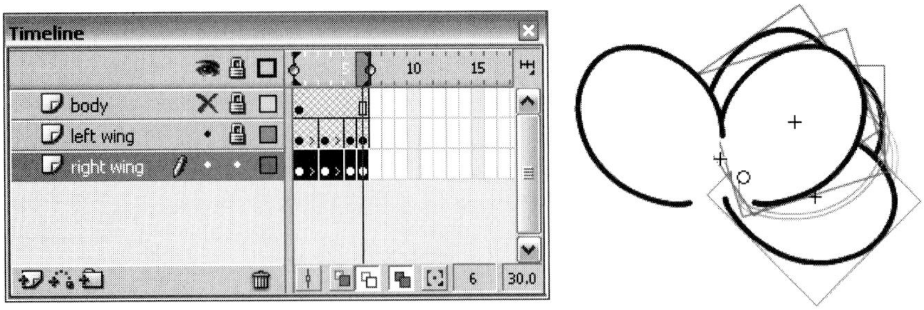

FIGURE 6.15 Reposition the wings to the right.

Text Movement

There are many ways to animate text. The easiest and most efficient way without needing to know any complicated code is to take a similar approach to the bee animation and use multiple movie clips architected together to display text movement. As shown in Figure 6.16, there are two different motions going on in the text animation we will be analyzing. Each letter animates in by scaling up as shown on the right side of Figure 6.16. While this is happening, the letter continually animates up and down as shown on the left side of Figure 6.16. The way these animations will be architected is that the movie clip of the letter scaling will be holding the movie clip of the letter animating up and down. Set your movie's frame rate to 30 fps by accessing the document properties.

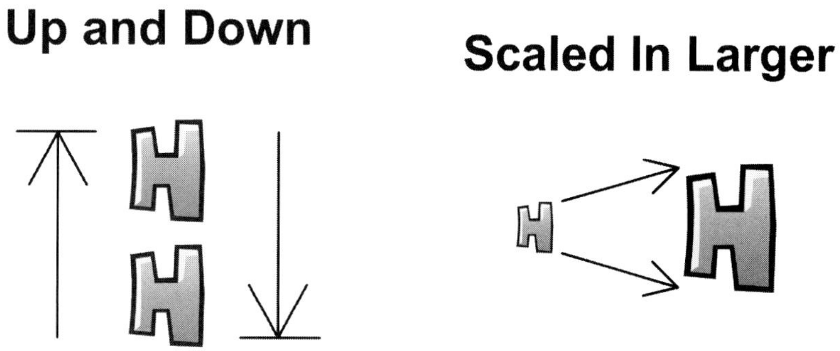

FIGURE 6.16 The two key animations portraying the text movement. Courtesy of Electrotank, Inc.

To further understand how this works, let's look at the movie clip that contains the letter animating up and down. As shown in Figure 6.17, this motion tween is made up of three keyframes.

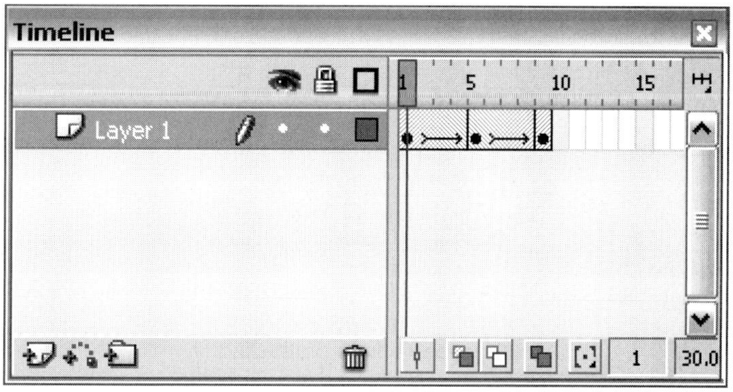

FIGURE 6.17 Timeline of the motion tween that makes the letter move up and down.

To see what is displayed in the three keyframes, we can look at the graphics placed side by side, as shown in Figure 6.18. Notice how in keyframes 1 and 3 the letter is placed in the same position, and the letter in keyframe 2 has a higher Y position. The animation of the letter moving up and down is straightforward and a perfect example of a simple motion tween.

FIGURE 6.18 The position of the letter graphics in the three keyframes of the motion tween. Courtesy of Electrotank, Inc.

To see how the letters are scaled in, we analyze the main movie clip that holds all the animated letters. Animating the letter H scaled in is done with a simple motion tween, as shown in Figure 6.19. We leave the first frame blank to establish visually no letters. The second frame holds the first keyframe of the H letter at a small size. This keyframe is set as a motion tween.

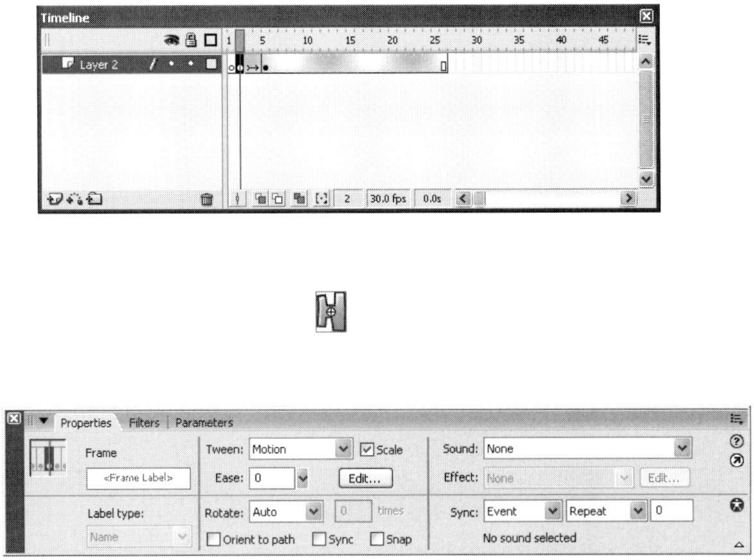

FIGURE 6.19 Timeline of the motion tween making the letter animate up, down, and scale in. Courtesy of Electrotank, Inc.

The last keyframe of the motion tween is on frame 5, which contains the H letter at its largest size, as shown in Figure 6.20. This is just one motion tween of one letter that will be placed in this movie clip.

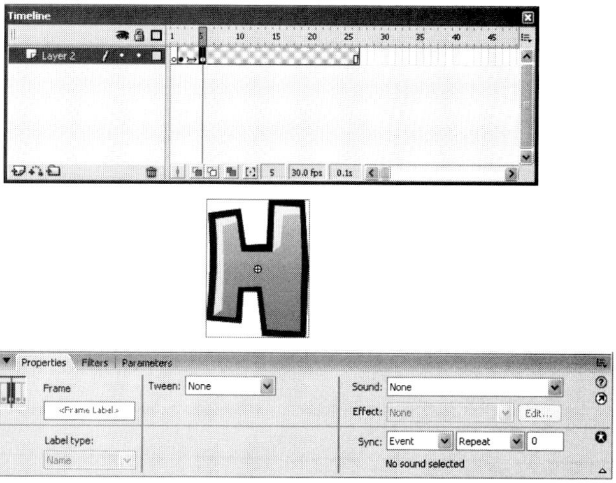

FIGURE 6.20 Last keyframe of the letter scaling in to its largest size. Courtesy of Electrotank, Inc.

Once we apply similar motion tweens to other letters and space the start of the tweens as shown in Figure 6.21, you can see how the animation of the letters scaling in will start to take shape.

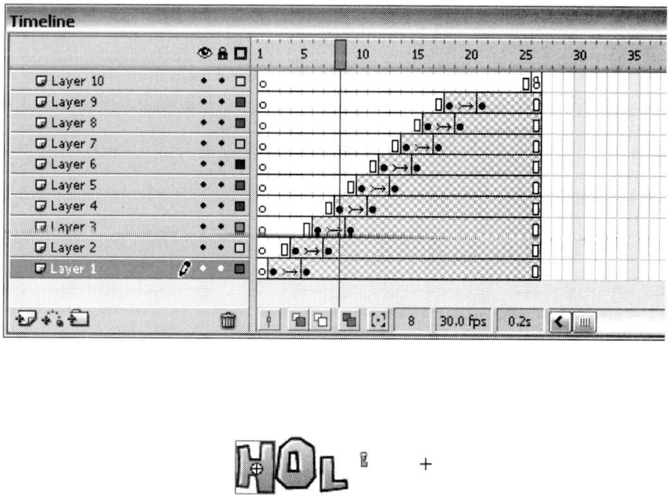

FIGURE 6.21 Adding more letters, tweening them to scale in, and spacing them out in the timeline gives you the effect shown here. Courtesy of Electrotank, Inc.

The Playhead is the pink rectangular box in the frame number line in the Timeline panel, which tells you what frame you are viewing in your animation. Moving the Playhead further along your timeline, you can see more of the letters scaling in, as shown in Figure 6.22.

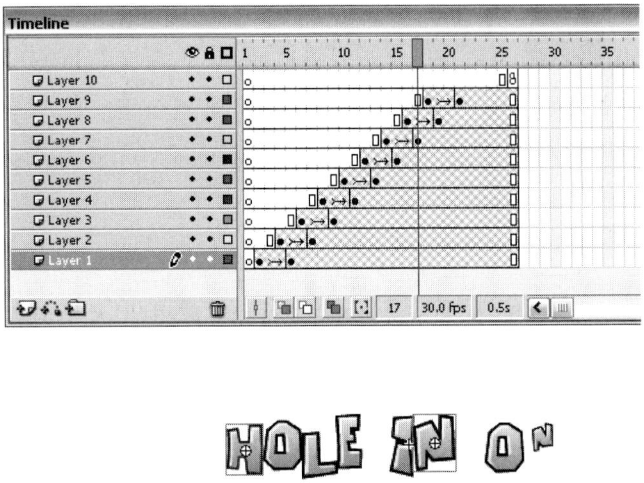

FIGURE 6.22 Moving the cursor further down the timeline, you can see the text message taking shape. Courtesy of Electrotank, Inc.

As shown in Figure 6.23, we can see the last frame of the animation and all the letters scaled in to their largest size.

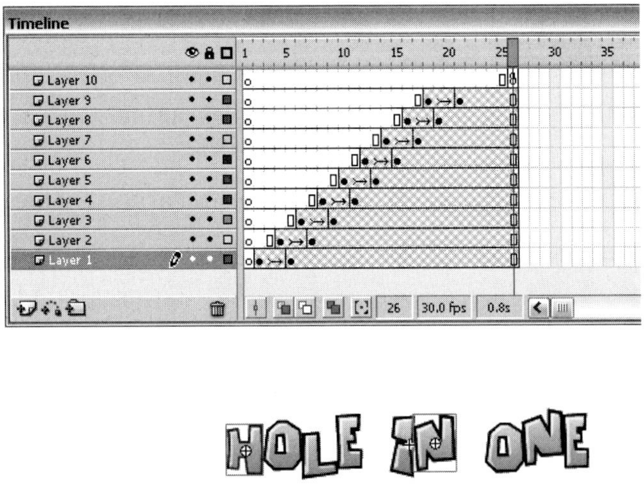

FIGURE 6.23 Last frame of the animation; all the text movie clips are done scaling in. Courtesy of Electrotank, Inc.

Bouncing Ball

When a ball bounces, it does not just go up and down. Several other elements come into play, like the squishing of the ball on impact, decrease in height of each bounce as the ball comes to a stop, or how fast the ball falls down and bounces back up. You could spend hours catching these details with the human eye, as when a ball bounces by it can happen fast. Let us create the path at which the ball will be moving. Create three new layers in Flash, and on the bottom layer, draw a line with the Line tool to create the ground on which the ball will bounce. Leave the middle layer blank, and with the top layer selected, make it a Motion Guide layer by clicking on the Motion Guide icon at bottom of the Timeline panel. In this top layer, draw the path you want the ball to animate on as shown in Figure 6.24.

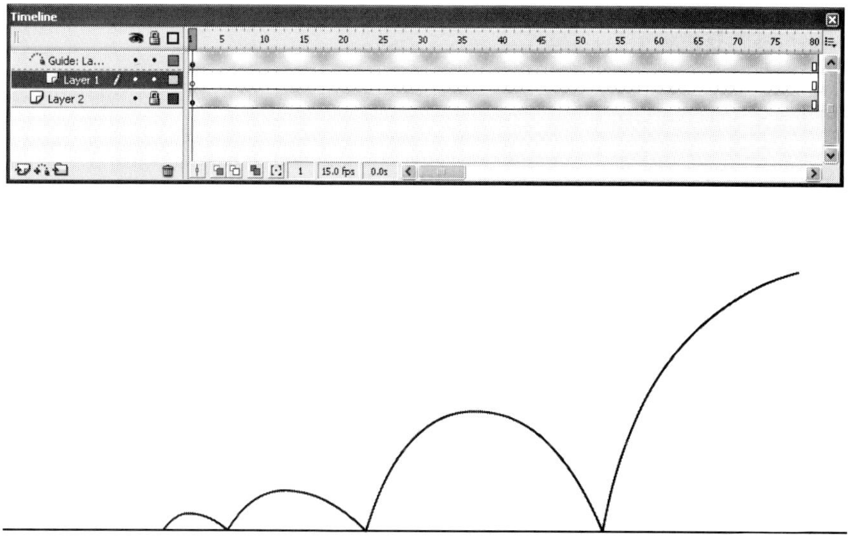

FIGURE 6.24 Create a motion path.

ON THE CD

On the middle layer, let us begin adding the base keyframes of the ball in key positions. There is a ball graphic provided on the companion CD-ROM in Chapter_6/ Exercises/tennisball.png. Import the png into Flash and convert it to a symbol. Create the following keyframes on the main timeline, and at each keyframe, change the position of the ball snapped along the path, as shown in Figure 6.25.

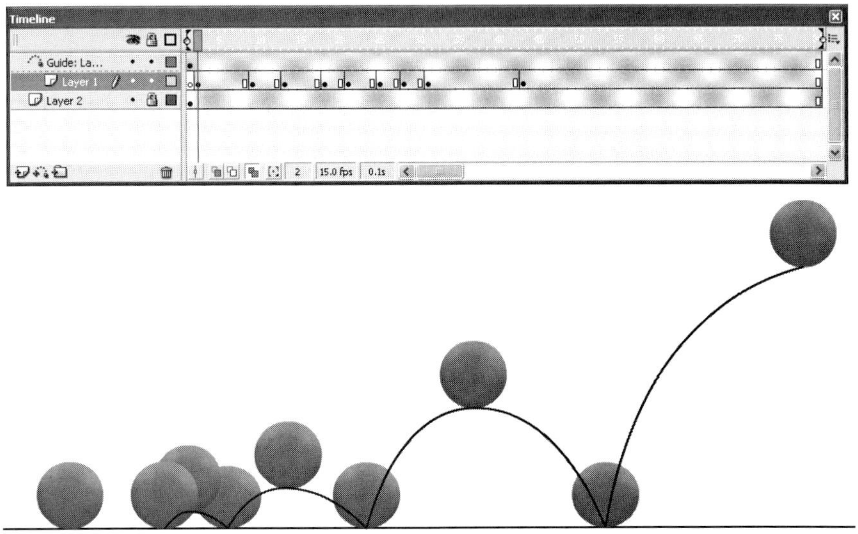

FIGURE 6.25 Add keyframes of the ball at different positions.

Select a keyframe, and in the Properties panel in the Tween drop-down box, select Motion and check the Snap checkbox. Repeat this step for every keyframe. Now, let us start to add the squish effect in this animation. To do so, we have to add more keyframes and make some minor graphic transforming. Select frame 8 and make it a keyframe, as shown in Figure 6.26.

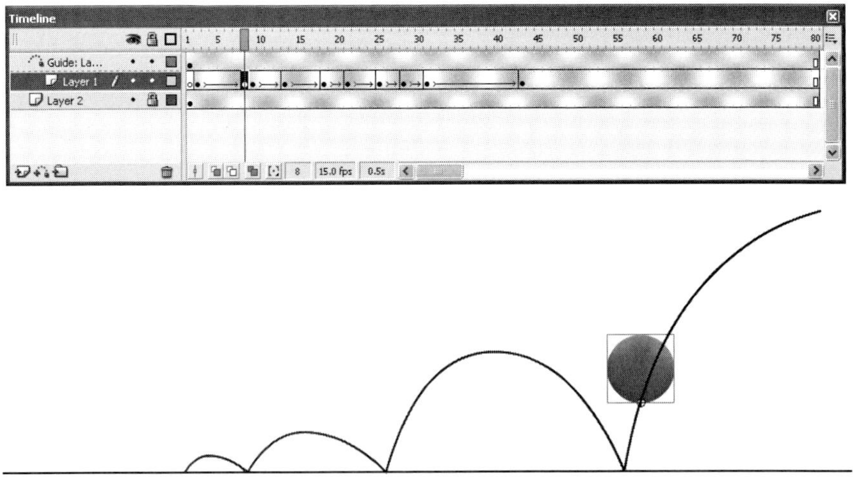

FIGURE 6.26 Add motion tween to keyframes and create a new keyframe.

Select frame 17 and make it a keyframe, as shown in Figure 6.27.

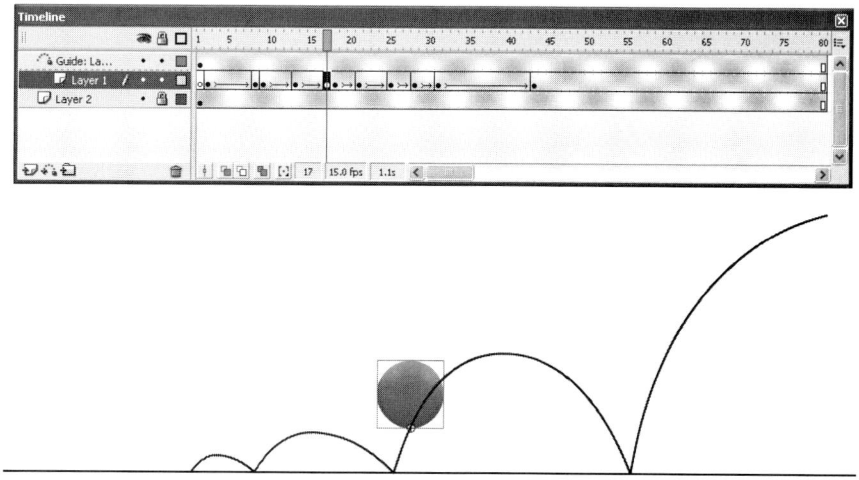

FIGURE 6.27 Make a new keyframe.

Select frame 9, and with the Free Transform tool, scale the ball vertically, making it look like it is squished, as shown in Figure 6.28.

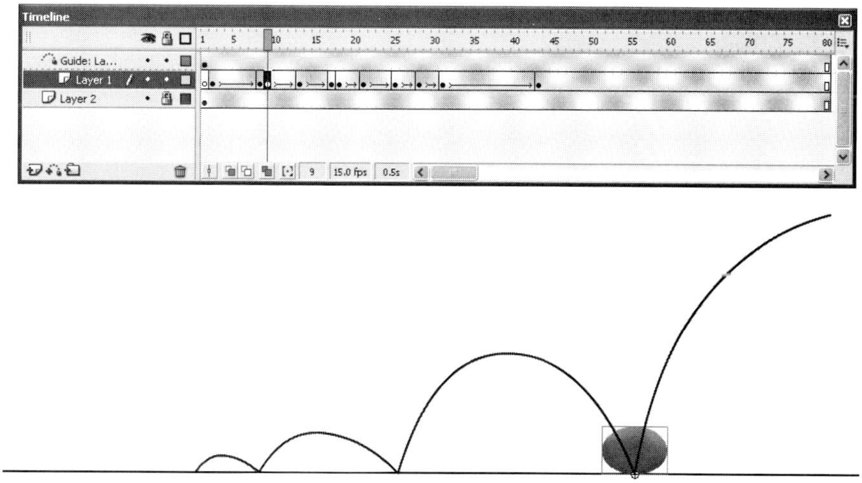

FIGURE 6.28 Make a new keyframe and scale the ball.

Select frame 18, and with the Free Transform tool, scale the ball vertically slightly less than on frame 9 since the ball is slowing down. Make it look squished, as shown in Figure 6.29.

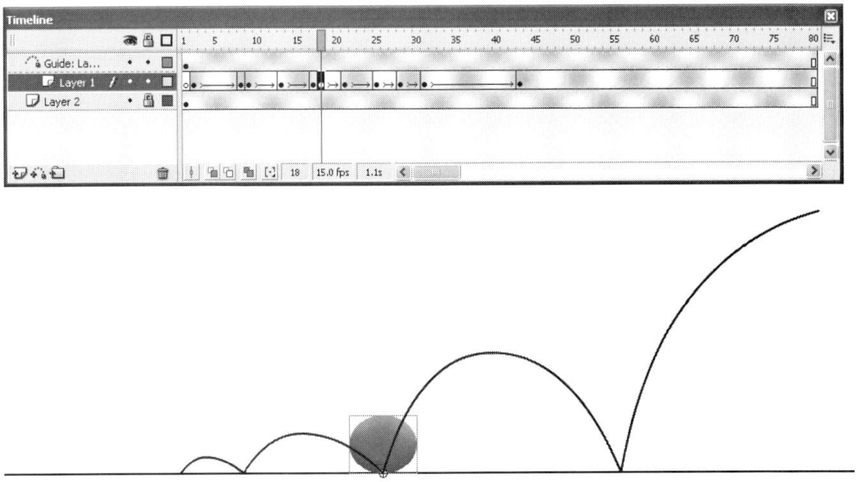

FIGURE 6.29 Make a new keyframe and scale the ball.

Select frame 10, and with the Free Transform tool, skew the ball to the left, making it look like it is in motion, as shown in Figure 6.30.

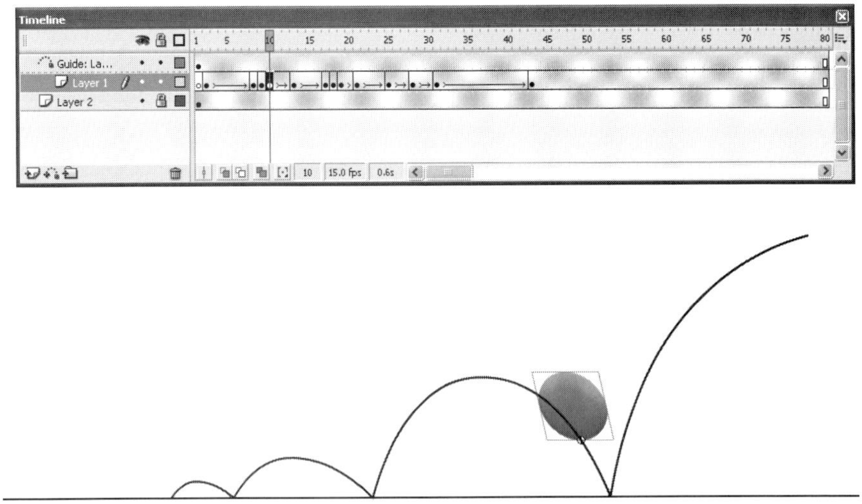

FIGURE 6.30 Make a new keyframe and skew the ball.

Select frame 19, and with the Free Transform tool, skew the ball to the left, slightly less than on frame 10 since the ball is slowing down. Make it look like it is in motion, as shown in Figure 6.31.

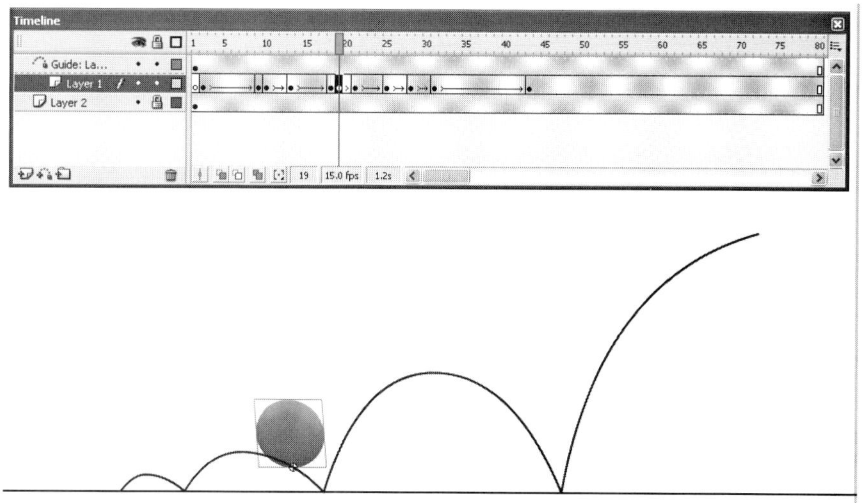

FIGURE 6.31 Make a new keyframe and skew the ball.

Figure 6.32 shows all the keyframes needed to depict the ball bouncing, and how a motion tween can handle the in-betweens for you.

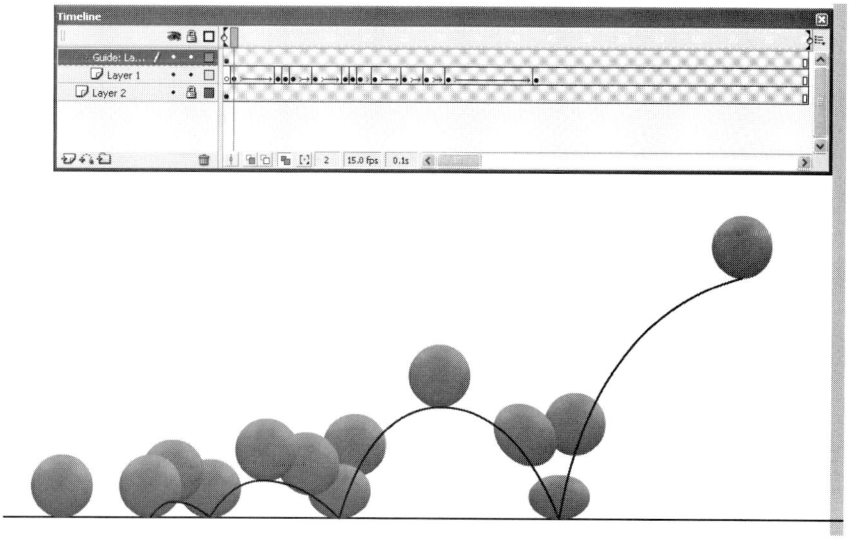

FIGURE 6.32 Every keyframe needed to replicate a ball bouncing.

ANIMATING SPECIAL EFFECTS

Special effects animation is a short-in-length animation or a series of two to four images that depict action or a reaction in your Web animation or game. *Special effects animation* is not a feature in Macromedia Flash; it is just a term used for short animations of this type. For instance, in a game when you complete a level and the number changes to show you that you have made it to the next level, a special effects animation will play to draw attention to the fact that the number changed. In a Web animation, if in the background you have a waterfall, it would only be natural to have water flowing down to make your background seem even more realistic. A small short looping animation would be great to show that: another example of a special effects animation. These short animations can add more depth and realism to any animation or game.

Sparkle

A sparkle special effects animation draws attention to any graphic it plays on and is a nice touch to make your graphics come alive. This sparkle animation was used in a puzzle game to signify a level change. The four keyframes used to create this effect are shown in Figure 6.33. Set your movie's frame rate to 24 fps by accessing the document properties.

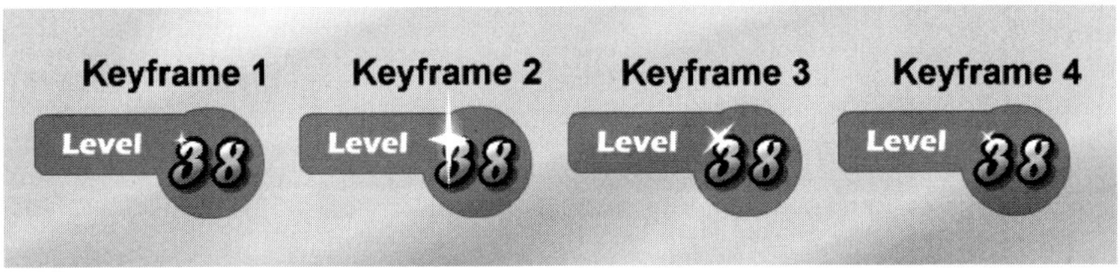

FIGURE 6.33 The four keyframes used in the motion tween of the sparkle animation.
Courtesy of Electrotank, Inc.

The four keyframes are used in a motion tween shown in Figure 6.34, which animates the in-between frames to display the full motion of the sparkle. Notice how on the first keyframe, the ease is set to 75. Ease controls how the tweened frames of animation between the keyframes are distributed and placed. For example, setting the ease to 75 will make the sparkle scale quickly and slow to the size of the next keyframe.

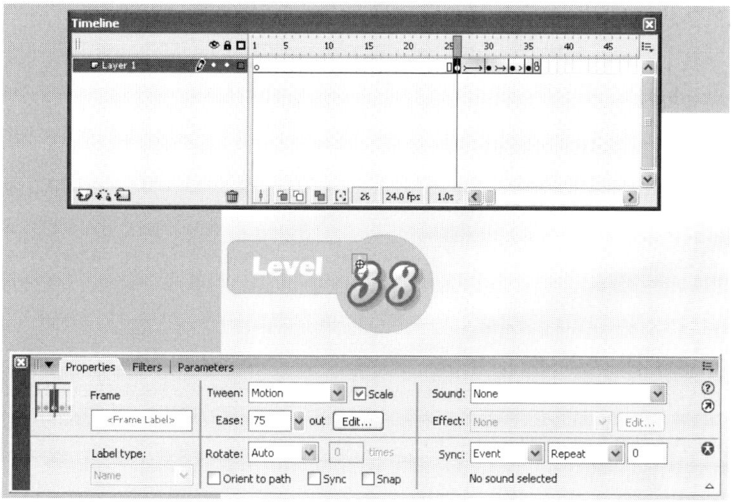

FIGURE 6.34 Keyframe 1 of the motion tween that makes the sparkle graphic scale in; ease 75 was used. Courtesy of Electrotank, Inc.

The second keyframe's ease is set to –75, as shown in Figure 6.35. This setting will make the sparkle graphic rotate slowly and then end quickly to the angle of the sparkle in the next keyframe.

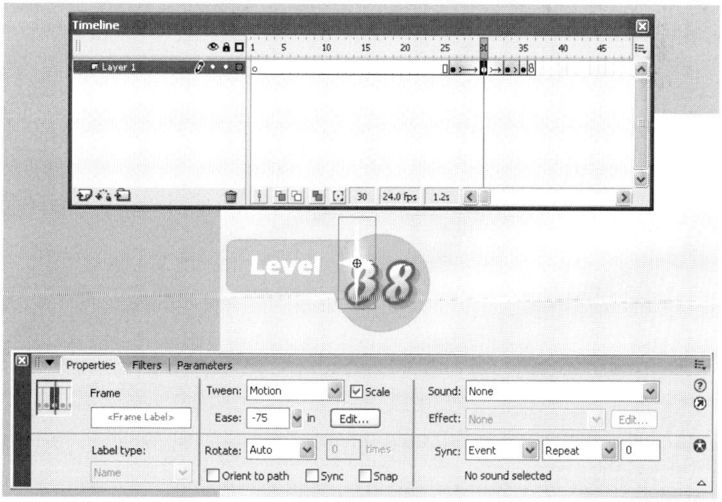

FIGURE 6.35 Keyframe 2 of the motion tween where an ease –75 was used. Courtesy of Electrotank, Inc.

The third keyframe is just a simple motion tween and does not have an ease value set to it; therefore, the tween frames will be distributed evenly between keyframes 3 and 4, as shown in Figure 6.36.

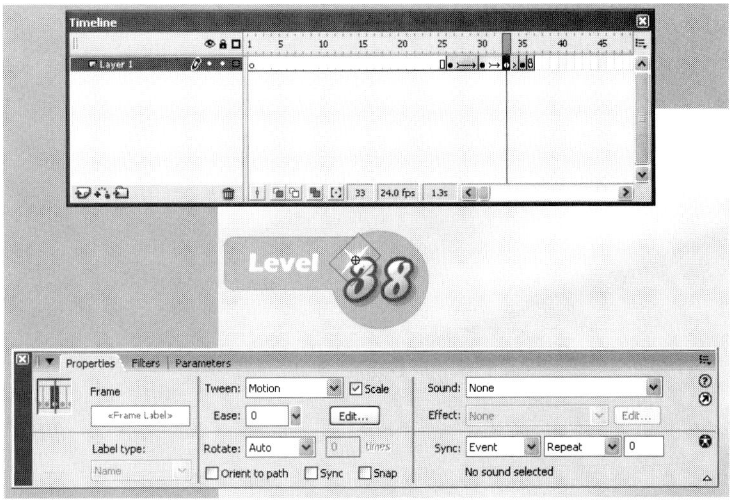

FIGURE 6.36 Keyframe 3, where the sparkle graphic is rotated and scaled down. Courtesy of Electrotank, Inc.

The fourth and last keyframe is not set to motion tween, since there is not another keyframe to tween to, as shown in Figure 6.37. This is normal, and only the first keyframe needs to be set to motion tween for a complete tween to take place.

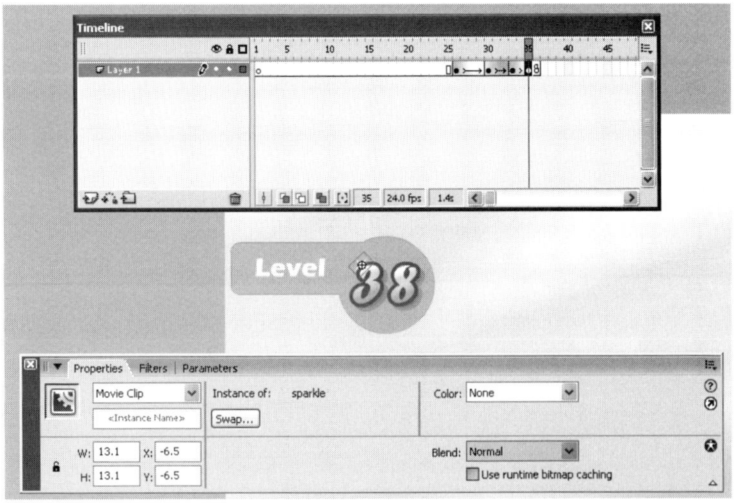

FIGURE 6.37 Keyframe 4 of the sparkle graphic where it is scaled down to end the animation. Courtesy of Electrotank, Inc.

Waterfall

Creating an effect of water falling is quite easy and can be done in Flash by combining several movie clips together with a small amount of keyframes. The water backdrop texture is made from a linear gradient, as shown in Figure 6.38. A variety of light and dark blue color swatches are used to give the rippling effect in the linear gradient. Set your movie's frame rate to 15 fps by accessing the document properties.

To make it look like the water is flowing down, we will create a white radial gradient texture, as shown in Figure 6.39. Notice how the Alpha percentage field is modified to make the gradient transparent.

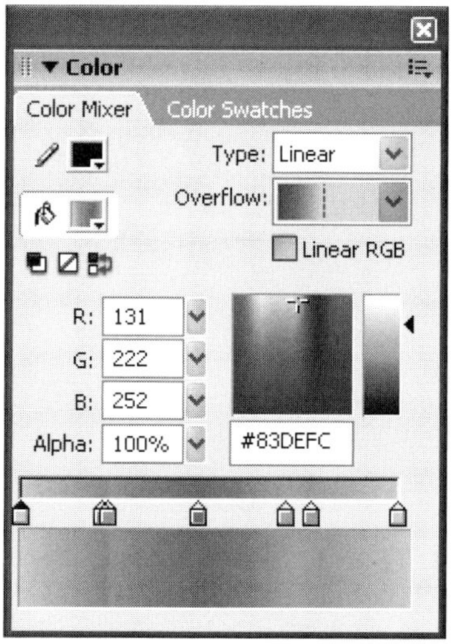

FIGURE 6.38 Linear gradient created for the water backdrop graphic.

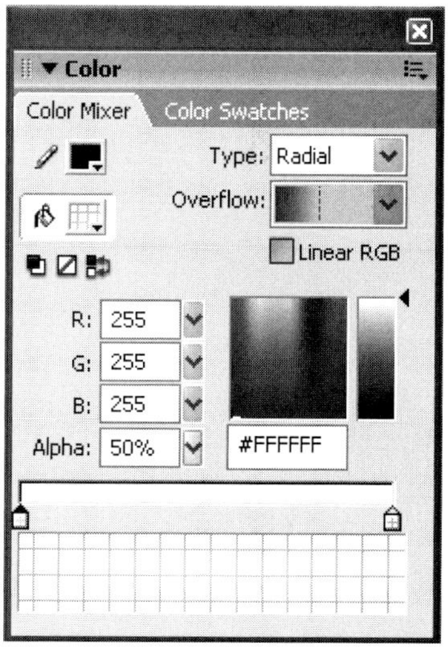

FIGURE 6.39 Radial gradient to be used with the water texture.

As shown in Figure 6.40, the water backdrop on the left is created with the Rectangle tool and with water linear gradient selected, which we just created. Select the rectangle with the Selection tool and execute the shortcut key to make it a symbol movie clip. On the right side of Figure 6.40, we start to create the water texture with the white alpha radial gradient we just created.

Execute the shortcut key command to group the first radial gradient and make two copies of it; place them next to each other, as shown in Figure 6.41. The Group feature is also found under Modify > Group.

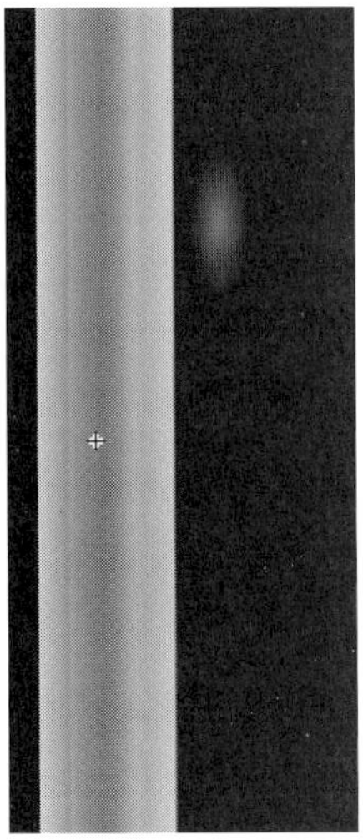

FIGURE 6.40 Water backdrop movie clip created and the start of the water texture. Courtesy of Electrotank, Inc.

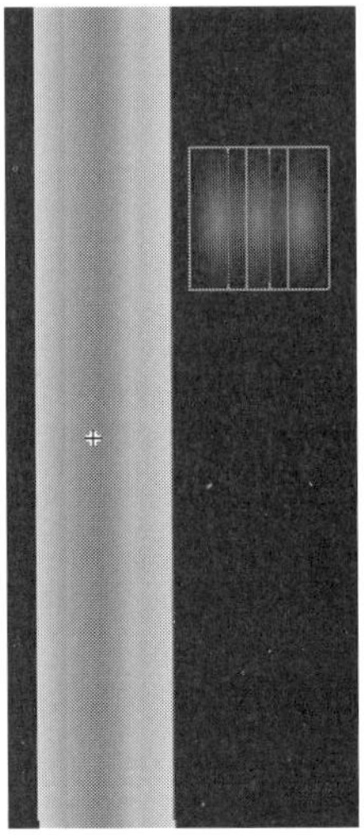

FIGURE 6.41 Radial gradient grouped, duplicated, and turned into a symbol movie clip. Courtesy of Electrotank, Inc.

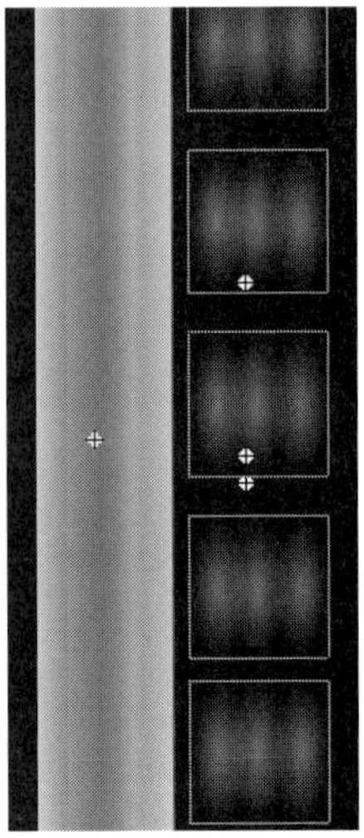

FIGURE 6.42 Water texture movie clip duplicated in a vertical row. Courtesy of Electrotank, Inc.

Select the three radial gradients with the Selection tool, and hold down the Shift key to select the last two gradients. Once selected, execute the shortcut key command to make these graphics a symbol movie clip. Duplicate the new water texture movie clip, duplicate it four more times, and place the copies in a vertical row, as shown in Figure 6.42.

This waterfall animation only needs four keyframes to make it look like it is looping, as shown in Figure 6.43. Create the first keyframe with the water backdrop movie clip and the water texture movie clips placed on top of it. To add another keyframe, select the first keyframe and access the menu items Insert > Timeline > Keyframe. With the second keyframe, select all the water textures, move them down about 20 pixels, and create a new keyframe by selecting the second keyframe and accessing the menu items Insert > Timeline > Keyframe. From the third keyframe, move the water textures down about 20 pixels and create a fourth keyframe from the third keyframe. On the fourth and last keyframe, select the water textures and move them down 20 pixels. If you play back the keyframes, it should look like the water texture is moving down.

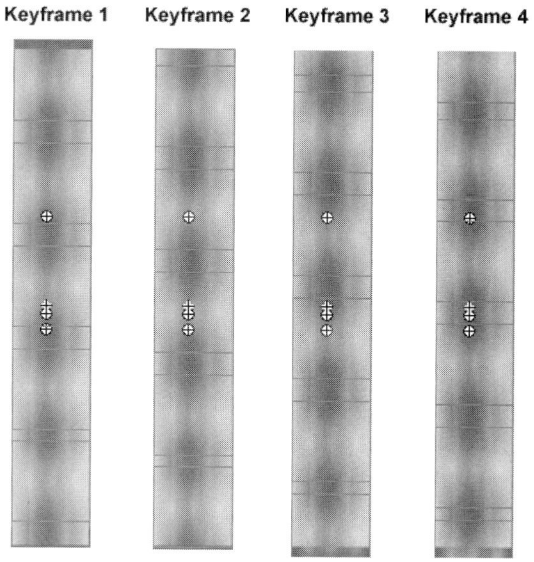

FIGURE 6.43 The final four keyframes that make up the waterfall special effect. Courtesy of Electrotank, Inc.

Reflection

ON THE CD

Anytime you have light hitting a metal or plastic surface, the light tends to return, creating a reflection. Here, we will take a logo and add some impact to it by applying a simple animated reflection. A reflection can be achieved by animating a white alpha gradient across your logo, but to replicate it perfectly, we will be masking the alpha gradient to only show up on the reflective part of the logo. There is a logo graphic provided on the companion CD-ROM in Chapter_6/6-44.png. Import the png into Flash and convert it to a symbol, as shown in Figure 6.44.

FIGURE 6.44 Import logo into Flash and convert to symbol.

Now, let us create the fill shape that will act as the mask. If you have a vector graphic of your logo, you will not need to created a fill shape. For this example, we have the fill shape already create on the companion CD-ROM in Chapter_6/6-45.fla. Open the file in Flash and copy and paste onto the raster logo. Once positioned, convert it to a symbol. Go inside this symbol and add a new layer on top of the first. Select the bottom layer with the graphic in it and make it a mask layer by selecting Modify > Timeline > Layer Properties. In the pop up menu, select the Mask radio button. Close the pop-up, and drag the top layer and position it underneath the masked layer, as shown in Figure 6.45.

ON THE CD

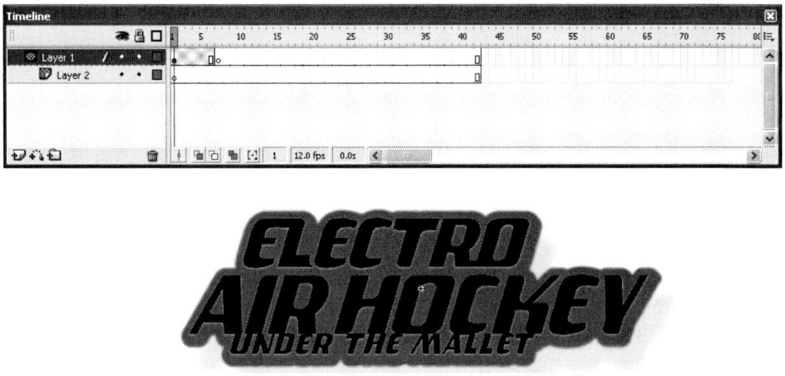

FIGURE 6.45 Making a masked layer.

We will construct our animated alpha gradient on the bottom blank layer. The first swatch from the left is #FFFFFF Alpha: 0%, the middle swatch is #FFFFFF Alpha: 50%, and the right swatch is #FFFFFF Alpha: 0%, as shown in Figure 6.46.

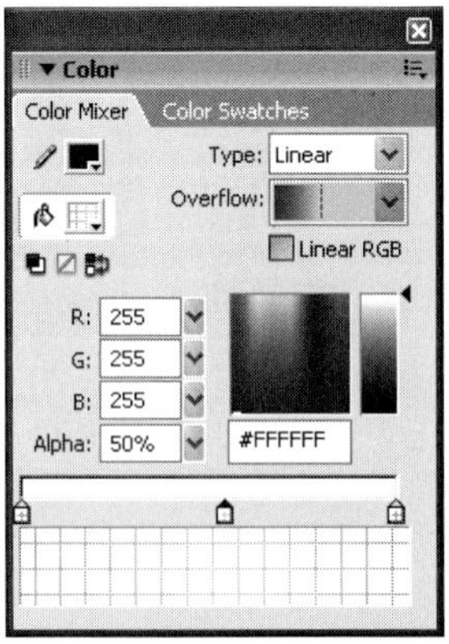

FIGURE 6.46 Creating the alpha radial gradient.

Create a keyframe on the blank layer, and place your gradient fill in the keyframe. Use the Rectangle tool to create the gradient fill with no line color. Use the Gradient Transform tool to modify the position and rotation of the radial gradient and place it, as shown in Figure 6.47.

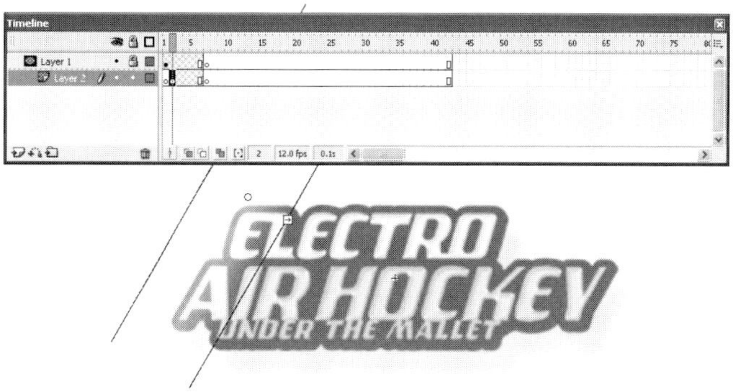

FIGURE 6.47 Placing the gradient on the blank layer.

Create a second keyframe on frame 6. Reposition the gradient with the Gradient Transform tool, as shown in Figure 6.48. Click on frame 2, and in the Properties panel select Shape in the Tween drop-down to make this keyframe a shape tween.

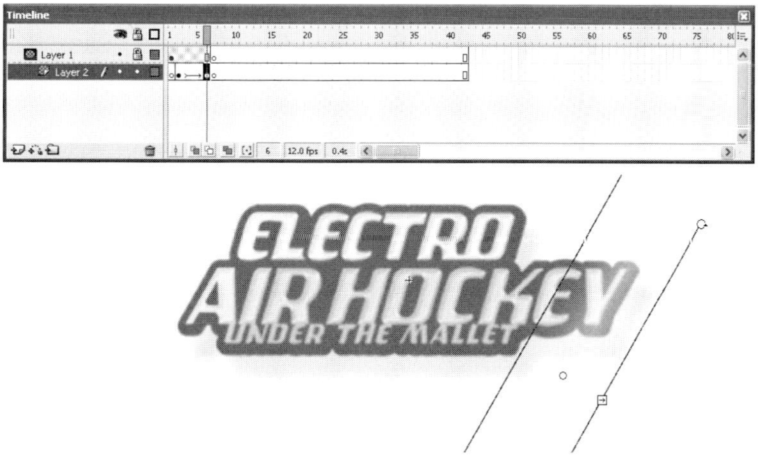

FIGURE 6.48 Create a second keyframe and change the position of the gradient.

Select and drag the player head in the Timeline panel to see your shape tween in action. The radial gradient should be moving from left to right when starting at frame 2. As shown in Figure 6.49, you can see how the radial gradient is applied and how it may affect the logo.

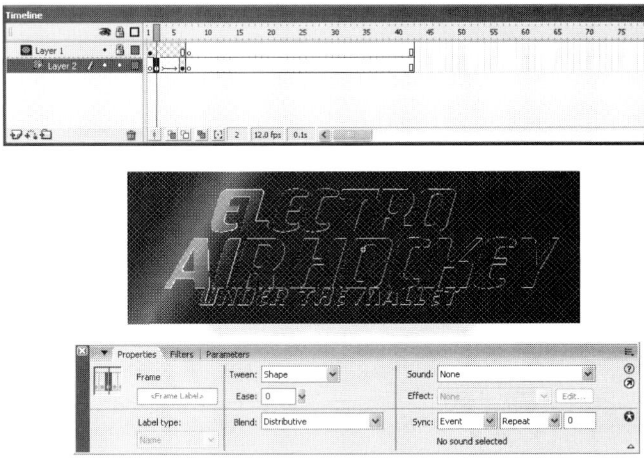

FIGURE 6.49 Verifying the shape tween animating properly.

As show in Figure 6.50, you can see the difference between frame 3 and frame 5, how the radial gradient animates across, and only shows up on the reflective parts of the logo.

FIGURE 6.50 Comparing frames and effective mask.

Fire

Animating fire can be a challenge. View a campfire burning and analyze how it moves. If you drew a looping animation of a fire, how would you get it to loop? Fire is always moving up, flames starting from the ground and flying up. It has a spiky curvy body to it. Studying fire more closely, we notice that to give the illusion that the flame is going up, you can animate it waving similar to an ocean wave. As the tip of the flame disappears, it seems to leave the body of the fame, as shown in Figure 6.51. Set the frame rate for this project to 30 fps, and when creating the keyframes in the Timeline panel, make them last for two frames.

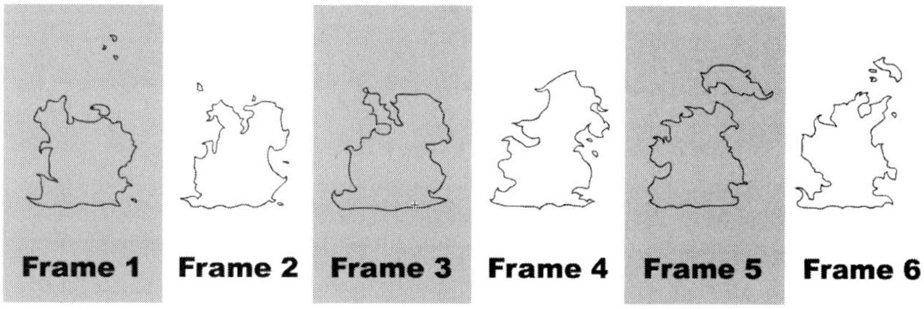

FIGURE 6.51 Analyzing the keyframes of a fire's complete motion.

Instead of explaining how to draw all six keyframes, we will review just one, and you can implement those steps to the other frames. First, draw the outline of the shape of the flame, as shown in Figure 6.52. Use the Line tool to place your lines, and switch to the Arrow tool to reposition and add the curve to the line. You can use the Pencil tool, but that will not give you an optimized outline.

To define the shape of the flame and other areas to color, we will be adding another outline inside, as shown in Figure 6.53

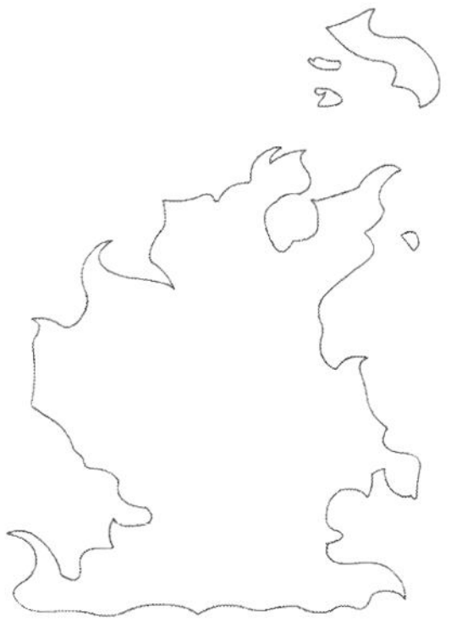

FIGURE 6.52 Draw the outlineof the flame.

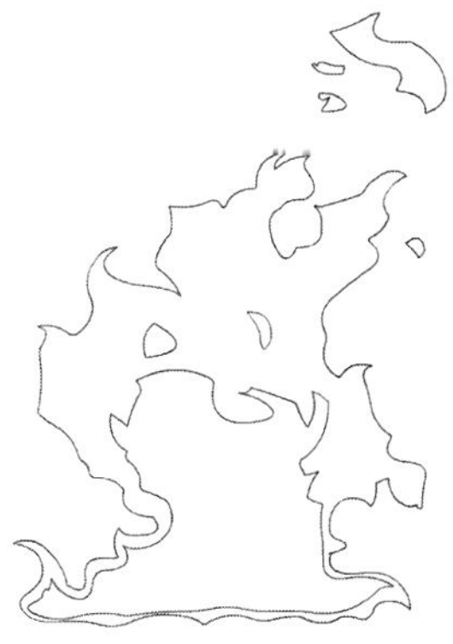

FIGURE 6.53 Draw another outline within the first.

To make sure we have enough detail, add another outline, and this time, make it between the last and first outlines, as shown in Figure 6.54.

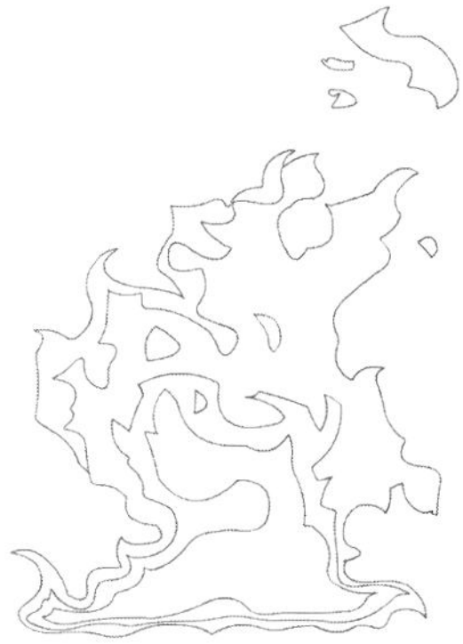

FIGURE 6.54 Drawing an outline between the last two.

Now that we are done defining the outlines, let us start coloring between these outlines. Create the following radial gradient with your Color Mixer panel; the left swatch is #FF9900 and the right swatch is #FF6600. Apply it with the Paint Bucket tool and position it with the Gradient Transform tool, as shown in Figure 6.55.

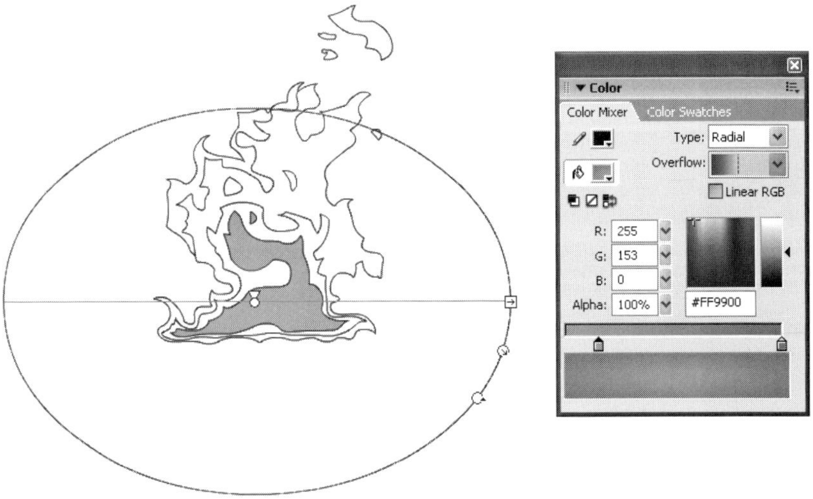

FIGURE 6.55 Create and apply the first radial gradient.

Create the following radial gradient with your Color Mixer panel; the left swatch is #FF6600 and the right swatch is #FF6600, Alpha: 75%. Apply it with the Paint Bucket tool and position it with the Gradient Transform tool, as shown in Figure 6.56.

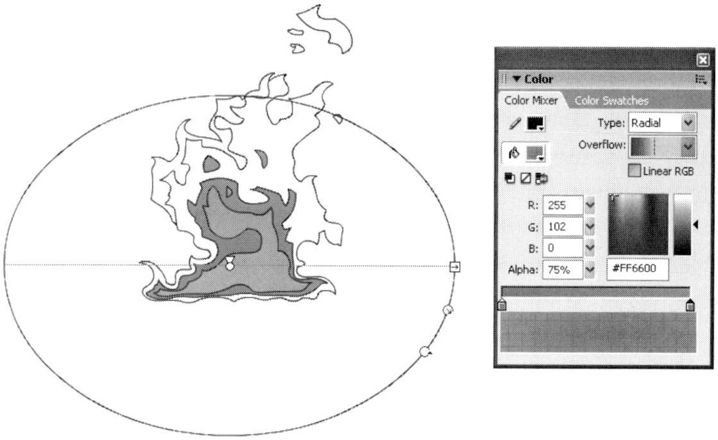

FIGURE 6.56 Create and apply the second radial gradient.

Create the following radial gradient with your Color Mixer panel; the left swatch is #CC3300 and the right swatch is #CC6600, Alpha: 50%. Apply it with the Paint Bucket tool and position it with the Gradient Transform tool, as shown in Figure 6.57.

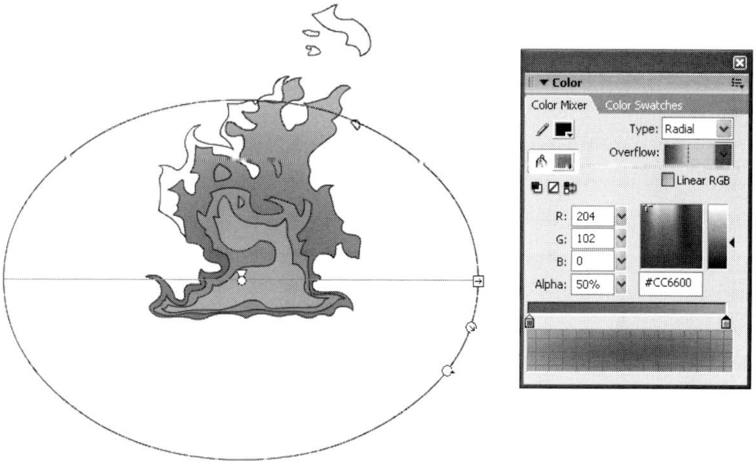

FIGURE 6.57 Create and apply the third radial gradient.

Create the following radial gradient with your Color Mixer panel; the left swatch is #990000, Alpha: 50%, and the right swatch is #996600, Alpha: 25%. Apply it with the Paint Bucket tool and position it with the Gradient Transform tool, as shown in Figure 6.58.

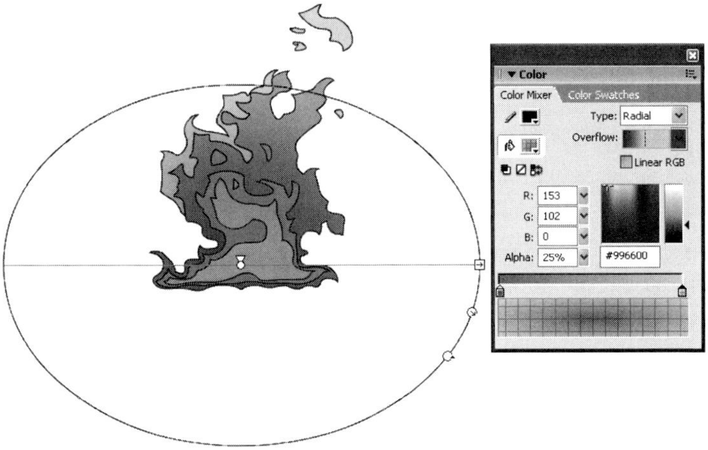

FIGURE 6.58 Create and apply the fourth radial gradient.

By coloring all six keyframes, you should have the same result, as shown in Figure 6.59. By placing them in the same position on each keyframe and playing the animation, you should have the fire in motion.

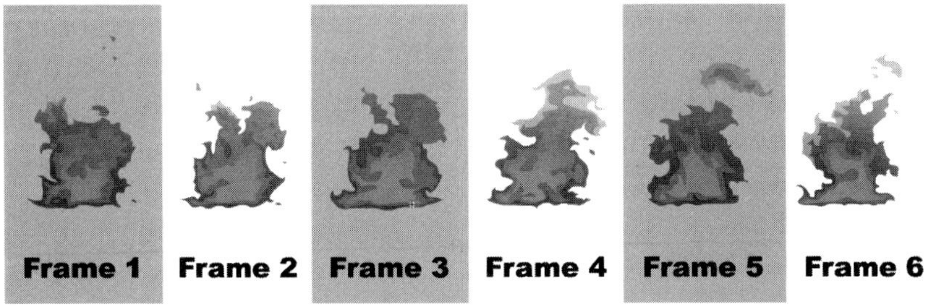

FIGURE 6.59 Analyzing the six colored keyframes.

SUMMARY

- Tween movie clips versus animating frame by frame to produce a smaller file size.
- Embed a movie clip with another movie clip, each containing independent animating graphics to create dynamic-looking movement.
- Animate movie clips in Macromedia Flash to create special effect animations quickly and easily.

EXERCISES

ON THE CD

The following exercises will put to use what you learned in this chapter. You will be creating floating bubbles, a bouncing tennis ball, flies flying, diamonds sparkling, and a reflecting car. The files for the following exercises are on the companion CD-ROM in the folders cited.

1. Create a floating bubble with the image given and the techniques you learned in the *Text Movement* section. Make your background color something other than black or white to see the bubble correctly since it is transparent. The image file is on the companion CD-ROM in Chapter_6/Exercises/bubble.png.
2. Create a bouncing tennis ball animation with the image given and the techniques you learned in the *Bouncing Ball* section. The image file is on the companion CD-ROM in Chapter_6/Exercises/tennisball.png.
3. Create a flying fly animation with the images given and the techniques you learned in the *Create Looping Animations* section. The image files are on the companion CD-ROM in Chapter_6/Exercises/flybody.png and Chapter_6/Exercises/flywing.png.
4. Add a sparkle effect animation on top of an image of an engagement ring with the techniques you learned in the *Sparkle* section. The image file is on the companion CD-ROM in Chapter_6/Exercises/diamond.jpg.
5. Add a reflection effect animation on top of an image of a sports car with the techniques you learned in the *Reflections* section. The image file is on the companion CD-ROM in Chapter_6/Exercises/car.jpg.

CHAPTER

7 TEXTURE TECHNIQUES

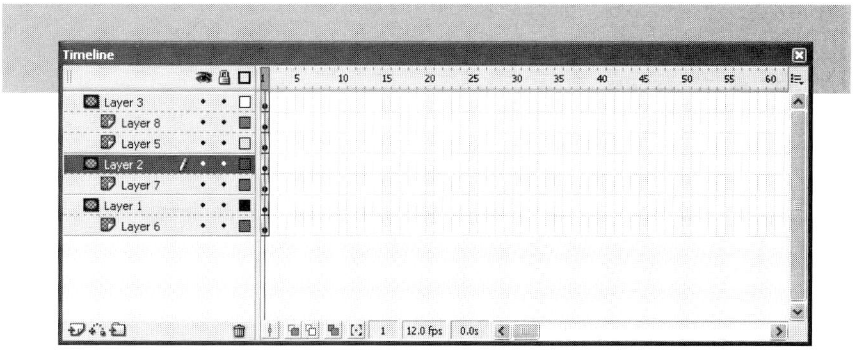

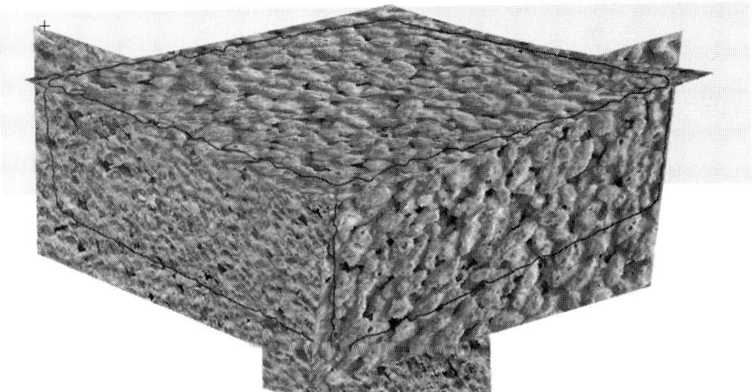

Whether it is the shirt on your back or the wooden desk you work at, all items around you have some type of visual texture. This chapter focuses on the many textures you may experience in everyday life, and unique techniques that will help you achieve illustrating just about anything you wish. Textures can be illustrated using vector graphics or even raster graphics. We know that not every type of texture is possible with vectors, so we show you how raster graphics can help where vectors leave off.

The texture of an object depends on what the object is made of, or the depth of the object's surface. For instance, the grain in wood is a swirl-shaped pattern, but the surface may be smooth to the touch, whereas a textured metal plate has a raised diamond-shaped pattern but no visual grain. Lighting in the environment plays a big part in the texture of the object. If the object is reflective, light or other objects in the background could show up on the surface of the object, and shadows could cast on the object changing how it looks. All of these elements should be considered if you want to make your illustrations in Flash more accurate representations of the real world.

VECTOR TEXTURES

You may be surprised with what the vector drawing tools found in Flash can do and the many textures that are possible. In this section, we explore textures such as basic plastic and photorealistic wood grain. A couple of different metal textures will be explained, and the porous surface from a sponge will be revealed. All of these techniques can be applied to your own projects, ranging from making your user interface futuristic with a metal texture, to applying the wood texture to your buttons for an earthy look.

Textured Metal Plate

Creating a textured metal plate in Flash is simple; it just requires a couple of layers of highlights to depict the look of metal, and an overlapping texture to represent the texture or feel of the metal. As shown in Figure 7.1, we use the Rectangle tool to create a radial gradient fill. If a line stroke is created along with the fill, it can be deleted, as it will not be needed. Use the Gradient Transform tool to edit the center point and scale of the radial gradient.

Create a new layer above the previous one. Open your Color Mixer panel and create a radial gradient with the following settings, as shown in Figure 7.2. The first swatch has a HEX value of #FFFFFF 30% Alpha, the second swatch #FFFFFF 20% Alpha, and the third swatch #FFFFFF 0% Alpha. Apply this radial gradient to your fill swatch in your Tool panel, and with the Rectangle tool, create a rectangle-shaped fill. Group and du-

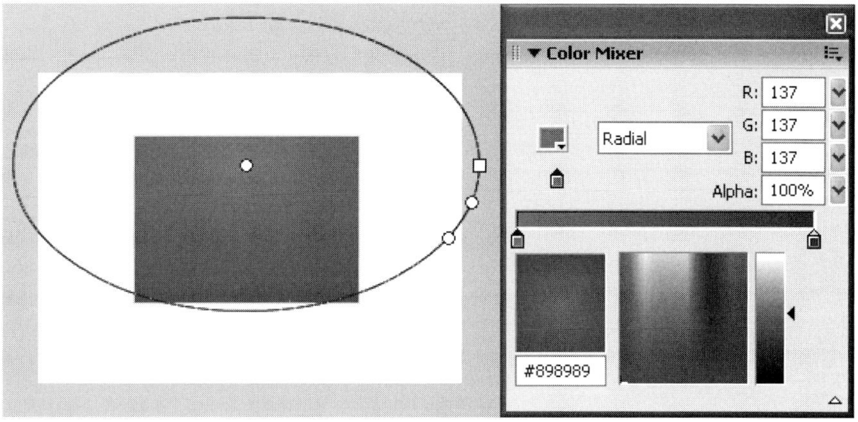

FIGURE 7.1 Create a rectangle fill with a radial gradient; position the gradient center point toward the top.

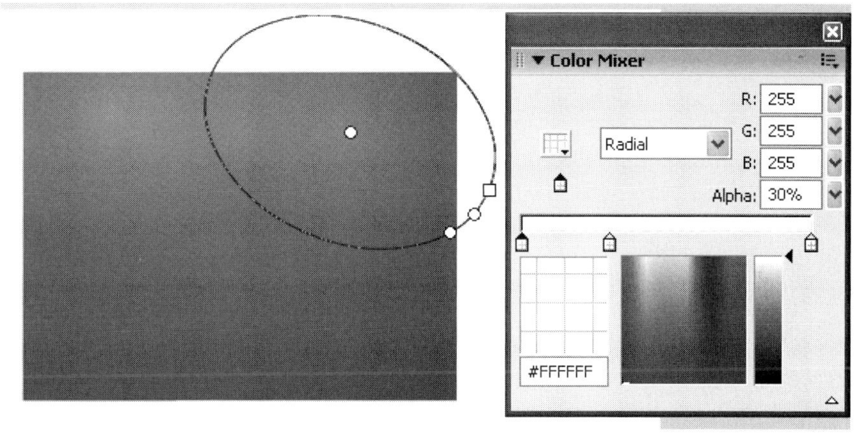

FIGURE 7.2 Create two alpha radial gradient fills to add highlights to the metal.

plicate the newly created fill by using the Group and Duplicate shortcut keys, and reposition it to the opposite side so you have two radial gradients adding highlights to your metal. In the menu, the Duplicate feature is located under Edit > Duplicate.

To focus on creating the texture of the metal plate, we will start by using the Line tool to draw one piece of the texture, as shown in Figure 7.3. Use the Selection tool to manipulate the lines that you will create with the Line tool to form the curved shape of the texture piece, a common shape found on pieces of metal. It will contain two outlined areas where fills will be placed.

Using the Selection tool, select the textured piece and use the appropriate shortcut keys to copy and paste the graphic to create a new one. Horizontally flip the newly created graphic; you can access the Flip Horizontal menu item in Modify > Transform > Flip Horizontal. With your arrow keys, reposition the graphic as shown in Figure 7.4.

FIGURE 7.3 With the Line tool, draw an outline that will define the shape of one piece of the metal texture.

FIGURE 7.4 Duplicate and horizontally flip the outline and position it down and to the left.

In four easy steps, we will create a horizontal texture.

For Step 1, select the two pieces of graphic with your Selection tool. Execute the shortcut keys to Copy and Paste in Place the graphic. In the menu, these features are located under Edit. By holding down your Shift key while pressing the down arrow key on your keyboard several times, you can reposition the newly created graphic vertically down. Repeat Step 1 until you have a column of about 11 to 12 graphics, as shown in Step 1 of Figure 7.5.

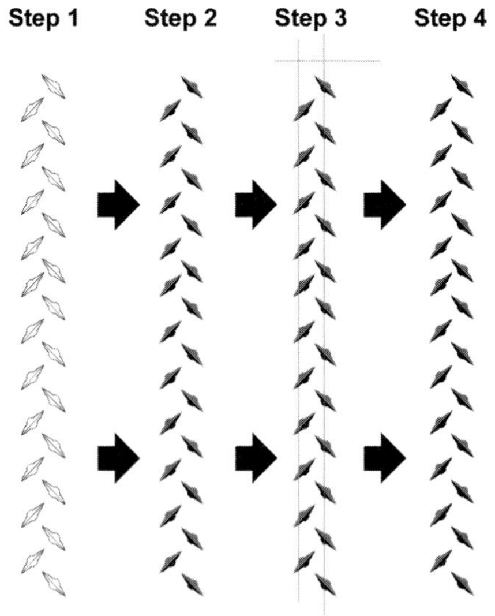

FIGURE 7.5 Duplicate the texture vertically down, fill the outlines with two different-colored fills, delete the outlines, and separate the two different-colored fills on different layers.

In Step 2, switch to your Paint Bucket tool, apply a light color in the areas on the top of each piece, and apply a dark color in the areas on the bottom of each piece.

In Step 3, to delete all the unwanted lines we used to define where fills will be applied, we draw three lines with the Line tool. This technique is used to connect all the individual line graphics so they can be selected quickly. Once your lines are drawn as shown in Step 3, use the Selection tool, double-click on any part of the line, and all the lines will be selected.

As shown in Step 4, delete the selected lines using the shortcut key. We need to place the light fills on their own layer and the dark fills on their own layer, so selecting and coloring the fills will be much easier. Create a new layer, select the light fills, and copy and paste them in place on the new layer.

As shown in Figure 7.6, we will be duplicating the vertical texture horizontally 16 times across. Use the technique of copying and pasting in place, and then reposition the graphic by holding down the Shift key and using the right arrow key. Make sure you do this technique one layer at a time, because if you select all and duplicate them, the new graphics will be pasted on one layer, and we need to keep the colored fills on their own layers. As you continue to create more columns of graphics, select as many as you can so the duplication process will go faster.

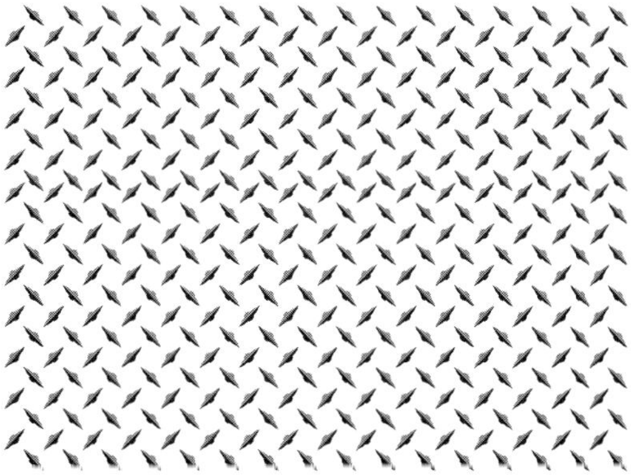

FIGURE 7.6 Duplicate the vertically tall texture 16 times horizontally.

Create a radial gradient, as shown in Figure 7.7, which will be applied to the light-colored fills. The first swatch is #FFFFFF 100% Alpha, the second swatch is #929292 100% Alpha, and the third swatch is #2B2B2B 100% Alpha. Select all the light-colored graphics, which should be on their own layer, and apply the radial gradient with the Paint Bucket tool, with the newly created gradient set to the fill swatch on the Tool panel.

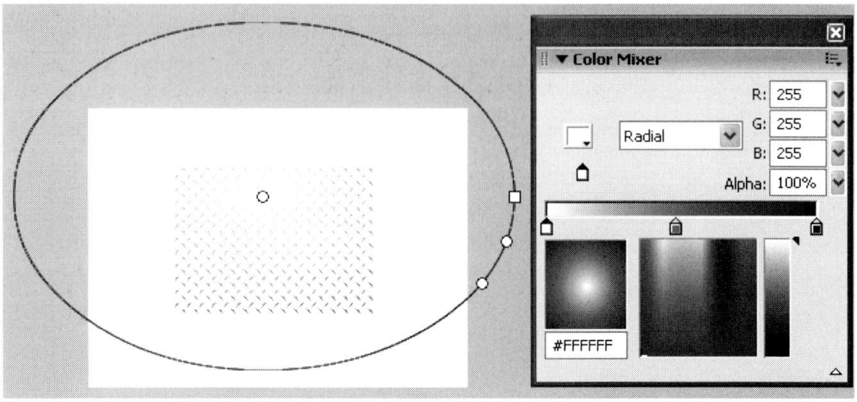

FIGURE 7.7 Create a radial gradient and apply it to the light-colored graphics.

To apply the radial gradient globally throughout all the fills, click on one of the fills with your Paint Bucket tool. To edit the center point and scale of the gradient, use the Gradient Transform tool.

Create a radial gradient, as shown in Figure 7.8, which will be applied to the dark-colored fills. The first swatch is #8B8B8B 100% Alpha, the second swatch is #646464 100% Alpha, and the third swatch is #242424 100% Alpha. Select all the dark-colored graphics, which should be on their own layer, and apply the radial gradient with the Paint Bucket tool, with the newly created gradient set to the fill swatch on the Tool panel. To apply the radial gradient globally throughout all the fills, click on one of the fills with your Paint Bucket tool. To edit the center point and scale of the gradient, use the Gradient Transform tool.

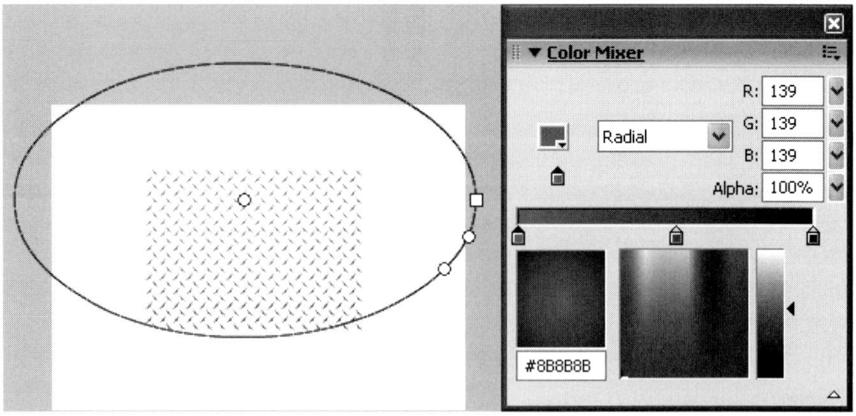

FIGURE 7.8 Create a radial gradient and apply it to the dark-colored graphics.

One of the many things that can be learned from this exercise is that layering gradient fills can give you dynamic-looking results that can portray how light reflects off certain objects, as shown in Figure 7.9.

FIGURE 7.9 Final illustration of the textured metal plate.

Plastic—Hard

There are many different types of plastics, and hard plastic reflects light differently than soft plastic does. For this tutorial, we will be creating hard plastic. Hard plastic surprisingly reflects light, making a sharp reflection on the surface. Each figure in this section contains more than one step of a certain task. Letters are used in the figures that correlate to a letter in the writing that explains fill configurations used in the Color Mixer.

As shown in Figure 7.10, our first task is to draw an outline of the basic shape of the funnel.

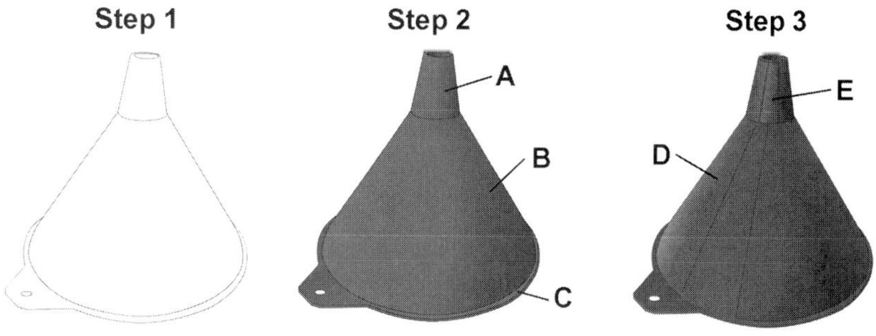

FIGURE 7.10 Create the base color for the funnel.

In Step 1, use the Line tool to plot your lines, and the Snap to Objects feature on to snap lines together precisely. Switch the Snap to Object feature off temporarily by holding down the G key as you are using the Line tool. Use the Selection tool to add curve to your lines.

In Step 2, apply the base color to the funnel with three gradients. Gradient A is a linear gradient with a color swatch of #004CCC in the middle of the color line, and a swatch of #002C80 to the far right. Gradient B is the same settings as the first gradient, but it is a radial gradient. Gradient C is a linear gradient similar to the first, but the color swatch is a little bit lighter with a HEX value of #003A9E.

For Step 3, use the Line tool to create outlines for where the base highlights will be placed. At the body of the funnel, we will be applying a linear gradient on each side to give a slight highlight on the side of the funnel. The linear gradient applied has two color swatches, one on each side of the color line set at #FFFFFF Alpha: 0% and #FFFFFF Alpha: 20%. At the tip of the funnel at E and on the left side of the tip, apply the following linear gradient that has three color swatches all set at #FFFFFF but different alpha settings. The left color swatch is Alpha: 0%, the middle swatch is Alpha: 15%, and the right swatch is 0%. Between these two gradients, apply #FFFFFF with Alpha: 20%. Once you are done adding the fills, delete the black outlines, as we will not need those.

Figure 7.11 is broken down into four steps, which will complete the main highlight.

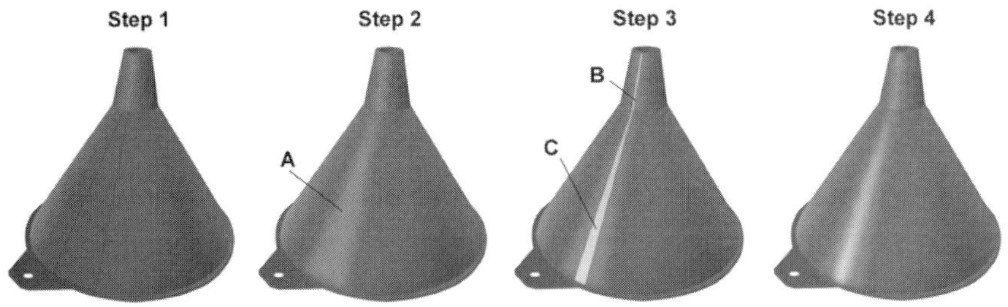

FIGURE 7.11 Add the base layer of highlight detail.

In Step 1, with the Line tool, draw an outline where the first highlight will be.

In Step 2, as A indicates, use the Paint Bucket tool and apply the solid fill #FFFFFF Alpha: 20%. Use the Selection tool to select the outline and delete it. Select the fill and convert it to a symbol. In the Properties panel, find the Filters tab, add a filter by pressing the + icon, and select Blur from the drop-down. Set the blur to 10 and the quality to High.

In Step 3, add a new layer on top and use the Line tool to create an outline for the last highlight. B is a solid fill set at #FFFFFF Alpha: 52%. C is a linear gradient with two color swatches, both set at #FFFFFF. The left swatch is Alpha: 30%, and the right swatch is set at 53%. This way, the 30% side meets the 52% fill at the tip, giving us the contrast we are looking for. Select these two fills and convert them to a symbol.

In Step 4, apply a blur filter effect set at 8 with quality High.

The next three steps define the last layer of highlights, as shown in Figure 7.12. This will be curved in shape and help define the object's shape.

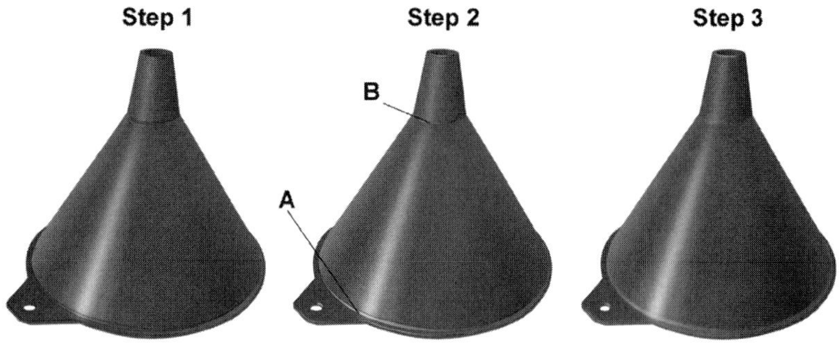

FIGURE 7.12 Add the last layer of curved highlights.

In Step 1, create a new layer and place it on top of all the previous layers. Use the Line tool and create curved outlines at the base and where the tip meets the body.

Then in Step 2, open the Color Mixer panel to create a solid fill of #FFFFFF Alpha: 35% and a linear gradient with two color swatches at each end of the color line, both #FFFFFF, but set one with Alpha: 0% and the other at Alpha: 35%. Apply the solid fill to the bottom outline and to B. Apply the linear gradient to A.

In Step 3, delete the outlines, select the fills, and convert them to a symbol. With the symbol selected in the Filter panel, apply a blur effect of 2, quality set at High.

Our last task is to add a shadow to the funnel. Create a new layer and place it at the bottom of all the other layers. Use the Lasso tool and select from the base color layer of the funnel to select a similar shape as shown in Figure 7.13, Step 1. Convert it to a symbol. In the Filter panel, apply a drop shadow effect, set blur at 3, Strength: 68%, Quality: High, Distance: 0, and check the hide object checkbox. Once you are done with the settings, use the Selection tool, select the shadow symbol, and use the arrow keys to move it around. Find the position where it is shown on the bottom and right side of the funnel.

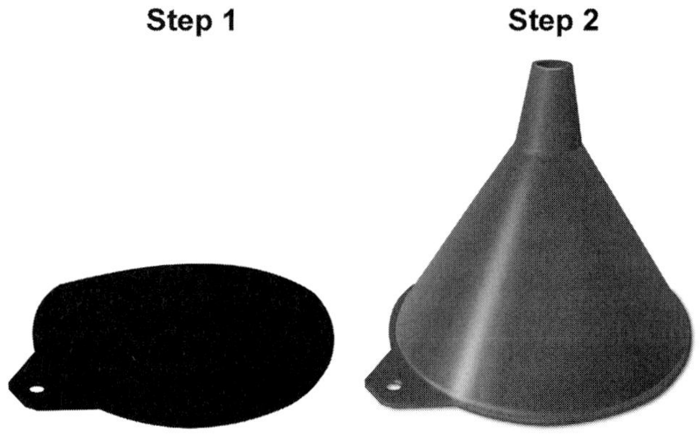

FIGURE 7.13 Add a shadow placed on a bottom layer.

Metal

The spatula we create here was chosen because of the reflections it gave off. It was not a perfect reflection like a mirror, but distorted, and had some interesting-looking highlights. As you can see in Figure 7.14, the basic shape of this metal spatula is quite simple. In Step 1, use the Line tool to create your outline and use the Selection tool to add curves to your lines. For Step 2, add depth to the spatula with the same technique with the Line and Selection tools.

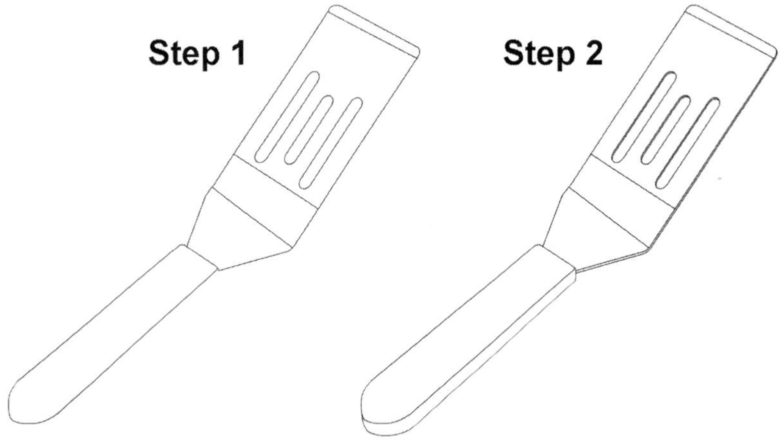

FIGURE 7.14 Create the outline of the spatula.

As shown in Figure 7.15, we will be defining the basic fills for the spatula. In Step 1, fill the top handle area with a black solid fill, #030D02. In the bottom side area, apply a linear gradient; this will define the slight highlight at the bottom of the handle. The linear gradient contains three color swatches, one at each end of the color line and one in the middle. The color swatches used are left: #384739, middle: #29342C, and right: #0F1C11. Apply this linear gradient with the Paint Bucket tool and edit it with the Gradient Transform tool so the lighter end is toward the bottom. In Step 2, fill A, create the following linear gradient with two color swatches both at each end of the color line; #1B2729 and #27383F. With the Gradient Transform tool, position the blue side toward the top. At the tip of the spatula, apply a solid fill of #213334. Step 3 will smooth the transition between the top and bottom fills. B and C are both the same linear gradient but positioned horizontally opposite from each other. The linear gradient has three color swatches: #FFFFFF, #52737A, and #2F4448. In Step 4, apply a linear gradient to the side of the metal part. This linear gradient contains the color swatches #61787C and #253738. Position this linear gradient with the darker end toward the top.

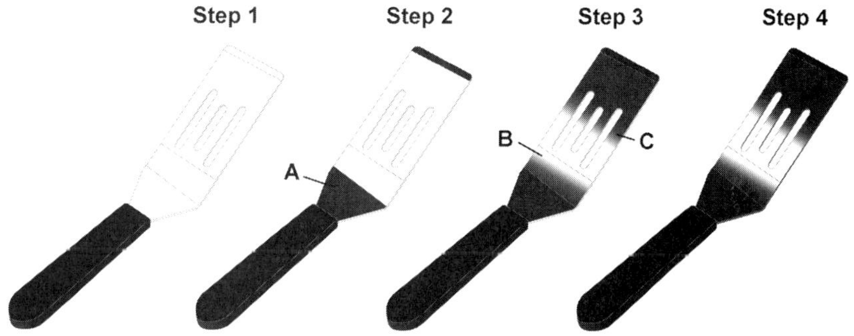

FIGURE 7.15 Add the basic fills of the spatula.

Next, we will be adding a layer of glare-like shine to the metal as shown in Figure 7.16 to make it seem quite reflective. The techniques we used on the funnel to create highlights will be used on the spatula. In Step 1, create a new layer and place it on top. Use the Line tool to create outlines at the three skinny holes in the spatula. Fill the outlines with #FFFFFF and delete the outlines. Convert these fills to a symbol and apply a blur effect of .5, quality: High. For Step 2, use the Pencil tool set at Smooth, and create the outlines for the next highlights. Apply fill A with #344B4A and fill B with #FFFFFF. Convert each of these fills to a symbol, and apply to fill A a blur effect of 2, quality: High, and fill B a blur

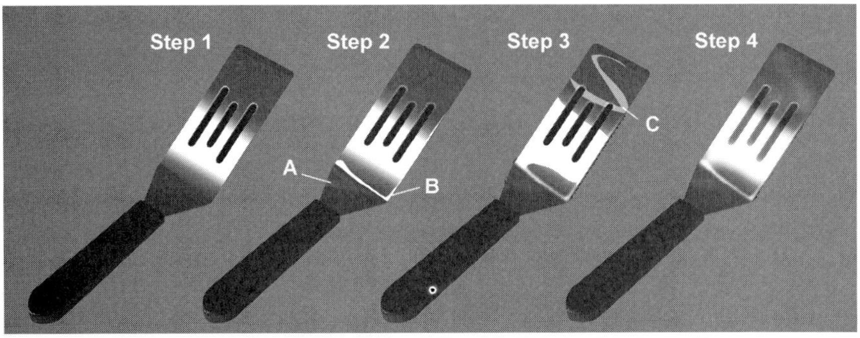

FIGURE 7.16 Add a layer of glares to the metal part.

effect of 1.25, quality: High. In Step 3, use the Pencil tool to draw the S-shaped outline and large lower area. Fill C with #FFFFFF, Alpha: 61%, and the large lower area with #FFFFFF. Convert each of these fills to a symbol, and apply to fill C a blur effect of 9, quality: High, and large lower fill blur effect of 10, quality: High.

Our last task is to create a drop shadow for the spatula. Create a new layer and place it at the bottom in relation to the other layers. The quickest way to create this shape is to select the handle graphic with the Lasso tool and copy and paste it on the new layer. Select the metal part base fill with the Lasso tool and copy and paste it on the new layer. With it still selected, use the Free Transform tool and skew it to match Figure 7.17. Select all fills on this new layer and change their fills to a black linear gradient that fade transparent of 70% on the end toward the top, as shown in Step 1. In Step 2, convert it to a symbol. In the Filter panel, apply a blur effect of 5, quality: Low. Once you are done with the set-

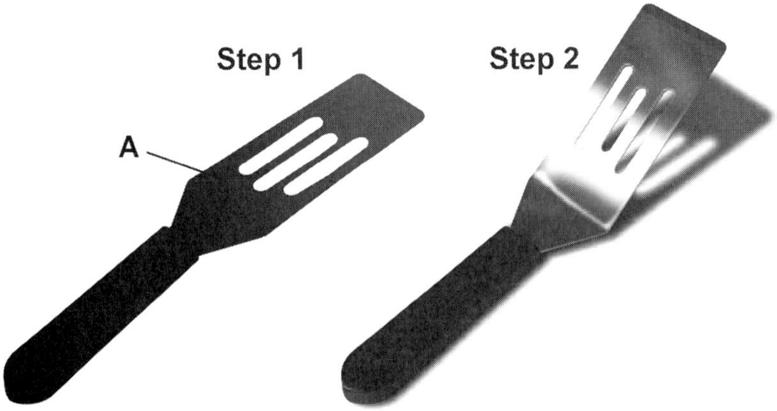

FIGURE 7.17 Add a shadow to the spatula.

tings, use the Selection tool to select the shadow symbol, and use the arrow keys to move it around. Find the position where it is shown on the bottom and right side of the spatula.

Chrome

Chrome seems to be much more reflective than just our normal metal and stretches the reflection like a funhouse mirror. Chrome is also found on car bumpers and coffee pots. Some figures in this section have a gray or black background to show white lines and detail, but you don't have to change your background color. We will be creating a chrome-looking dog bowl. Our first task is to create the basic outlines of this object as shown in Figure 7.18. In Step 1, use the Oval tool and Line tool to build out the top, bottom, and sides of the bowl. In Step 2, use the Pencil tool to create the outlines for the funhouse mirror-shaped reflections.

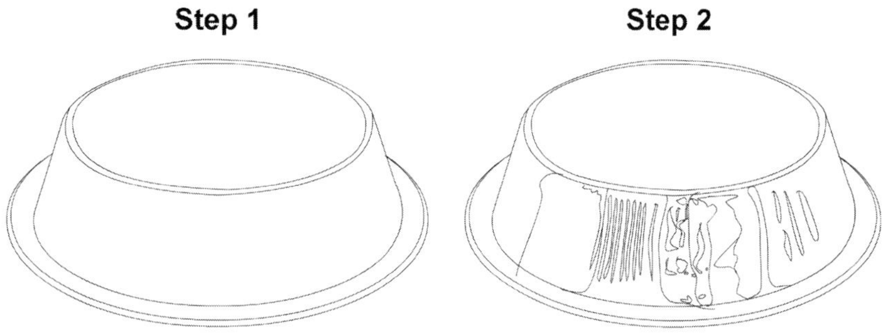

FIGURE 7.18 Create basic outline of the bowl.

In this task, we'll apply solid color and linear gradients to the outlined areas and apply a blur effect, as shown in Figure 7.19. In Step 1, apply several different solid fills and linear fills. Fill A is a linear gradient with three color swatches: #181A19, #3A3A32, and #5B5851. Fill B is a linear gradient with two color swatches: #B6B1AB and #606266. Fill C is a linear gradient with two color swatches: #71654F and #413B2F. Fill D is a linear gradient with two color swatches: #454443 and #1A1A1A. Once you are done applying the fills, delete the outlines and select the fills. Convert them to a symbol and apply a blur effect of 1.25 on quality: High.

In this task, we will be creating the base color for the inside of the bowl, as shown in Figure 7.20. In Step 1, start by creating an outline by using the Oval tool to create an oval, and use the Selection tool to modify it. In Step 2, apply the fills with the Paint Bucket tool to create the base color. Fill A is comprised of four color swatches: #262926, #383A34, #333331, and #181C1B. Fill B is a solid fill of #32352A. Fill C is a linear gradient made up of two color swatches: #30322C and #403E2F. Once you are done applying fills, remove the outlines and select the fills. Once selected, convert them to a symbol. Apply a blur effect of 3 with quality: Medium.

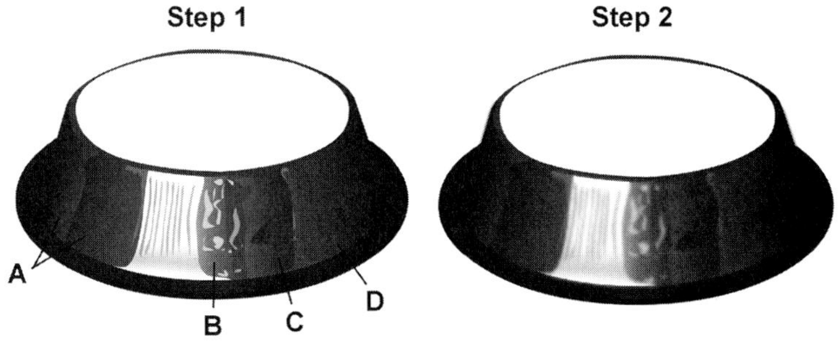

FIGURE 7.19 Add the base layer of fill.

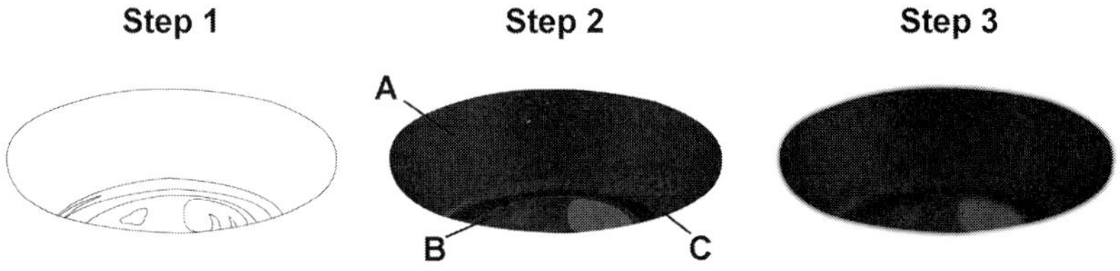

FIGURE 7.20 Add the base layer of fill for the inside of the bowl.

As shown in Figure 7.21, we will be adding side highlights to the bowl. In Step 1, create a new layer and place it at the top. Create an outline of the shape shown and apply fill A. Fill A is a radial gradient made of four color swatches: #565751 Alpha: 100%, #565751 Alpha: 50%, #565751 Alpha: 50%, and #565751 Alpha: 100%. Once gradient is applied, delete the outline, convert it to a symbol, and apply a blur effect of 2 on quality: High. Step 2, create a new layer on top, and create another outline in the shape shown in Step 2. Fill B is a radial gradient with four color swatches: #8A9CB2 Alpha: 57%, #8A9CB2 Alpha: 30%, #8A9CB2 Alpha: 30%, and #8A9CB2 Alpha: 57%.

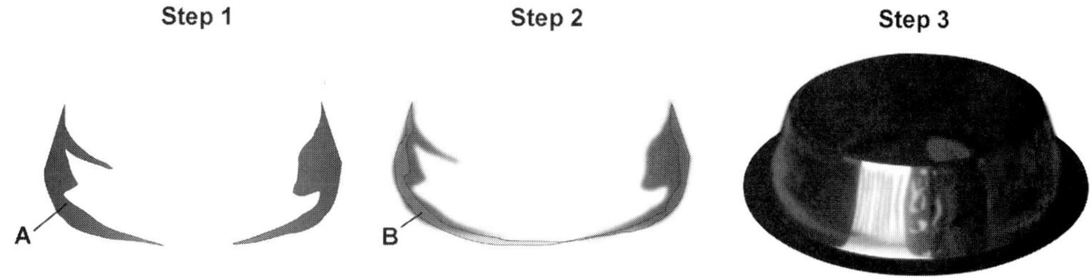

FIGURE 7.21 Add the first layer of side highlights.

Create a new layer and place it above all the previous layers. In Step 1, use the Pencil tool to create an outline, which will be where you will place a solid fill of #FFFFFF with Alpha: 16%. Select and delete the outlines, as they will not be needed anymore. In Step 2, select the fills and convert them to a symbol. Apply a blur filter to the symbol with a value of 3 and quality: High, as shown in Figure 7.22.

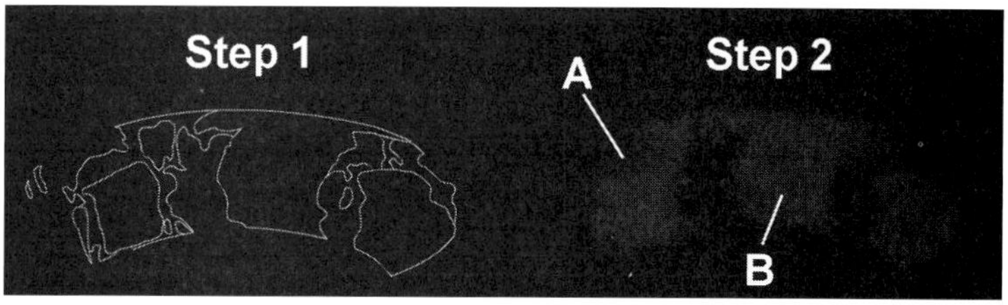

FIGURE 7.22 Add highlight for the inside of the bowl.

Create a new layer and place it above all the previous layers. In Step 1, use the Pencil tool to create an outline, which will be where you will place a solid fill of #F4F4F6. Select and delete the outlines, as they will not be needed anymore. In Step 2, select the fills and convert them to a symbol. Apply a blur filter to the symbol with a value of 3 and quality: High, as shown in Figure 7.23.

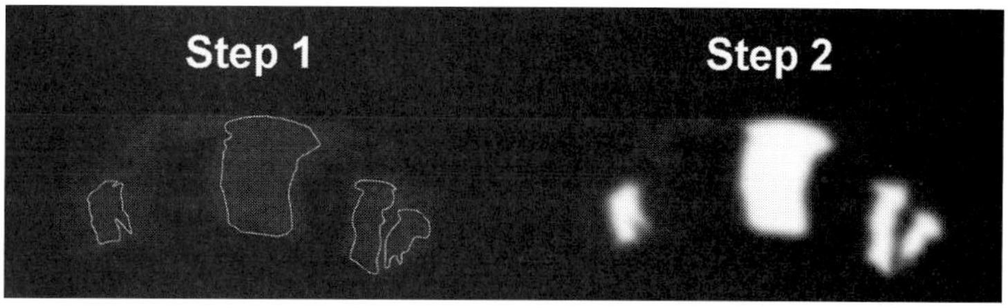

FIGURE 7.23 Add a second layer of highlight to the inside of the bowl.

In this next task, we will be creating a raised part in the chrome in the shapes of little fish. In Step 1, on the same layer, use the Pencil tool to create an outline, which will be where you will place a solid fill of #000000, as shown in Figure 7.24. Select and delete the outlines, as they will not be needed anymore. In Step 2, select the fills and convert them to a symbol. Apply a bevel filter to the symbol with a value of 1, strength: 100%; Shadow: #666666, Highlight: #FFFFFF, angle: 72, distance: 1 and quality: High. Check the Knockout checkbox and set the type to inner.

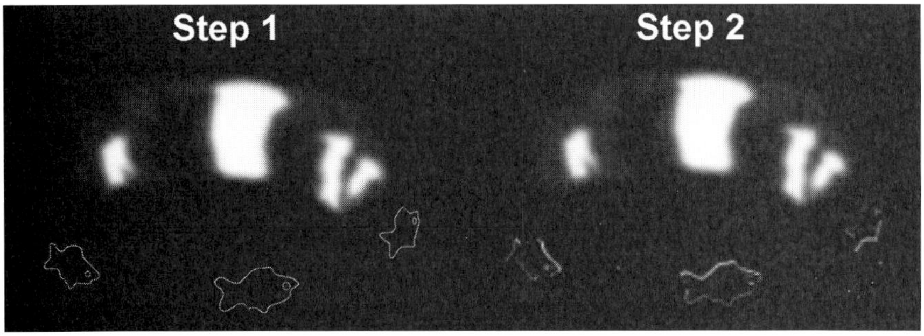

FIGURE 7.24 Add the last layer of highlight inside the bowl.

Create a new layer and place it above all the previous layers. In Step 1, use the Pencil tool to create an outline, which will be where you will place a solid fill of #FFFFFF, as shown in Figure 7.25. Select and delete the outlines, as they will not be needed anymore. In Step 2, select the fills and convert them to a symbol. Apply a blur filter to the symbol with a value of 1.25 and quality: High.

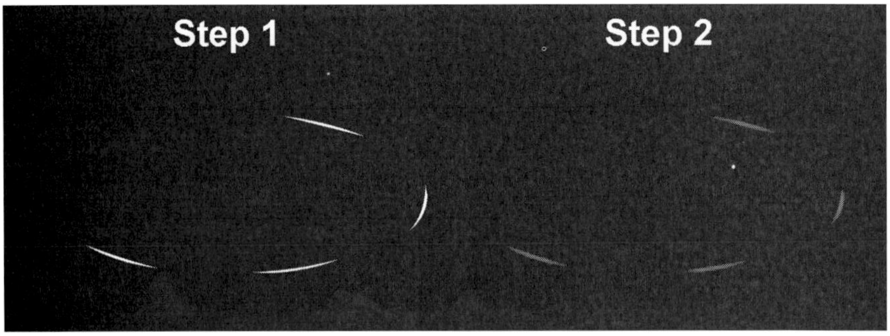

FIGURE 7.25 Add highlight trim on the rim of the bowl.

Create a new layer and place it at the bottom from the previous layers. In Step 1, use the Pencil tool to create an outline, which will be where you will place a solid fill of #000000, as shown in Figure 7.26. Select and delete the outlines, as they will not be needed anymore. In Step 2, select the fills and convert them to a symbol. Apply a drop shadow filter to the symbol with a value of 3, strength: 56%, quality: High, color: #000000, angle: 45, distance: 0, and check the Hide Object checkbox.

FIGURE 7.26 Create a shadow of the bowl.

Sponge

A porous object like a sponge seemed like a perfect vector texture to create, because it contains hard edges, circular craters, and is usually one color. For the first task, create an outline, a foundation for the base color fills, as shown in Figure 7.27. In Step 2, apply three linear gradient fills to the outline and delete the outlines when done. Fill A contains two color swatches at each end of the color line: #5BB230 and #57992B. Place it so the lighter green is toward the bottom and the dark green is at the top. Fill B contains two color swatches at each end of the color line: #4CA81F and #408F1C. Place it so the lighter green is on the right and the dark green is to the left. Fill C contains two color swatches at each end of the color line: #2B8514 and #165D00. Place it so the lighter green is on the left and the dark green is to the right.

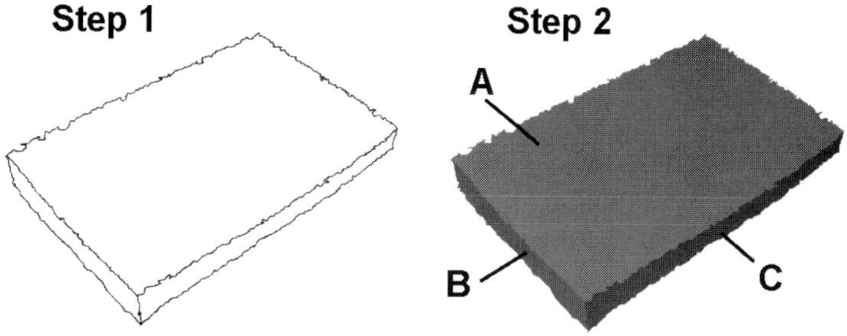

FIGURE 7.27 Create a base color for the sponge.

Create two textures that will act as our porous craters for the sponge's surface. We create two so when we duplicate them throughout the surface, it does not look repetitive. To create them, simply use the Pencil tool to draw the outlines and apply dark green fills to them with the Paint Bucket tool. When you are done coloring them, make each a symbol, as shown in Figure 7.28. This way, when they are duplicated, our file size will be optimized.

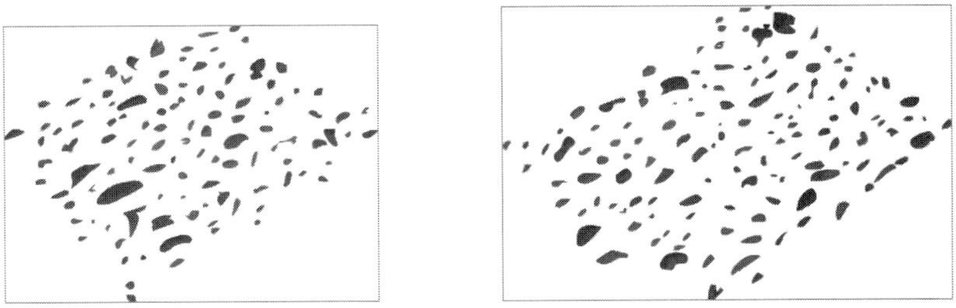

FIGURE 7.28 Create two textures that will soon be applied on top of the base color.

Duplicate more of the same texture by using the Duplicate quick key command when you have a texture selected. Position and rotate the textures with the Free Transform tool, as shown in Figure 7.29.

You probably noticed there were some gaps in the sponge that did not have any textures, so to fix that, we will be drawing in filler textures. Use the same technique you used to create your first textures to draw the filler textures, as shown in Figure 7.30.

FIGURE 7.29 Apply the textures on top of the base color.

FIGURE 7.30 Add filler textures where needed.

Now we will begin to create textures for the sides of the sponge. We could try to use the same symbol technique, but this area is very skinny and contains a drastic gradient in the background, so we will be drawing in the texture similar to the filler textures. Use the Pencil tool to create the outlines, a foundation for the base color fills, as shown in Figure 7.31.

FIGURE 7.31 Draw outlines for the side textures.

In Step 1, apply a linear gradient fill to the outlines and delete the outlines when done, as shown in Figure 7.32. Fill A contains two color swatches at each end of the color line: #49A21F and #295C12. Place it so the lighter green is toward the bottom and the dark green is at the top. In Step 2, apply a linear gradient fill to the outlines and delete the outlines when done. Fill B contains two color swatches at each end of the color line: #1E620D and #154301. Place it so the lighter green is toward the bottom and the dark green is at the top.

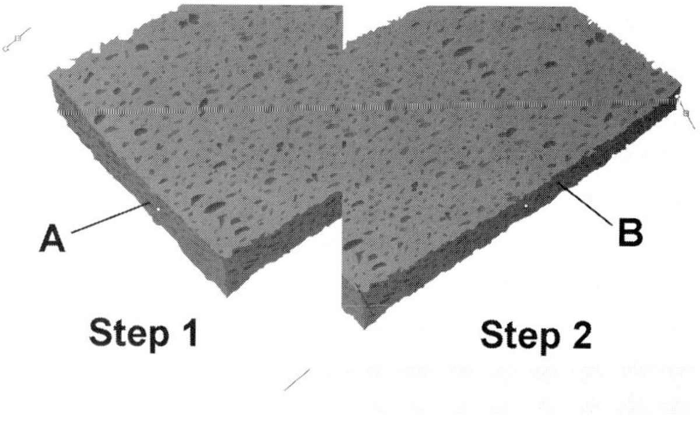

FIGURE 7.32 Apply fills to the outlines.

Create a new layer and place it at the bottom from the previous layers. In Step 1, use the Pencil tool to create an outline, which will be where you will place a solid fill of #243300, as shown in Figure 7.33. Select and delete the outlines, as they will not be needed anymore. In Step 2, select the fills and convert them to a symbol. Apply a blur filter to the symbol with a value of 3 and quality: High.

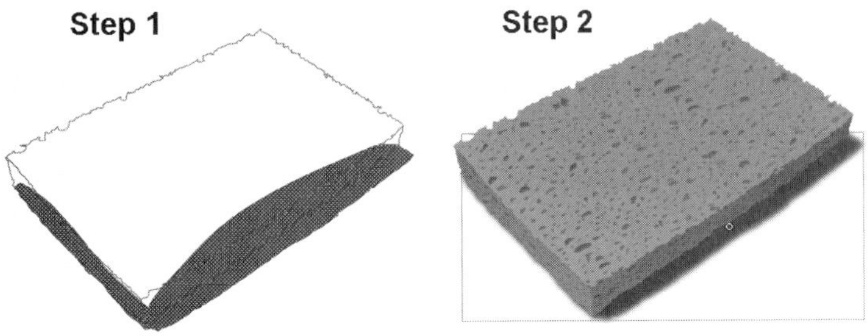

FIGURE 7.33 Create a drop shadow for the sponge.

Wood

Wood textures are always popular, as they can be applied to any object and become photorealistic looking. They can be applied to user interface elements to give an earthy feel. For the first task, create an outline, a foundation for the base color fills, as shown in Figure 7.34. Use the Pencil tool set at Smooth to achieve the curvy lines of the grain.

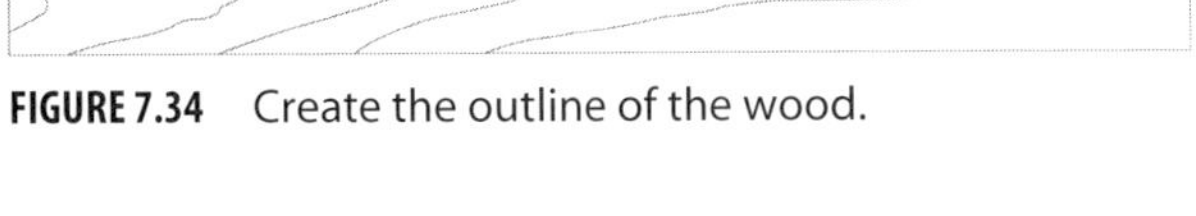

FIGURE 7.34 Create the outline of the wood.

In this next task, we will be applying the base color for the wood. It is made up of linear and radial gradients, as shown in Figure 7.35. In Step 1, apply linear gradient fills to the skinny horizontal outlines. The linear gradient used contains two color swatches at each end of the color line:

#EFD0A2 and #E6C28B. Place it so the lighter brown is toward the bottom and the darker brown is at the top. In Step 2, apply a radial gradient fill to the curved outlines and delete the outlines when done. Fill B contains two color swatches, the lighter brown placed in the center of the gradient: #EFD0A2 and #E5C088. Place it so the lighter brown is to the left and the darker brown is to the right.

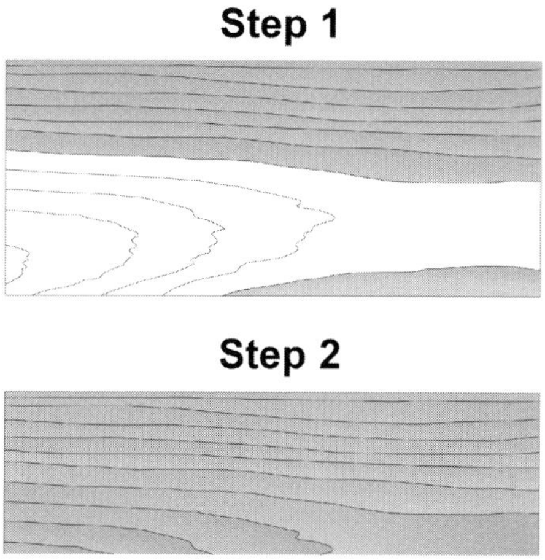

FIGURE 7.35 Apply the base color of the wood.

Create a texture that will act as our wood grain for the wood's surface. To do so, simply use the Line tool, draw one line, and then apply a curve to it with the Selection tool. Then, draw another line connecting both ends to the first line and apply a curve to the new line. You should have a thin splinter shape; fill the outline with a solid fill with a value of #CEA166, as shown in Figure 7.36. When you are done coloring, delete the outlines and convert it to a symbol; this way, when they are duplicated our file size will be optimized.

FIGURE 7.36 Create a grain texture.

Duplicate more of the same texture by using the Duplicate quick key command when you have the texture selected. Position and rotate the textures with the Free Transform tool, as shown in Figure 7.37.

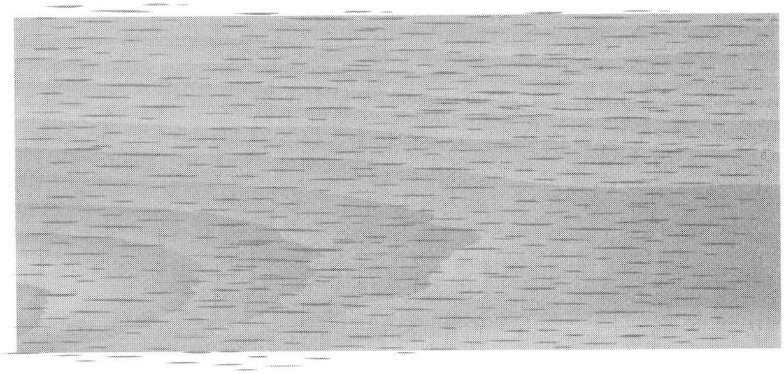

FIGURE 7.37 Apply the grain texture to the wood.

BITMAP TEXTURES

Bitmaps have their place in Flash, and one of the roles they can play is adding subtle or grainy texture that could not normally be achieved with the vector drawing tools alone. Be aware that implementing bitmap textures in your project will increase the file size quite a bit, but we will be reviewing a few techniques that will save you a couple hundred kilobytes. Since bitmaps are square, we will be masking them to achieve the shape we desire. With bitmaps, we will be able to achieve objects like a crispy rice treat to the swirling rock texture of a marble slab.

Rice Treat

These crispy and sticky rectangle rice treats are yummy to the taste buds, but who knew they would be yummy in Flash? With their simple rectangular shape, most of the work will be done in the rice treat texture we will be applying. To begin, we will create the fill shapes that will be used as the mask shapes, as shown in Figure 7.38. Create an outline, and use 3-point perspective, which was explained in Chapter 4, "Illustration Techniques." Once you have your rectangle shape, replace the straight lines with bumpy lines, as shown in Step 1. This will give your treat the correct surface to match the texture we will be using. In Step 2, use the Paint Bucket tool to apply any color fills to each area; just make sure the three fills are different in HEX value so they do not meld together.

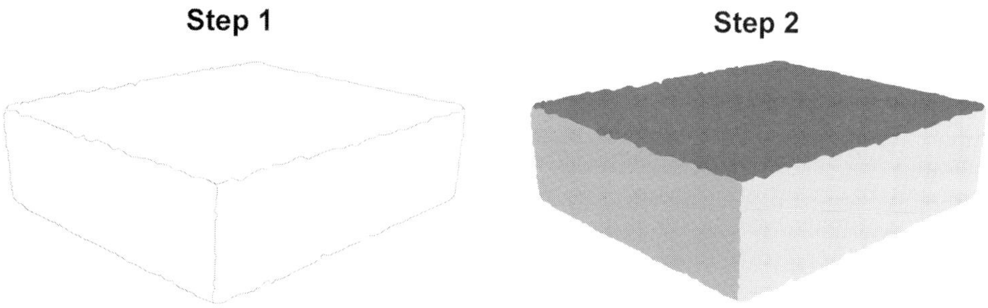

FIGURE 7.38 Create the mask shapes.

Select the mask shapes and convert to symbol. Go inside the symbol by double-clicking it. Put each fill shape on its own layer. Add a new layer under each of the first three layers with the mask shapes in them. Import the rice texture into Flash by using the quick key command to Import Image. You will find the two rice textures we will be using in Chapter_7, treat1.jpg and treat2.jpg on the companion CD-ROM. Place treat1 on the blank layers below the top mask shape and the right-side mask shape. Place treat2 on the blank layer below the left mask shape. Double-click on each mask shape layers, click the Mask radio button in the pop up, and click OK. This should make that layer a mask layer. Now, click and drag the layers with the textures in them and place them under the mask layer you want to associate it with. This should change the icons in the layers to the Mask Hierarchy icons, as shown in Figure 7.39. To see the mask at work, make sure all layers are locked. Another content layer has been added with a solid fill of light orange and a transparency, which will tint the color of the top texture.

ON THE CD

We will be tinting the other sides to light orange on the main Timeline on a new layer, because we will be adding linear gradients to blend them together, as shown in Figure 7.40. In Step 1, create an outline and fill the left area with a solid fill of #DA9958, Alpha: 38%, and fill in the right area with a solid fill of #D07E2F, Alpha: 52%. In Step 2, blend the fills together by applying linear gradients in the three areas marked. Fill A is a linear gradient with two color swatches: #F8EBDF, Alpha: 39% and #DA9958, Alpha: 38%. Fill B is a linear gradient with two color swatches: #DA9958, Alpha: 36% and #DA9958, Alpha: 57%. Fill C is a linear gradient with three color swatches: #D07E2F, Alpha: 18%, #D07E2F, Alpha: 17%, and #D07E2F, Alpha: 52%.

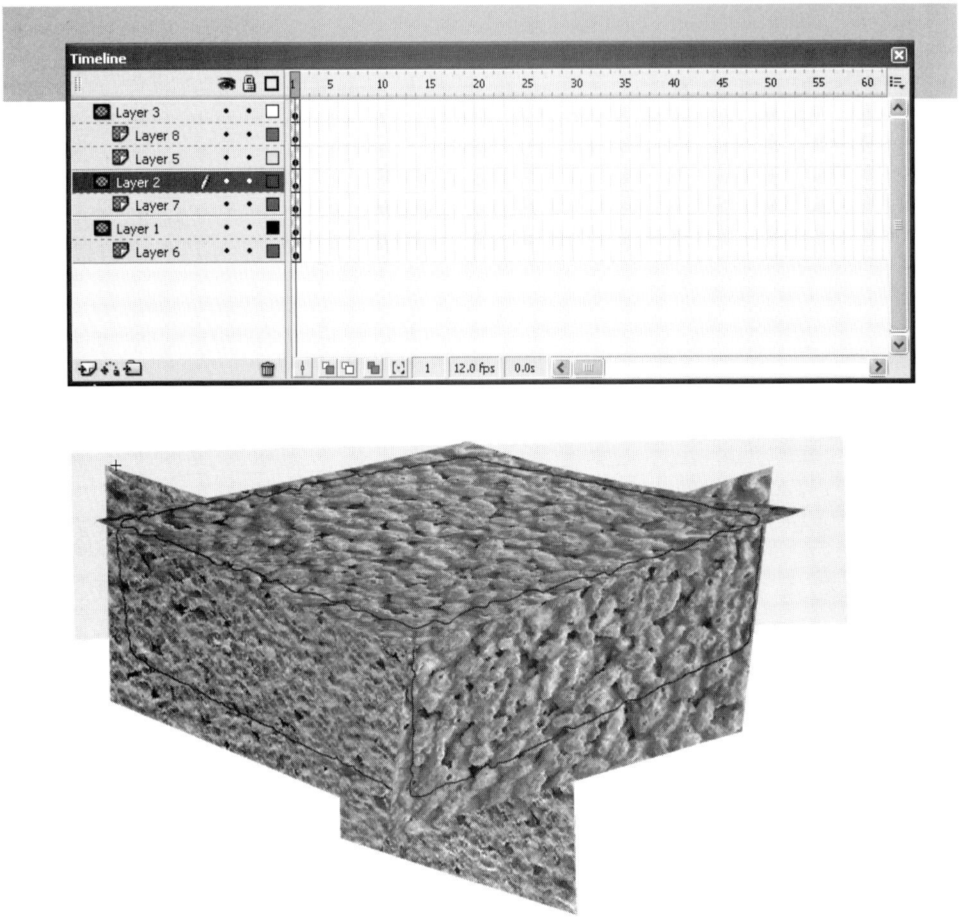

FIGURE 7.39 Incorporating the mask shapes with the texture bitmap.

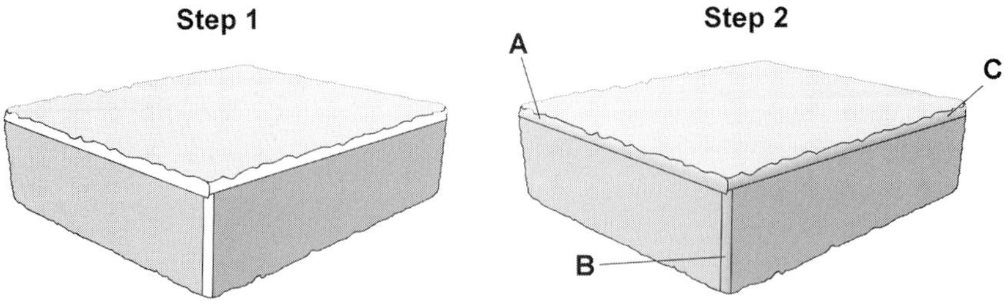

FIGURE 7.40 Create a fill overlay.

In this task, we will be creating a drop shadow for the rice treat, as shown in Figure 7.41. This shadow will be a bit different from others, as we will be adding a shadow and a ground reflection. Create a new layer and place it below the other layers. In Step 1, create an outline of the shadow and apply a solid fill of #000000, delete the outlines, and convert the fill to a symbol. Apply a drop shadow filter on it and set it to blur 5, strength: 62%, quality: High, color: #4D2F11, angle: 45, distance: 0, and check the Hide Object checkbox. In Step 2, create the reflection by drawing an outline and divide it in half. In each side, we will be adding the same linear gradient, but each skewed differently to make a pointing down shape. The linear gradient contains two color swatches: #8B551F, Alpha: 20% and #8B551F, Alpha: 75%.

FIGURE 7.41 Create a shadow for the object.

FIGURE 7.42 The final rendering of the rice treat.

On the same layer as the drop shadow, apply a simple radial gradient to give the rice treat a backdrop. The radial gradient contains two color swatches: #E8BF97 and #DA9958. Position the lighter color toward the center of the gradient. You'll get something like Figure 7.42.

Cardboard Box

Everyone loves to receive a package in the mail or a present for a special occasion, so all of us should be familiar with the object we are about to create. This cardboard box is quite simple in shape, and the textures we will be using bring it to life. To begin, we will be creating the fill shapes that will be used as the mask shapes, as shown in Figure 7.43. Create an outline, and use 2-point perspective, explained in Chapter 4.

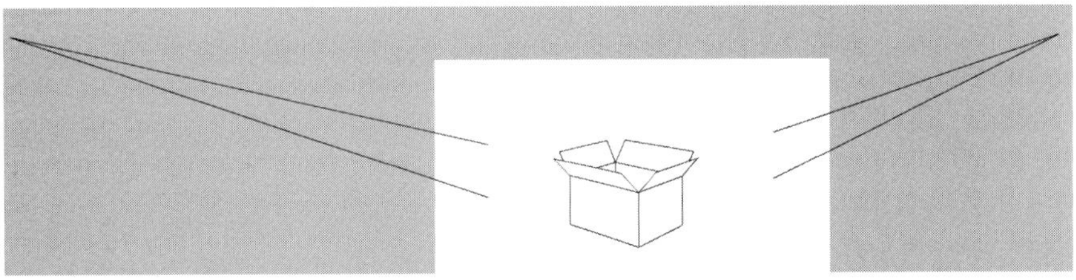

FIGURE 7.43 Outline created with 2-point perspective.

Use the Paint Bucket tool to apply any color fills to each area; just make sure the three fills are different in HEX value so they do not meld together, as shown in Figure 7.44. Delete the outlines and convert the fills to a symbol.

FIGURE 7.44 Create the mask shapes.

ON THE CD

Go inside the symbol by double-clicking it. Put each fill shape on its own layer. Add a new layer under each of the first layers with the mask shapes in them. Import the cardboard textures into Flash by using the quick key command to Import Image. You will find the two cardboard textures we will be using on the companion CD-ROM in Chapter_7, cardboard1.jpg and cardboard2.jpg. Place cardboard1 on the inner flap mask layers, and cardboard2 on all the other mask layers. Double-click on each mask shape layers, click the Mask radio button in the pop up, and click OK. This should make that layer a mask layer. Now, click and drag the layers with the textures in them and place them under the mask layer you want to associate it with. This should change the icons in the layers to the Mask Hierarchy icons, as shown in Figure 7.45. Use the Free Transform tool to change the position, rotation, and skew of the textures to get the look for a specific side of the box. To see the mask at work, make sure all layers are locked.

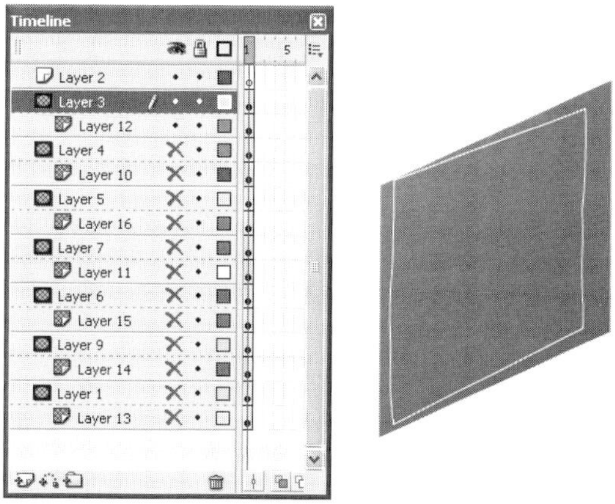

FIGURE 7.45 Incorporating the mask shapes with the texture bitmap.

Lock all the layers, and your box should look like the one shown in Figure 7.46.

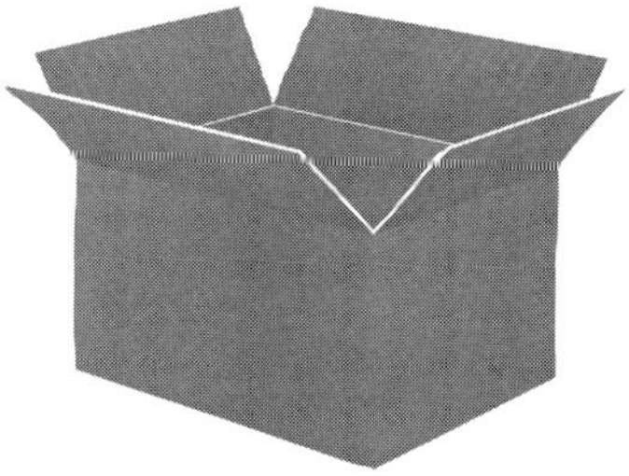

FIGURE 7.46 Box with mask layers locked.

By using the same outlines we used in the beginning, apply linear gradients to create a fill overlay that will give the cardboard box depth, as shown in Figure 7.47. In Step 1, apply linear gradients throughout the

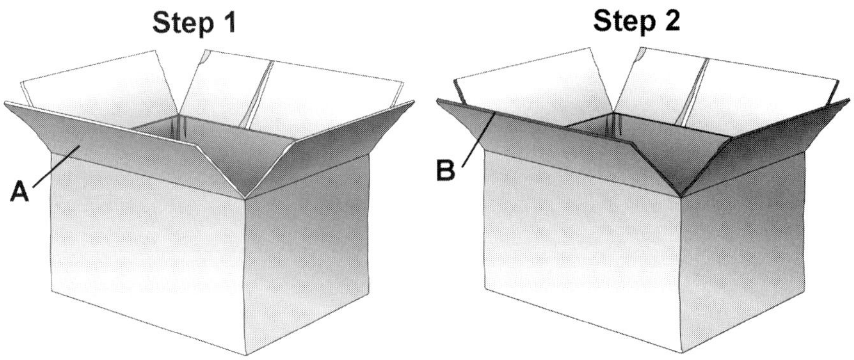

FIGURE 7.47 Create a fill overlay.

outlines. All these linear gradients are similar but with different degrees of transparency. Fill A is a linear gradient with two color swatches: #000000, Alpha: 18% and # #000000, Alpha: 36%. Position the lighter side at the bottom and the darker side toward the top. In Step 2, apply solid fills to the trim of the cardboard box to give it more definition and the minor details that will make it seem more realistic. Area B contains two solid fills: #AE8359 and #55402B.

Add dents and wrinkles on the inner part of the cardboard box by applying solid fills with the HEX values #FFFFFF, Alpha: 9% and #000000, Alpha 15%, as shown in Figure 7.48.

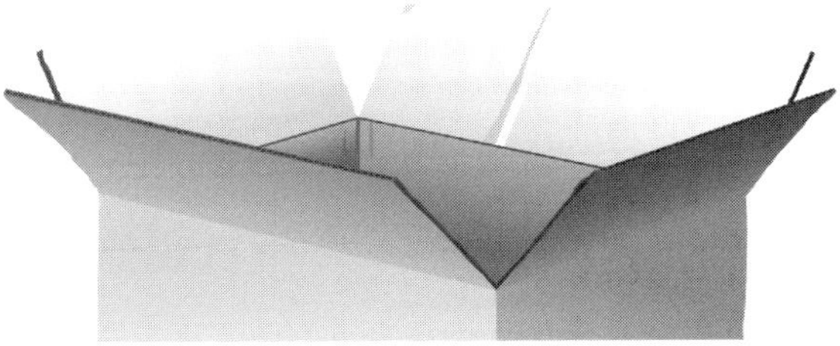

FIGURE 7.48 Adding more detail to the trim.

Create a new layer and place it at the bottom from the previous layers. In Step 1, use the Pencil tool to create an outline, where you will place a solid fill of #00FF00, as shown in Figure 7.49. Select and delete the outlines, as they will not be needed anymore. In Step 2, select the fills and convert them to a symbol. Apply a drop shadow filter to the symbol with a value of 4, strength: 68%, quality: High, color: #000000, angle: 45, distance: 0, and check the Hide Object checkbox.

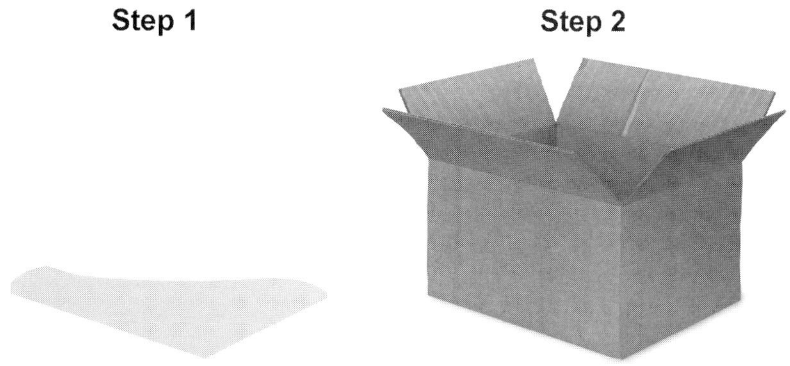

FIGURE 7.49 Create a shadow for the box.

Baseball Cap

Baseball caps keep the sun out of your eyes, keep your head warm, and sometimes keep your face concealed while you're in public, but the cap we will create here just shows us how a simple fabric texture can go a long way in making an object look photorealistic. To begin, we will be creating the fill shapes that will be used as the mask shapes, as shown in Figure 7.50. Create a basic outline of the baseball cap, as shown in Step 1. In Step 2, use the Paint Bucket tool to apply any color fills to each area; just make sure the solid fills are different in HEX value so they do not meld together.

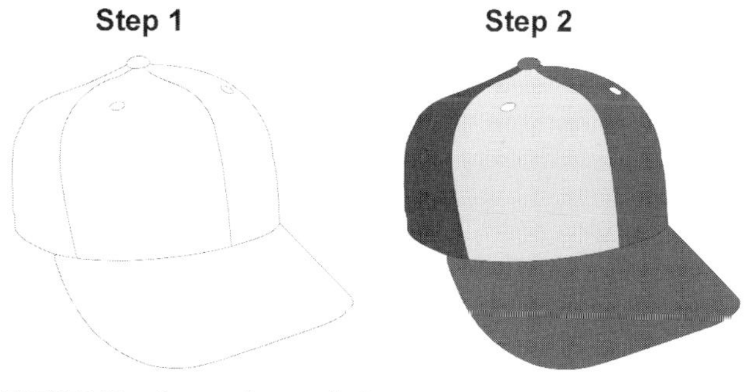

FIGURE 7.50 Create the mask shapes.

ON THE CD

Select the solid fills and convert them to a symbol. Go inside the symbol by double-clicking it. Put each fill shape on its own layer. Add a new layer under each of the first layers with the mask shapes in them. Import the fabric texture into Flash by using the quick key command to Import Image. You will find the fabric texture on the companion CD-ROM in

Chapter_7, hatfabric_small.jpg. Place hatfabric_small in the blank layers, and use the Free Transform tool to change the position, rotation, and skew of the textures to get the look for a specific part of the baseball cap. Double-click on each mask shape layers, click the Mask radio button in the pop up, and click OK. This should make that layer a mask layer. Now, click and drag the layers with the textures in them and place them under the mask layer you want to associate it with. This should change the icons in the layers to the Mask Hierarchy icons, as shown in Figure 7.51. To see the mask at work, make sure all layers are locked.

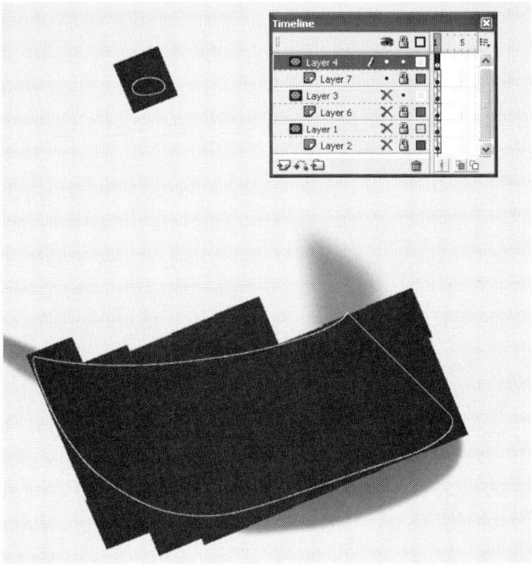

FIGURE 7.51 Incorporating the mask shapes with the texture bitmap.

Lock all the layers, and your cap should look like the one in Figure 7.52.

FIGURE 7.52 Cap with mask layers locked.

By using the same outlines we used in the beginning, apply gradients to create a fill overlay that will give the baseball cap depth, as shown in Figure 7.53. In Step 1, get the outline prepared for the areas where we will be applying gradients. In Step 2, apply gradients to the bill of the cap and the top button. Apply solid fills to the round cut-out holes on the top. Fill A is a linear gradient with two color swatches: #09071B, Alpha: 0% and #09071B, Alpha: 100%. Position the lighter side to the left and the darker side to the right side. In Step 2, apply fill B, which contains a linear gradient with four color swatches: #09071B, Alpha: 0%, #09071B, Alpha: 100%, #09071B, Alpha: 100%, and #09071B, Alpha: 0%.

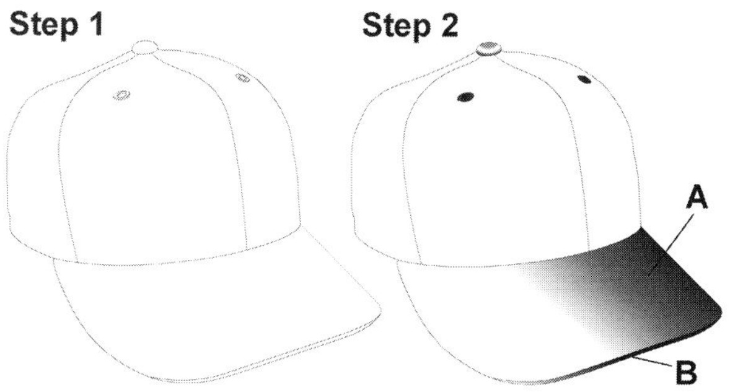

FIGURE 7.53 Adding a fill overlay.

By using the same outlines we used in the beginning, we will be adding more lines to define the stitching on the baseball cap, as shown in Figure 7.54. In Step 1, prepare the outline for the areas where we will be applying more lines. In Step 2, use the Line tool to create the new stitch lines. To create the stitch pattern in the line, go in the Properties panel and apply the following settings to the line: .25, type: dashed, dash: 4, with 2 pts. Apply a linear gradient to the stitches on the bill with two color swatches: #09071B, Alpha: 33% and #09071B, Alpha: 100%.

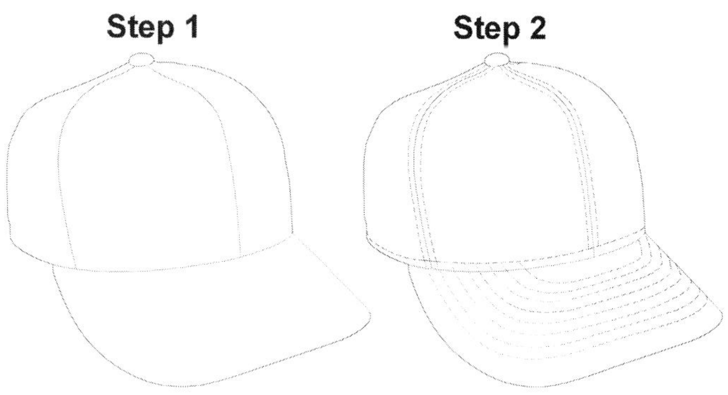

FIGURE 7.54 Adding line overlay.

Create a new layer and place it above all the previous layers. We will be adding another layer of fill overlay to add depth to the body of the baseball cap, as shown in Figure 7.55. In Step 1, use the Pencil tool to create an outline, which will be where you will place the same linear gradient throughout. The linear gradient contains two color swatches: #09071B, Alpha: 33% and #09071B, Alpha: 100%. Apply them with the Paint Bucket tool, and modify their position and rotation with the Gradient Transform tool. Select and delete the outlines, as they will not be needed anymore. In Step 2, select the fills and convert them to a symbol. Apply a blur filter to the symbol with a value of 5 and quality: High.

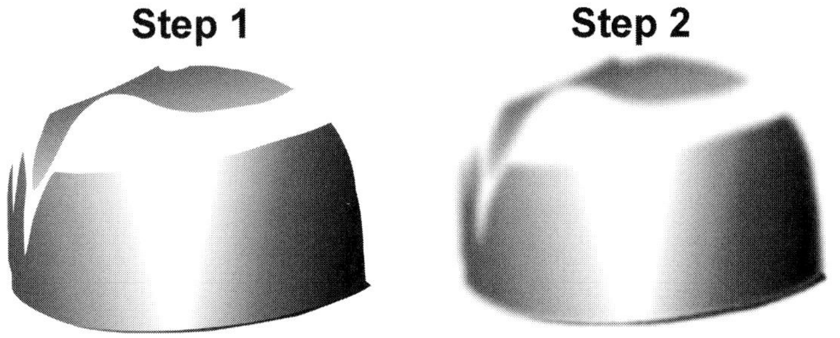

FIGURE 7.55 Adding more fill overlay.

Create a new layer and place it at the bottom of the previous layers. In Step 1, you can see how the baseball cap looks with all the layers of depth and detail, as shown in Figure 7.56. In Step 2, use the Pencil tool to create an outline, which will be where you will place a solid fill of #3C4353. In the left side and bottom areas, we will be adding a radial gradient that contains two color swatches: #22282B and #485362.

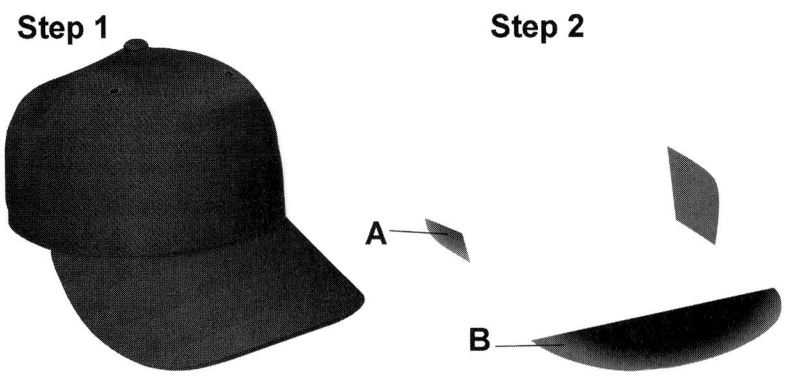

FIGURE 7.56 Creating shadow for the cap.

FIGURE 7.57 Final rendering of the cap.

Select the two bottom radial gradients and convert them to a symbol. Apply a blur filter to the symbol with a value of 1.5 and quality: High. Select the top solid fill and convert it to a symbol. Apply a blur filter to the symbol with a value of 8 and quality: High.

Serving Board

This tutorial is a great example of how you can incorporate vector textures with bitmap textures. Here, we use the great qualities of the small file size of vectors and complicated patterns that bitmaps can portray to achieve a supreme photorealistic look. To begin, we will be creating an outline that will be used as the mask shapes. Create a basic outline of the serving board, as shown in Figure 7.58.

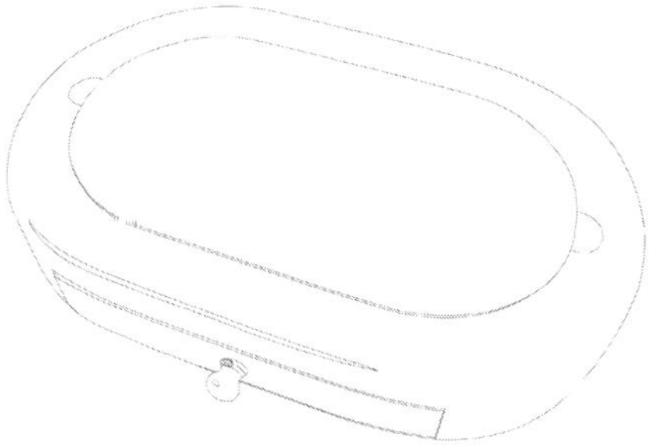

FIGURE 7.58 Create an outline of the serving board.

Here, we will be creating a mask shape and applying the vector wood texture we created earlier in this chapter, as shown in Figure 7.59. In Step 1, use the Paint Bucket tool to apply any color fill to the entire area. In

FIGURE 7.59 Create a mask shape and apply it to the vector texture.

Step 2, select the fill and convert it to a symbol. In that symbol, create a new layer, import the vector wood texture, and duplicate it throughout.

Here, we will be creating a mask shape and applying a bitmap marble texture, as shown in Figure 7.60. In Step 1, use the Paint Bucket tool to apply any color fill to the center part of the outline area. In Step 2, select the fill and convert it to a symbol. In that symbol, create a new layer and import the marble texture into Flash by using the quick key command to Import Image (in the menu, File > Import > Import to Stage). The marble texture we will be using is on the companion CD-ROM in Chapter_7, marble.jpg. Place marble in the blank layer and use the Free Transform tool to change the position, rotation, and skew of the textures to get the look for the flat surface of the serving board. Double-click on the mask shape layer, click the Mask radio button in the pop up, and click OK. This should make that layer a mask layer. Now, click and drag the layer with the texture in it and place it under the mask layer you want to associate it with.

ON THE CD

FIGURE 7.60 Create a mask shape and apply it to a bitmap texture.

By using the same outlines we used in the beginning, apply gradients to create a fill overlay that will give the serving board depth, as shown in Figure 7.61. In Step 1, prepare the outline for the areas where we will be applying gradients. In Step 2, apply gradients to detailed areas of the serving board. Fill A is a radial gradient with five color swatches: #FFFFFF, Alpha: 100%, #FFFFFF, Alpha: 38%, #FFFFFF, Alpha: 0%, #321600, Alpha: 0%, and #321600, Alpha: 100%. Fill B is a solid fill of #FFFFFF, Alpha: 36%. Convert Fill B to a symbol and apply a blur filter to it of 1.5, quality: High. Fill C is a linear gradient with four color swatches: #FFFFFF, Alpha: 100%, #FFFFFF, Alpha: 28%, #FFFFFF, Alpha: 69%, and #FFFFFF, Alpha: 0%. Convert Fill C to a symbol and apply a blur filter to it of 1.5, quality: High. Fill D is a radial gradient with two color swatches: #542201, Alpha: 72% and #542201, Alpha: 0%. Fill E is a radial gradient with three color swatches: #321600, Alpha: 100%, #321600, Alpha: 36%, and #FFFFFF, Alpha: 28%.

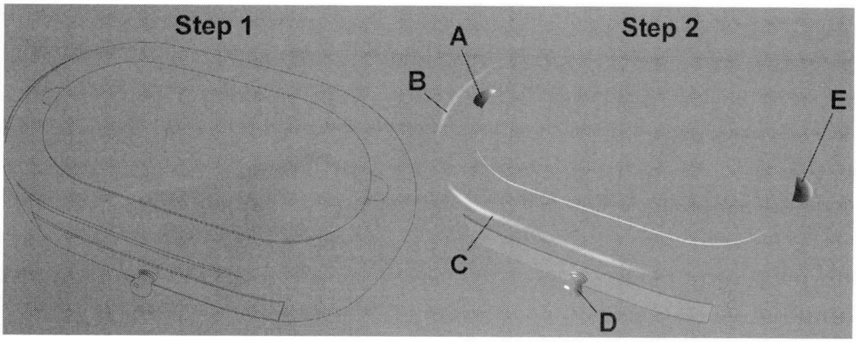

FIGURE 7.61 Creating fill overlays.

Create a new layer and place it above all the previous layers. We will be adding another layer of fill overlay to add depth to the sides of the serving board, as shown in Figure 7.62. In Step 1, create an outline on each side where linear gradients will be applied. Fill A linear gradient contains two color swatches: #614316, Alpha: 0% and #614316, Alpha: 80%. Apply them with the Paint Bucket tool, and modify their position and rotation with the Gradient Transform tool. Fill B linear gradient contains two color swatches: #614316, Alpha: 0% and #614316, Alpha: 80%. Select and delete the outlines, as they will not be needed anymore. In Step 2, select the fills and convert them to a symbol. Apply a blur filter to the symbol with a value of 5 and quality: High. Apply a mask to this symbol with the shape of the entire serving board so the blur will not bleed outside the object.

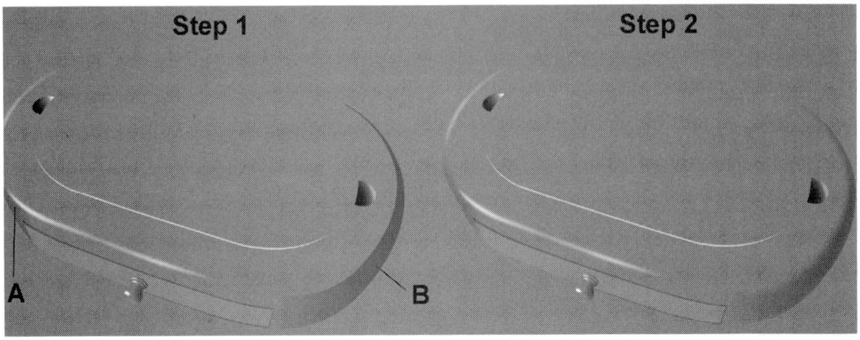

FIGURE 7.62 Creating more fill overlays.

Create a new layer and place it on top of all the other layers. Create a fill the shape of the marble surface and apply the following linear gradient that contains six color swatches: #91FFFF, Alpha: 0%, #91FFFF, Alpha: 22%, #91FFFF, Alpha: 0%, #91FFFF, Alpha: 0%, #91FFFF, Alpha: 26%, and #91FFFF, Alpha: 0%. This will add glare to the marble surface as shown in Figure 7.63.

FIGURE 7.63 Adding glare to the marble surface.

Create a new layer and place it at the bottom of the previous layers. In Step 1, create a fill shape that will be used as the shape that will be blurred, as shown in Figure 7.64. In Step 2, convert the fill to a symbol and apply a drop shadow filter to the symbol with a value of 12, strength: 62%, quality: High, color: #000000, angle: 45, distance: 0, and check the Hide Object checkbox.

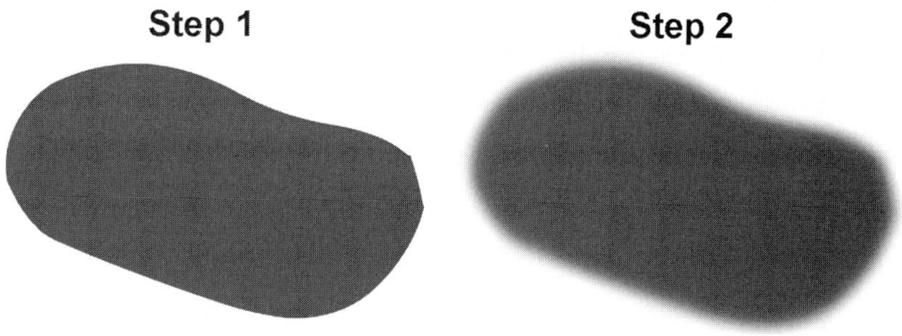

FIGURE 7.64 Creating a shadow for the serving table.

With all the layers visible, you should have the rendering of the serving board as shown in Figure 7.65.

FIGURE 7.65 Final rendering of the serving table.

SUMMARY

- Use the drawing tools to achieve photorealistic textures such as plastic, metal, chrome, wood, and even sponge.
- Integrate bitmap images into your vector graphics to save time replicating those photorealistic textures.
- Mask a bitmap image to make it the shape you desire.

EXERCISES

ON THE CD

The following exercises will put to use what you learned in this chapter. You will be creating a metal fork, a hammer with a wooden handle, a slice of bread, and a stack of rocks. The files for the following exercises are on the companion CD-ROM in the folders cited.

1. Create a metal-looking fork from the image provided. Use the techniques learned in this chapter, especially the ones you learned while creating the metal to achieve the shine found in the fork. The jpg file is located on the companion CD-ROM in Chapter_7/Exercises/fork.jpg.
2. Create a hammer with a wooden handle from the image provided. Use the techniques learned in this chapter, especially the ones you learned while creating the wood texture. The jpg file is located on the companion CD-ROM in Chapter_7/Exercises/hammer.jpg.
3. Create a slice of bread from the image provided. Use the techniques learned in this chapter, especially the ones you learned while creating the rice treat and baseball cap to achieve the grainy texture found in the slice of bread. The jpg file is located on the companion CD-ROM in Chapter_7/Exercises/bread.jpg.
4. Create a stack of rocks from the image provided. Use the techniques learned in this chapter, especially the ones you learned while creating the cardboard box and serving board to achieve the texture and light and shadow found in the stack of rocks. The jpg file is located on the companion CD-ROM in Chapter_7/Exercises/rocks.jpg.

CHAPTER

8

NOVICE TUTORIALS

This chapter consists of novice tutorials of normal everyday items. We will be using techniques learned in Chapter 4, "Illustration Techniques" and applying them to a pen, CD-ROM, and a few other objects. These tutorials put to use the *illustration approach* of creating outlines, base color, and detail, which makes for efficient examples. Most of the figures in this chapter encompass a couple of steps within a single task, which gives you a dashboard look at the changes that lie ahead. We strongly recommend that you have the source file open relating to the current tutorial you are reviewing, as not every detail is covered in the text.

PEN

A highlighter pen is the perfect novice item. The shape of it is cylinder in nature, and the cap on it has a neat crosshatching design to it, which will make nice areas to fill with solid color. The logo on the pen can be a bit challenging but is easily reproduced, as it is made up of the fonts Arial, Arial Black, and Arial Narrow. We begin by creating the base color for the pen, as shown in Figure 8.1. In Step 1, draw an outline of the basic shape of the pen. Use the Line tool to plot your lines with the Snap to Objects feature on to snap lines together precisely. Switch the Snap to Object feature off temporarily by holding down the G key as you are using the Line tool. Use the Selection tool to add curve to your lines. In Step 2, apply the base color to the pen. Use a solid fill for the cap and use two linear gradients for the body of the pen. In Step 3, apply detail to the top of the cap.

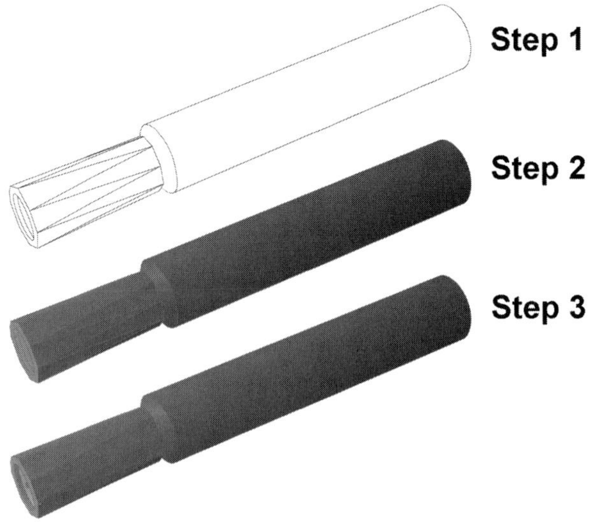

FIGURE 8.1 Creating the base color of the pen.

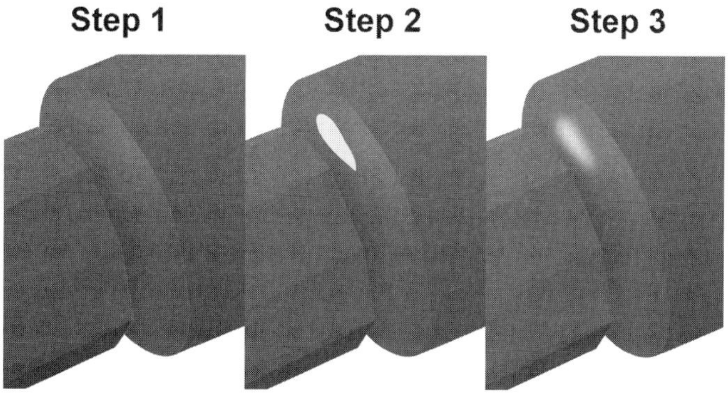

FIGURE 8.2 Adding detail where the cap and pen meet.

In this next task, we will be adding a highlight where the cap meets the body of the pen, as shown in Figure 8.2. In Step 1, use a preexisting outline and paste it on a new layer on top of the previous layers. For Step 2, with the Pencil tool, draw a small oval and apply a solid fill of #FFFFFF. In Step 3, convert the fill to a symbol and apply a blur filter with the value 2, quality: Low.

To create the logo on the pen, we will be plotting lines to help guide us to the correct position and curve our letters should be, as shown in Figure 8.3. In Step 1, use the Line and Selection tools to create your outlines, and fill the proper areas with a solid fill of #000000. In Step 2, use the Text tool to write out the smaller text, and use the Free Transform tool to rotate and skew the text to get it to sit in that slant position. For Step 3, delete all the outlines, as you will not need them anymore.

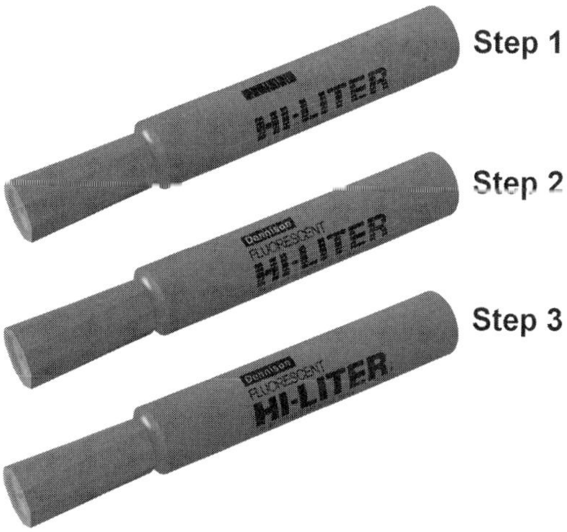

FIGURE 8.3 Creating a logo on the pen.

In these next steps, we will be creating a drop shadow with two layers of shadow to achieve the look of the pen body and tip of the cap touching the ground, as shown in Figure 8.4. In Step 1, with the Line tool, draw the area where the base shadow will be. Apply a solid fill to the area and delete the lines. For Step 2, convert the fill to a symbol and apply a drop shadow filter of 13, strength: 50%, quality: Low, color: #000000, angle: 45, distance: 0, and check the Hide Object checkbox. In Step 3, repeat steps 1 and 2 to create another shadow, but create it on a new layer above the rest and at a smaller size.

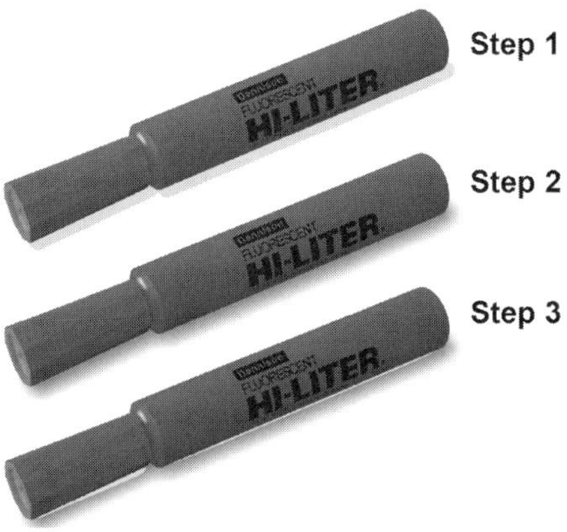

FIGURE 8.4 Creating a shadow for the pen.

Convert the fill to a symbol and apply a drop shadow filter of 9, strength: 48%, quality: High, color: #000000, angle: 45, distance: 0, and check the Hide Object checkbox. Now the pen is complete, as shown in Figure 8.5.

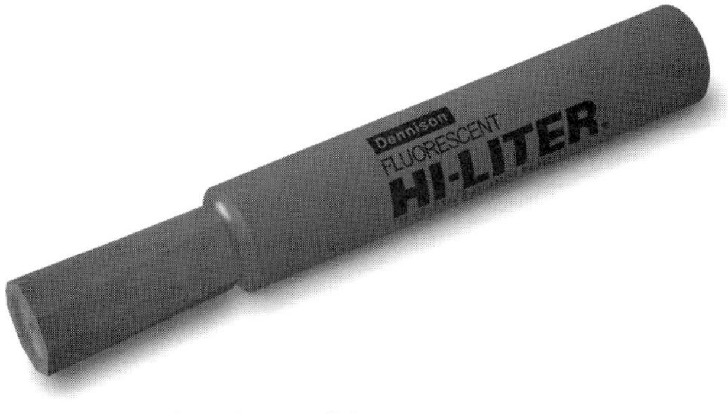

FIGURE 8.5 Final rendering of the pen.

ChapStick®

Almost everyone is familiar with ChapStick, which is the subject of our next tutorial. It is quite similar to the pen, has a base color, layer of color overlay, and some text and a logo. To begin, we will be drawing the base color of the ChapStick, as shown in Figure 8.6. In Step 1, use the Line tool to create your outline, and use the Selection tool to add curves to your lines. For Step 2, add linear gradients to the cap of the outlines. Use the Gradient Transform tool to line the gradient up with the outlines. In Step 3, add linear gradients to the trim and bottom part of the outlines. Finally, in Step 4, apply a solid fill for the black part of the ChapStick and a linear gradient for the red trim within the black area.

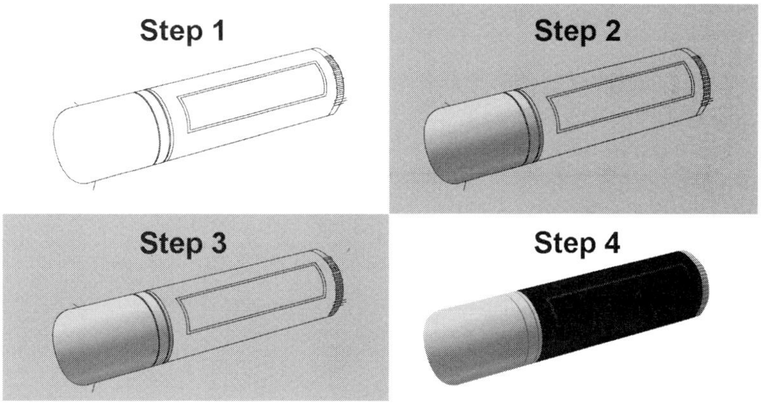

FIGURE 8.6 Creating the base color of the ChapStick.

In this task, we will be adding a gradient overlay to define the highlight on the top of the cap, as shown in Figure 8.7. In Step 1, with the Line tool, draw an outline where the highlight will be. In Step 2, use the Paint Bucket tool and apply a radial gradient that has a transparency so it fades out. Finally, use the Selection tool to select the outline and delete it.

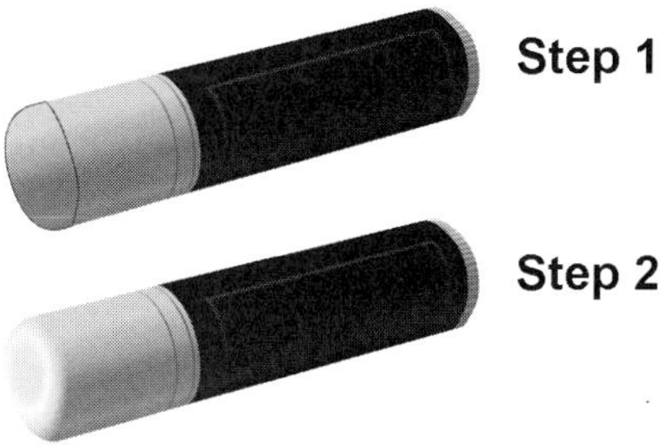

FIGURE 8.7 Adding a fill gradient overlay.

To create the logo on the ChapStick, we will be using the Pencil tool to draw the outlines, as shown in Figure 8.8. In Step 1, use the Pencil tool and create your outlines. In Step 2, use the Pencil tool again to draw the outlines for the small text at the bottom. The last line of text is so small you can just make shapes that look like words and that will be fine. Then, in Step 3, apply the same fill used on the cap to color in the text outlines. Delete all the outlines as you will not need them anymore.

FIGURE 8.8 Creating the logo on the ChapStick.

In these next steps, we will be creating a drop shadow, as shown in Figure 8.9. In Step 1, with the Line tool, draw the area where the base shadow will be. Apply a solid fill to the area and delete the lines. In Step 2, convert the fill to a symbol and apply a blur filter of 4 and quality: Low.

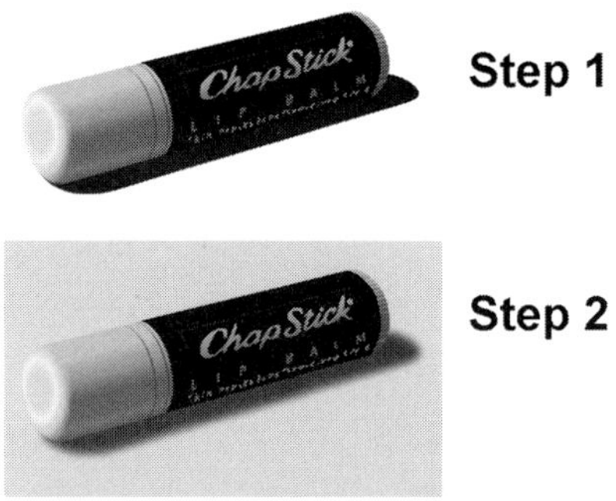

FIGURE 8.9 Creating a shadow for the ChapStick.

MANGA CHARACTER

The manga character was drawn for an Electrotank game called *Electro Air Hockey: Under the Mallet,* released in 2003. In this section, we review how the character was constructed and the coloring techniques used to achieve the dynamic gradients. To start, we will be constructing the black ink-looking outline, as shown in Figure 8.10. In Step 1, sketch out your manga character, scan it into your computer, and import it into Flash to be traced. For Step 2, place the sketch on the bottom layer, while you use the Brush tool to trace the sketch drawing. While drawing your fill lines, make sure they are as optimized as possible by optimizing the line width as you go.

Now that the ink-looking fill lines are rendered, let us start to color the character, as shown in Figure 8.11. In Step 1, use the Paint Bucket tool to apply different color fills to the character. For Step 2, use the Line tool to divide the areas based on where gradients will be placed, making it easier to connect the gradients.

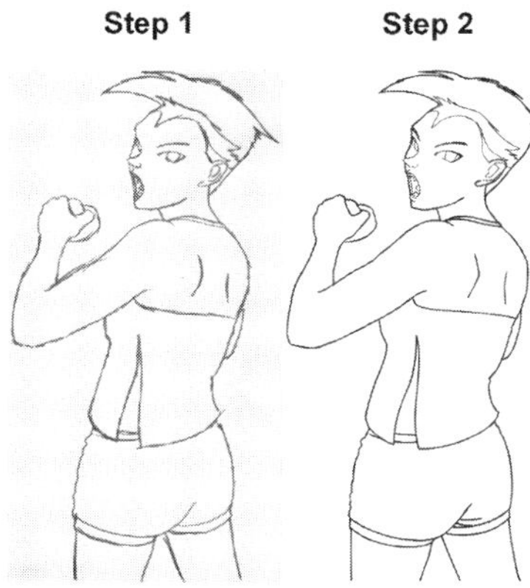

FIGURE 8.10 Sketch, trace, and create the fill outlines for our manga character.

FIGURE 8.11 Add your base color, dividing lines, and then gradients.

Here, we will analyze how the arm gradients were blended together, as shown in Figure 8.12. In Figure 8.13, you can see how the two radial gradients were seamlessly connected together. By using the same radial gradient on both sides and modifying the scale of the gradient, a perfect match can be made.

With the final rendering of the character finished (Figure 8..14), you can see the impact linear and radial gradients can have in adding depth and shape to the character.

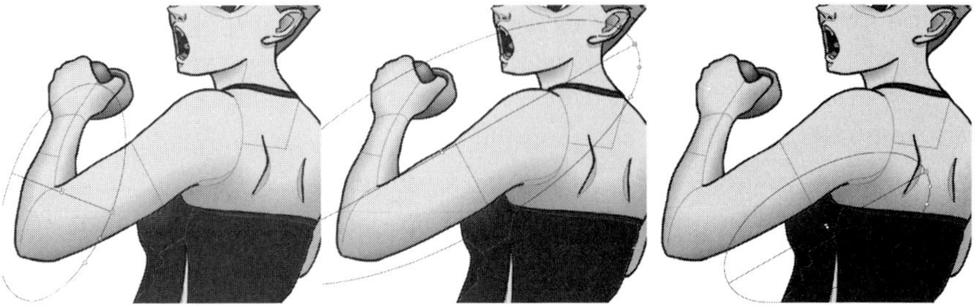

FIGURE 8.12 Detailed diagram of arm gradients.

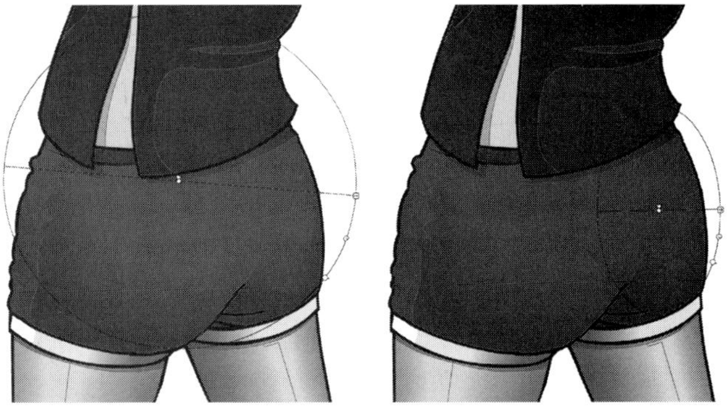

FIGURE 8.13 Detailed diagram of rear end gradients.

FIGURE 8.14 Final rendering of our manga character.

SCREW DRIVER

This simple object shows how solid fills can represent the metal part of a screwdriver, as shown in Figure 8.15. In Step 1, create the basic outline for the screwdriver with the Line tool and Selection tool. In Step 2, use the same tools to add more outline detail. In Step 3, use the Color Mixer panel and the Paint Bucket tool to apply solid fills to the metal part of the screwdriver.

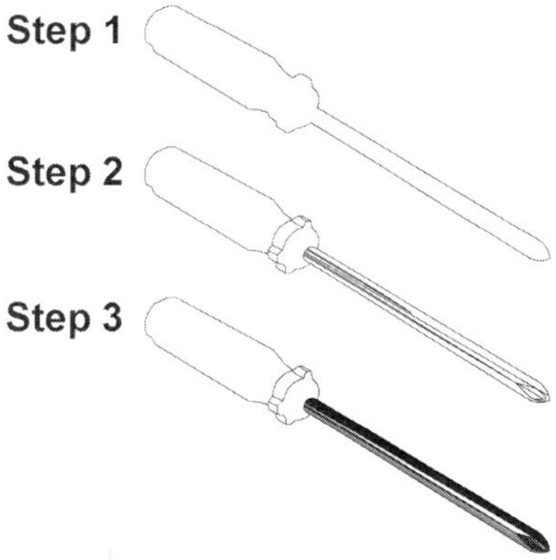

FIGURE 8.15 Create the outlines and start adding the base color.

In Step 1, use the Line tool to add more outline detail where fill color will be placed, as shown in Figure 8.16. In Step 2, apply a linear gradient on the top and bottom part of the screwdriver. Fill A is a linear gradient with five color swatches: #002760, #002A69, #002760, #003D80, and #003D80. Fill B is a linear gradient with two color swatches: #014082 and #0F6AA3. Apply solid fills to the area where the metal part of the screw connects to the plastic part.

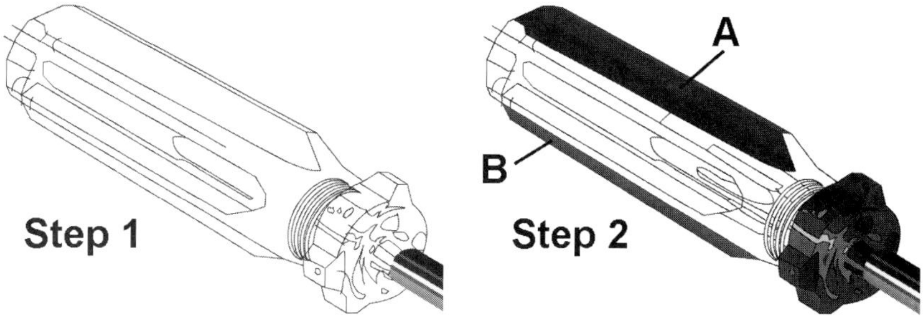

FIGURE 8.16 Add more base color.

In this task, we will be creating the base color for the inside of the screwdriver handle, as shown in Figure 8.17. In Step 1, apply the fills with the Paint Bucket tool to create the base color. Fill A is a solid fill of #004274. Fill B is a solid fill of #544D43. Fill C is a solid fill of #464E50. In Step 2, once you are done applying fills, remove the outlines, select the fills, and convert them to a symbol. Apply a blur effect of 1.5 with quality: Low.

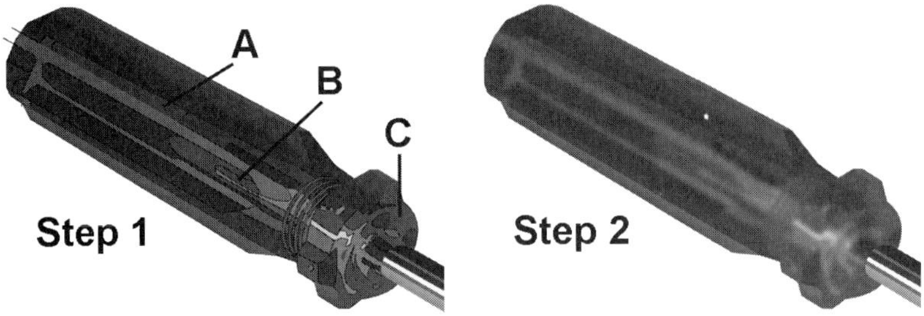

FIGURE 8.17 Add the final layer of base color.

In this last task, you will be adding a shadow to the screwdriver. Create a new layer and place it at the bottom of all the other layers. In Step 1, use the Lasso tool and select from the base color layer of the screwdriver to select a similar shape as shown in Figure 8.18. Convert it to a symbol, and in the Filter panel apply a drop shadow effect, set blur at 5, strength: 70%, quality: High, color: #000000, angle: 45, distance: 0, and check the Hide Object checkbox. Once you are done with the settings, use the Selection tool to select the shadow symbol, and use the arrow keys to move it around. Find the position where it is shown on the top and right side of the screwdriver.

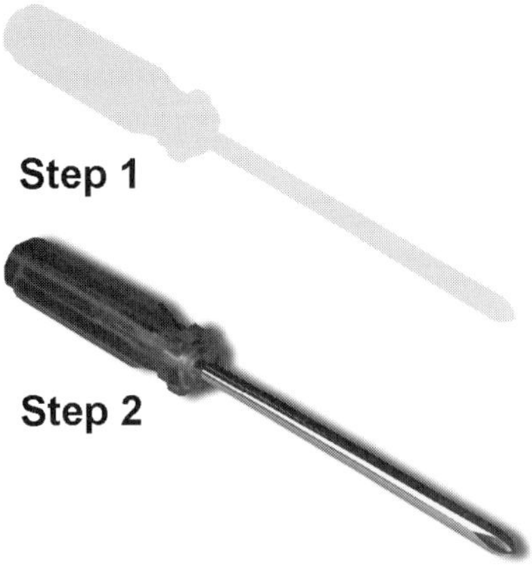

FIGURE 8.18 Create a shadow for our screwdriver.

Pool Balls and Cue Stick

Re-creating the sharp highlights found in the reflection on a pool ball's surface is possible in Flash by using the same approach of layering gradient graphics and the alpha color setting to make certain color swatches transparent. To start, we must use the Oval tool to create outlines that will define where fills will be placed. Use the Line and Selection tools to create dividing curves within the initial circle outlines, as shown in Figure 8.19.

FIGURE 8.19 Use the Oval and Line tools to draw outlines defining the basic shape of three pool balls.

Create four different-colored radial gradients, all with the same swatch positions, with the Color Mixer, as shown in Figure 8.20. The blue radial gradient used to color the top ball contains the color swatches #070922 100% Alpha, and #161F94 100% Alpha. The dark purple radial gradient used to color the middle left ball contains the color swatches #110809 100% Alpha, and #530348 100% Alpha. The yellow radial gradient used to color the stripe on the lower right ball contains the color swatches #6A4904 100% Alpha, #B87908 100% Alpha, and #F8CD02 100% Alpha. The white radial gradient used to color the white part of the ball contains the color swatches #2D3317 100% Alpha, #927E63 100% Alpha, and #FBF2E3 100% Alpha. Apply the radial gradients with the Paint Bucket tool, and edit the center point and scaling of the gradient with the Gradient Transform tool.

Draw outlines with the Line and Selection tools to define where gradient and solid fills will be placed, as shown in Figure 8.21. Since pool balls are very shiny, the reflective areas will be small and thin.

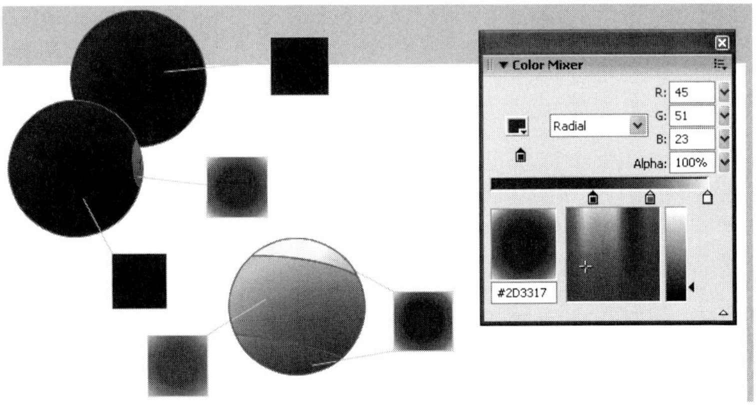

FIGURE 8.20 Several radial gradients are created and applied to the outlines. All lines are selected and deleted.

FIGURE 8.21 Using the Line tool, outlines are created to define where the highlight fills will be applied.

With the Color Mixer, create a linear gradient that will be used for the main highlights, as shown in Figure 8.22. The settings of this linear gradient are #FAFCFF 0% Alpha, #FAFCFF 10% Alpha, #FAFCFF 10% Alpha, and #FAFCFF 0% Alpha. Apply a solid white fill to the square-shaped outlines on the dark purple and yellow striped balls.

Using the Text tool, type the number 9 and use the Free Transform tool to rotate and scale the number so it looks like it is printed on the ball, as shown in Figure 8.23.

Use the Pencil tool and draw a circle at the base of all the balls. This area will be where the shadow radial gradient will be placed, as shown in Figure 8.24. To make sure this line does not interfere with previous fills or shapes, create a new layer and place it below all other layers.

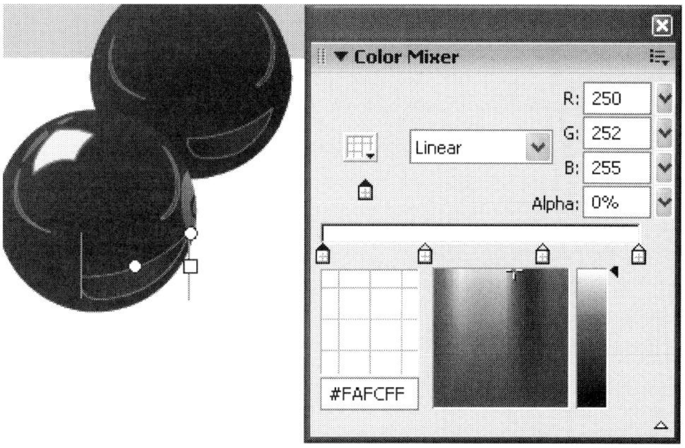

FIGURE 8.22 Gradient and solid fills are applied to the outlined areas and all lines are deleted.

FIGURE 8.23 With the Text tool, the number 9 is created and repositioned with the Free Transform tool.

FIGURE 8.24 The Pencil tool is used to create a circular outline to define the shadow.

Create a radial gradient with the Color Mixer, as shown in Figure 8.25. This radial gradient will be used to portray the shadow of the balls and contains the color swatches #002020 100% Alpha, and #002020 0% Alpha. Apply the radial gradients with the Paint Bucket tool, and edit the center point and scaling with the Gradient Transform tool. Once you are done applying the gradients, select the outlines and delete them, as they will not be needed.

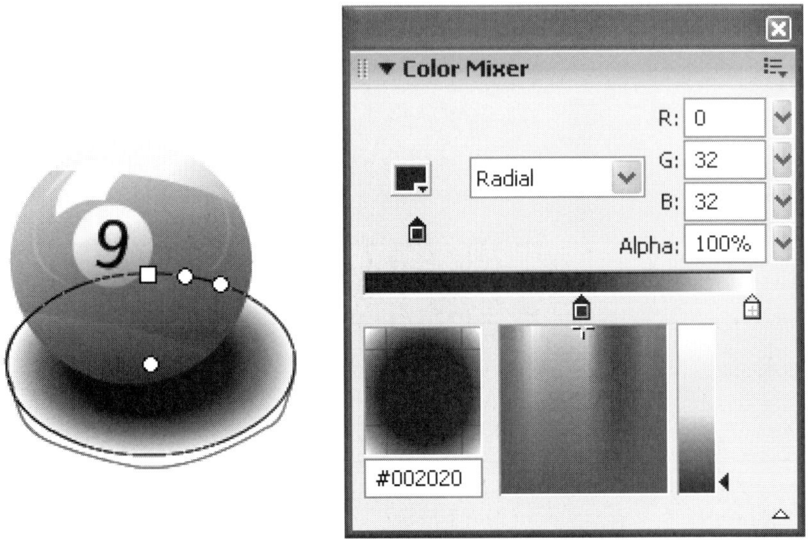

FIGURE 8.25 Radial gradient is created and applied to the shadow-outlining areas.

To create an outline defining the shape of the cue stick, use the Line tool to plot your lines, and use the Selection tool to create curved lines, as shown in Figure 8.26.

FIGURE 8.26 Using the Line and Selection tools, outlines are created that define the cue stick.

Create four different colored fills with the Color Mixer, as shown in Figure 8.27. The linear gradient used to color the top long area of the cue stick contains the color swatches #E6D3C2 100% Alpha, #F0DEC6 100% Alpha, #BFA98E 100% Alpha, #8C6F53 100% Alpha, #6F6146 100% Alpha, and #4A3C21 100% Alpha.

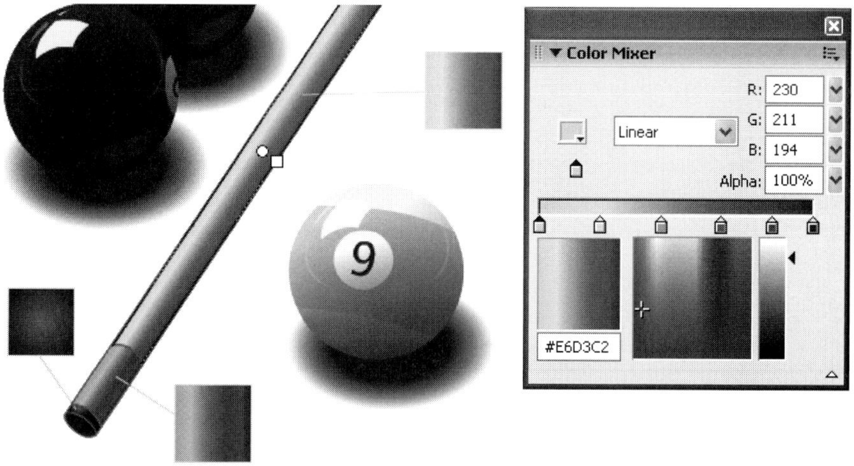

FIGURE 8.27 A solid fill and three gradients are created and applied to the cue stick outline.

As shown in Figure 8.28, the gray linear gradient used to color the lower area of the cue stick contains the color swatches #BEB7AF 100% Alpha, #D0C9BF 100% Alpha, #87877B 100% Alpha, #5A523F 100% Alpha, #615D44 100% Alpha, and #342616 100% Alpha. The dark radial gradient used to color the end of the cue stick contains the color swatches #8E8680 100% Alpha and #1E160D 100% Alpha. The dark solid fill used to color the tip part of the cue stick contains the color swatch #292212 100% Alpha. Apply the radial gradients and solid fill with the Paint Bucket tool, and edit the center point and scaling of the gradient with the Gradient Transform tool.

Once the cue stick is colored, select the outlines and delete them. Use the Line tool to create an outlined area where the shadow linear and radial gradients will be applied, as shown in Figure 8.29.

The radial gradient used to color the shadow of the pool balls is reused for the cue stick shadow. Use the Color Mixer panel to create a linear version of that radial gradient and save it. Apply the linear and radial versions of the shadow gradient with the Paint Bucket tool, and connect the gradients by editing the center point and scaling with the help of the Gradient Transform tool, as shown in Figure 8.30.

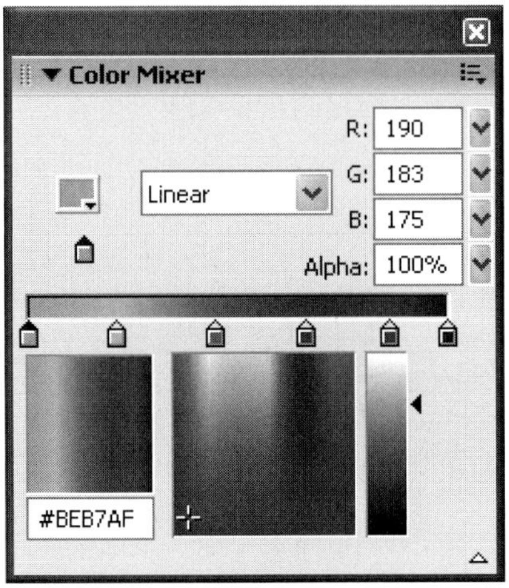

FIGURE 8.28 Linear gradient created for the bottom part of the cue stick.

FIGURE 8.29 Create an outline with the Line tool that will define the area where the shadow fills will be placed.

FIGURE 8.30 Apply the gradients to the outline areas.

To create a ground on which these items will sit, we will be using the Color Mixer panel to make a new radial gradient, as shown in Figure 8.31. The radial gradient contains the color swatches #336699 100% Alpha and #15293D 0% Alpha. Apply the radial gradients with the Paint Bucket tool, and edit the center point and scaling with the Gradient Transform tool.

FIGURE 8.31 Create a radial fill that will act as the ground on which the objects sit.

CD-ROM

A CD-ROM was originally chosen for this book because it seemed to be an easy exercise—a wrong assumption. Although creating it was easy, getting the surface to look reflective and believable was another matter. This CD object is a perfect example of how using many linear gradients can portray a brilliant reflection or glare. For the first task, create an outline, a foundation for the base color fills, as shown in Figure 8.32. In Step 2, apply a couple of gradient fills to the outline. Fill A is a radial gradient that contains three color swatches: #48543D, #3D533E, and #57992B. Fill B is a radial gradient that contains four color swatches: #151C22, #968E77, #786A4D, and #857D4E. Fill C is a linear gradient that contains two color swatches: #4C7E7D and #82B0AB. Fill D is a radial gradient that contains four color swatches: #367876, #1C575B, #5E9A74, and #3E6B4A.

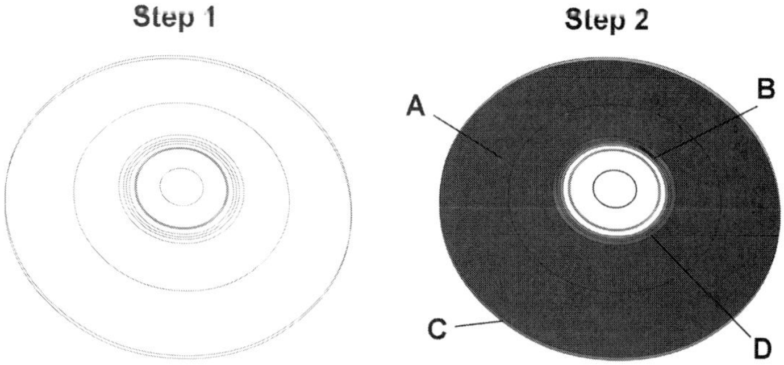

FIGURE 8.32 Create the outlines and add a base color to the CD-ROM.

As shown in Figure 8.33, use outlines to define the middle radius, paste them on a new layer, and apply a radial gradient with four color swatches: #487959, #487139, Alpha: 85%, #516134, Alpha: 54%, and #405A37, Alpha 39%.

FIGURE 8.33 Add a gradient overlay.

Next, we will be adding a shadow to the CD, so create a new layer and place it at the bottom of all the other layers, as shown in Figure 8.34. In Step 1, select the base color from the previous tasks and paste it on the new layer. In Step 2, convert it to a symbol, and in the Filter panel, apply a drop shadow effect, set blur at 3, strength: 40%, quality: High, color: #000000, angle: 45, distance: 0, and check the Hide Object checkbox. Once you are done with the settings, use the Selection tool to select the shadow symbol, and use the arrow keys to move it around. Find the position on the bottom, right side of the CD as shown in Figure 8.34.

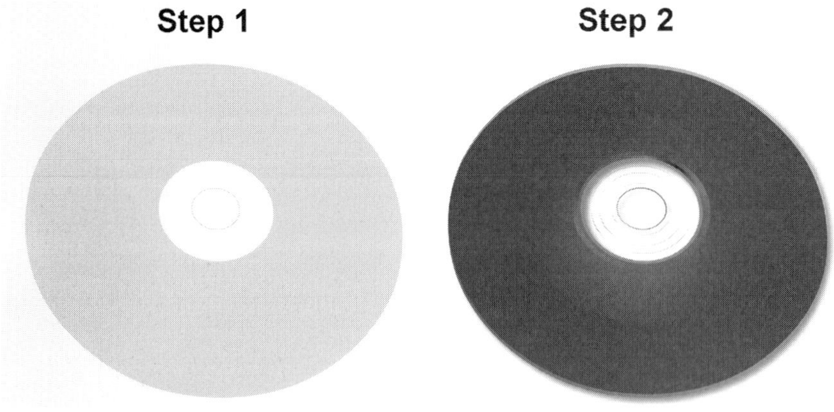

FIGURE 8.34 Create a drop shadow.

The next three steps will define the CD's detail glare that forms on the surface, as shown in Figure 8.35. In Step 1, create a new layer and place it on top of all the previous layers. Use the Line tool and the outlines, which all radiate from the center. In Step 2, open the Color Mixer panel to create the linear gradients. Fill A is a linear gradient that contains three color swatches: #3CA3AC, Alpha: 99%, #48AC4A, and #898562. Fill B is a linear gradient that contains four color swatches: #6FFFE6, #89FEC2, #D7B1EC, and #4FD4E7. Fill C is a linear gradient that contains two color swatches: #1D5AEB, Alpha: 70% and #46BD61, Alpha: 70%. Fill D is a linear gradient that contains three color swatches: #2AA3DA, #2DD178, and #967D92. In Step 2, create more outlines on the right side and apply the linear gradients. Fill E is a linear gradient that contains two color swatches: #34A7AE, Alpha: 50% and #11BBA1, Alpha: 83%. Fill F is a linear gradient that contains two color swatches: #3DAE6E, Alpha: 77% and #7174A7, Alpha: 80%. Fill G is a linear gradient that contains three color swatches: #2666DD, Alpha: 10%, #2895B1, Alpha: 22%, and #2CCC7D, Alpha: 21%.

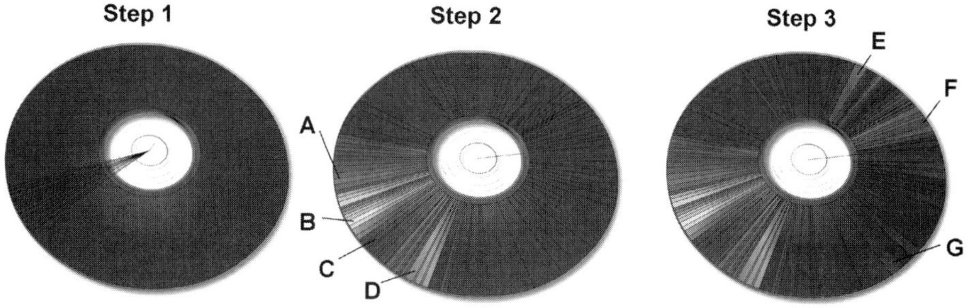

FIGURE 8.35 Add a layer of detailed color overlay.

Select all the linear gradients we just finished applying, convert them to a symbol, and apply a blur filter of 1.5, quality: High. Your final render will look like Figure 8.36.

FIGURE 8.36 Final rendering of the CD-ROM.

SUMMARY

- Use the Line and Selection tools for more control over vector fills and to keep the number of vector points to a minimum.
- Define the shape of an object with simple linear gradients, as in the Pen and ChapStick examples.
- Line up a radial gradient to blend into a linear gradient to create different complex shaped gradients.

EXERCISES

ON THE CD

The following exercises will put to use what you learned in this chapter. You will be creating a piece of sour candy, a lit candle, an origami paper bird, three lollipops, and a cup of coffee. The files for the following exercises are on the companion CD-ROM in the folders cited.

1. Create a small circle-shaped sour candy piece from the image provided. Duplicate the original and add a blur filter to make the others look like they are out of focus. The jpg file is on the companion CD-ROM in Chapter_8/Exercises/sour candy.jpg.
2. Create a lit candle from the image provided. Use the blur filter to achieve the glow in the flame and slight highlights on the candle. The jpg file is on the companion CD-ROM in Chapter_8/Exercises/candle.jpg.
3. Create an origami paper bird from the image provided. Linear gradients should do the trick to achieve the paper look. The jpg file is on the companion CD-ROM in Chapter_8/Exercises/origami.jpg.
4. Create three lollipops from the image provided. Layer a couple of gradient fill overlays to portray the hard candy surface. The jpg file is on the companion CD-ROM in Chapter_8/Exercises/lollipops.jpg.
5. Create a coffee cup with coffee in it from the image provided. Use techniques learned from this chapter to achieve the soft shadows on the ceramic. The jpg file is on the companion CD-ROM in Chapter_8/Exercises/coffee cup.jpg.

CHAPTER

9 ADVANCED TUTORIALS

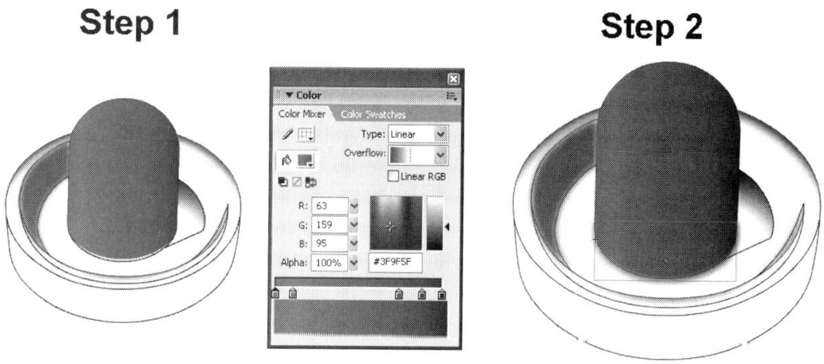

This tutorial chapter shows the full illustrating potential of Macromedia Flash. Whether you are trying to reproduce a small glass jar or looking to achieve a photorealistic-looking object like a human, this program can make it happen. In each tutorial, there is much detail to cover and much of it is spread throughout the figures and written material, so it is a good idea to review all details. Since the steps in these tutorials are production-level tasks, they will be repetitive at times; however, working through all the steps is well worth the result. We encourage you to reference the appropriate source Flash file on the companion CD-ROM while working on a specific tutorial, as not all details will be explained here.

ON THE CD

MALLET

An air hockey mallet is a neat piece of plastic, and the curvy shadows and highlights make for a challenging tutorial. To start, we will be creating an outline, which will be used to add color to our object, as shown in Figure 9.1. In Step 1, use the Line and Oval tools to draw the outline of the mallet. In Step 2, apply a radial gradient fill that will act as the base color. The radial gradient contains two color swatches: #6CDD9B and #46B071.

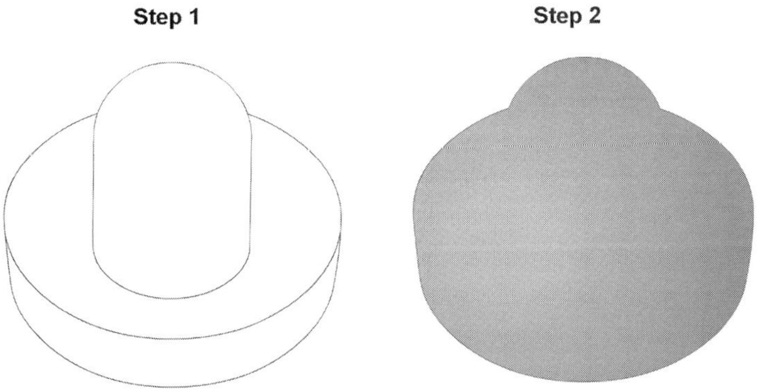

FIGURE 9.1 Creating the base color of the mallet.

In Step 1, add more detail to the outline with the Line tool. In Step 2, apply a radial gradient that contains two color swatches: #000A1E, Alpha: 0% and #000A1E, Alpha: 100%, as shown in Figure 9.2.

On a new layer, start defining the shape of the mallet, as shown in Figure 9.3. In Step 1, use the Line tool to create the outline for the curve shape, apply a green fill to the area, and delete the outlines. In Step 2, convert the fills to a symbol and apply a blur filter of 5 with a quality: Low.

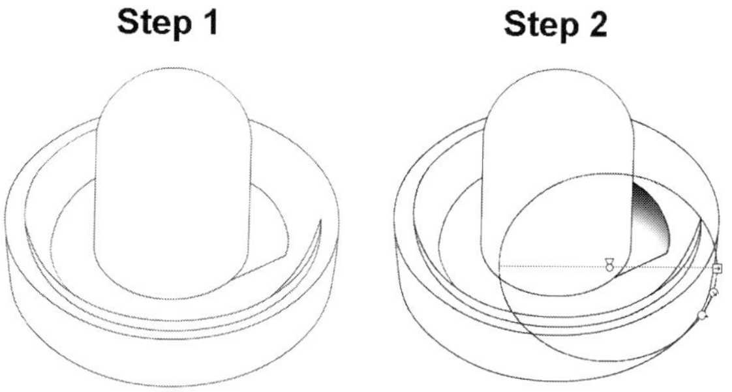

FIGURE 9.2 Add detail to the outlines and apply a radial gradient to it.

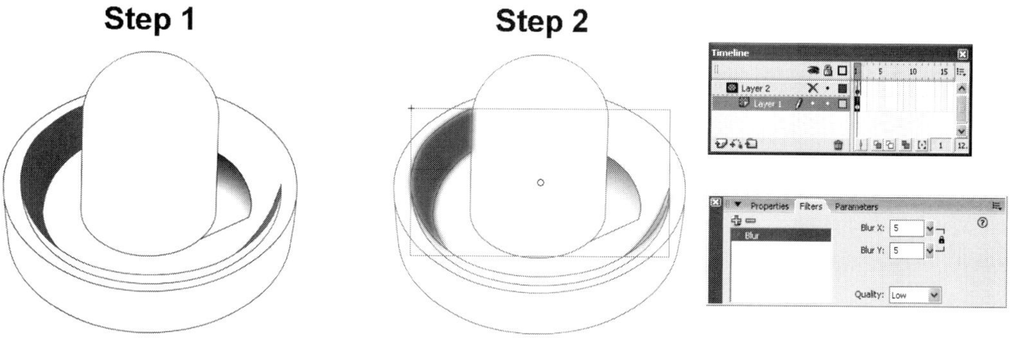

FIGURE 9.3 Add more color definition to the mallet.

As shown in Figure 9.4, in Step 1, apply a radial gradient that contains two color swatches: #39A464, Alpha: 100% and #5BC78B, Alpha: 0%, which will define the inner shadow. In Step 2, apply a radial gradient that contains two color swatches—#5BC78B, Alpha: 0% and #348F58, Alpha: 100%—to define the outer shadow.

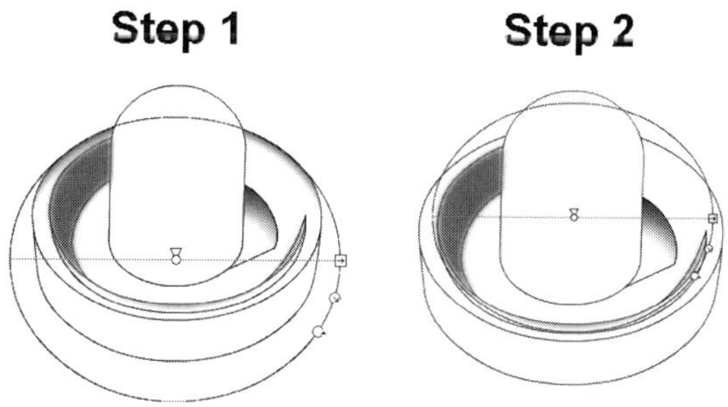

FIGURE 9.4 Add a radial gradient on the underside of the mallet.

Create a base linear gradient that will define the handle of the mallet, as shown in Figure 9.5. In Step 1, apply a linear gradient that contains five color swatches: #3F9F5F, #41A766, #18833F, #0E6B37, and #044826. In Step 2, use the Lasso tool to select the bottom part of the handle fill, duplicate it, make it a symbol, and apply a blur filter of 5 with quality: Low, which will blend the base of the handle to the center of the mallet.

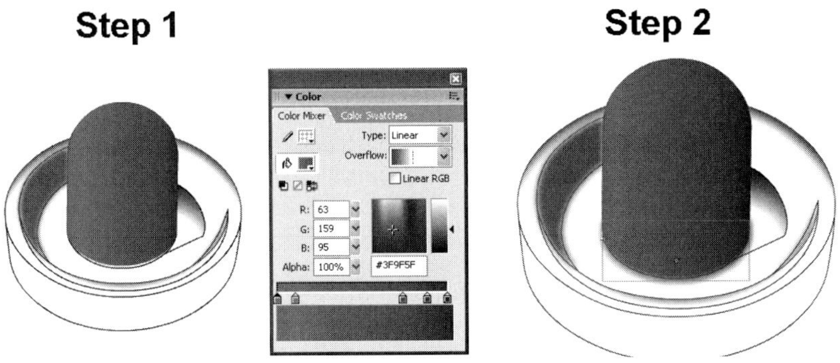

FIGURE 9.5 Add a base gradient to the handle of the mallet.

Apply a linear gradient to the side of the mallet (Figure 9.6), select the linear fill, and convert it to a symbol. The linear gradient used contains five color swatches: #8CB97E, #67AB72, #346A39, #274B25, and #0C261B. Apply a blur filter to it with the value of 2 with quality: High.

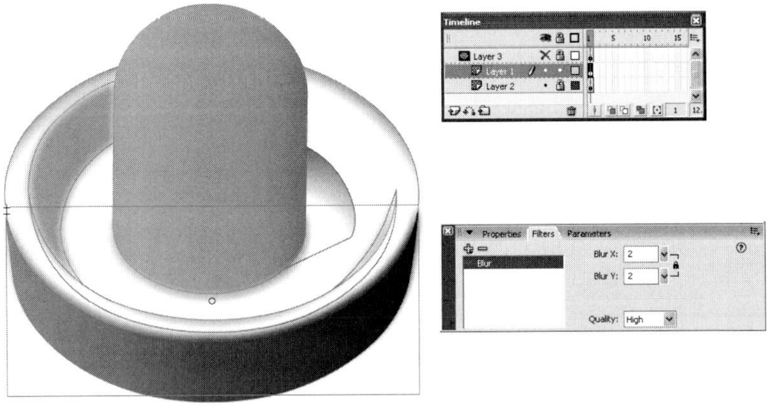

FIGURE 9.6 Apply a linear gradient to the side of the mallet.

In this next task, we will be adding a shadow and highlight to the mallet, as shown in Figure 9.7. In Step 1, create a solid fill shape that portrays the handle casting a shadow on the base of the mallet. Convert that fill to a symbol and apply a blur filter with a value of 5 and quality: High. In Step 2, create splinter-shaped white linear gradients that will represent sharp highlights. Apply a blur filter with a value of 1 and quality: High.

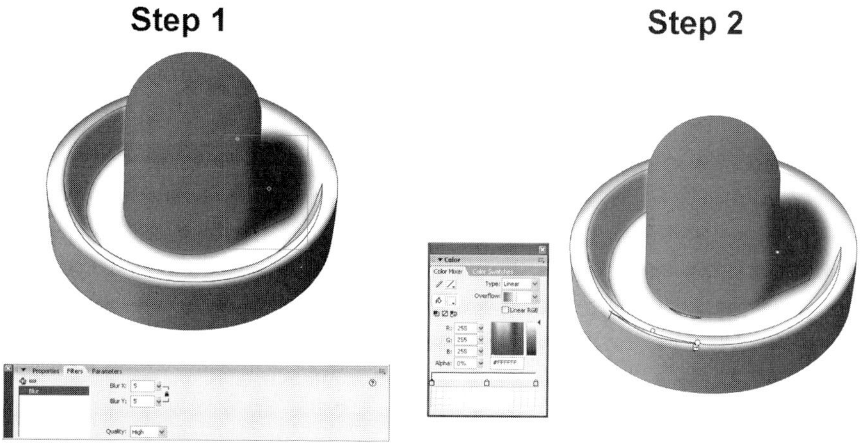

FIGURE 9.7 Add a shadow the handle is casting.

The handle of the mallet contains an interesting shaped gradient, which previous versions of Flash could not replicate. Since we now have the power of the blur filter, we can achieve this dynamic gradient shape with a couple of layers of blurred gradient overlays, as shown in Figure 9.8. In Step 1, create a raindrop-shaped fill and apply a radial gradient to it. In Step 2, convert the radial gradient to a symbol and apply a blur filter to it.

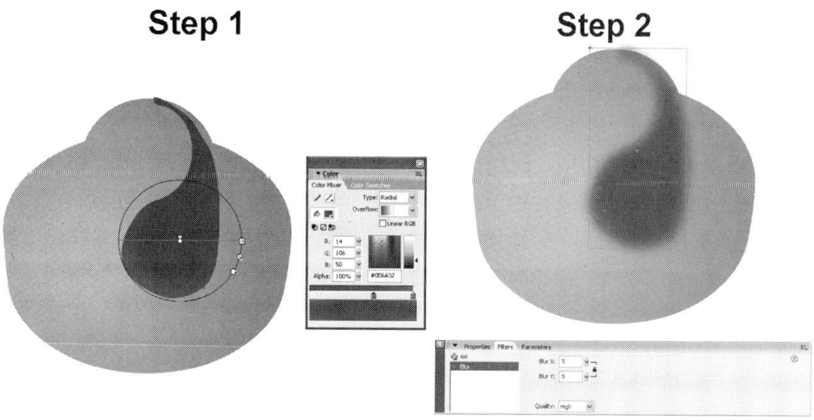

FIGURE 9.8 Add a layer of gradient overlay to define the shape of the handle.

Use the same technique to layer another gradient overlay on top, which will blend the two together (Figure 9.9). In Step 1, create a slimmer raindrop-shaped fill and apply a radial gradient to it. Convert the radial gradient to a symbol and apply a blur filter to it. In Step 2, create a side splinter-shaped fill and apply a linear gradient to it. Convert the linear gradient to a symbol and apply a blur filter to it.

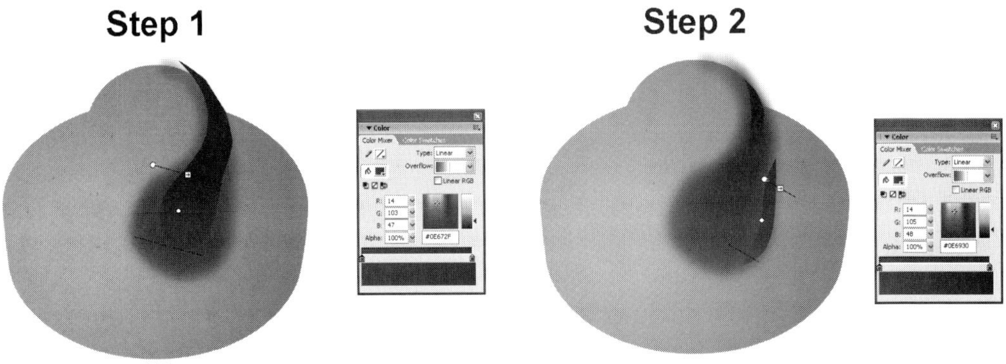

FIGURE 9.9 Add a second layer of gradient overlay.

Since all these gradient fills will be blurred and we only want the blur filter to show up on the inside, we create a mask to trim the blur on the right side and bottom, as shown in Figure 9.10.

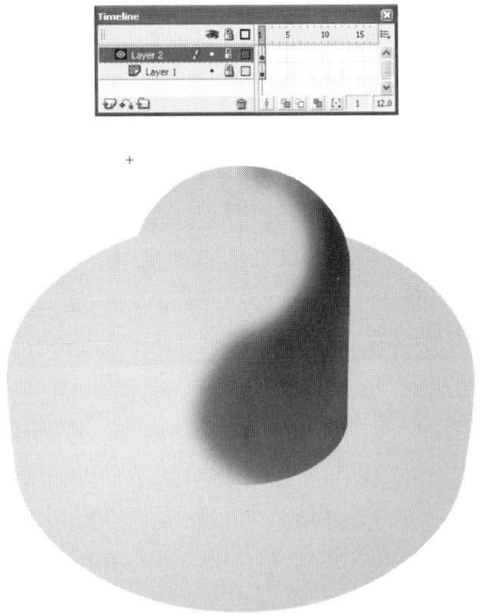

FIGURE 9.10 Mask the gradient overlays so they do not bleed on the right and bottom.

On a new layer, apply a radial gradient that will portray a main highlight, making the top of the handle look quite round, as shown in Figure 9.11.

In these next steps, we will be creating a drop shadow, as shown in Figure 9.12. With the Line tool, draw the area where the base shadow will be. Apply a solid fill to the area and delete the lines. Convert the fill to a symbol and apply a blur filter of 3 and quality: High.

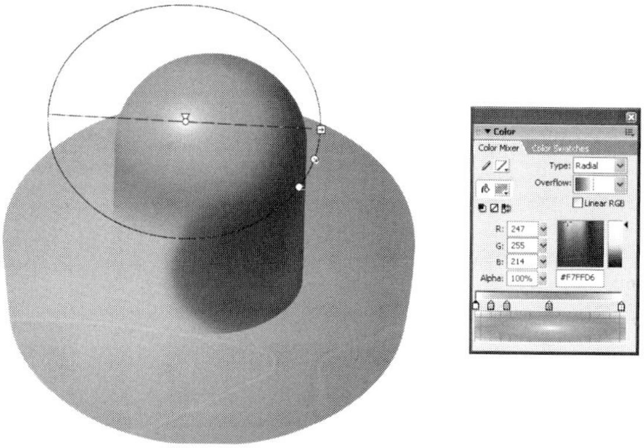

FIGURE 9.11 Add a gradient overlay to define the round top of the handle.

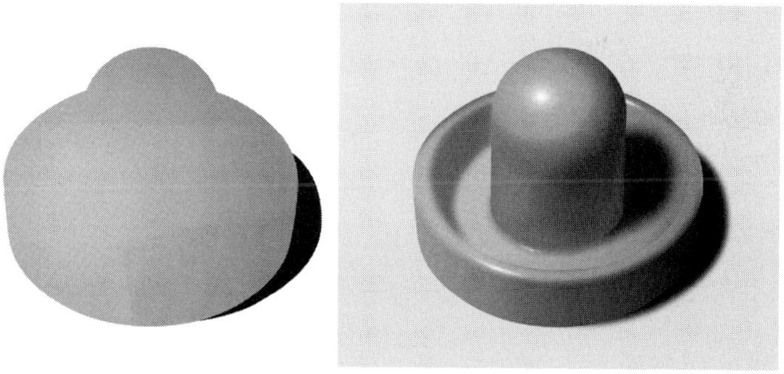

FIGURE 9.12 Create a drop shadow for the mallet.

JAR

This jar is made of glass and has a plastic top. Glass is an interesting element because it may look invisible if there are no objects around it to reflect off it. Start by creating the outlines and apply gradients to the lid, as shown in Figure 9.13.

Define the lid with two curved fill shapes, that once blurred will portray a shadow and highlight trim on the lid, as shown in Figure 9.14.

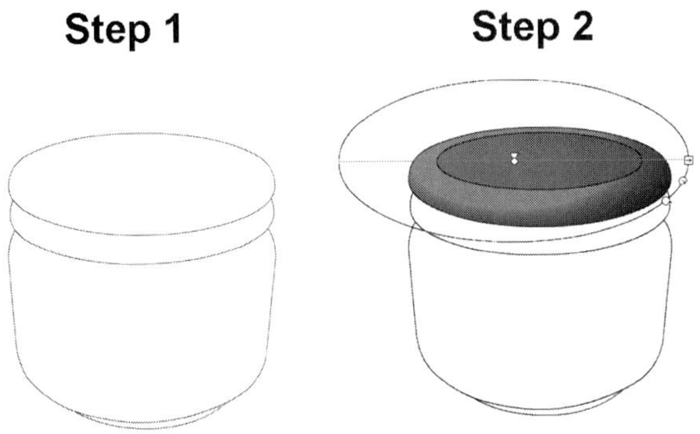

FIGURE 9.13 Create the outline and base gradients for the lid.

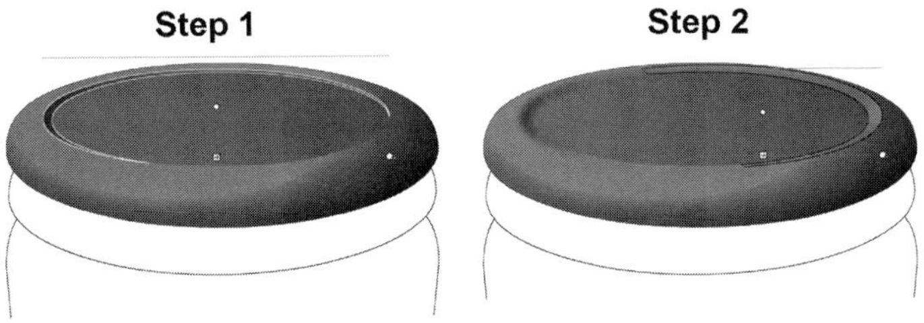

FIGURE 9.14 Further define the shape of the lid.

To add more depth to the lid, apply two linear gradient fills layered on top of each other and applied with a blur filter, as shown in Figure 9.15.

FIGURE 9.15 Add a shadow to the side of the lid.

Add a layer of highlights using the same technique as used on the shadow gradients, as shown in Figure 9.16.

A quick trick to render the bottom part of the lid is to make the top part we just finished a symbol, duplicate it, and place the new one lower and underneath the first, as shown in Figure 9.17.

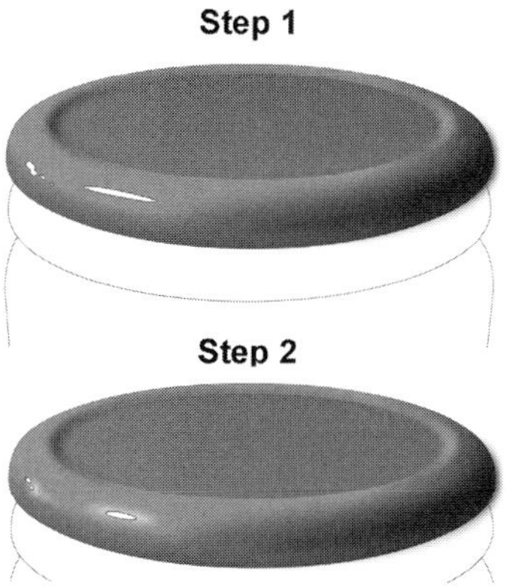

FIGURE 9.16 Add a highlight to the side of the lid.

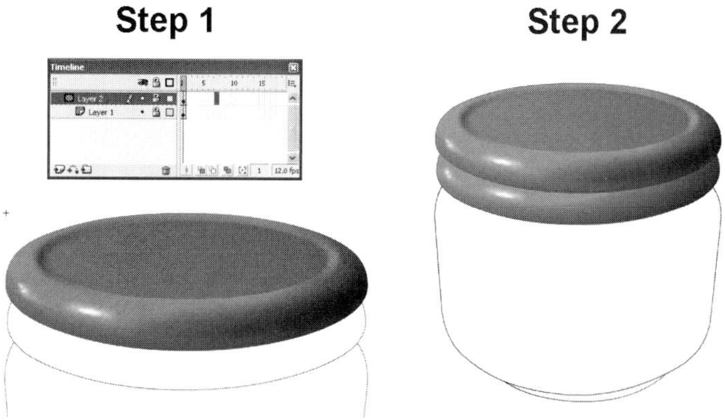

FIGURE 9.17 Duplicate the lid to form the bottom part of the lid.

To make sure both lid graphics do not look repetitive, we will be adding a shadow, which the top lid will be casting on the bottom part of the lid, as shown in Figure 9.18.

In this next task, we will be adding the first layer of reflections to the sides of the glass jar, as shown in Figure 9.19. In Step 1, define the outlines more and apply several solid fills. In Step 2, on a new layer draw a larger glare and apply a transparent linear gradient. Convert this linear gradient to a symbol and apply a blur filter to it to make it fuzzy looking.

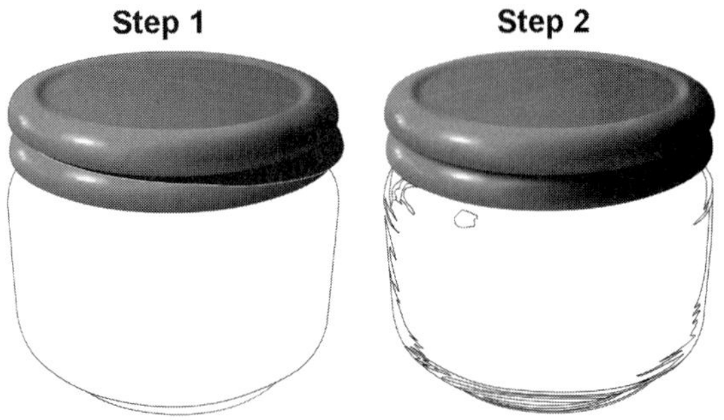

FIGURE 9.18 Add a shadow that the top lid casts on the bottom lid, and add outlines for the glass body of the jar.

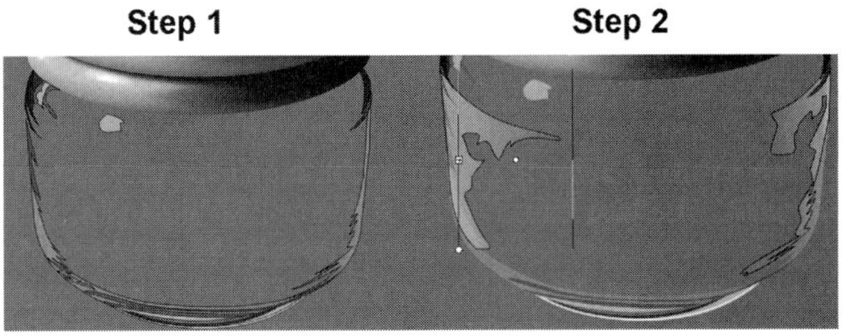

FIGURE 9.19 Create fill overlays for the glass.

Define the outlines a little more on the base and apply radial gradients to blend the bevel-type swirl look, as shown in Figure 9.20.

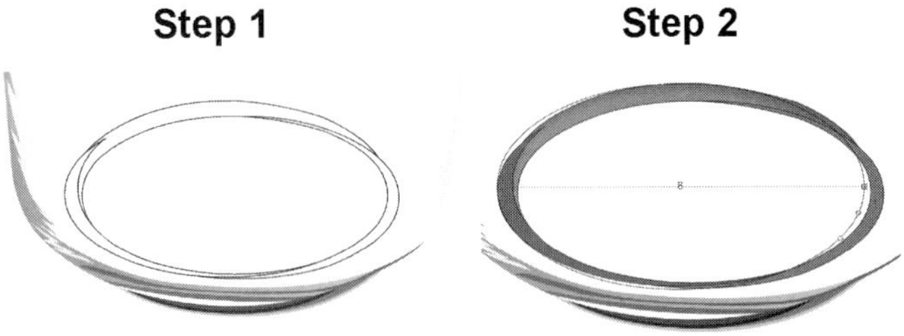

FIGURE 9.20 Create another layer of fill overlays to define the bottom part of the glass.

Start to define the base of the glass jar with linear and radial gradients, as shown in Figure 9.21. In Step 1, apply a radial gradient with the Paint Bucket tool and position it with the Gradient Transform tool. In

Step 2, add another layer of transparent radial gradient to blend the center gradient with the base.

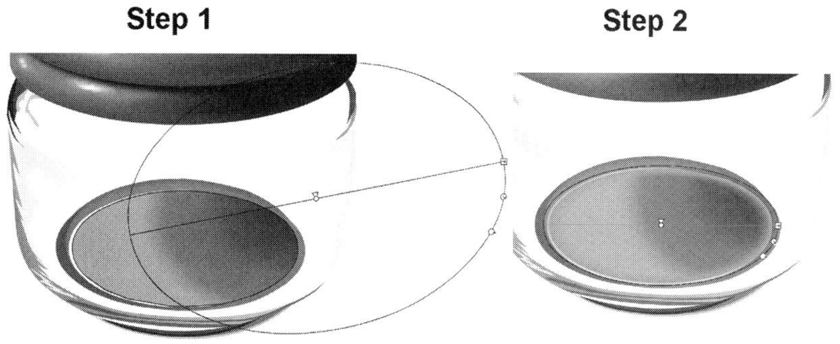

FIGURE 9.21 Define the radial gradient on the bottom of the glass.

In the next three steps, we will be adding three different layers of transparent gradients to add shine and glare to the glass jar, as shown in Figure 9.22. In Step 1, create a curved shape and apply a linear gradient that contains two color swatches: #FDFEFF, Alpha: 30% and #FEFEFC, Alpha: 66%. Convert the fills to a symbol and apply a blur filter with the value of 6 and quality: High. In Step 2, create a wavy and curved shape and apply a linear gradient that contains two color swatches: #FDFEFF, Alpha: 6% and #FEFEFC, Alpha: 30%. Convert the fills to a symbol and apply a blur filter with the value of 1.5 and quality: High. In Step 3, create a curved shape and apply a linear gradient that contains two color swatches: #FDFEFF, Alpha: 49% and #FEFEFC, Alpha: 100%. Convert the fills to a symbol and apply a blur filter with the value of 1.5 and quality: Low.

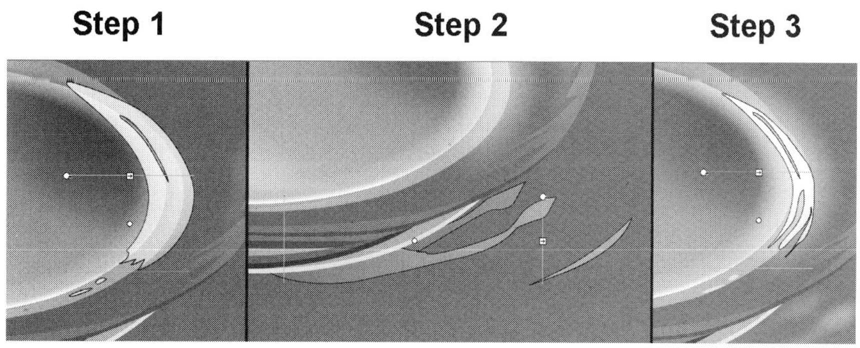

FIGURE 9.22 Add three areas of highlights for the base of the jar.

Create a new layer and place it at the bottom of all the other layers. Create a base shadow linear fill, as shown in Figure 9.23. The linear gradient contains two color swatches: #37412E, Alpha: 85% and #172435, Alpha: 75%. Convert the fills to a symbol and apply a blur filter with the value of 5 and quality: High.

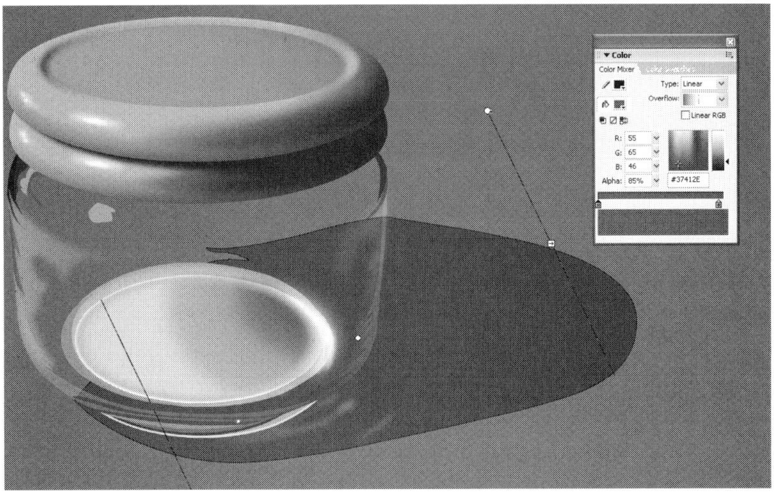

FIGURE 9.23 Create the base shadow for the jar.

On a new layer above the layer we were just working with, add two reflection fill overlays, as shown in Figure 9.24. In Step 1, create a bunch of curved shapes and apply a linear gradient that contains two color swatches: #3694D1, Alpha: 0% and #3694D1, Alpha: 75%. Convert the fills to a symbol and apply a blur filter with the value of 7 and quality: High. In Step 2, create a wavy and curved shape and apply a solid fill with a value of #A8A3A0, Alpha: 62%. Convert the fills to a symbol and apply a blur filter with the value of 5 and quality: High.

FIGURE 9.24 Add two gradient overlays to add reflection to the glass casts on the ground.

In the next four steps, we will be adding mints inside the jar, as shown in Figure 9.25. In Step 1, create the outlines with the Pencil tool. In Step 2, start applying the solid fills to the green and yellow mints. In Step 3, apply the solid fills to the pink mints. In Step 4, apply the solid fills to the rest of the mints.

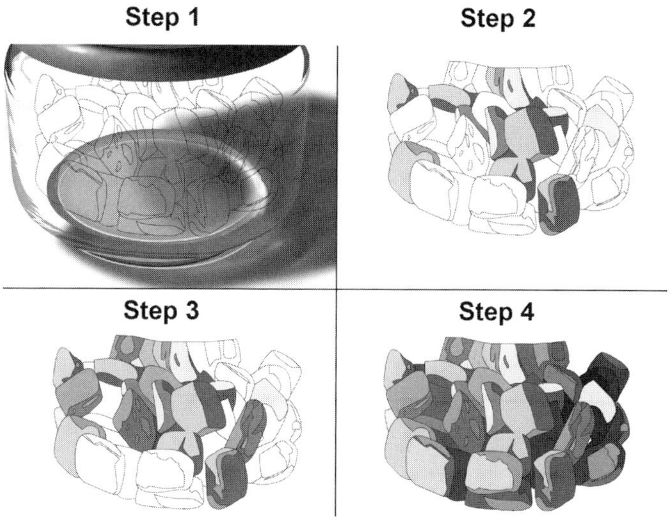

FIGURE 9.25 Add a bunch of mints to the inside of the jar.

Delete the outlines when you are done applying the fills, and convert all the fills to a symbol. Apply a blur filter with the value of 1.25 and quality: High, as shown in Figure 9.26.

FIGURE 9.26 The final rendering of the jar.

SAFETY PIN

The safety pin tutorial is a perfect example of a single layer of simple gradients matched together to portray a metal object. Unlike the stainless steel pan, the safety pin does not contain many additional layers of transparent gradients. To start, use the Line tool to plot lines, and add curves to them with the Selection tool. To create the loop in the object, use the Oval tool to create a perfect circle curve, as shown in Figure 9.27.

Use the Line tool to block off certain areas of the outline. This will ensure that when we apply gradients, they are applied where we want them, as shown in Figure 9.28.

FIGURE 9.27 Use the Line and Selection tools to create an outline drawing of a safety pin.

FIGURE 9.28 Drawn lines separating different areas where fills will be applied.

With the Color Mixer panel, create a radial gradient that will be used to color the thin area of the pin, as shown in Figure 9.29. This radial gradient contains the color swatches #0E1134 100% Alpha, #FEFBF9 100% Alpha, #3144AE 100% Alpha. It will be placed on the upper thin area. To create the radial gradient for the lower thin area of the pin, switch the position of the first and third color swatches, which will give an opposite gradient to the first one we created.

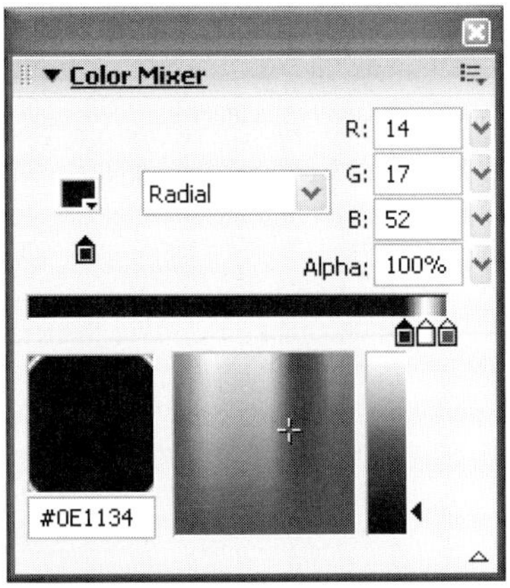

FIGURE 9.29 Create a radial gradient that will be applied to one side of the pin.

With the Paint Bucket tool, apply the two different radial gradients to the areas shown in Figure 9.30. Use the Gradient Transform tool to edit the center position, rotation, and scale of the gradient.

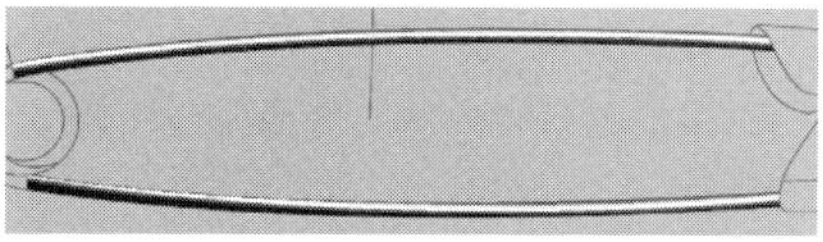

FIGURE 9.30 Apply the radial gradient to the top thin area. Reverse the order of the color swatches to make the radial gradient used in the bottom thin area.

Create two more radial gradients that will be used to fill the loop area of the object. The first radial gradient as shown in Figure 9.31 contains the color swatches #0E1134 100% Alpha and #FEFBF9 100% Alpha.

The second radial gradient as shown in Figure 9.32 contains the color swatches: #4453CB 100% Alpha, #0E1134 100% Alpha, #0E1134 100% Alpha, and #FEFBF9 100% Alpha.

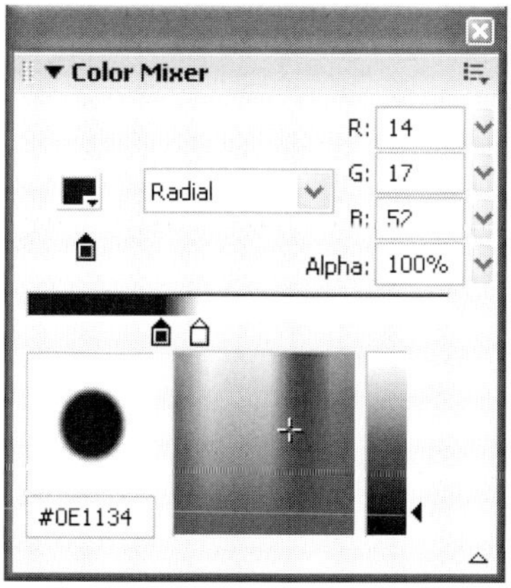

FIGURE 9.31 Create a radial gradient used for the top left.

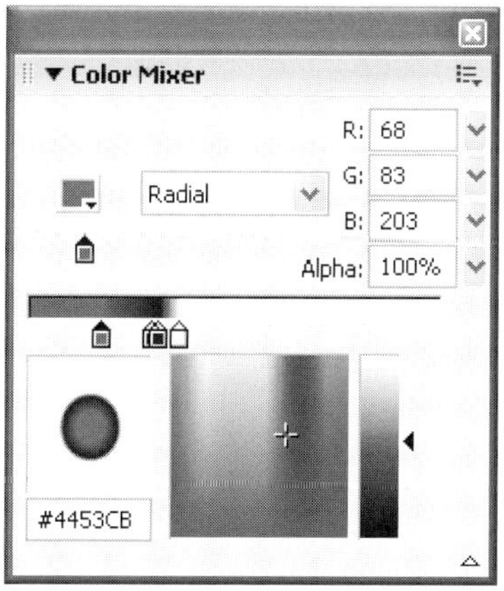

FIGURE 9.32 Create a radial gradient used for the inner right loop.

Apply the first radial gradient in the small curved area at the top left, and apply the second radial gradient to the middle right curved area, as shown in Figure 9.33.

The first radial gradient is used to close the loop, but the two color swatches are switched to create a gradient on the opposite side, so the dark blue is on the outer area of the gradient, as shown in Figure 9.34.

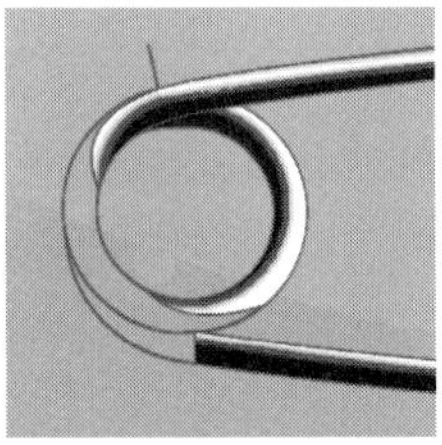

FIGURE 9.33 Apply both radial gradients making sure the inner top- left gradient connects with the top radial gradient.

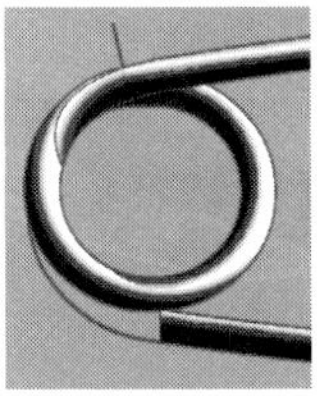

FIGURE 9.34 Reverse the order of the color swatches in the radial gradient made in Figure 9.31 and apply it to the left area of the loop.

As shown in Figure 9.35, create a radial gradient that contains the color swatches #FEFBF9 100% Alpha, #0E1134 100% Alpha, #0E1134 100% Alpha, and #4453CB 100% Alpha.

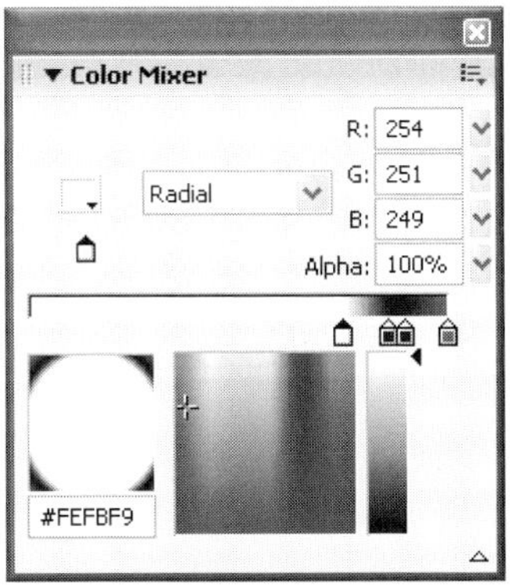

FIGURE 9.35 Create a radial gradient for the bottom curved area.

Apply the radial gradient to the bottom-left curved area of the pin, as shown in Figure 9.36. Use your Gradient Transform tool to reposition the gradient so it matches up with the one touching it. With the Line tool, block off part of the thin area of the pin and fill it with a new linear gradient consisting of two color swatches: #090B22 and #3144AE.

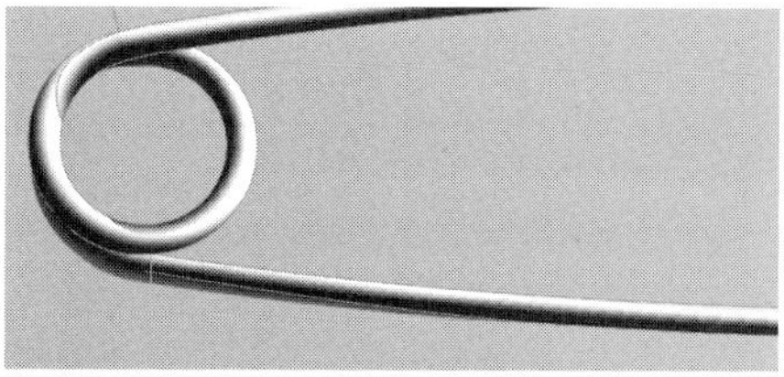

FIGURE 9.36 Apply the gradient to the bottom outlined area and make sure it connects with the bottom radial gradient. Cut off an area of the bottom radial gradient and continue the newly applied radial gradient.

Create a linear gradient that will be the dominant gradient in this part of the pin; all other gradients next to it must connect seamlessly to it. The gradient contains four color swatches: #4453CB 100% Alpha, #FEFBF9 100% Alpha, #FEFBF9 100% Alpha, and #0E1134 100% Alpha, as shown in Figure 9.37.

Reuse the colors employed in the previous linear gradient to create the new gradients with the hand-drawn lines pointed out, as shown in Figure 9.38.

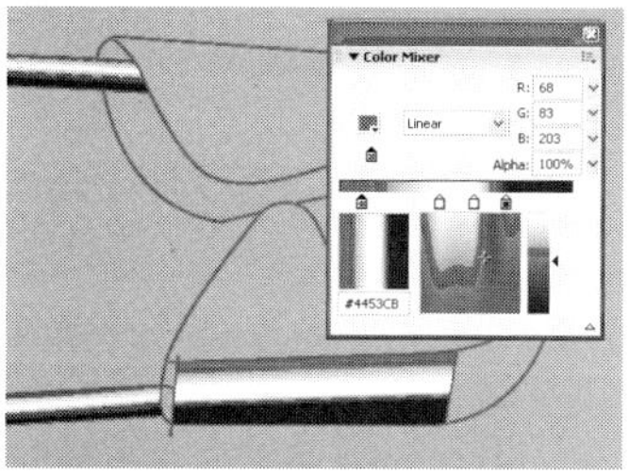

FIGURE 9.37 Create a linear gradient and apply it to an area of the pin.

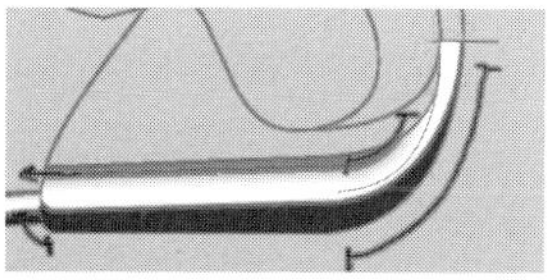

FIGURE 9.38 Notice the hand-drawn lines showing how newly added gradients interact with other fills around them.

Create a new radial gradient as shown in Figure 9.39, containing the color swatches #FEFBF9 100% Alpha, #4453CB 100% Alpha, #4453CB 100% Alpha, and #0E1134 100% Alpha. Notice how we continually create new gradients depending on our needs, but the color swatches remain similar; this way, we have better odds of gradients connecting perfectly with each other.

To fill in the underside of the pin, we will need to create a dark color swatch, as shown in Figure 9.40. The area is divided into two parts: the left area will hold a linear gradient, and the right side will hold a radial gradient. Both will connect forming a faint gradient. The linear gradient contains the two color swatches: #162050 100% Alpha and #070B1D 100% Alpha. To create the radial version of this gradient, click on the Fill drop-down menu and select Radial. Apply the two gradients with the Paint Bucket tool, and edit the center point and scale of the gradients with the Gradient Transform tool.

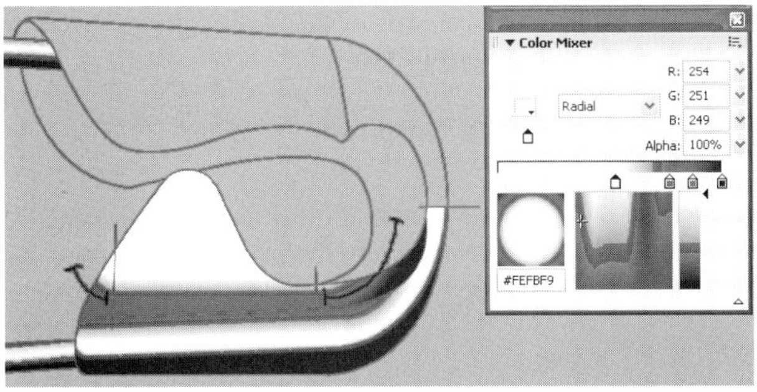

FIGURE 9.39 Create a new gradient and apply it and other already-created gradients to the outlined areas.

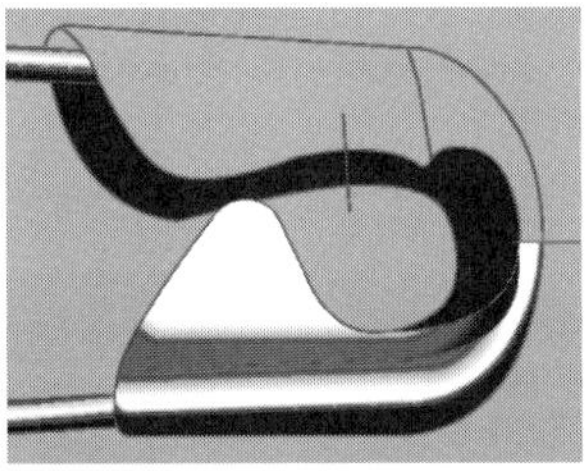

FIGURE 9.40 Apply a dark blue fill and gradient to the inner area of the pin.

Create a linear gradient that will portray the highly reflective area at the top as shown in Figure 9.41. This linear gradient contains six color swatches: #FEFBF9 100% Alpha, #4453CB 100% Alpha, #0E1134 100% Alpha, #FEFBF9 100% Alpha, #4453CB 100% Alpha, and #0E1134 100% Alpha. Notice that the hand-drawn lines show how the two radial gradients interact with each other. The color swatches included in these gradients are #FEFBF9 100% Alpha and #0E1134 100% Alpha. Reverse the position of the color swatches to create the other gradient.

To further define the linear gradient and make the reflective colors pop out more, use the Line tool to block off certain areas to be ready to add some solid fills and a linear gradient. As pointed out in Figure 9.42, the two solid colors are #345CB8 and #0E1134. The linear gradient contains three color swatches: #293992 100% Alpha, #A2BAF2 100% Alpha, and #0E1134 100% Alpha. Apply the fills with the Paint Bucket tool and position the linear gradient with the Gradient Transform tool. Make sure you select and delete all lines, as we will not need them anymore.

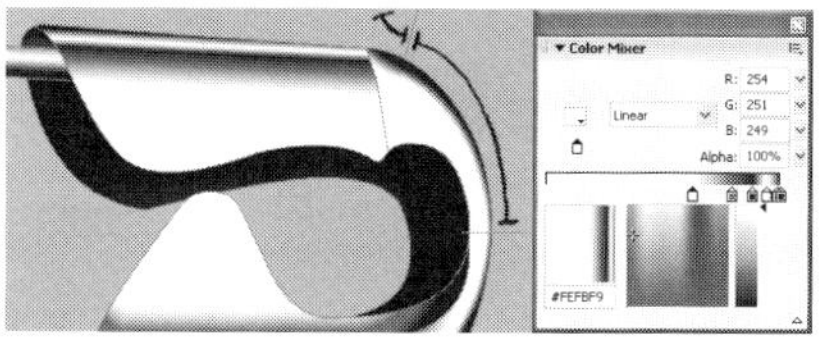

FIGURE 9.41 Create a linear gradient and apply it to the top outlined area. Notice the hand-drawn lines showing how two of the gradients should be applied.

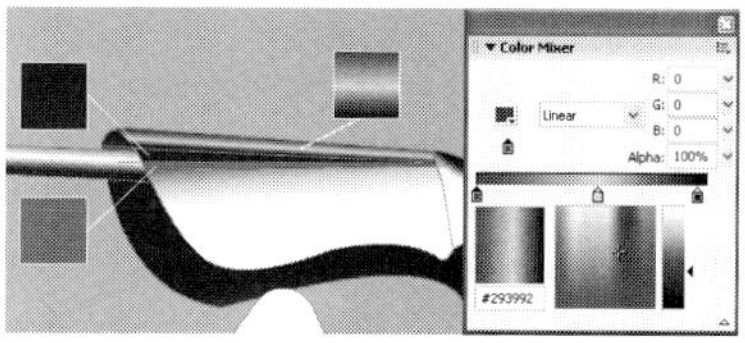

FIGURE 9.42 Create a linear gradient and two solid fills applied to the top area of the pin.

Since this object is quite thin and the shadow it casts is very thin, we can get away with using a transparent solid fill to portray a shadow being cast. In two easy steps, we will have a shadow drawn. Create a new layer and place it below the layer we have been working with. Execute the shortcut key command to Select All Graphics and Copy Them. Click your cursor on the new layer you just created so we are editing in that layer, and Paste in Place the copied graphics on the new layer. With the newly pasted graphics still selected, open the Color Mixer panel and create a solid black fill with 15% Alpha. Setting up this solid fill with the graphics selected will change the fills to this new-colored fill. With your arrow keys, reposition the graphic as shown in Figure 9.43. With the newly colored fill still selected, execute the shortcut key to Copy and Paste in Place, change the Alpha setting to 25%, and position it between the real graphic and the first black graphic we created.

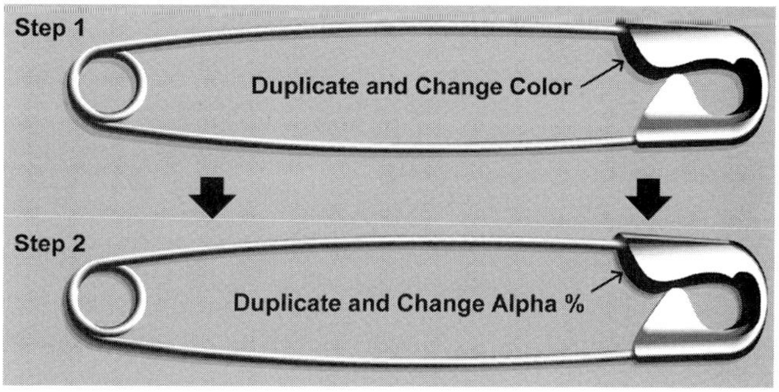

FIGURE 9.43 Create a drop shadow in two easy steps.

Use the Select All shortcut key, found in the menu under Edit > Select All, to select all the graphics. Then, bring up the Transform panel, type 43 in the Rotate text field, and press the Enter key to execute the rotation, as shown in Figure 9.44. To create a ground on which the pin sits, we will be using the Color Mixer panel to make a new radial gradient. The radial gradient contains two color swatches: #999999 100% Alpha and #526B94 100% Alpha. Create a new layer, place it below all the other layers, and create a rectangle shape with the new radial gradient we made. Use the Gradient Transform tool to edit the center position, rotation, and scale of the gradient.

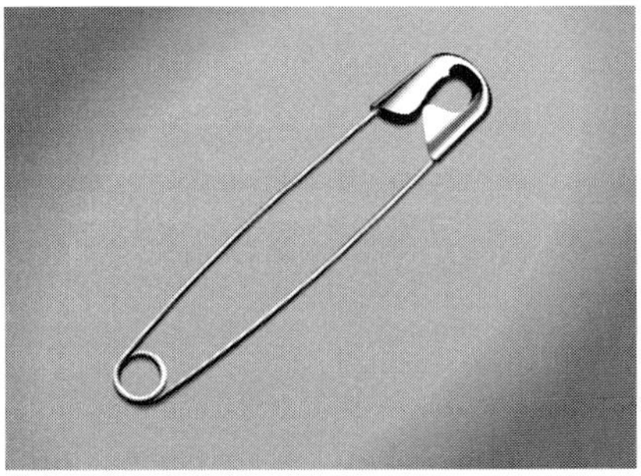

FIGURE 9.44 Rotate the pin and apply a radial gradient in the background.

APPLE

Illustrating a realistic-looking apple in Flash is not easy, although if you follow this tutorial step by step you will have the knowledge to produce an object with a heavy texture like this apple. A Fuji apple like this one is not your average shiny red apple you are used to seeing. A Fuji apple is yellow with orange and red pointy, elongated textures. To make these textures look real, you must use several layers of them. To start, we will need to create an outline of the apple. First, use the Line tool and plot your points, as shown in Figure 9.45.

Switch to the Selection tool and grab the center of the lines to add curves to the lines, as shown in Figure 9.46.

With the Color Mixer panel, create a yellow radial gradient and apply it to the circular outline, as shown in Figure 9.47. The radial gradient contains four color swatches: #ECF991 100% Alpha, #ECF991 100% Alpha, #E6E673 100% Alpha, and #D1D127 100% Alpha. Reposition the center and scale the gradient with the Gradient Transform tool. Select and delete the outline once you are done applying the radial gradient.

Going forward, we will be creating many different types of outlines with the Line tool. To make sure we stay consistent with the initial shape of the apple, use the Ink Bottle tool, and add a stroke outline to the yellow radial gradient. Select that outline, delete it, and paste it on a new

FIGURE 9.45 Use the Line tool to plot your outlines.

FIGURE 9.46 With the Selection tool, add curves to your straight lines.

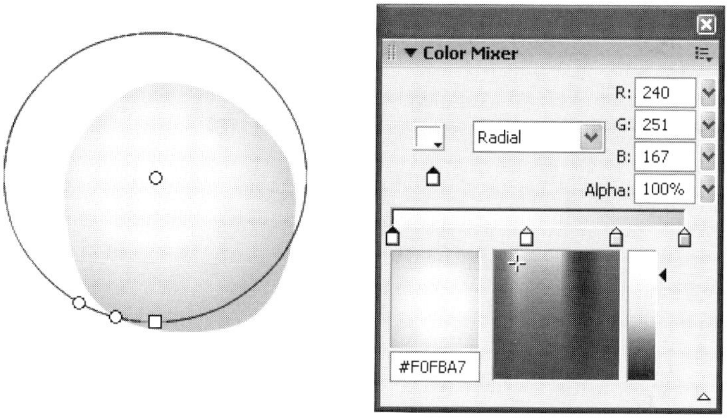

FIGURE 9.47 Create a radial gradient and apply it to the outlined area.

layer where you will be working on the new texture, as shown in Figure 9.48. On this new layer positioned above the first one, use the Line and Selection tools to define the shape of this new texture outline. Try to use as few vector points as possible when plotting your points. This will be the base texture, so it does not need to be very detailed.

With the Color Mixer panel, create a light red radial gradient and apply it to the base texture outline, as shown in Figure 9.49. The radial gradient contains two color swatches: #D02F2F 3% Alpha and #D02F2F 10% Alpha. Reposition the center and scale the gradient with the Gradient Transform tool. Select and delete the outline once you are done applying the radial gradient.

FIGURE 9.48 Using the Line tool, create outlines that will define where a fill will be applied.

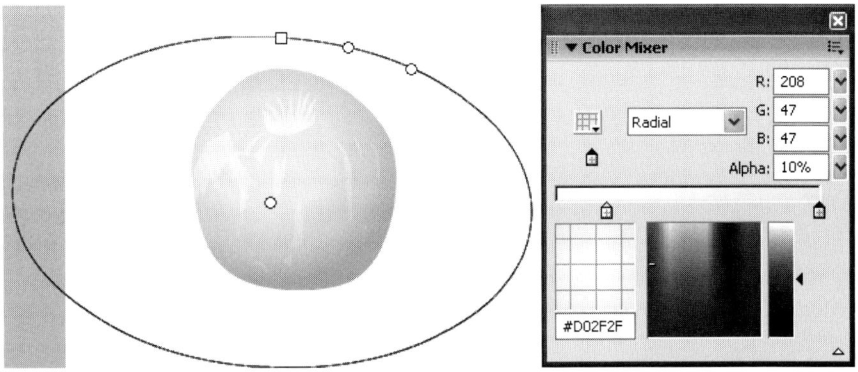

FIGURE 9.49 Apply a radial gradient to the outlined area.

Create a new layer and place it above all the other layers. Acquire the outline of the shape of the apple and paste it in place on this new layer. With the Line and Selection tools, define the shape of a more complicated texture outline, as shown in Figure 9.50. Make sure to illustrate this texture in two pieces, which will hold differently positioned gradients. Although this texture should be more detailed than the last one, make sure you are using as few vector points as possible.

Focusing on coloring the bottom detailed texture, the top texture has been placed on a new layer and the layer has been hidden for the moment. With the Color Mixer panel, create a light red radial gradient and apply it to the detailed texture outline, as shown in Figure 9.51. The radial gradient contains three color swatches: #D02F2F 3% Alpha, #D02F2F 10% Alpha, and #D02F2F 41% Alpha. Reposition the center and scale the gradient with the Gradient Transform tool. Select and delete the outline once you are done applying the radial gradient.

FIGURE 9.50 With the Line and Selection tools, draw two outlines where more detail will be.

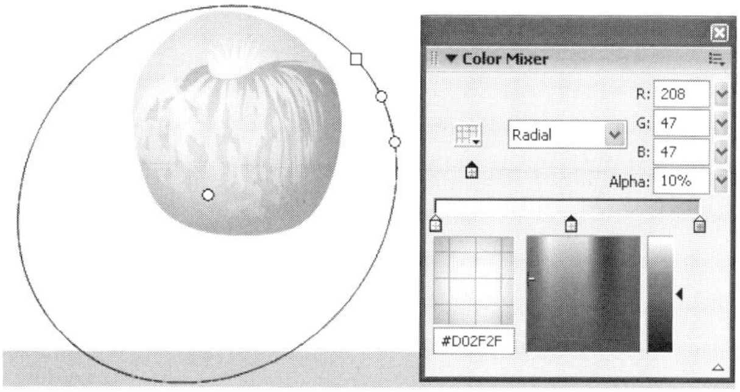

FIGURE 9.51 Create a radial gradient and apply it to the lower outline area.

Unhide the top texture outline and hide the bottom texture layer. With the Color Mixer panel, create another light red radial gradient and apply it to the detailed texture outline, as shown in Figure 9.52. The radial gradient contains two color swatches: #D02F2F 0% Alpha and #D02F2F 100% Alpha. Reposition the center and scale the gradient with the Gradient Transform tool. Select and delete the outline once you are done applying the radial gradient.

Create a new layer on top of all the previous layers, and use the Line and Selection tools to create the final level of detailed texture outline, as shown in Figure 9.53.

Apply the last gradient you created to this outline, reposition the center, and scale the gradient with the Gradient Transform tool, as shown in Figure 9.54. Select and delete the outline once you are done applying the radial gradient.

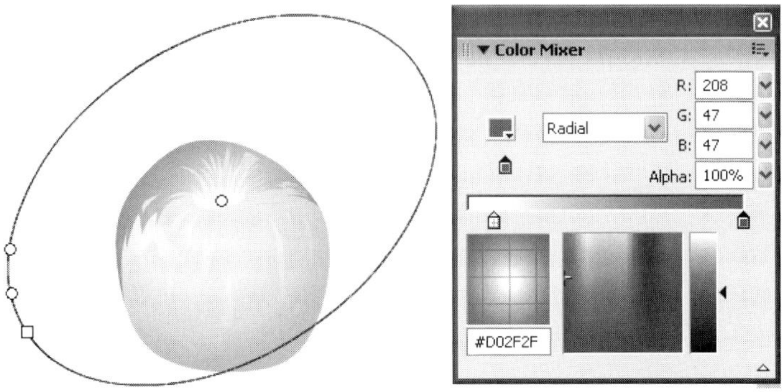

FIGURE 9.52 Create a more visible gradient and apply it to the upper outline area.

FIGURE 9.53 With the Line and Selection tools, draw another outline.

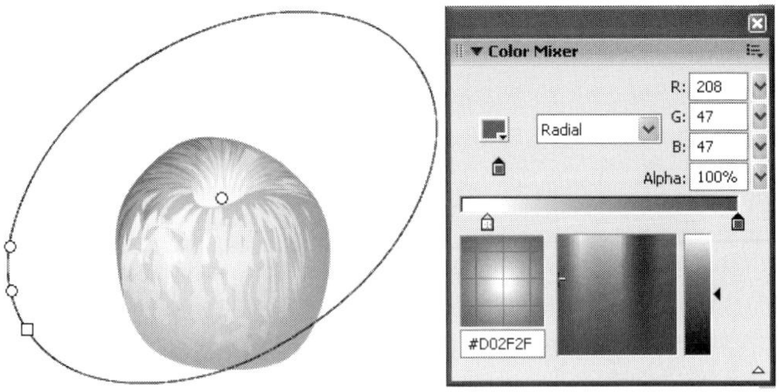

FIGURE 9.54 Apply a similar gradient to the outlined area.

On the same layer, use the Line and Selection tools to create the final level of detailed texture outline accenting the lower top, as shown in Figure 9.55.

FIGURE 9.55 With the Line and Selection tools, draw an outline that will define the top-front detail in the apple.

Using the same radial gradient, apply it to the outline, reposition the center, and scale the gradient with the Gradient Transform tool, as shown in Figure 9.56. Select and delete the outline once you are done applying the radial gradient.

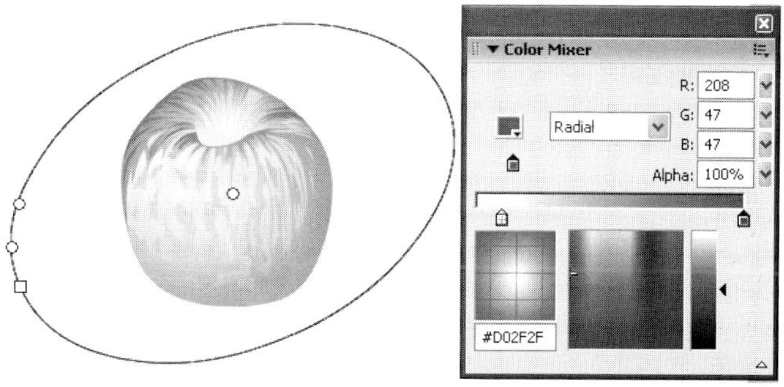

FIGURE 9.56 Apply the radial gradient to the outlined area.

Again, acquire the outline shape of the apple, and Copy and Paste in Place on a new layer, as shown in Figure 9.57.

With the Color Mixer panel, create a transparent dark red radial gradient that will define the apple's roundness, as shown in Figure 9.58. The radial gradient contains three color swatches: #5F1616 0% Alpha, #5F1616 36% Alpha, and #5F1616 96% Alpha. Reposition the center and scale the gradient with the Gradient Transform tool. Select and delete the outline once you are done applying the radial gradient.

FIGURE 9.57 Create an outline of the apple by applying the Ink Bottle tool on the first yellow radial gradient we created. Select the outline, delete it, and paste it on a new layer above all other layers.

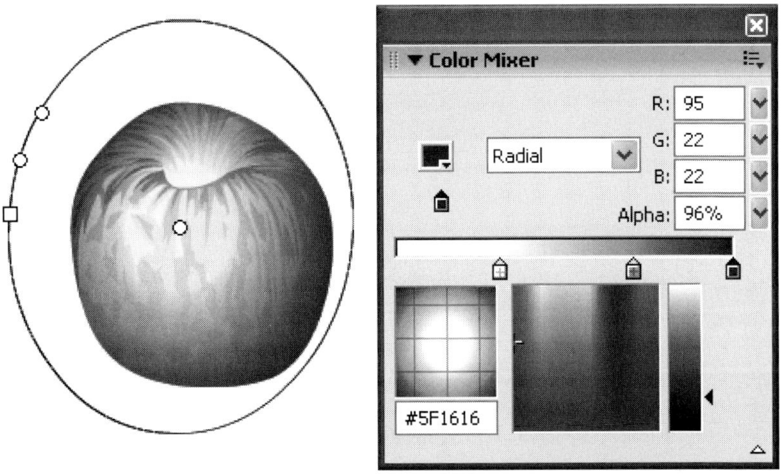

FIGURE 9.58 Apply a newly created gradient that will act as the overall shadow defining the apple's roundness.

To define the stem, and to center the light green color and white highlights, an additional layer will be needed. Use your Line and Selection tools and draw the necessary outlines, as shown in Figure 9.59. Since the white highlights require an odd shape to make the apple look more realistic, we cannot replicate it with a normal radial gradient. Different levels of solid transparent fills will do the trick, which is why so many outlines are needed.

FIGURE 9.59 Create outlines that will define the highlights and stem area.

The stem is colored with a radial gradient with two color swatches: #3D2E03 100% Alpha and #806335 100% Alpha. The tip of the stem is colored with a solid fill with a HEX value of #C9A365. The center light green radial gradient as shown in Figure 9.60 contains two color swatches: #95BB39 50% Alpha and #95BB39 0% Alpha. The white highlights are colored with the same #FFFFFF white solid fill and set at different Alpha settings. The closer to the center of the outlines, the higher the percentage of Alpha used. For example, the white fill used on the inside may have an Alpha setting of 80%, but the white fill used on the outside may have an Alpha setting of 5%.

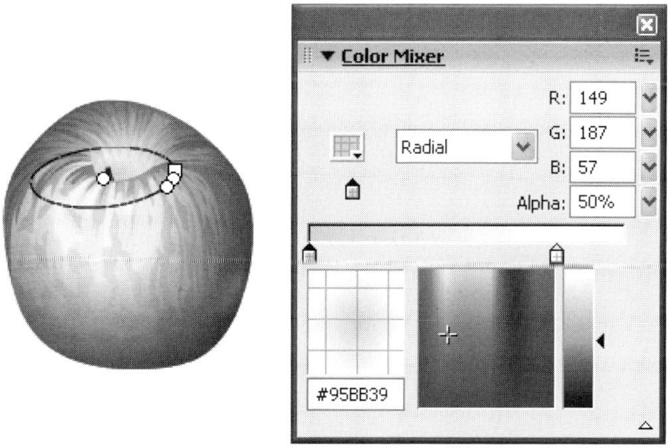

FIGURE 9.60 Apply white fills to the highlight area outlines with different levels of Alpha.

Apply a green radial gradient to the center area and brown solid fills for the stem, making the apple look more realistic.

The surface of a Fuji apple is not perfectly smooth, so we will be creating a radial gradient that will be used to create textures to make the apple look like it has blemishes on the surface. With the Color Mixer panel, create a green and yellow radial gradient, as shown in Figure 9.61. The radial gradient contains two color swatches: #95BB39 100% Alpha and #ECF991 100% Alpha. Use the Oval tool to create the radial gradient, and turn it into a symbol movie clip by accessing the menu items Modify > Convert to Symbol.

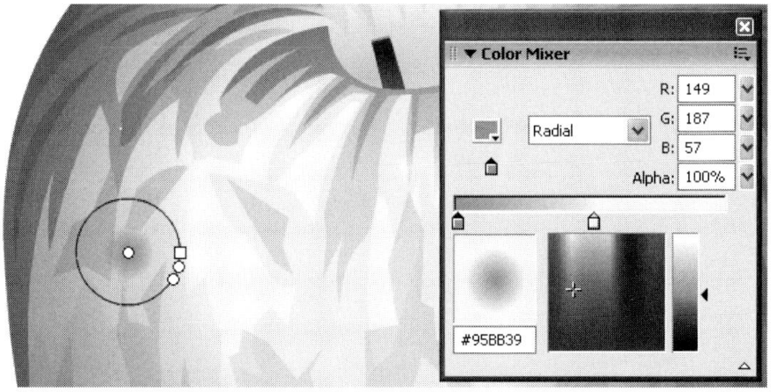

FIGURE 9.61 Create a similar green radial gradient that we will use to depict blemishes in the apple's surface.

Duplicate the green and yellow radial gradient movie clip randomly across the apple; feel free to change the size of the gradient with the Free Transform tool, as shown in Figure 9.62.

FIGURE 9.62 Duplicate the green radial gradient movie clip, resize it, and position it in many places.

Create a new layer and position it at the bottom of the layers we have been working with. On it, create a circle with the Oval tool; this is where the shadow radial gradient will be placed, as shown in Figure 9.63.

Create a new radial gradient with the Color Mixer panel, as shown in Figure 9.64. The radial gradient contains three color swatches: #000000 75% Alpha, #000000 25% Alpha, and #000000 0% Alpha. Apply the radial gradients with the Paint Bucket tool, and edit the center point and scaling of the gradient with the Gradient Transform tool.

FIGURE 9.63 Create a circular line that will define the area where the first shadow will be placed.

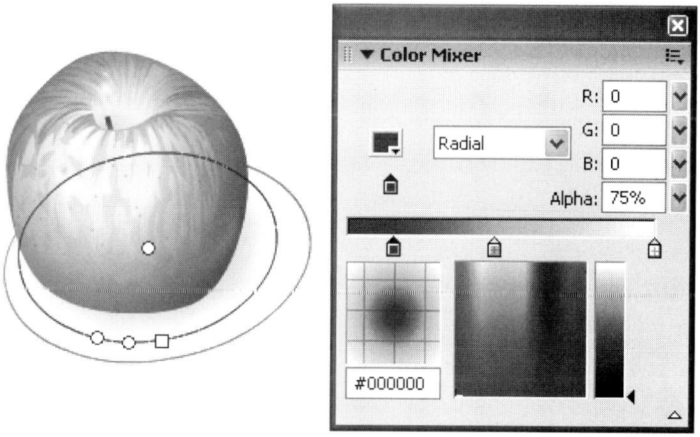

FIGURE 9.64 Create and apply a radial gradient that will define the inner shadow.

Create a new layer and position it at the bottom of all the layers. On it, create a circle with the Oval tool. Select the first oval, Copy and Paste in Place, and scale it down to create another smaller circle; repeat this to create a third smaller circle. With the Line tool, divide the circles in half, as shown in Figure 9.65.

FIGURE 9.65 Create three circular lines that will define the area where the second and more prominent shadow will be placed. Divide the circles in half with a line.

Create a new radial gradient with the Color Mixer panel, as shown in Figure 9.66. The radial gradient contains two color swatches: #3D2E03 100% Alpha and #7B5509 20% Alpha. Apply the radial gradient to the left side with the Paint Bucket tool, and edit the center point and scaling of the gradient with the Gradient Transform tool.

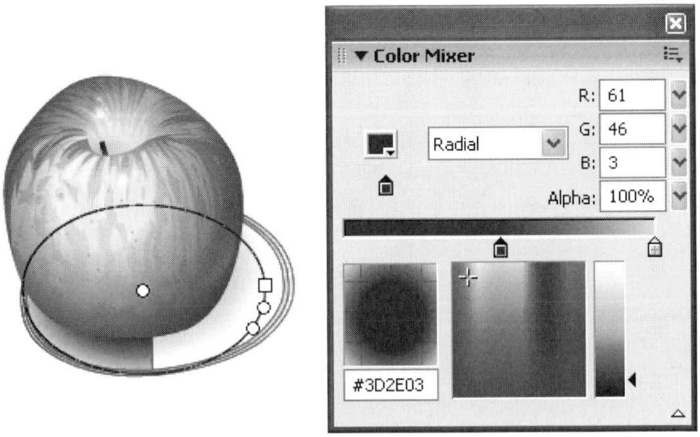

FIGURE 9.66 Create and apply a radial gradient to the left half of the center outline.

Apply the same radial gradient to the right side with the Paint Bucket tool, and edit the center point and scaling of the gradient with the Gradient Transform tool, as shown in Figure 9.67. Apply the same radial gradient to the two outer outlined areas, but decrease the Alpha percentage in the color swatches the further out the gradient fill is. For example, the closer outer outline to the center is decreased to 14% Alpha, and the outmost outline is decreased to 5% Alpha.

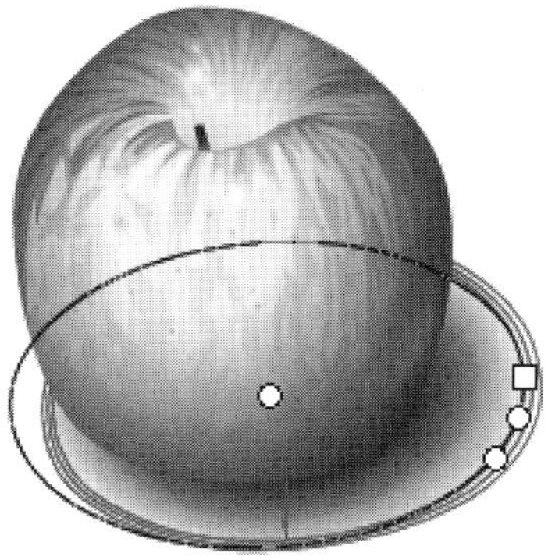

FIGURE 9.67 Apply the same gradient to the right center area, and edit it to match the size of the area. Apply the same gradients to the two other outer circle areas, but lower the Alpha color settings so they are increasingly transparent as they go out.

The final rendering of the apple as shown in Figure 9.68 shows how, with the combination of optimized layered textures and transparent gradients, you can produce a realistic-looking apple.

FIGURE 9.68 Final illustration of the apple.

Bell Pepper

Illustrating a bell pepper may seem easy at first; in actuality, it was one of the most difficult to plan as to how all the gradients would interact with each other to get the final look. Although this object may not contain as many textures as the apple, the bell pepper requires several layers of transparent gradients to define its shape. Making it even more difficult is the seamless "s" shaped flowing gradients required to define the bumps and uneven surfaces of the object. To start defining the basic outline shape of the object, use the Line tool to plot the lines, and use the Selection tool to modify the lines and give them a more curved shape, as shown in Figure 9.69.

Adding more lines to the graphic defines the object's shape and where basic gradients could be applied, as shown in Figure 9.70.

FIGURE 9.69 With the Line tool, draw an outline of the bell pepper. Use the Selection tool to make the lines curved.

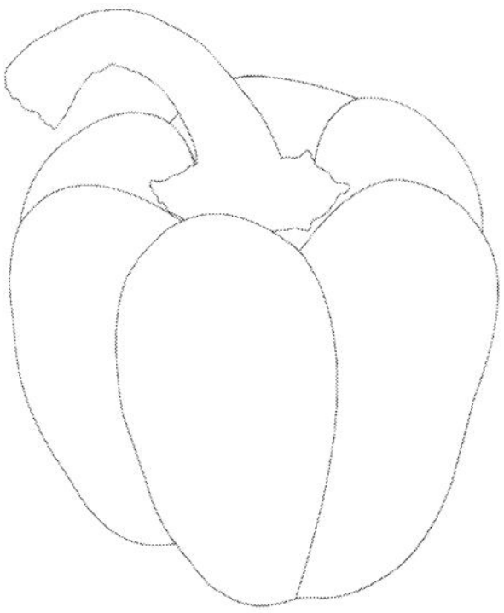

FIGURE 9.70 Continue to use the Line and Selection tools to define the shape of the bell pepper.

Using the Line tool, the outlines are further divided to define areas where fills will be applied, as shown in Figure 9.71.

The first part of the bell pepper we will be coloring is the red body of the object. Before any complicated gradients can be laid down, we must create the base color of the body. Remember, we will be reusing a handful of colors, and it will be noted when a gradient will be used for a second time. Create a new radial gradient with the Color Mixer panel, as shown in Figure 9.72. The radial gradient contains two color swatches: #CB190D 100% Alpha and #670000 100% Alpha. Apply the radial gradient with the Paint Bucket tool, and edit the center point and scaling of the gradient with the Gradient Transform tool.

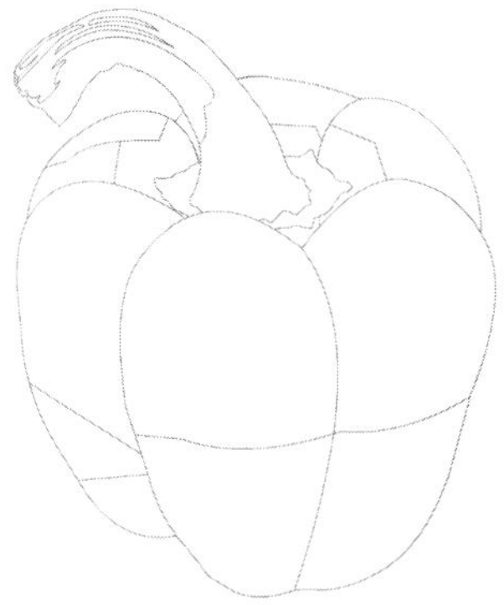

FIGURE 9.71 Use the Line tool to create separations between different areas of the bell pepper.

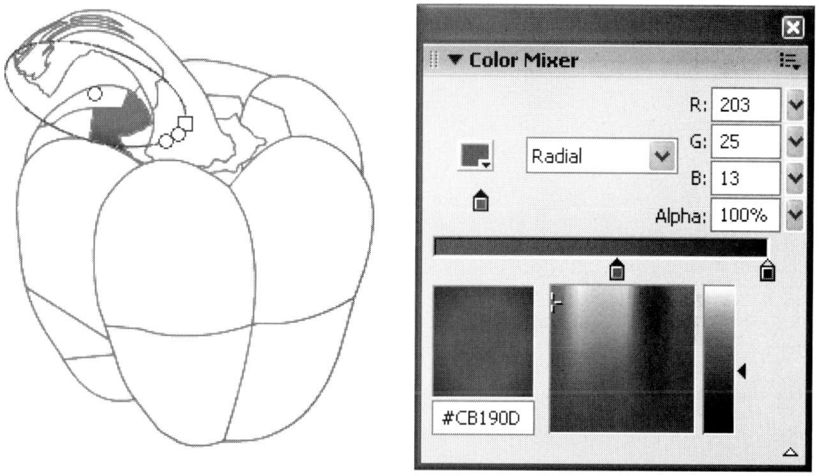

FIGURE 9.72 Create and apply a radial gradient, giving the bell pepper more shape.

Use the same radial gradient we just created, but switch the placement of the two color swatches and apply it to the area shown in Figure 9.73. Use the Gradient Transform tool to line up the two gradients.

Create a new radial gradient with the Color Mixer panel, as shown in Figure 9.74. The radial gradient contains two color swatches: #BC100C 100% Alpha and #670000 100% Alpha. Apply the radial gradient with the Paint Bucket tool, and edit the center point and scaling of the gradient with the Gradient Transform tool.

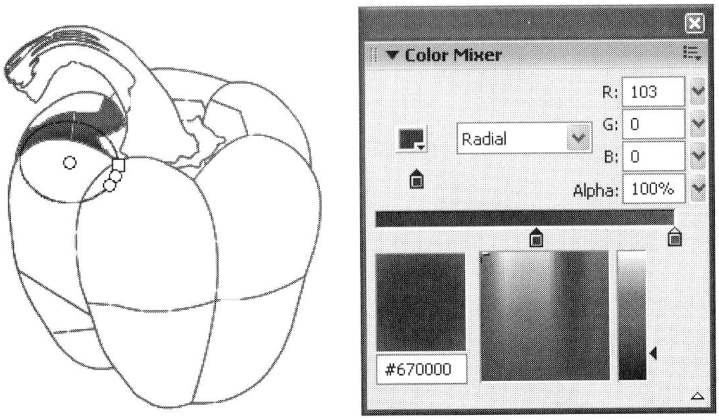

FIGURE 9.73 Create and apply a radial gradient connecting to the first gradient.

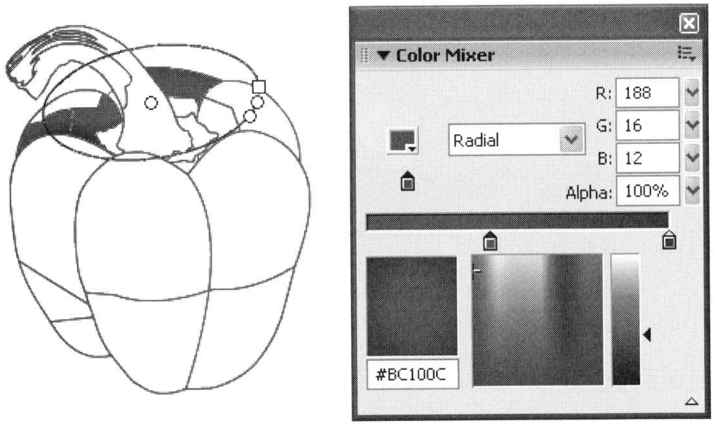

FIGURE 9.74 Create and apply a radial gradient defining the back part of the bell pepper.

Apply the same radial gradient we just created with the Paint Bucket tool, and edit the center point and scaling of the gradient with the Gradient Transform tool, as shown in Figure 9.75.

Create a new radial gradient with the Color Mixer panel, as shown in Figure 9.76. The radial gradient contains three color swatches: #BC100C 100% Alpha, #670000 100% Alpha, and #1A0B04 100% Alpha. Apply the radial gradient with the Paint Bucket tool to both of the inside areas defining the shadow of the base of the stem. Edit the center point and scaling of the gradient with the Gradient Transform tool.

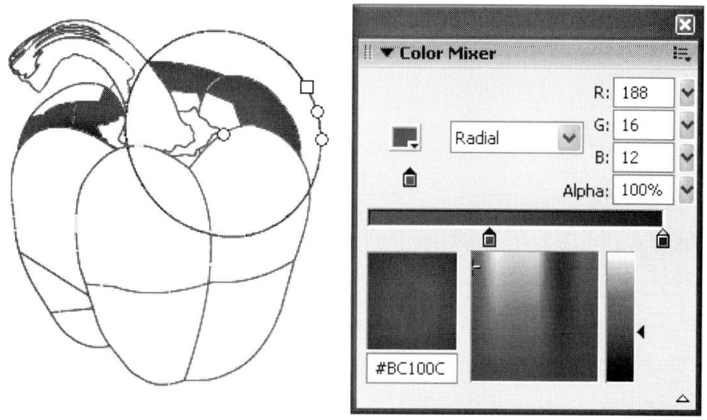

FIGURE 9.75 Using the same gradient, apply it to the area below.

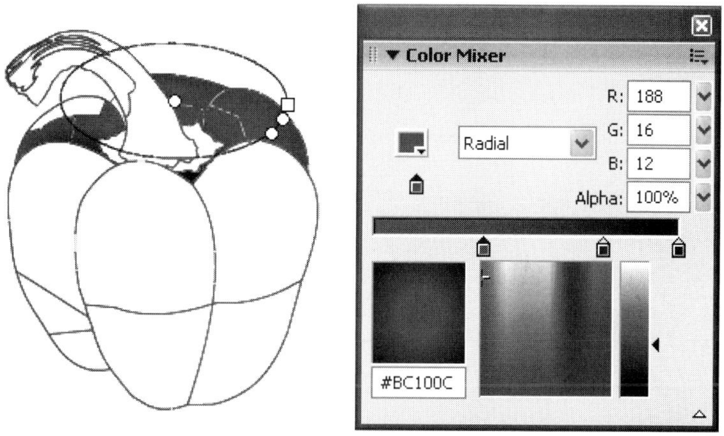

FIGURE 9.76 Use a darker, modified radial gradient and apply it to the areas close to the center of the bell pepper.

Create a new radial gradient with the Color Mixer panel, as shown in Figure 9.77. The radial gradient contains three color swatches: #8A120A 100% Alpha, #7A0000 100% Alpha, and #8A120A 100% Alpha. Apply the radial gradient with the Paint Bucket tool to the top three areas, and edit the center point and scaling of the gradient with the Gradient Transform tool.

Create a new radial gradient with the Color Mixer panel, as shown in Figure 9.78. The radial gradient contains three color swatches: #8A120A 100% Alpha, #8A120A 100% Alpha, and #720905 100% Alpha. Apply the radial gradient with the Paint Bucket tool to the two bottom areas, and edit the center point and scaling of the gradient with the Gradient Transform tool.

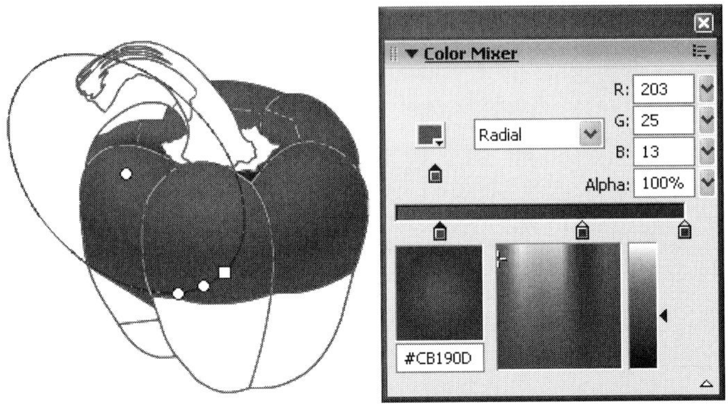

FIGURE 9.77 Create a radial gradient and apply it to the three main areas of the bell pepper, defining the object's shape.

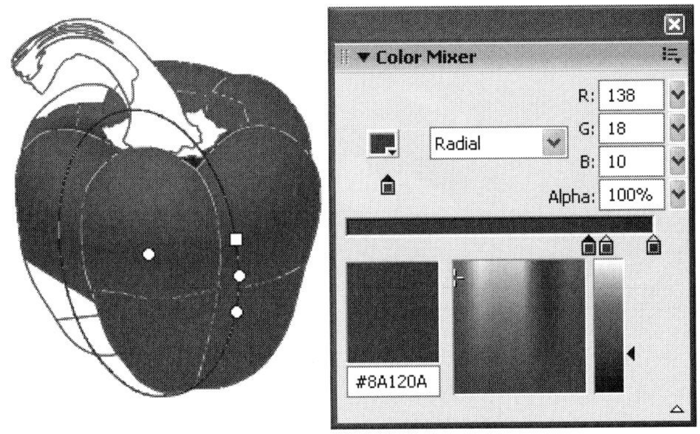

FIGURE 9.78 Create and apply a radial gradient in the two bottom outlined areas of the bell pepper.

Create a new radial gradient with the Color Mixer panel, as shown in Figure 9.79. The radial gradient contains three color swatches: #8A120A 100% Alpha, #A3140A 100% Alpha, and #670000 100% Alpha. Apply the radial gradient with the Paint Bucket tool to the bottom left area, and edit the center point and scaling of the gradient with the Gradient Transform tool.

The last outlined areas to fill will be done with three solid fills, and their HEX values are labeled in Figure 9.80. Once you have finished laying down the base body color of the object, delete the unnecessary lines so you can see how the gradients line up with each other.

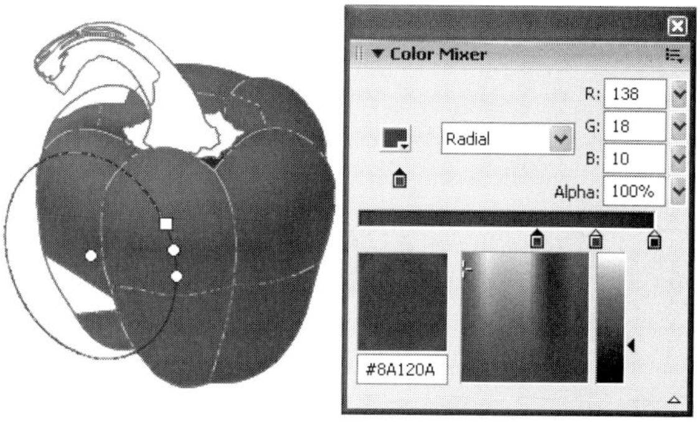

FIGURE 9.79 To define the bottom left tip of the bell pepper, create and apply a radial gradient.

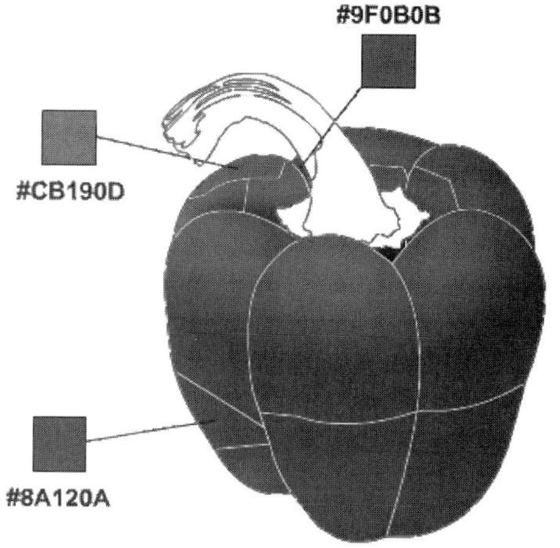

FIGURE 9.80 Apply three different solid fills to the outlined areas.

With the Line and Selection tools, add more detail to the outlines defining the stem as shown in Figure 9.81, since it will contain several gradients.

Starting at the base of the stem, we need to create a radial gradient that will define the bumpy highlights in the leafy-looking base, as shown in Figure 9.82. The radial gradient contains two color swatches: #606416 100% Alpha and #313301 100% Alpha. Apply the radial gradient with the Paint Bucket tool to the bottom left area, and edit the center point and scaling of the gradient with the Gradient Transform tool. Make the gradient darker or with less contrast for some of the less prominent bumps.

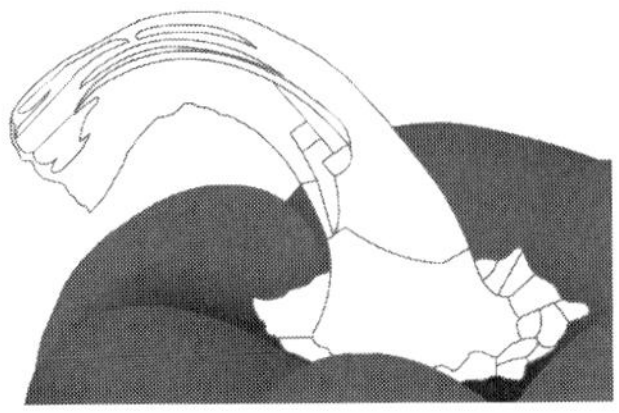

FIGURE 9.81 Focus on the stem and add further outlines, blocking off areas to make places for certain fills.

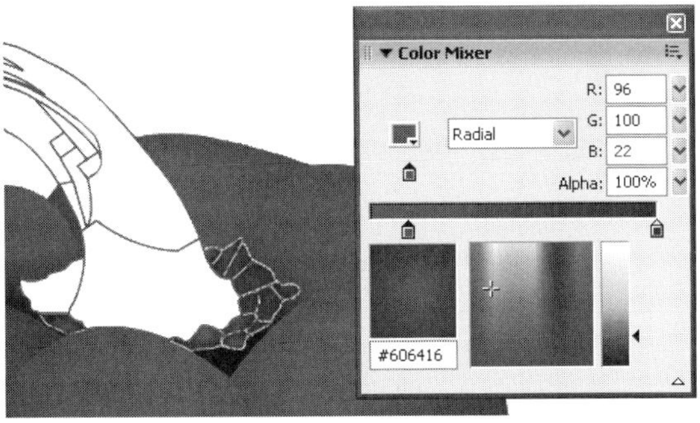

FIGURE 9.82 Create and apply a dark green gradient to the particular areas toward the base of the stem.

Create a new radial gradient with the Color Mixer panel, as shown in Figure 9.83. The radial gradient contains five color swatches: #281E03 100% Alpha, #333103 100% Alpha, #414604 100% Alpha, #464E05 100% Alpha, and #323F03 100% Alpha. Apply the radial gradient with the Paint Bucket tool to the base area of the stem, and edit the center point and scaling of the gradient with the Gradient Transform tool.

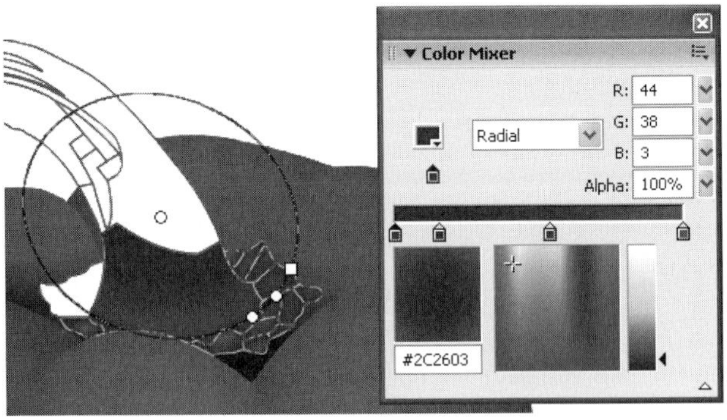

FIGURE 9.83 Create and apply a radial gradient defining the curvature of the stem.

Create a new radial gradient with the Color Mixer panel, as shown in Figure 9.84. The radial gradient contains four color swatches: #2C2603 100% Alpha, #2C2603 100% Alpha, #343509 100% Alpha, and #5F630B 100% Alpha. Apply the radial gradient with the Paint Bucket tool to the top area of the stem, and edit the center point and scaling of the gradient with the Gradient Transform tool.

Create a linear and radial gradient, both including the same color swatches, to be applied to the three top areas designated for highlight fills, as shown in Figure 9.85. The color swatches used in these gradients are #7E8625 100% Alpha and #5B5F0A 100% Alpha. Apply the radial gradient with the Paint Bucket tool to the top highlight areas of the stem, and edit the center point and scaling of the gradient with the Gradient Transform tool.

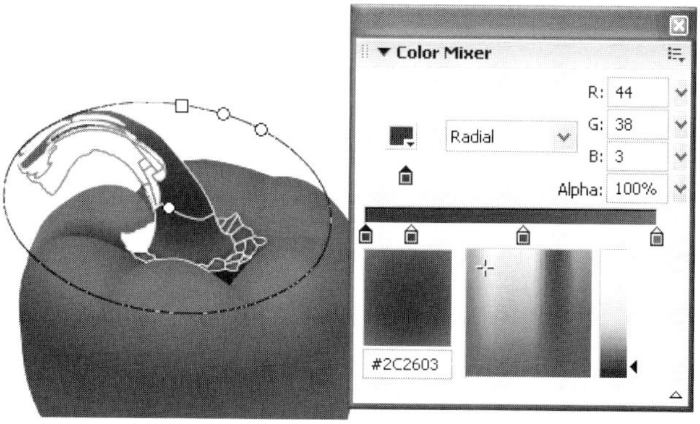

FIGURE 9.84 Create a modified gradient of the previous one created and apply it to the top area of the stem.

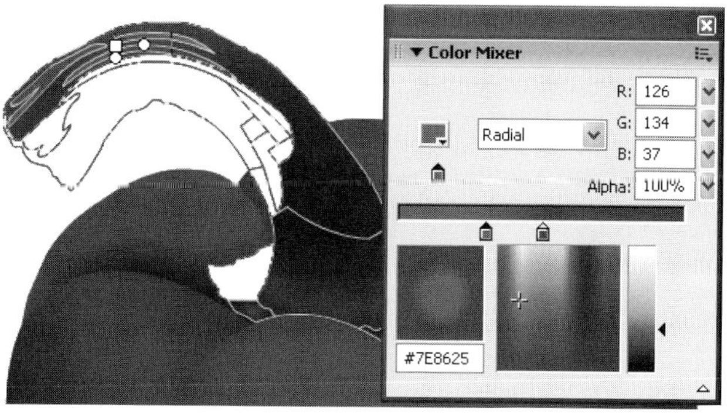

FIGURE 9.85 Add highlights to the top areas of the stem with linear and radial gradients of the same color.

Create a new radial gradient with the Color Mixer panel, as shown in Figure 9.86. The radial gradient contains two color swatches: #1C110A 100% Alpha and #736714 100% Alpha. Apply the radial gradient with the Paint Bucket tool to the underside of the stem, and edit the center point and scaling of the gradient with the Gradient Transform tool.

Create radial and linear gradients using the same color swatches to create the gradients you need to form the complicated path shown in Figure 9.87. Notice the hand-drawn line to point out the path of how the gradients should connect. The color swatches used in these many variations of gradients are #2D2904 100% Alpha, #1C110A 100% Alpha, and #2D2904 100% Alpha.

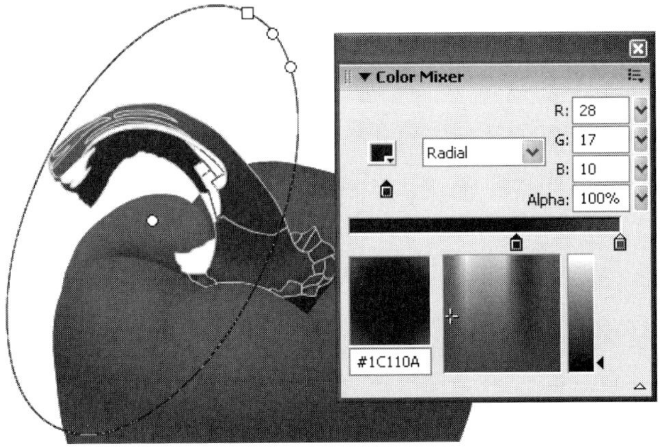

FIGURE 9.86 Create and apply a radial gradient to the underside of the stem.

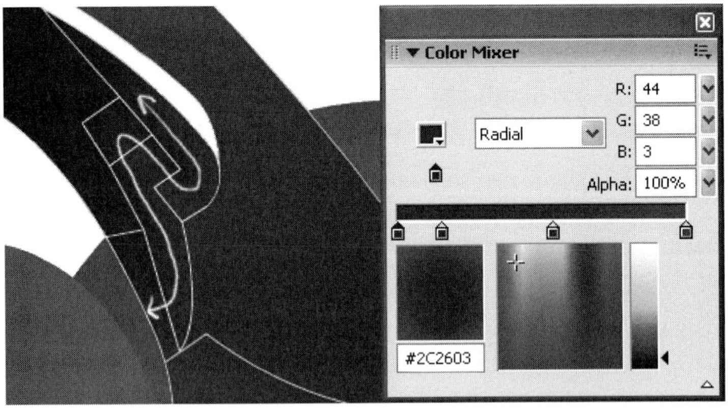

FIGURE 9.87 Create many variations of the same gradient and match them up to define the curvy part of the stem. Notice the hand-drawn line showing how the gradients should connect together.

Create a linear gradient to fill in the remaining outlined areas, as shown in Figure 9.88. The linear gradient has two color swatches: #2A1F0B 100% Alpha, and #51540A 100% Alpha. Apply the linear gradient with the Paint Bucket tool, and edit the center point and scaling of the gradient with the Gradient Transform tool.

Create a new layer and position it at the bottom under the previous layer. On it, use the Line and Selection tools to create an outline. This is where the shadow radial gradients will be placed, as shown in Figure 9.89.

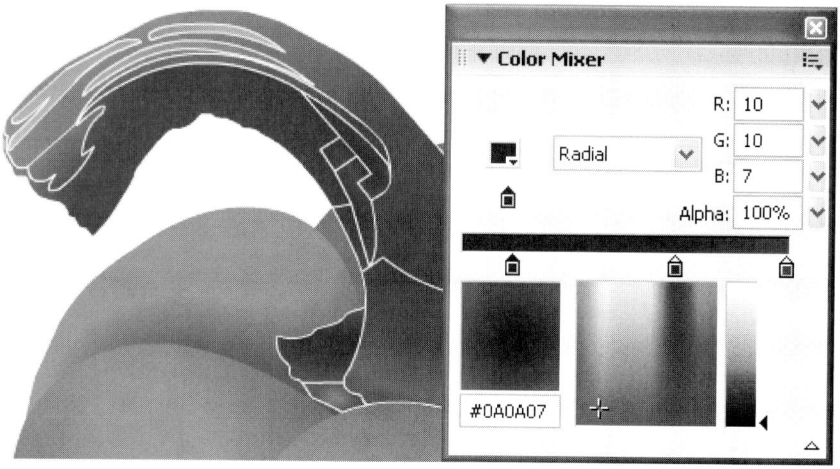

FIGURE 9.88 Fill in the last areas of the stem with dark green linear gradients.

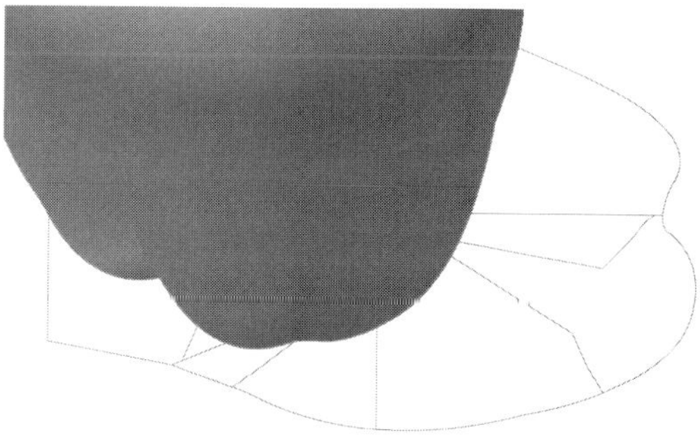

FIGURE 9.89 Using the Line and the Selection tools, draw the outline that will define how the shadow will form.

Create a new radial gradient with the Color Mixer panel, as shown in Figure 9.90. The radial gradient contains four color swatches: #251616 0% Alpha, #251616 55% Alpha, #251616 40% Alpha, and #251616 0% Alpha. Apply the radial gradients with the Paint Bucket tool, and edit the center point and scaling of the gradient with the Gradient Transform tool. A modified radial gradient will be needed for the slight inner curves. To create them, reverse the order of the color swatches.

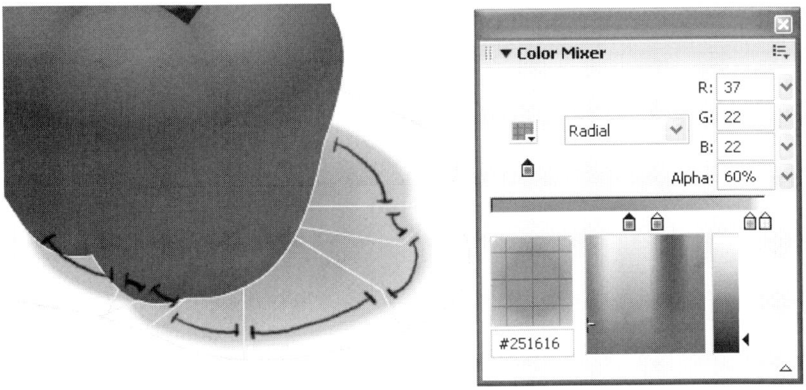

FIGURE 9.90 Create a gradient and use a couple of variations of swatch placement to get the radial gradients to match up. Notice the hand-drawn lines showing how one gradient flows into the next.

Notice the hand-drawn lines showing how each gradient is positioned to line up with the next.

Create more shadows defining the shape of the bell pepper by adding on a new layer. These transparent radial gradients contain two color swatches: #350000 0% Alpha and #350000 100% Alpha. Use the Rectangle or Oval tool to apply them to the new layer, as shown in Figure 9.91.

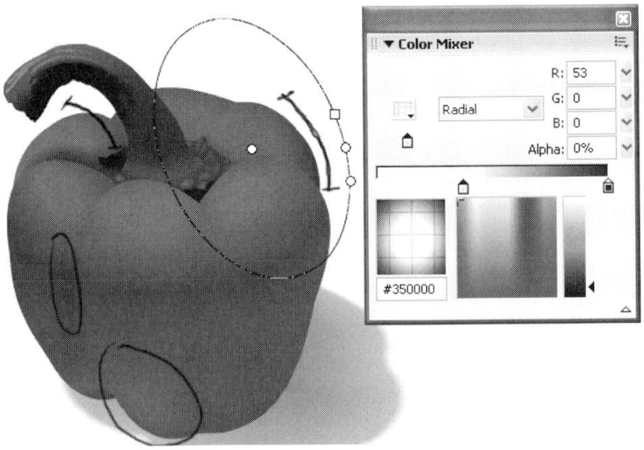

FIGURE 9.91 Adding more shadows with an added layer of radial gradients; notice the hand-drawn lines pointing out their placement.

Creating the curvy gradient can be difficult, but if you use similar-colored gradients and position your fills in the right places, it can be quite easy. Create a new layer, and with the Line tool, create the outlines to define where the radial gradients will be placed. Create a new radial gradient with the Color Mixer panel, as shown in Figure 9.92. The radial gradient contains three color swatches: #330000 0% Alpha, #330000 35% Alpha, and #330000 60% Alpha. Reverse the positions of the color swatches for the opposite-turning gradient. Apply the radial gradients with the Paint Bucket tool, and edit the center point and scaling of the gradient with the Gradient Transform tool.

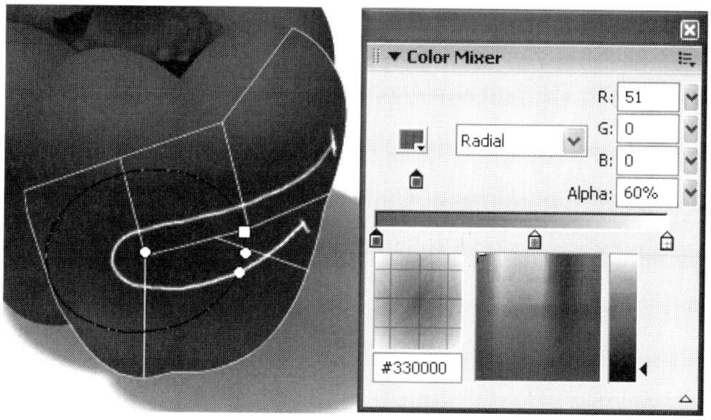

FIGURE 9.92 Create outlines and apply radial gradients that will define the curvy shadow on the right side of the bell pepper. The hand-drawn lines point out the flow of the gradients.

Create a white transparent radial gradient that will define the highlights of the bell pepper. Create a new radial gradient with the Color Mixer panel, as shown in Figure 9.93. The radial gradient contains four color swatches: #FCF1B8 65% Alpha, #FAEEAF 40% Alpha, #EDF198 10% Alpha, and # EDF198 0% Alpha. Apply the radial gradient with the Oval tool by drawing a fill where the highlights are needed. Edit the scaling of the gradient with the Gradient Transform tool. Different variations of this gradient are needed, so adjust the color settings to achieve other gradient combinations.

Create a new layer and position it at the bottom under all the layers we have been working with. On it, use the Line and Selection tools to create an outline; this is where the shadow radial gradients will be placed, as shown in Figure 9.94. Create a new radial gradient with the Color Mixer panel. The radial gradient contains two color swatches: #251616

40% Alpha and #251616 0% Alpha. Apply the radial gradients with the Paint Bucket tool, and edit the center point and scaling of the gradient with the Gradient Transform tool. A modified radial gradient will be needed for the slight inner curves. To create them, reverse the order of the color swatches.

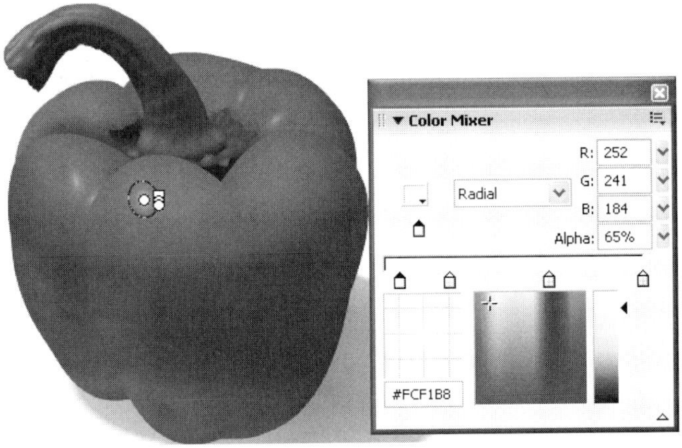

FIGURE 9.93 Add small highlights to make the bell pepper seem more realistic.

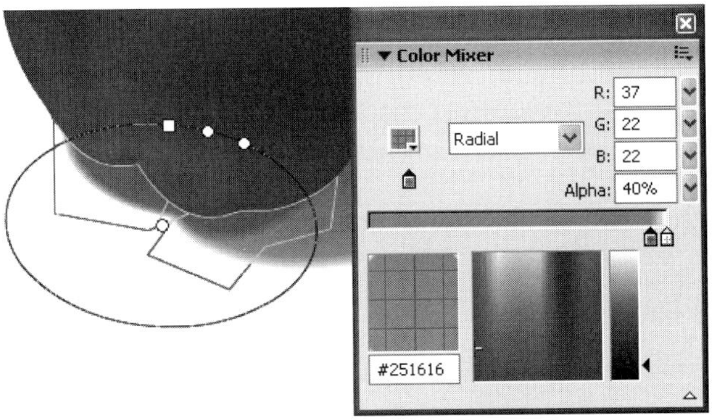

FIGURE 9.94 Create outlines and apply gradient fills that define the strongest shadow.

Reviewing the final illustration of the bell pepper in Figure 9.95, what really stands out as the most important lesson of this tutorial is that if you tightly integrate many linear and radial gradients, almost any type of surface can be replicated in vector. Layering transparent radial gradients gives an image a more dynamic look.

FIGURE 9.95 Final illustration of the bell pepper.

HUMAN FIGURE

Reproducing a photorealistic human has always been a sought-after skill. Many attempts have resulted in a lack of photorealistic quality, or images with the trace bitmap look, riddled with chaotic, uncompressed vectors resulting in a huge file size. With the introduction of the simple blur filter, complicated shaped gradients are possible, which are found a lot in the human face and clothing. The image used here is yours truly, who posed for the camera and used the developed picture as reference. To start defining the basic outline shape of the object, use the Line tool to plot the lines, and use the Selection tool to modify the lines and give them a more curved shape, as shown in Figure 9.96. Start with the head and work your way down, finishing at the shoes.

FIGURE 9.96 Create the outline of the human body.

Shoes

Define more outline detail in the shoes with the Line and Selection tools, as shown in Figure 9.97.

Begin to apply radial gradients to the green lip of the shoe, as shown in Figure 9.98.

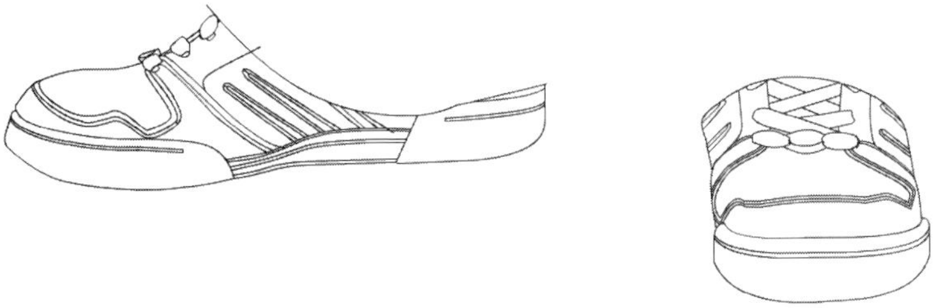

FIGURE 9.97 Focus on the shoes and define more detail in the outline.

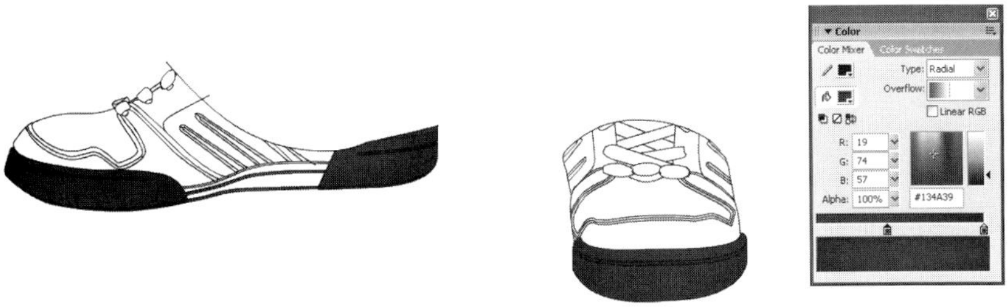

FIGURE 9.98 Apply a base layer of gradients.

Apply radial gradients in different shades of gray, which will define the shape of the shoe, as shown in Figure 9.99. Fill A is a radial gradient containing two color swatches: #5E6877 and #47515A. Fill B is a radial gradient containing three color swatches: #AEB4B7, #8D979C, and #6D7781. Fill C is a radial gradient containing three color swatches: #565F65, #8D9A9C, and #95A2A6. Fill D is a radial gradient containing three color swatches: #124334, #1E6A53, and #124334. Fill E is a radial gradient containing three color swatches: #58666B, #75848A, and #58666B.

Pants

Fill the pant outline area with a linear gradient, as shown in Figure 9.100. This linear gradient contains six color swatches: #12151A, #12171A, #10171E, #10171E, #0C1319, and #0D1112. This gradient is meant to be subtle in its transition, as it will be the base color for the pants.

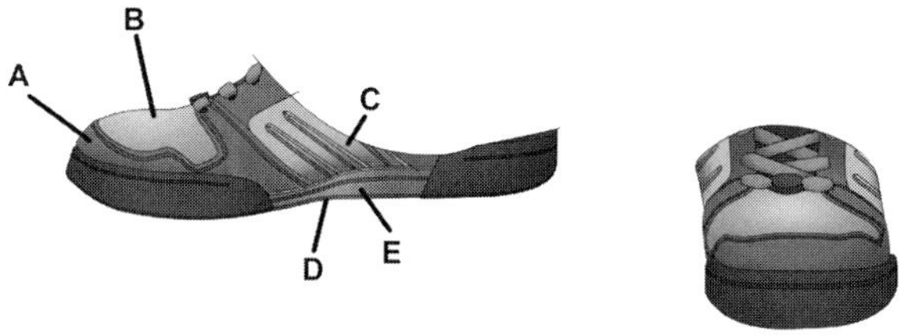

FIGURE 9.99 Add more gradients to define the shape of the shoe.

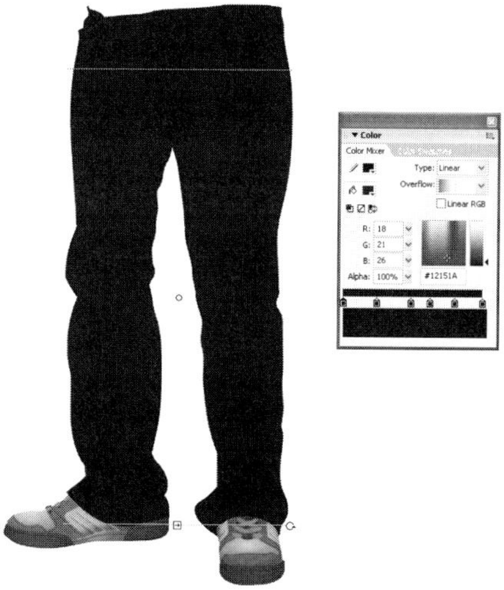

FIGURE 9.100 Create the base color of the pants.

In this task, we will be adding the shadow and highlights to the pants, which will define the depth and shape of the pants, as shown in Figure 9.101. In Step 1, create a new layer and use the Pencil tool to draw the shape of the first shadow fill overlay. Apply a solid fill of #0A0C0B, Alpha: 10%. In Step 2, delete the outlines, convert the fills to a symbol, and apply a blur filter with a value of 1.5 and quality: High. In Step 3, use the Pencil tool to draw the shape of the wrinkles on the right leg and apply linear and radial gradients to add depth. Convert these gradients to a symbol and apply a blur filter. In Step 4, use the Pencil tool to draw the shape of the wrinkles on the left leg, and apply linear and radial gradients to add depth. Convert these gradients to a symbol and apply a blur filter. In Step 5, visualize all the layers of overlays to view the final rendering of the pants.

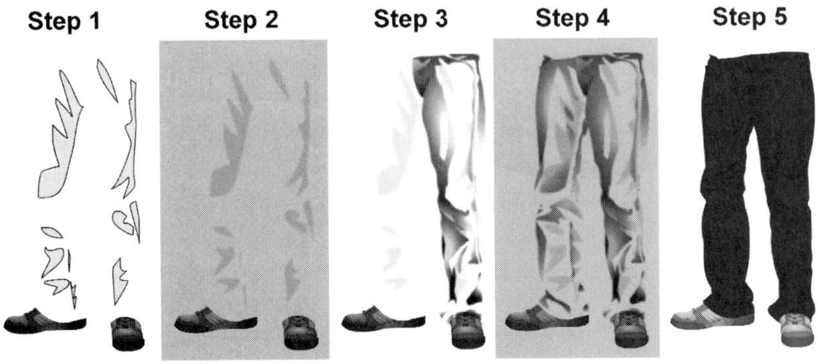

FIGURE 9.101 Dashboard view of the gradient overlays added to the pants.

Shirt

Add more detail to the outline of the shirt with the Pencil tool, as shown in Figure 9.102.

FIGURE 9.102 Define more detail in the shirt and arm outlines.

Apply the base gradient colors of the shirt, as shown in Figure 9.103. Fill A is a linear gradient containing two color swatches: #0E2515 and #18241A. Fill B is a radial gradient containing three color swatches: #1C5427, #13281B, and #080E0A. Fill C is a linear gradient containing two color swatches: #174D29 and #0B2B26. Fill D is a linear gradient containing 12 color swatches: #1C311F, #739370, #286028, #7C9A77, #406A44, #87A280, #527A55, #869D7B, #4F714A, #699768, #306134, and #3C4F28.

Apply linear gradients to the stripes in the shirt and rotate them to get the slant gradient look, as shown in Figure 9.104. Fill A is a linear gradient containing seven color swatches: #AA9155, #C9AF76, #715E31, #796828, #B19767, #C2A578, and #A47C41. Fill B is a linear gradient containing seven color swatches: #82817D, #9D9D9D, #515151, #515151, #8C8C8C, #9D9D9D, and #737373. Fill C is a linear gradient containing six color swatches: #AA9155, #C9AF76, #715E31, #796828, #B19767, and #B3915D. Fill D is a linear gradient containing six color swatches: #808080, #9D9D9D, #515151, #515151, #8C8C8C, and #888888.

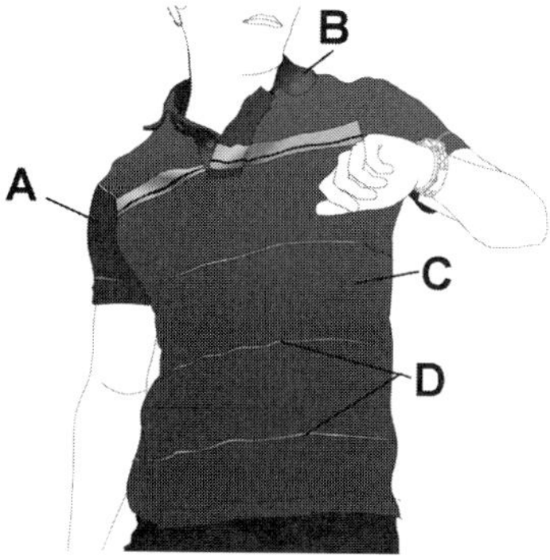

FIGURE 9.103 Apply the base gradients to the shirt outlines.

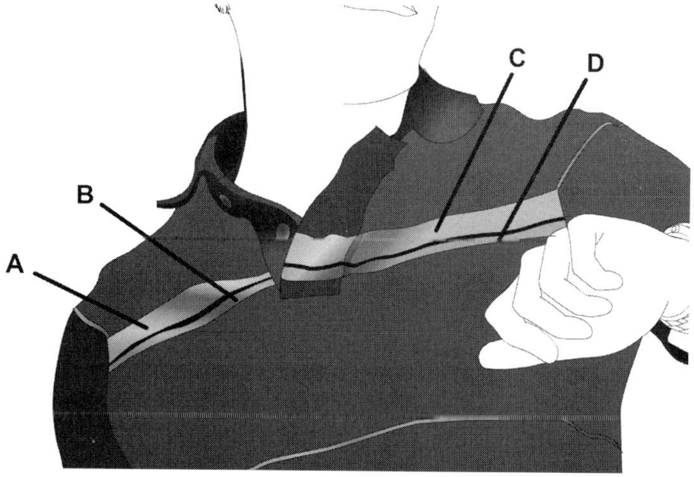

FIGURE 9.104 Apply linear gradients to replicate wrinkles in the cloth.

Create a new layer and use the Pencil tool to draw the shape of the wrinkles in the shirt, as shown in Figure 9.105. Apply gradients to the outlines, and delete the outlines when done applying the gradients. Fill A is a radial gradient containing three color swatches: #050706, Alpha: 37%, #050706, Alpha: 15%, and #050706, Alpha: 5%. Fill B is a radial gradient containing three color swatches: #050706, Alpha: 37%, #050706, Alpha: 27%, and #050706, Alpha: 5%. Fill C is a linear gradient containing two color swatches: #050706, Alpha: 71% and #050706, Alpha: 5%. Fill D is a linear gradient containing two color swatches: #050706, Alpha: 42% and #050706, Alpha: 10%. Fill E is a linear gradient containing two color swatches: #050706, Alpha: 48% and #050706, Alpha: 5%.

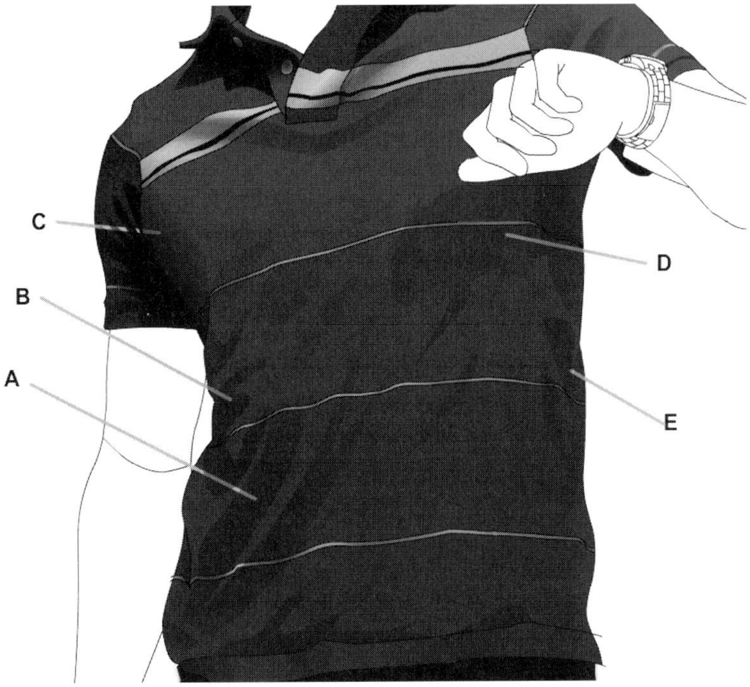

FIGURE 9.105 Add first layer of gradient overlay to define more wrinkles in the shirt.

Select all the gradients, convert them to a symbol, and apply a blur filter with a value of 1.25 and a quality: High, as shown in Figure 9.106.

Arms

Apply linear gradients to define the detail in the watch, as shown in Figure 9.107. Fill A is a linear gradient that contains six color swatches: #808080, #BDBDBD, #8A8A8A, #D5D5D5, #888888, and #4D4D4D. Fill B is a linear gradient that contains three color swatches: #959595,

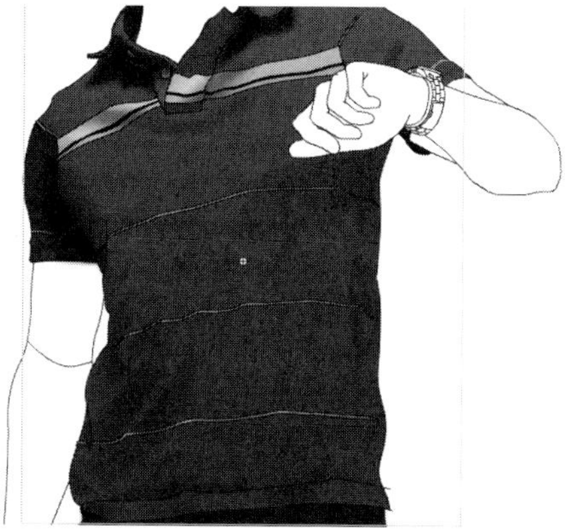

FIGURE 9.106 Apply a blur filter to the shirt.

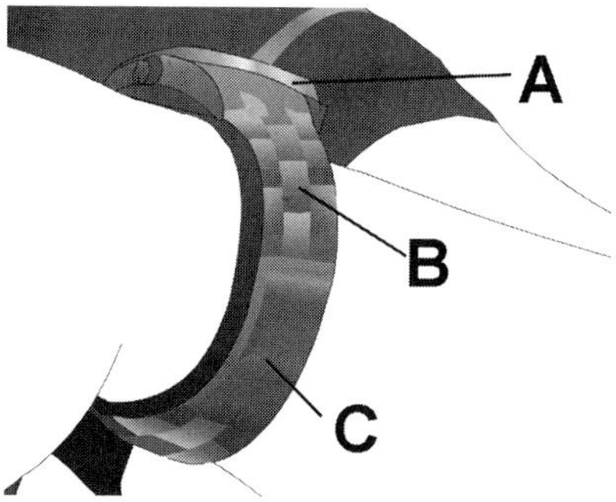

FIGURE 9.107 Apply gradient fills to the watch to define its shape.

#7C7C7C, and #4D4D4D. Fill C is a linear gradient that contains nine color swatches: #575757, #777777, #4A4A4A, #494949, #494949, #575757, #454545, #434343, and #262626.

In this next task, we will be adding gradient fills to the arm to define its shape, as shown in Figure 9.108. First, fill in the base color of the arm. Fill A is a radial gradient that contains three color swatches: #85461D, #6B3C1D, and #4D2E1C. Fill B is a radial gradient that contains three color swatches: #85461D, #6B3C1D, and #55321D. Fill C is a radial gradient that contains two color swatches: #6B3C1D and #4D2E1C. Second, add a layer of gradients to do define the shadow. Fill D is a linear gradient that contains five color swatches: #481F0B, Alpha: 65%, #481F0B, Alpha: 5%, #481F0B, Alpha: 0%, #481F0B, Alpha: 5%, and #481F0B, Alpha: 65%. Fill E is a radial gradient that contains two color swatches: #481F0B, Alpha: 0% and #481F0B, Alpha: 58%. Finally, add a detailed layer of gradient overlays that add another layer of shadow and a layer of highlights. Fill F is a linear gradient that contains three color swatches: #492F1E, #24211A, and #070707. Fill G is a radial gradient that contains two color swatches: #4F3220, Alpha: 73% and #492F1E, Alpha: 21%. Fill H is a solid fill with a value of #884E26, Alpha: 80%. Fill I is a linear gradient that contains two color swatches: #232019, Alpha: 12% and #232019, Alpha: 100%. Fill J is a solid fill with a value of #855A50, Alpha: 31%.

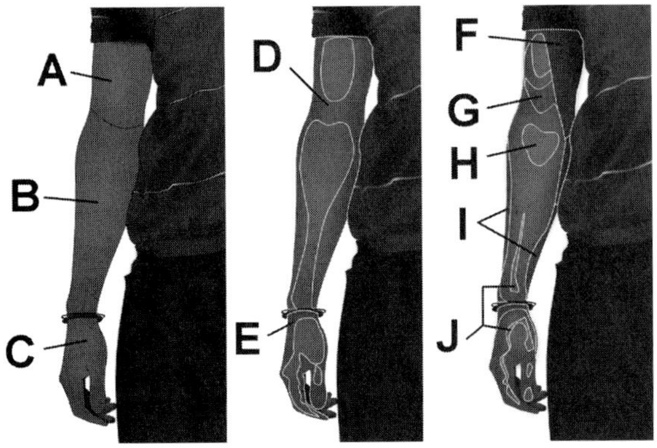

FIGURE 9.108 Dashboard look into how the left arm's shape is defined.

Apply a base gradient to the right arm and apply a shadow detail, as shown in Figure 9.109. The letters A, B, and C point out the different gradients used.

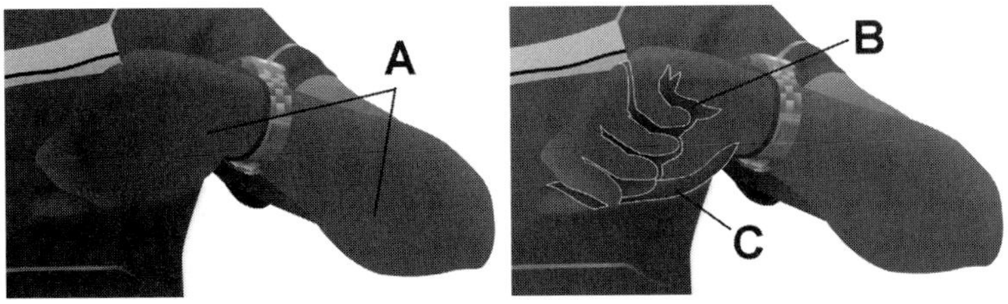

FIGURE 9.109 Defining the shape of the right hand.

On a new layer, apply a layer of detail gradients to the right arm, as shown in Figure 9.110. The letters A, B, and C point out the different gradients used.

Add a layer of small sharp highlights that accent the hand, making it look shimmering in the light. Create outlines, apply solid fills, convert them to a symbol, and apply a blur filter to them, as shown in Figure 9.111. The letters A and B point out the different gradients used.

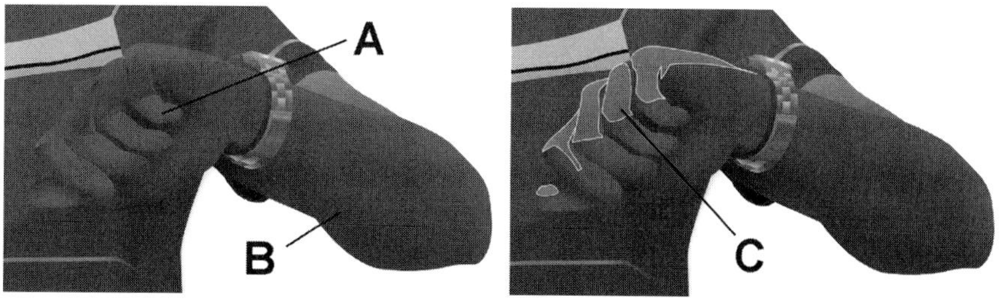

FIGURE 9.110 Adding highlights to the right arm.

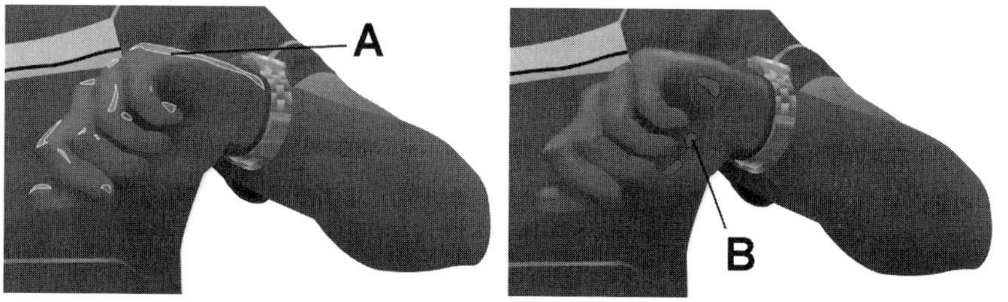

FIGURE 9.111 Adding a layer of sharp highlights.

Head

The shapes on the face are constructed the same way as the arms with layers of gradient overlays. Start by applying a base fill to the face, as shown in Figure 9.112. Then, apply the first layer of gradients and apply a blur filter to them. Finally, apply a darker layer of gradients that are then applied a blur filter. The letters A, B, C, D, E, F, and G point out the different gradients used.

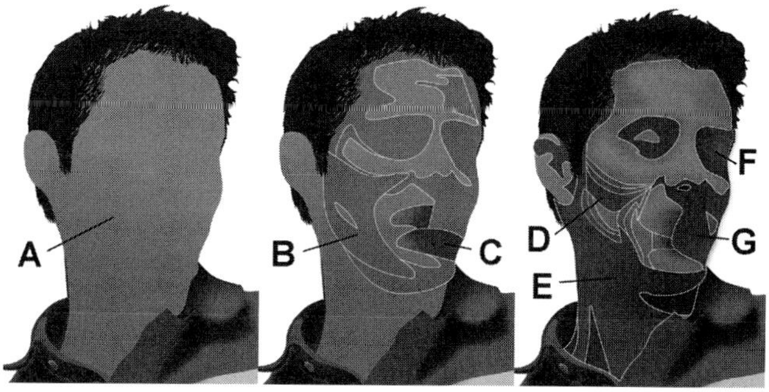

FIGURE 9.112 Add layers of gradient overlay to define the face's depth.

To add more depth under the chin, highlights on the forehead, and accents on the lip, we will be adding another layer of detail, as shown in Figure 9.113. The letters A, B, C, and D point out the different gradients used.

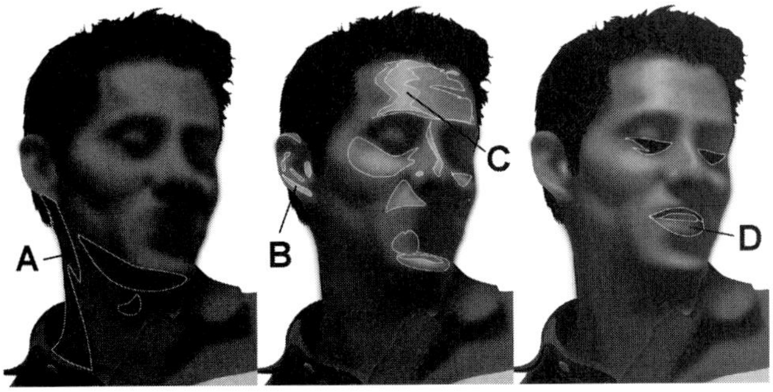

FIGURE 9.113 Add another layer of gradient overlay defining the highlights in the face.

Shadow

Use the Pencil tool to create an outlined area where the shadow linear gradient will be applied, as shown in Figure 9.114.

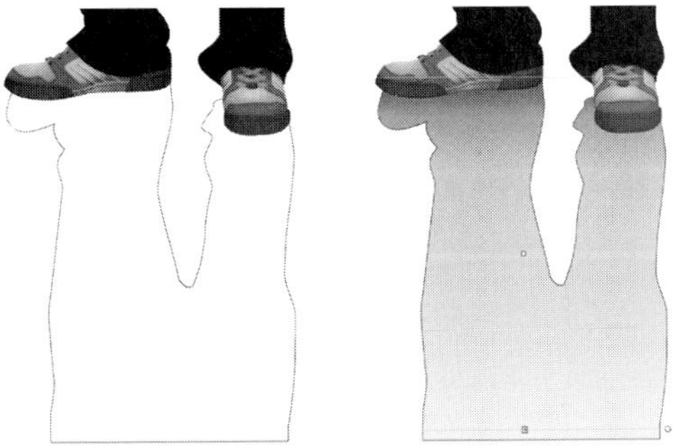

FIGURE 9.114 Create the shadow that the human casts.

Apply a blur filter to the shadow fill to give it the blur effect, shown in Figure 9.115.

FIGURE 9.115 Final rendering of a human.

SUMMARY

- Layer multiple optimized textures and repeating textures in a pattern or at random to make your illustrations look more realistic, especially if your object is very detailed.
- Use the Filter feature to quickly blur a graphic and make it look out of focus.
- Apply detail to your object in layers to allow the least amount of graphics needed to portray the detail.
- Use a linear gradient to easily create wrinkles in a shirt.

EXERCISES

ON THE CD

The following exercises will put to use what you have learned in this chapter. You will be creating a metal gear, plastic flamingo, strawberry, rose, and a human face. The files for the exercises are on the companion CD-ROM in the folders cited.

1. Create a metal gear from the image provided. Use the techniques you learned in the last three chapters to achieve that sharp metal look. The jpg file is on the companion CD-ROM in Chapter_9/Exercises/gear.jpg.
2. Create a plastic flamingo from the image provided. This image has similar qualities as the other plastic objects we have drawn in this book. The jpg file is on the companion CD-ROM in Chapter_9/Exercises/plastic flamingo.jpg.
3. Create a juicy strawberry from the image provided. Fruits and vegetables always tend to be a challenge to illustrate in Flash, but this strawberry has nice shadow and highlights, which are possible to replicate in Flash. The jpg file is on the companion CD-ROM in Chapter_9/Exercises/strawberry.jpg.
4. Create a beautiful rose from the image provided. Use radial gradients to capture this rose's realistic petals. The jpg file is on the companion CD-ROM in Chapter_9/Exercises/rose.jpg.
5. As the last exercise in the book, challenge your Flash illustrating skills and illustrate a human face, perhaps your own face from an old photograph. Use the techniques in this chapter to achieve the dynamic shapes needed to portray a human's face.

APPENDIX

A DEVELOPER RESOURCES

The Web sites and books cited here are excellent resources for general illustration, animation, digital illustration, Flash resource sites, and recommended supplies.

GENERAL ILLUSTRATION AND ANIMATION RESOURCES

Resource Sites

Harold Olejarz
www.olejarz.com/arted/perspective
This is a great site if you want to learn more about how perspective drawing is done, and provides interactive lessons to better learn the subject.

deviantART
www.deviantart.com
This huge community site is comprised of artists from around the globe, and their artwork.

Books

How to Draw What You See by Rudy De Reyna
Watson-Guptill Publications
ISBN: 0823023753; $16.95; *www.watsonguptill.com*
This book contains great lessons and techniques on how to draw from still life.

The Figure: The Classic Approach to Drawing and Construction by Walt Reed and Robin Hazlewood
Writers Digest Books
ISBN: 0891340971; $21.99
If you ever wanted to master how to draw human figures, this is the book for you.

Cartoon Animation (How to Draw and Paint series #26) by Preston Blair
Walter Foster Publications
ISBN: 0929261518; $7.95; *www.walterfoster.com*
These small books are great if you want to learn basic animation techniques. They even break an animation down to the frame and analyze how the motion is produced.

Perspective Made Easy by Ernest Norling
Dover Publications
ISBN: 0486404730; $8.95; *www.doverpublications.com*
A great book that makes understanding perspective simple and easy to learn. It covers the many basic types of perspectives and is worth checking out.

Creative Lighting Techniques for Studio Photographers by Dave Montizambert
Amherst Media
ISBN: 1584280034; $29.95; *www.amherstmedia.com*
When drawing an object from still life, it is always good to have the best lighting on your object, since that will dictate how your object will turn out. This book does a great job of explaining several techniques that come in handy when lighting an object or objects.

The Encyclopedia of Illustration Techniques by Catharine Slade
Running Press
ISBN: 0762400838; $49.99; *www.newriders.com*
This is one of those great books that cover many different drawing styles and drawing in different mediums. Experimenting with different mediums like chalk pastel or watercolor is a great way to expand your artistic talent.

Digital Illustration Resources

Resource Site

Vectorkid
www.vectorkid.com
This author's personal Web site devoted to illustrating in Flash, especially photorealistic illustration in Flash. This site has attracted many visitors and continues to amaze every visitor with the unbelievable vector works.

Book

Bert Monroy: Photorealistic Techniques with Photoshop® & Illustrator® by Bert Monroy

New Riders

ISBN: 0735709696; $49.99; *www.newriders.com*

Bert Monroy's books are always a treat, and his talent to produce photorealistic imagery in Photoshop and Illustrator continues to inspire many. Definitely check out this book if you are into photorealistic drawing.

FLASH RESOURCES

Resource Sites

Flashkit

www.flashkit.com

A site that has everything you need to know about Flash and has one of the biggest Flash communities.

ElectroServer

www.electro-server.com

ElectroServer is a powerful socket-server that enables developers to create multiuser applications. With the support of some amazing features such as server-side ActionScript, server plug-ins, and database support, developers can bring multiplayer Flash gaming and multiuser applications further than ever before.

RECOMMENDED HARDWARE

Following are the drawing supplies you should pick up if you are looking to purchase a scanner, graphics tablet, or light box.

Scanner

CanoScan LiDE 20

www.usa.canon.com

High Retail: $49.99, 48-bit for over 281 trillion possible colors, up to 600 × 1200 dpi resolution, Windows® and Mac supported. Check the Web site for details.

Graphics Tablets

Wacom Intuos2 6x8

www.wacom.com

High Retail: $299.99, Tablet Dimensions: 13.5" × 10.2" × .6". Active Area: 6"× 8", Pressure Levels: 1024, Resolution: 2540 dpi, Max. data rate: 200 pps, Accuracy: +– .01", Tilt Range: 50°–60°, Windows and Mac supported. Check the Web site for details.

Wacom Graphire3 6x8

www.wacom.com

High Retail: $199.95, Tablet Dimensions: 10.85" × 10.12 × .71" , Active Area: 5.94" × 8.22" , Pressure Levels: 512, Windows and Mac supported. Check the Web site for details.

Miscellaneous Drawing Supplies

LIGHT TRACER®

www.artograph.com

High Retail: $39.95, 10" × 12" (25 × 30 cm) acrylic work surface, Standard 12", 8-watt daylight fluorescent (included), Lamp provides 7500 hours of use. Check the Web site for details.

APPENDIX

B ABOUT THE CD-ROM

The CD-ROM accompanying this book contains files to assist you in your illustrating ventures. The files are separated by chapter, and in the chapter folders are Flash source files and any images available. Even though a project may span across a certain number of figures the source is named after the first figure. Example: The Mallet in Chapter 9 is called 9-1.fla. Refer to the system requirements presented here to ensure your system meets the minimum requirements.

To use the items on the CD-ROM, simply select the folder you want to use and then select the appropriate files. Again, be sure you have the necessary hardware and software to run these files.

SYSTEM REQUIREMENTS

Windows

Macromedia Flash
600 MHz Intel Pentium III processor or equivalent
Windows 98 SE (4.10.2222 A), Windows 2000, or Windows XP
128 MB RAM (256 MB recommended)

Macintosh

Macromedia Flash
500 MHz PowerPC G3 processor
Mac OS X 10.2.6 and later, 10.3
128 MB RAM (256 MB recommended)

INDEX